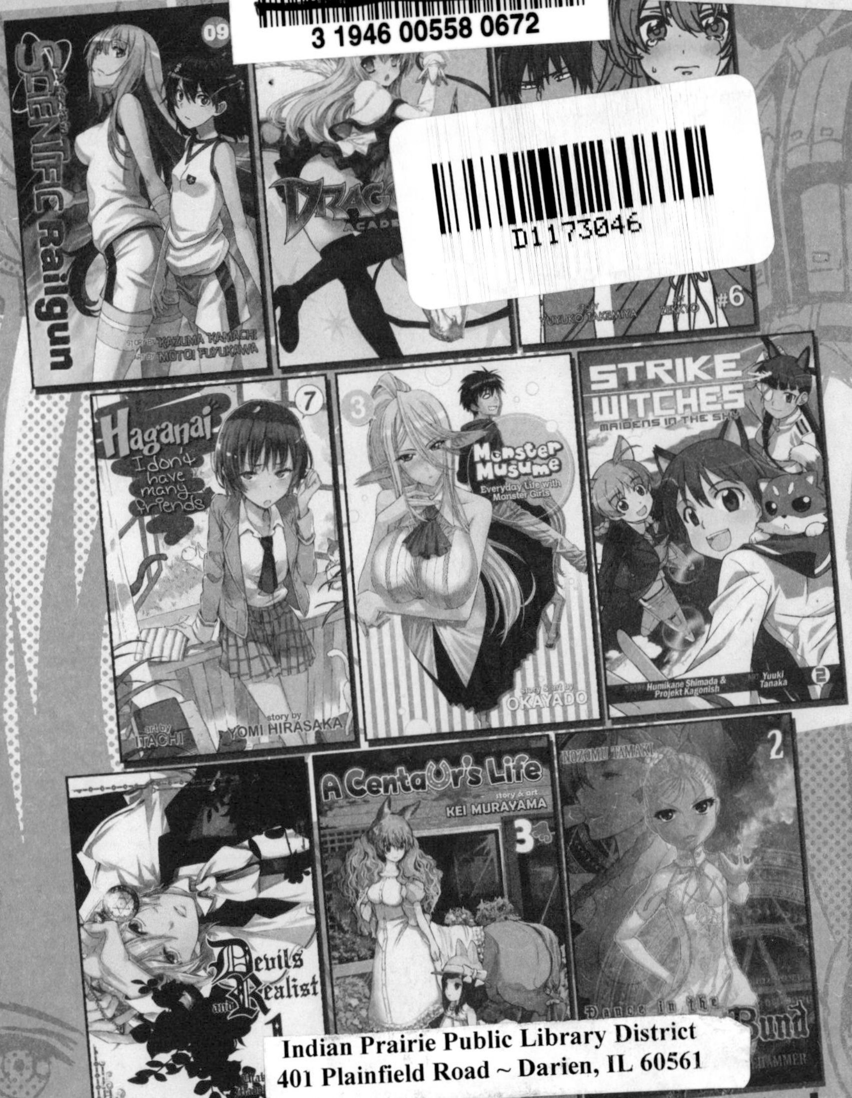
Scientific Railgun
09
STORY BY KAZUMA KAMACHI
ART BY MOTOI FUYUKAWA
Dragon Academy
Yuyuko Takemiya
Zekkyo
#6
Haganai
I don't have many friends
7
art by ITACHI
story by YOMI HIRASAKA
3
Monster Musume
Everyday Life with Monster Girls
story & art by OKAYADO
STRIKE WITCHES
MAIDENS IN THE SKY
Humikane Shimada &
Projekt Kagonish
Yuuki Tanaka
2
Devils and Realist
1
A Centaur's Life
story & art
KEI MURAYAMA
3
NOZOMU TAMAKI
2
Dance in the Vampire Bund

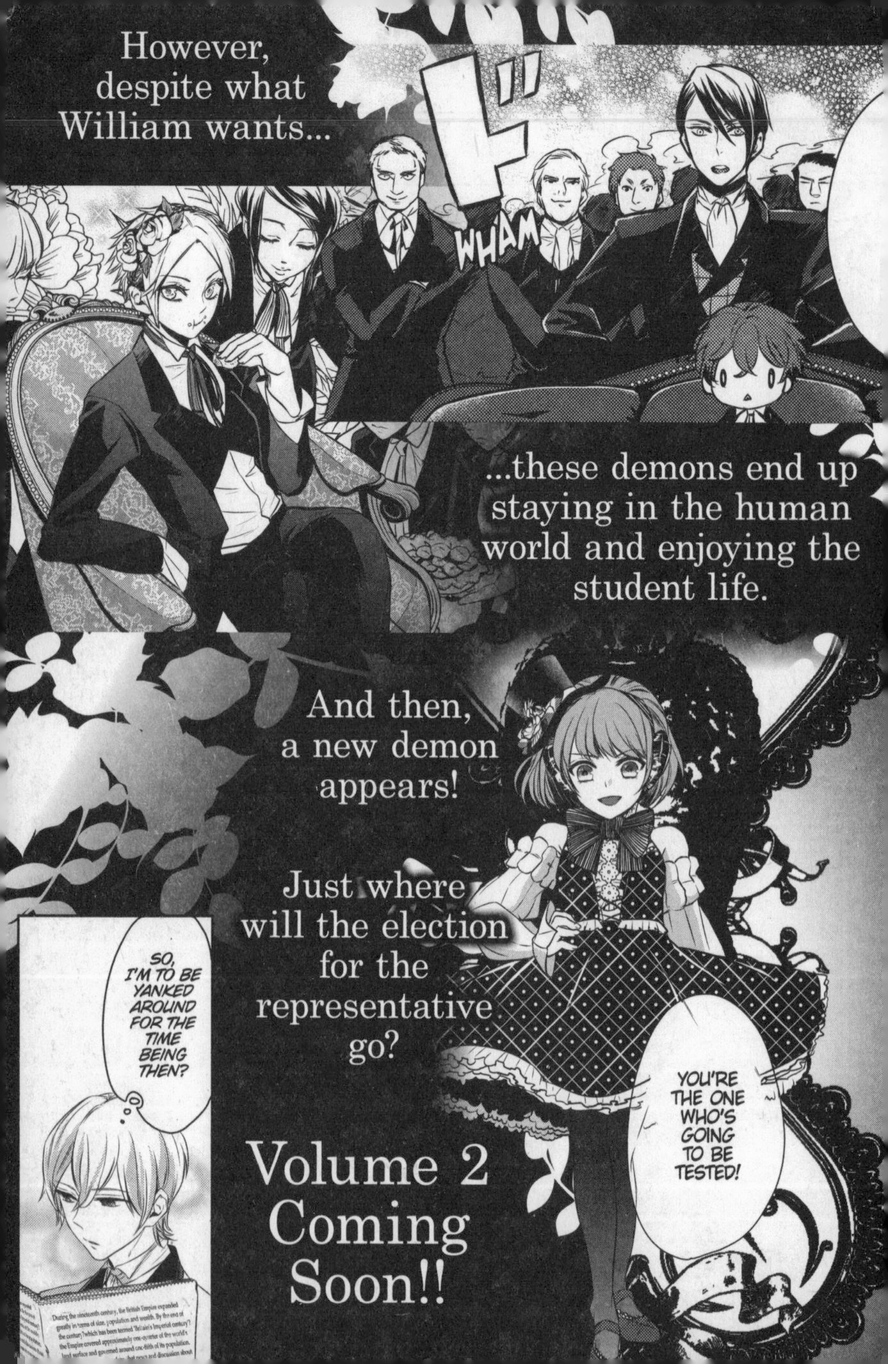

However, despite what William wants...
ド
WHAM
...these demons end up staying in the human world and enjoying the student life.
And then, a new demon appears!
YOU'RE THE ONE WHO'S GOING TO BE TESTED!
Just where will the election for the representative go?
SO, I'M TO BE YANKED AROUND FOR THE TIME BEING THEN?
During the nineteenth century, the British Empire expanded greatly in terms of size, population and wealth. By the end of the century, which has been termed 'Britain's Imperial century' the Empire covered approximately one-quarter of the world's land surface and governed around one-fifth of its population.
Volume 2 Coming Soon!!

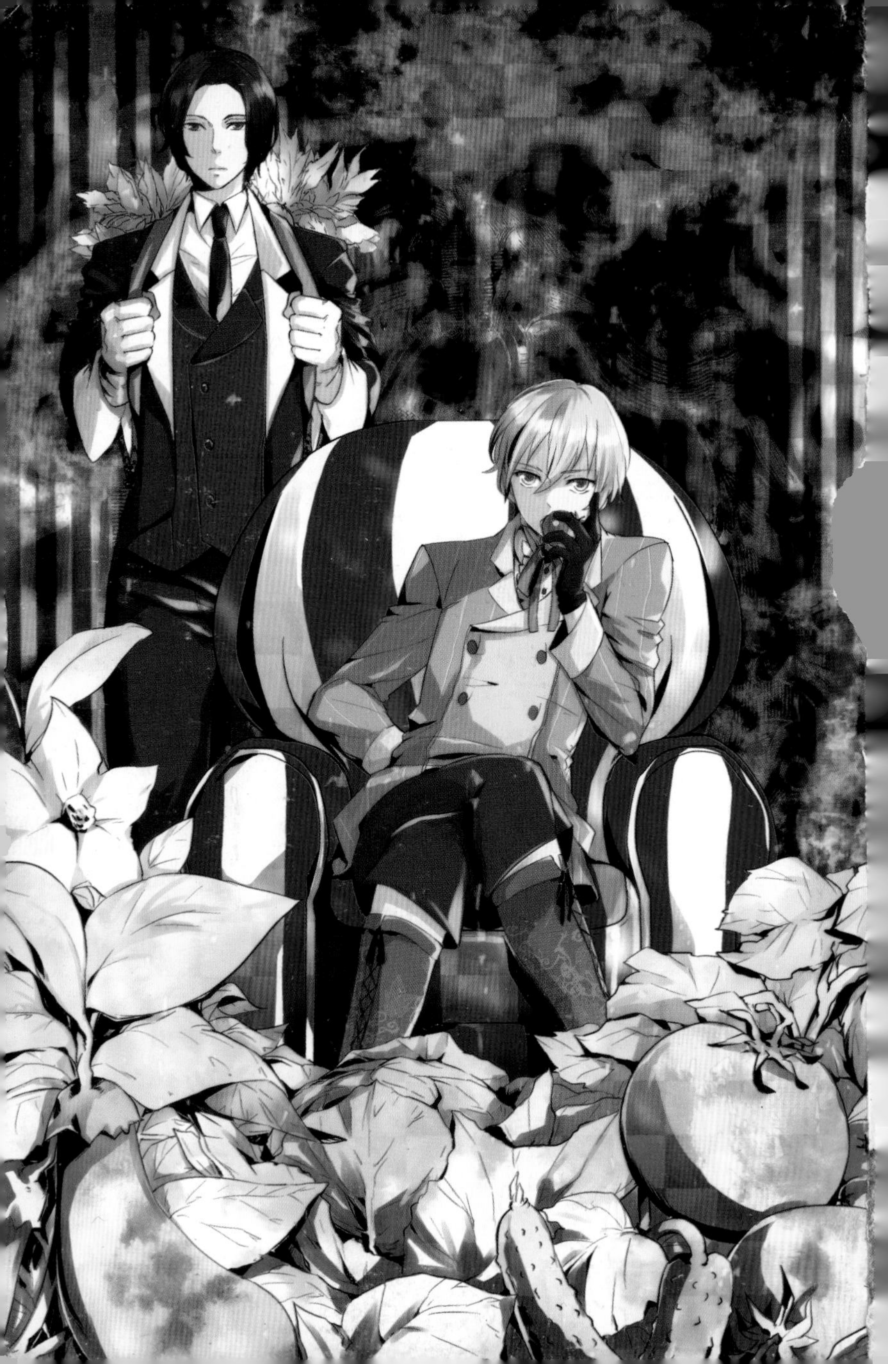

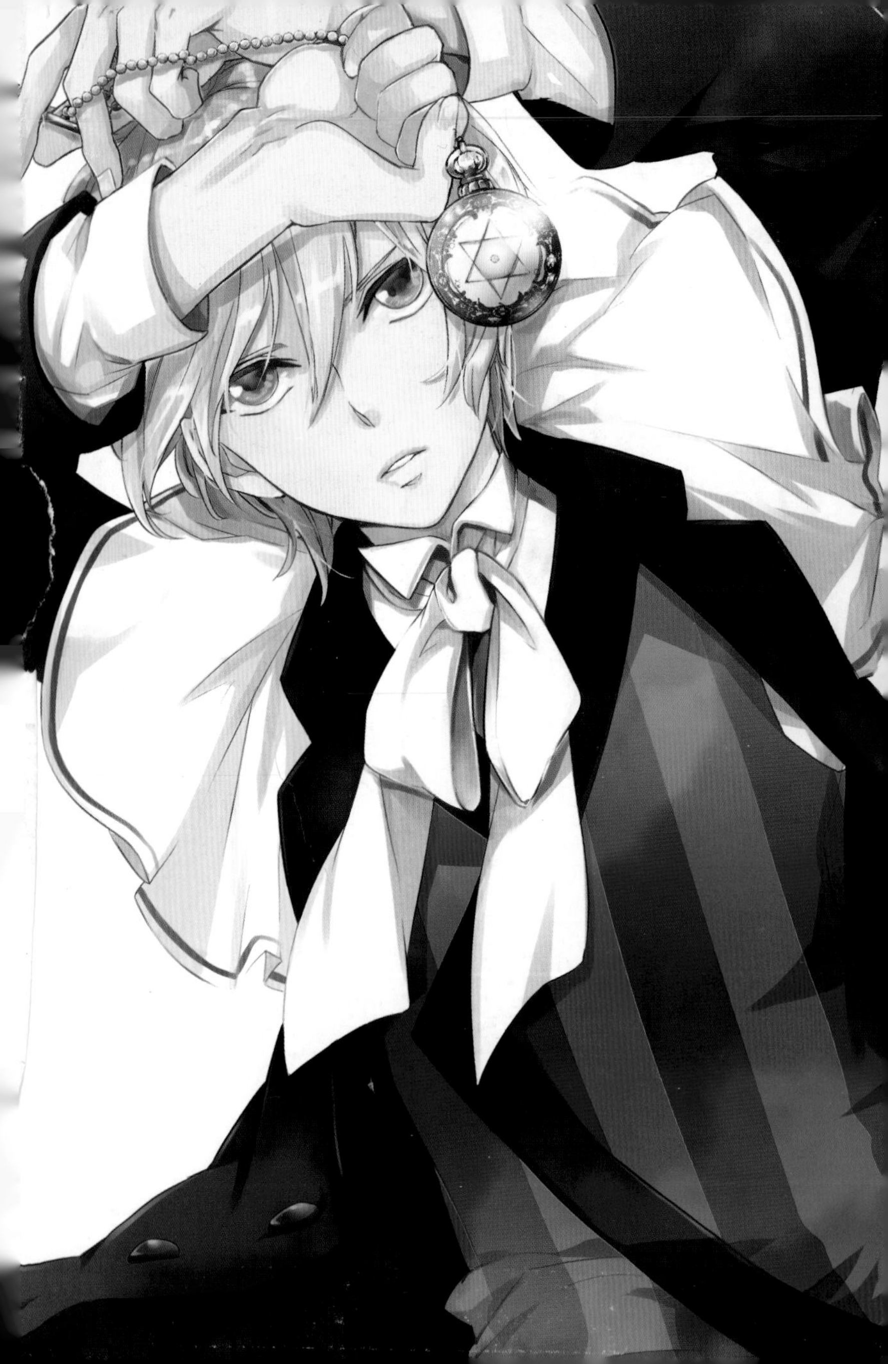

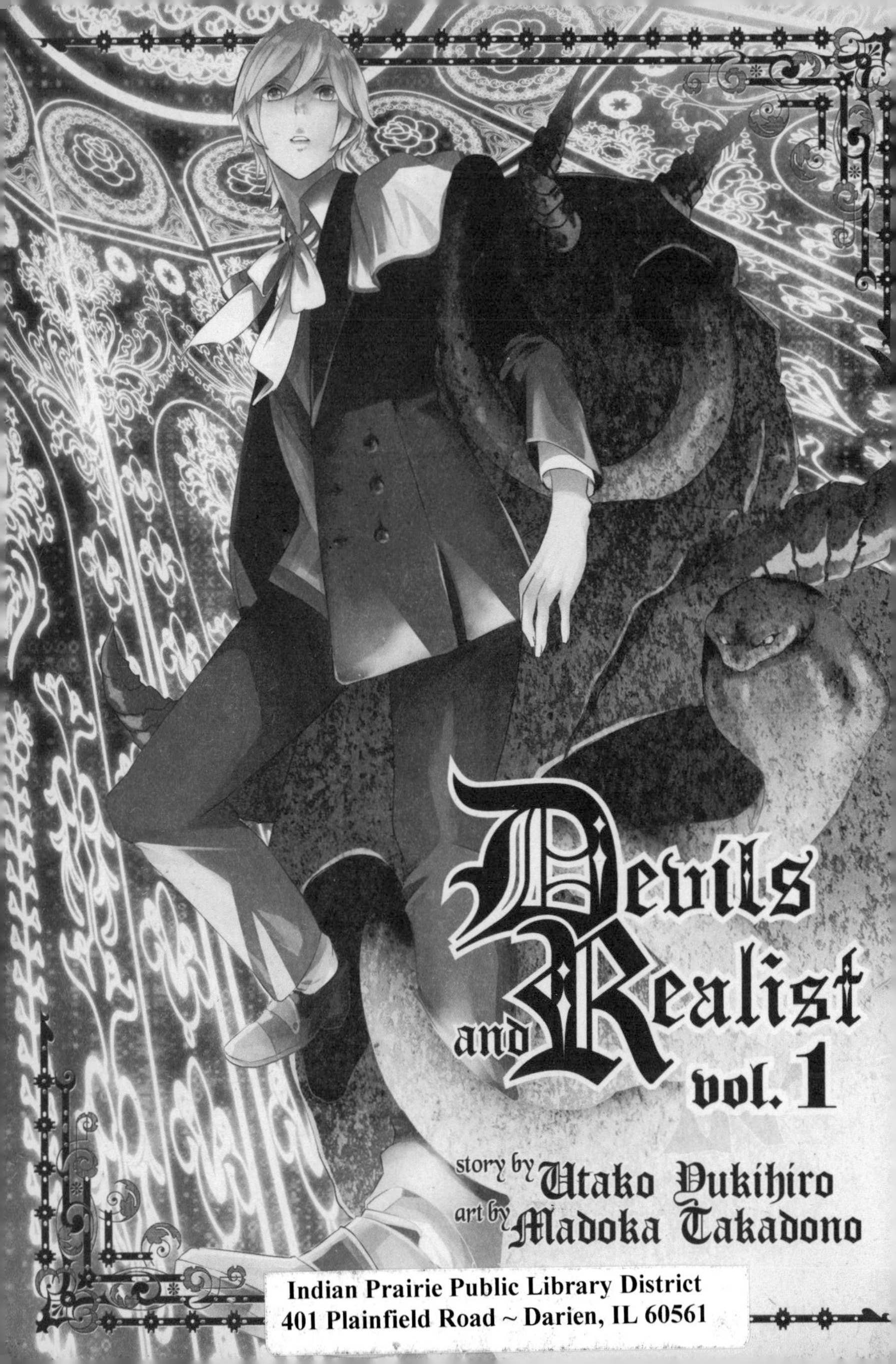
Devils and Realist
vol. 1
story by Utako Yukihiro
art by Madoka Takadono

SEVEN SEAS ENTERTAINMENT PRESENTS

Devils and Realist

art by UTAKO YUKIHIRO / story by MADOKA TAKADONO   VOLUME 1

TRANSLATION
Jocelyne Allen

ADAPTATION
Danielle King

LETTERING
Roland Amago

LAYOUT
Bambi Eloriaga-Amago

COVER DESIGN
Nicky Lim

PROOFREADER
Lee Otter

MANAGING EDITOR
Adam Arnold

PUBLISHER
Jason DeAngelis

MAKAI OUJI: DEVILS AND REALIST VOL. 1
© Utako Yukihiro/Madoka Takadono 2010
First published in Japan in 2010 by ICHIJINSHA Inc., Tokyo.
English translation rights arranged with ICHIJINSHA Inc., Tokyo, Japan.

Seven Seas books may be purchased in bulk for educational, business, or
promotional use. For information on bulk purchases, please contact Macmillan
Corporate & Premium Sales Department at 1-800-221-7945 (ext 5442)
or write specialmarkets@macmillan.com.

Seven Seas and the Seven Seas logo are trademarks of
Seven Seas Entertainment, LLC. All rights reserved.

ISBN: 978-1-626920-32-3

Printed in Canada

First Printing: April 2014

10 9 8 7 6 5 4 3 2 1

FOLLOW US ONLINE: **www.gomanga.com**

READING DIRECTIONS

This book reads from *right to left*, Japanese style.
If this is your first time reading manga, you start
reading from the top right panel on each page and
take it from there. If you get lost, just follow the
numbered diagram here. It may seem backwards at
first, but you'll get the hang of it! Have fun!!

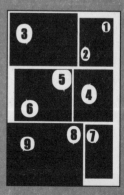

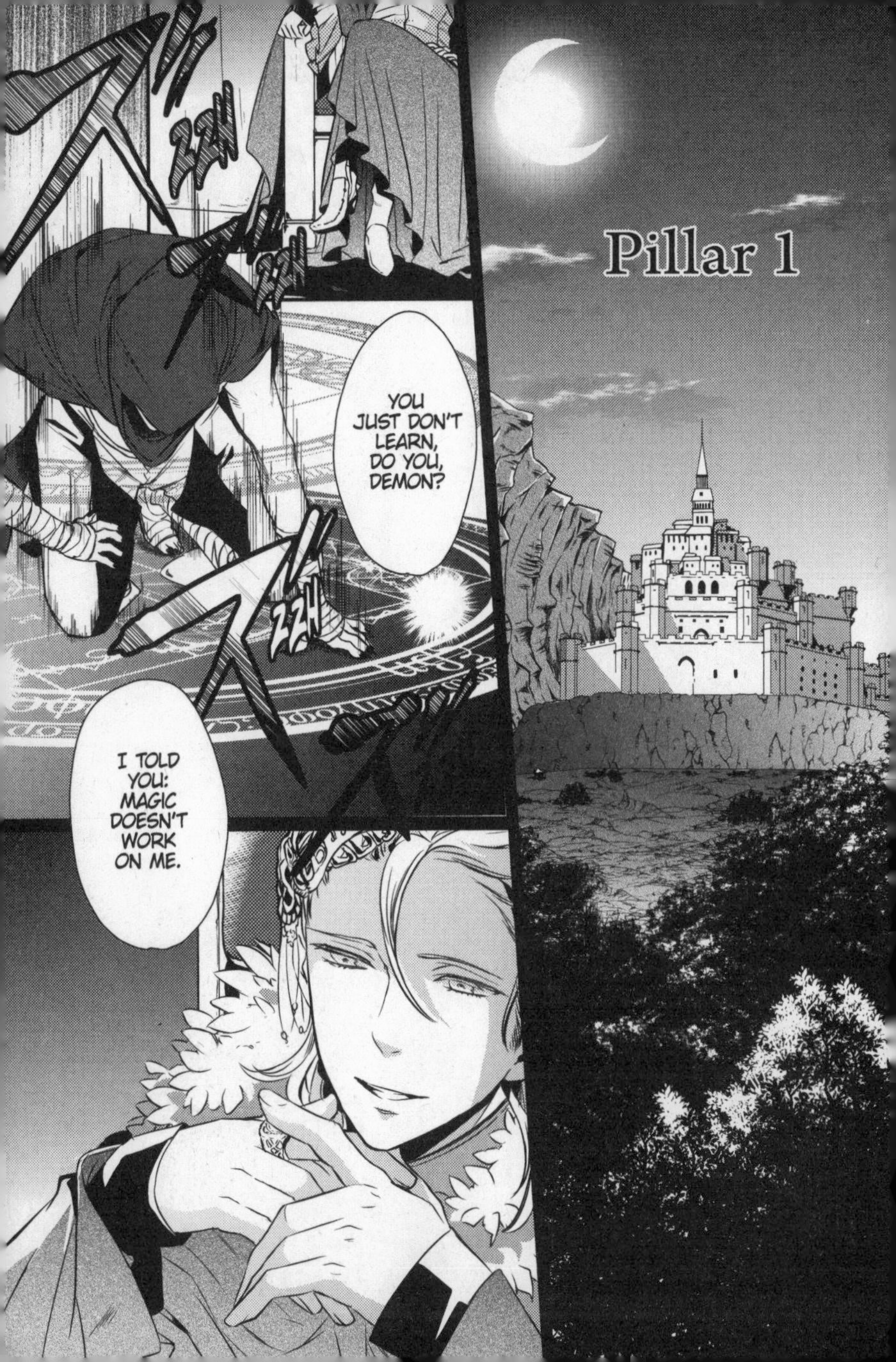
Pillar 1
ZZH
ZZH
ZZH
YOU JUST DON'T LEARN, DO YOU, DEMON?
I TOLD YOU: MAGIC DOESN'T WORK ON ME.

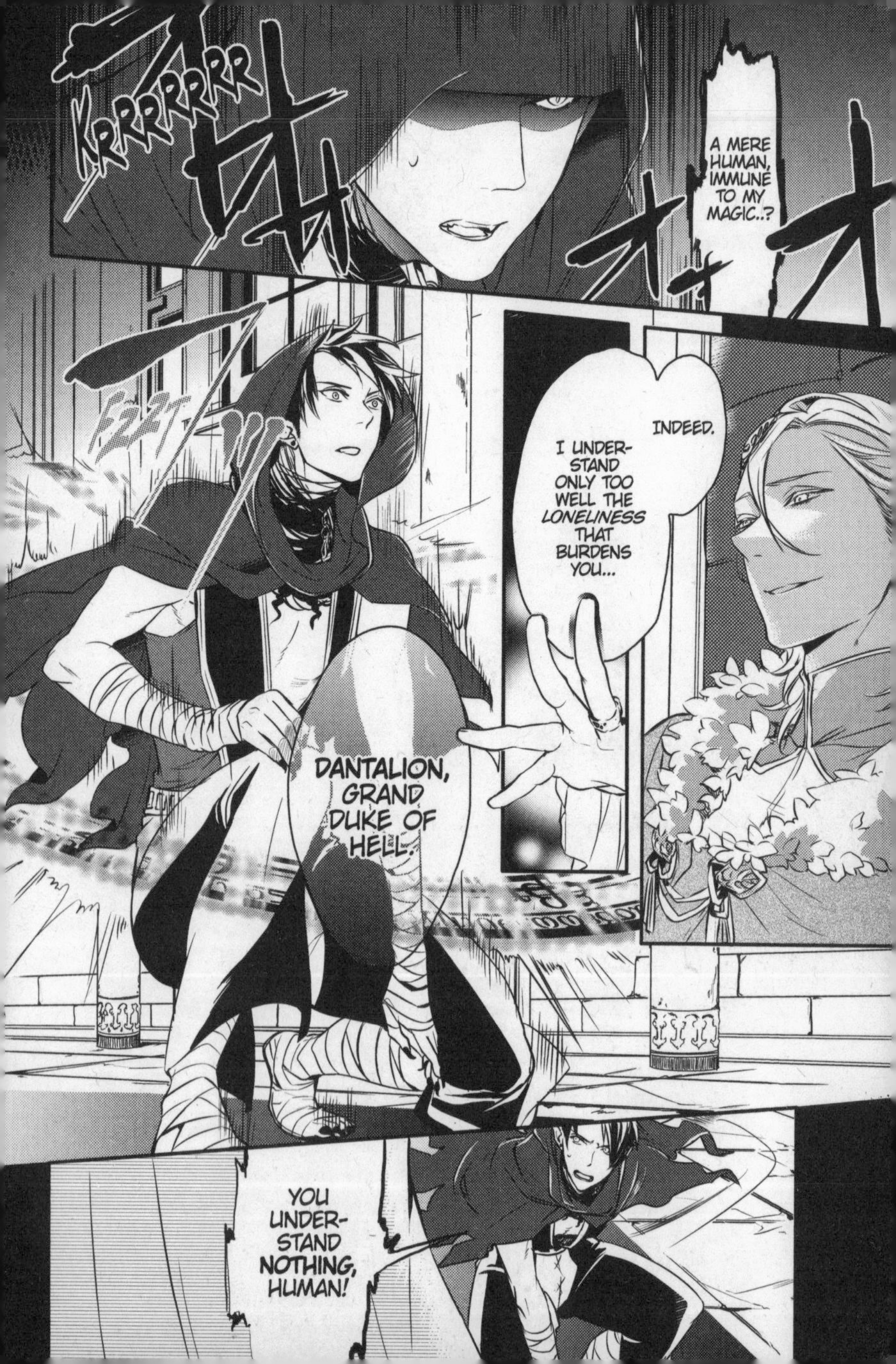
A MERE HUMAN, IMMUNE TO MY MAGIC..?
KRRRRRRR
INDEED.
I UNDERSTAND ONLY TOO WELL THE LONELINESS THAT BURDENS YOU...
DANTALION, GRAND DUKE OF HELL.
YOU UNDERSTAND NOTHING, HUMAN!

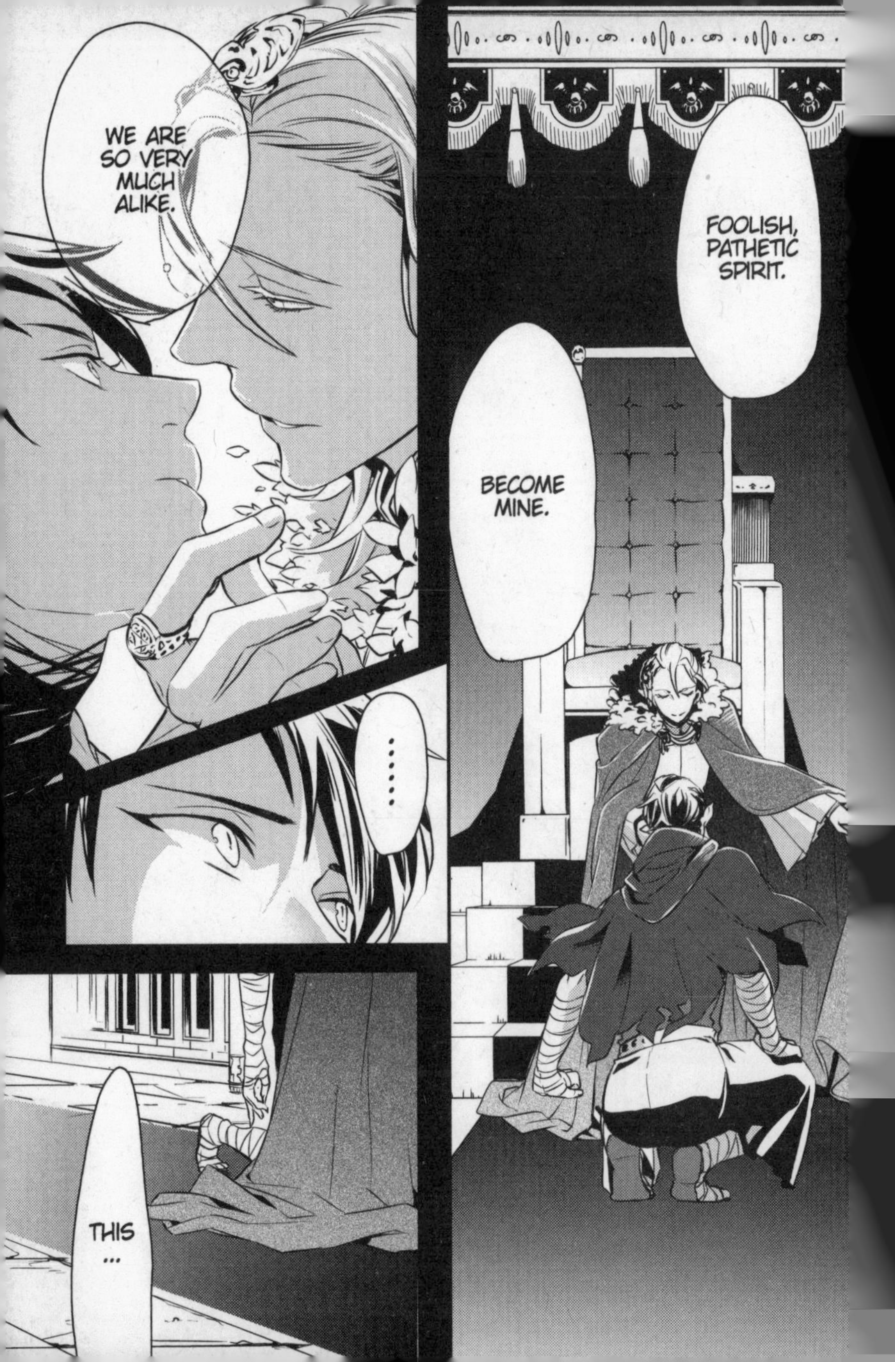
FOOLISH, PATHETIC SPIRIT.
BECOME MINE.
WE ARE SO VERY MUCH ALIKE.
......
THIS ...

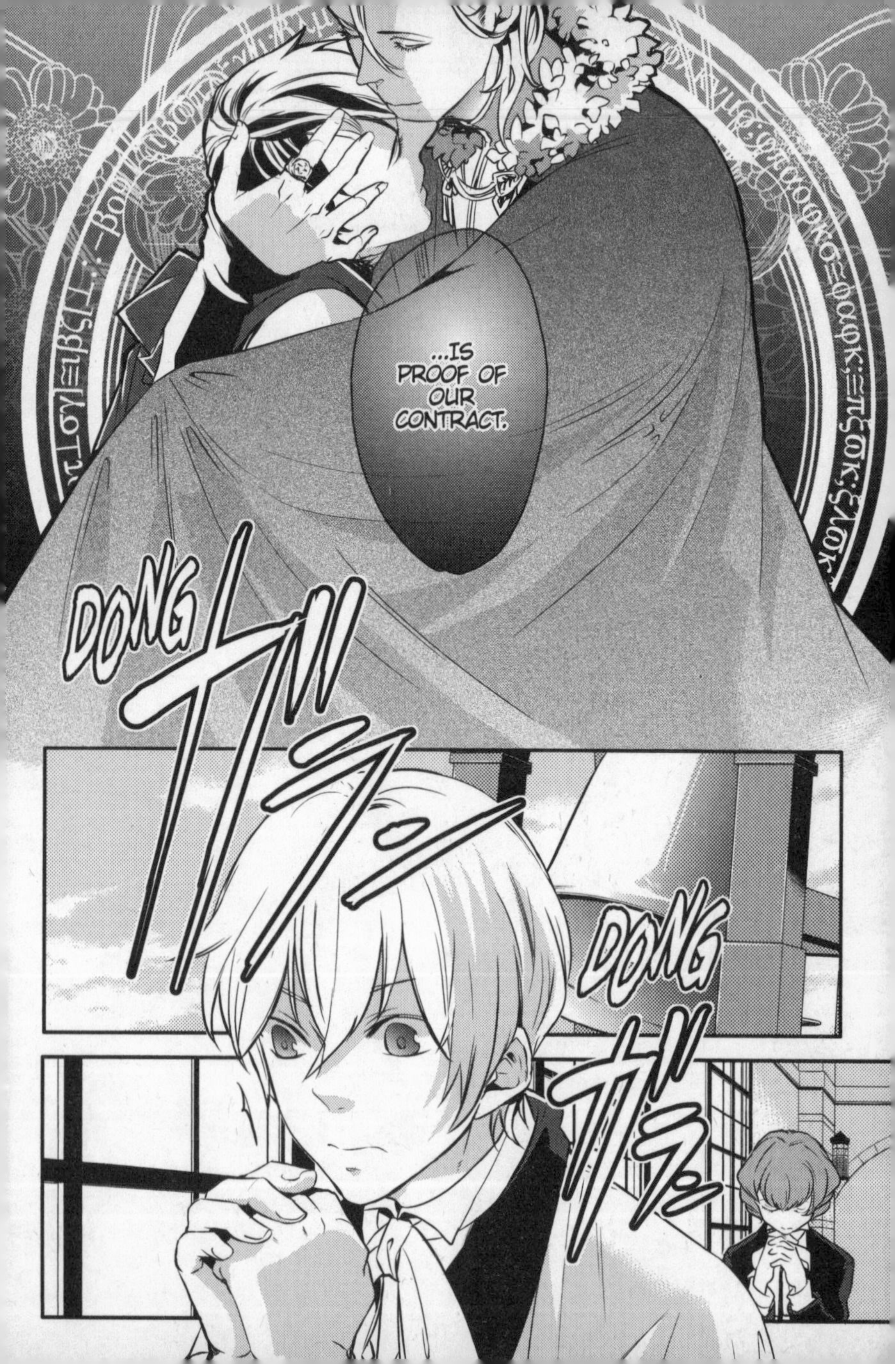
...IS PROOF OF OUR CONTRACT.
DONG
DONG

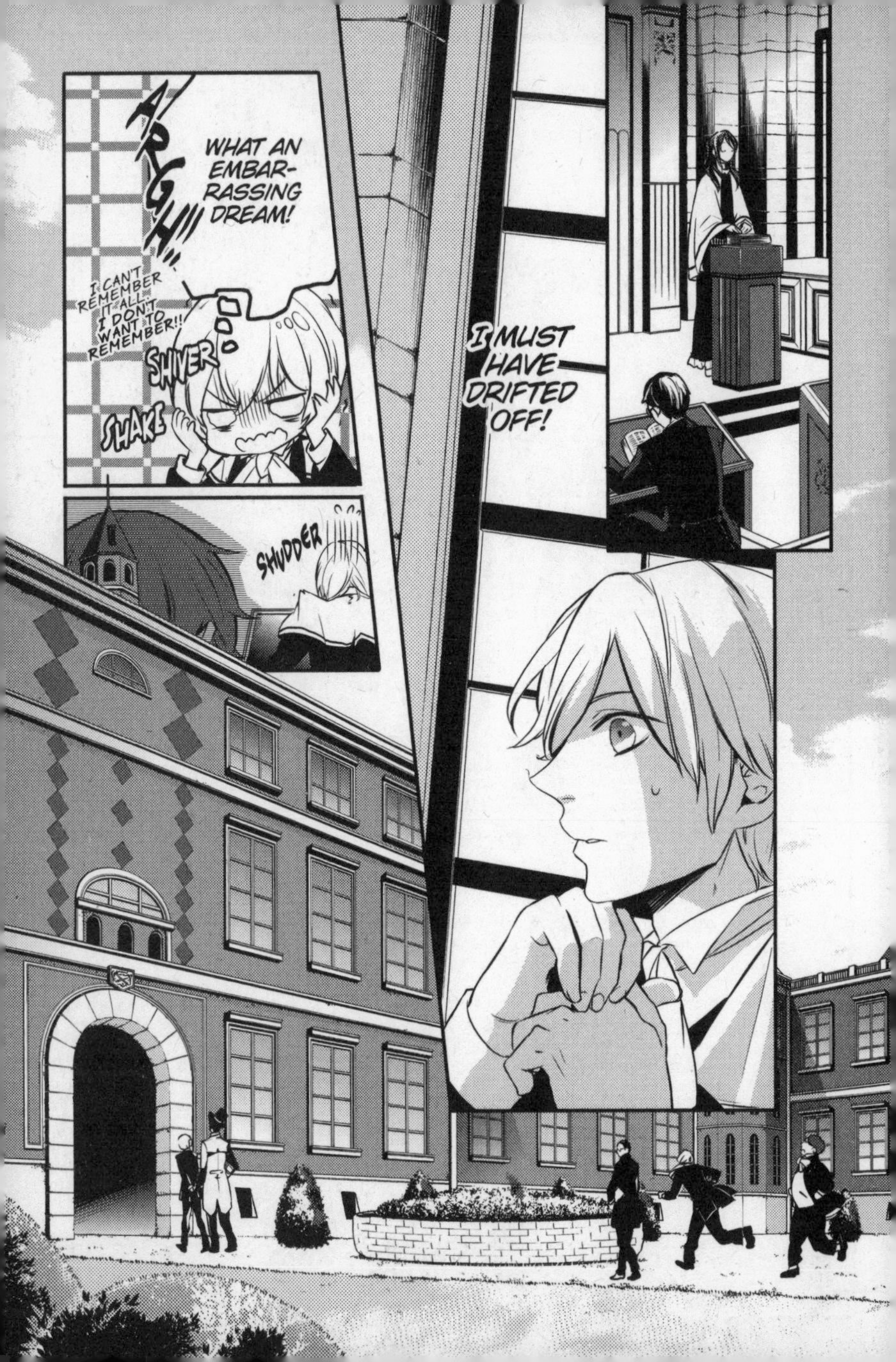
I MUST HAVE DRIFTED OFF!
WHAT AN EMBAR-RASSING DREAM!
ARGH!!!
I CAN'T REMEMBER IT ALL. I DON'T WANT TO REMEMBER!!
SHIVER
SHAKE
SHUDDER

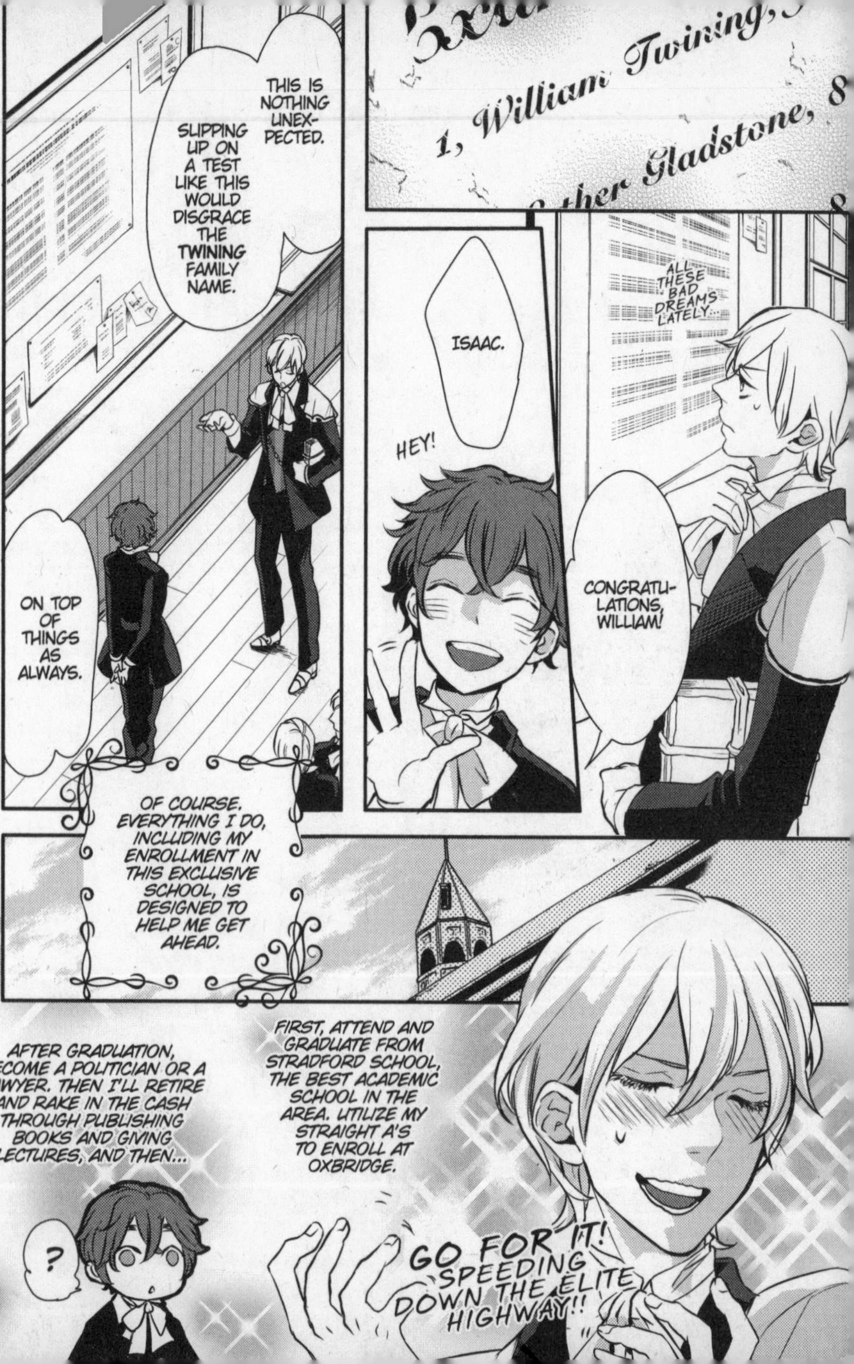
1, William Twining, 8
Gladstone, 8
ALL THESE BAD DREAMS LATELY...
CONGRATULATIONS, WILLIAM!
ISAAC.
HEY!
THIS IS NOTHING UNEXPECTED.
SLIPPING UP ON A TEST LIKE THIS WOULD DISGRACE THE TWINING FAMILY NAME.
ON TOP OF THINGS AS ALWAYS.
OF COURSE. EVERYTHING I DO, INCLUDING MY ENROLLMENT IN THIS EXCLUSIVE SCHOOL, IS DESIGNED TO HELP ME GET AHEAD.
FIRST, ATTEND AND GRADUATE FROM STRADFORD SCHOOL, THE BEST ACADEMIC SCHOOL IN THE AREA. UTILIZE MY STRAIGHT A'S TO ENROLL AT OXBRIDGE.
AFTER GRADUATION, BECOME A POLITICIAN OR A LAWYER. THEN I'LL RETIRE AND RAKE IN THE CASH THROUGH PUBLISHING BOOKS AND GIVING LECTURES, AND THEN...
GO FOR IT! SPEEDING DOWN THE ELITE HIGHWAY!!
?

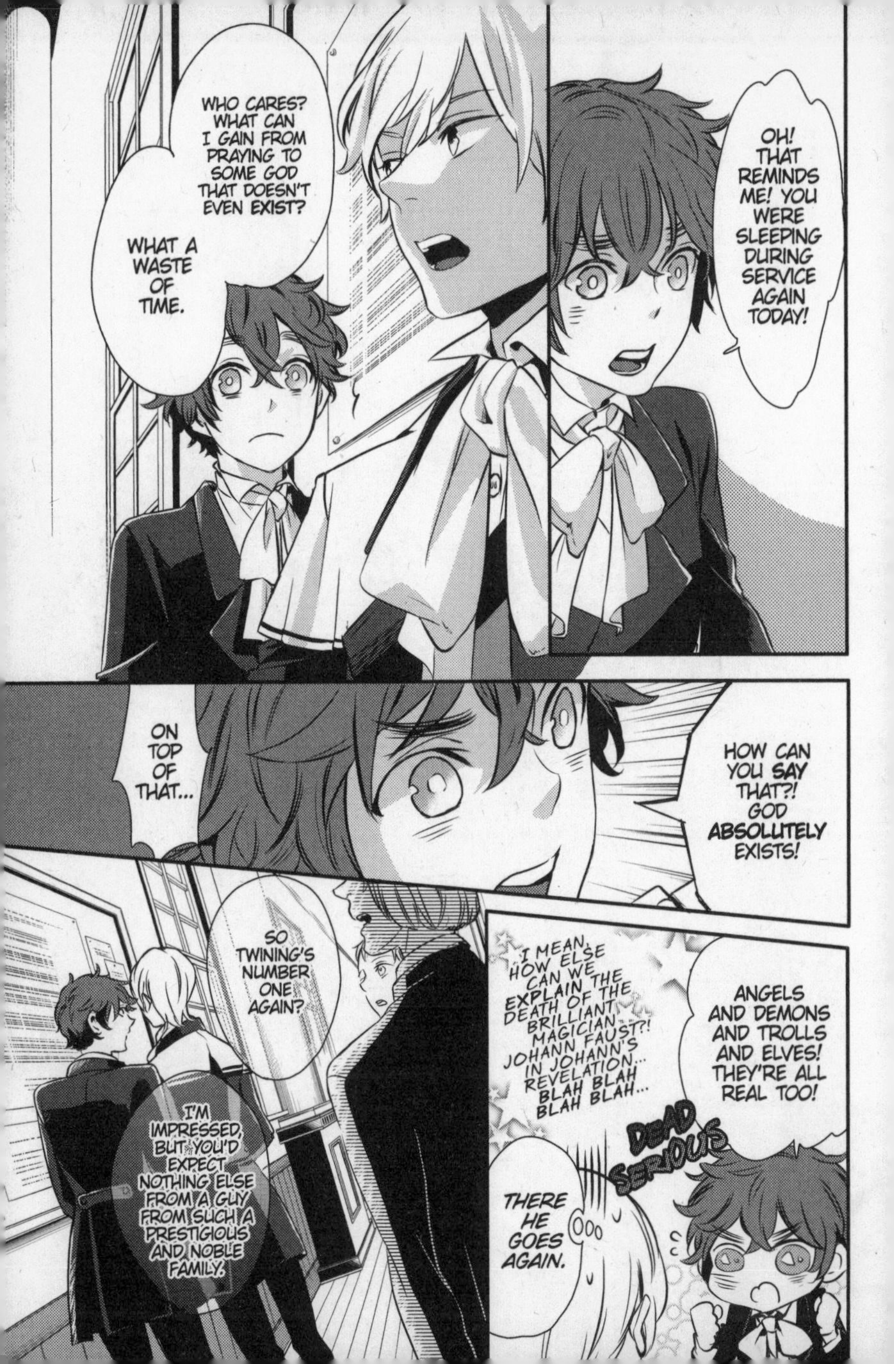
OH! THAT REMINDS ME! YOU WERE SLEEPING DURING SERVICE AGAIN TODAY!
WHO CARES? WHAT CAN I GAIN FROM PRAYING TO SOME GOD THAT DOESN'T EVEN EXIST?
WHAT A WASTE OF TIME.
HOW CAN YOU SAY THAT?! GOD ABSOLUTELY EXISTS!
ON TOP OF THAT...
ANGELS AND DEMONS AND TROLLS AND ELVES! THEY'RE ALL REAL TOO!
I MEAN, HOW ELSE CAN WE EXPLAIN THE DEATH OF THE BRILLIANT MAGICIAN JOHANN FAUST?! IN JOHANN'S REVELATION... BLAH BLAH BLAH BLAH...
DEAD SERIOUS
THERE HE GOES AGAIN.
SO TWINING'S NUMBER ONE AGAIN?
I'M IMPRESSED, BUT YOU'D EXPECT NOTHING ELSE FROM A GUY FROM SUCH A PRESTIGIOUS AND NOBLE FAMILY.

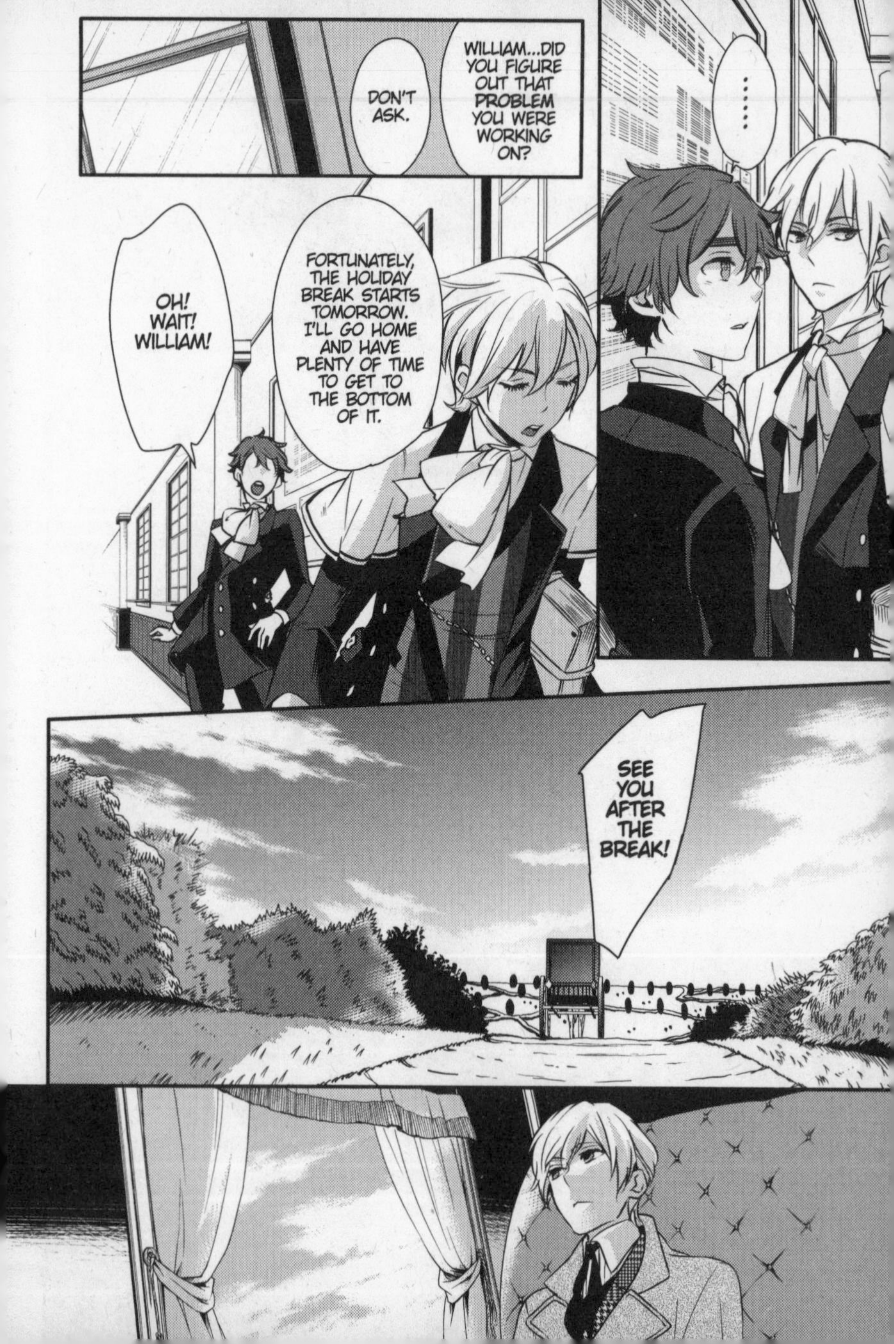
......
WILLIAM...DID YOU FIGURE OUT THAT PROBLEM YOU WERE WORKING ON?
DON'T ASK.
FORTUNATELY, THE HOLIDAY BREAK STARTS TOMORROW. I'LL GO HOME AND HAVE PLENTY OF TIME TO GET TO THE BOTTOM OF IT.
OH! WAIT! WILLIAM!
SEE YOU AFTER THE BREAK!

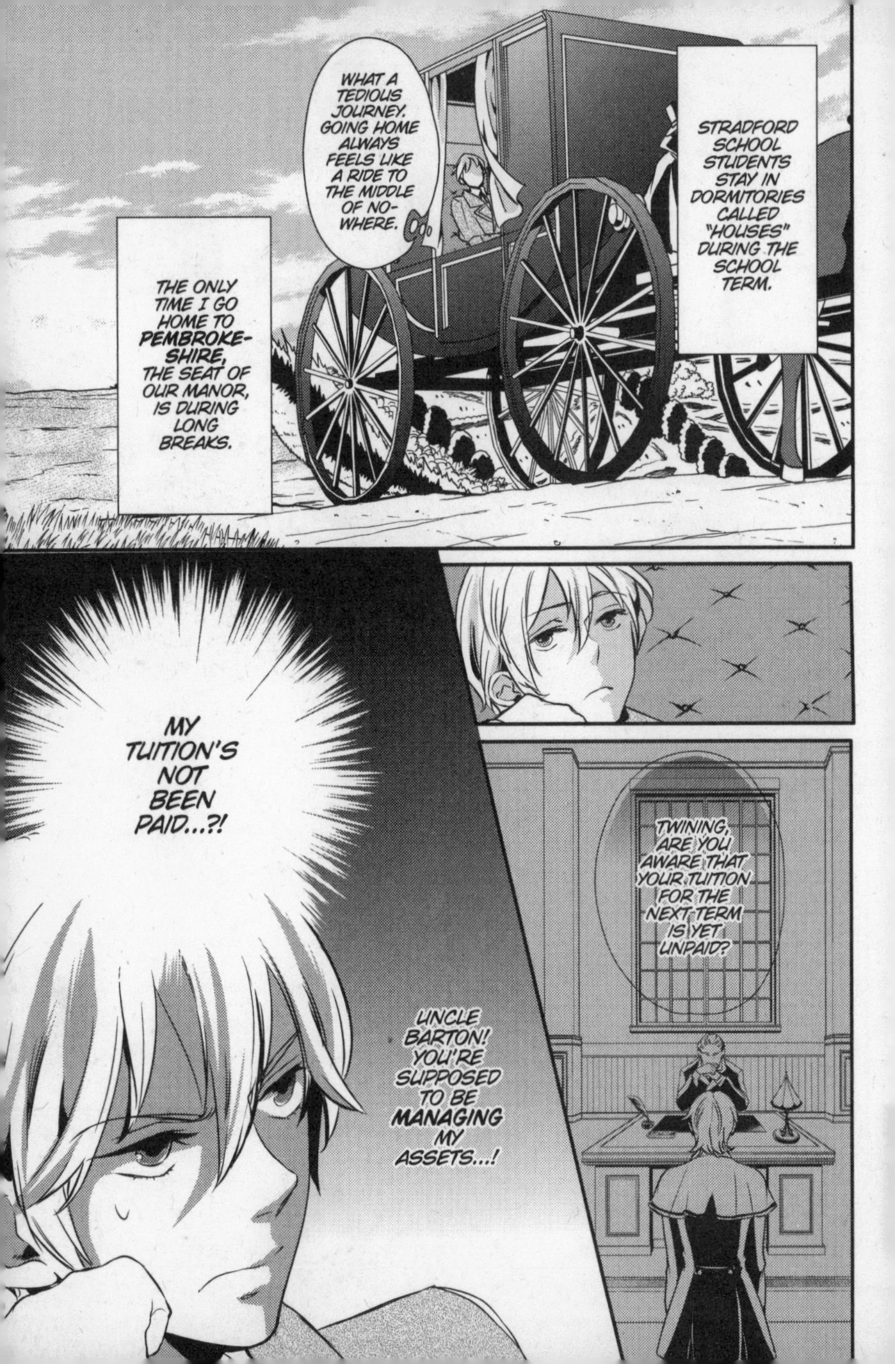
STRADFORD SCHOOL STUDENTS STAY IN DORMITORIES CALLED "HOUSES" DURING THE SCHOOL TERM.
WHAT A TEDIOUS JOURNEY. GOING HOME ALWAYS FEELS LIKE A RIDE TO THE MIDDLE OF NO-WHERE.
THE ONLY TIME I GO HOME TO PEMBROKE-SHIRE, THE SEAT OF OUR MANOR, IS DURING LONG BREAKS.
TWINING, ARE YOU AWARE THAT YOUR TUITION FOR THE NEXT TERM IS YET UNPAID?
MY TUITION'S NOT BEEN PAID...?!
UNCLE BARTON! YOU'RE SUPPOSED TO BE MANAGING MY ASSETS...!

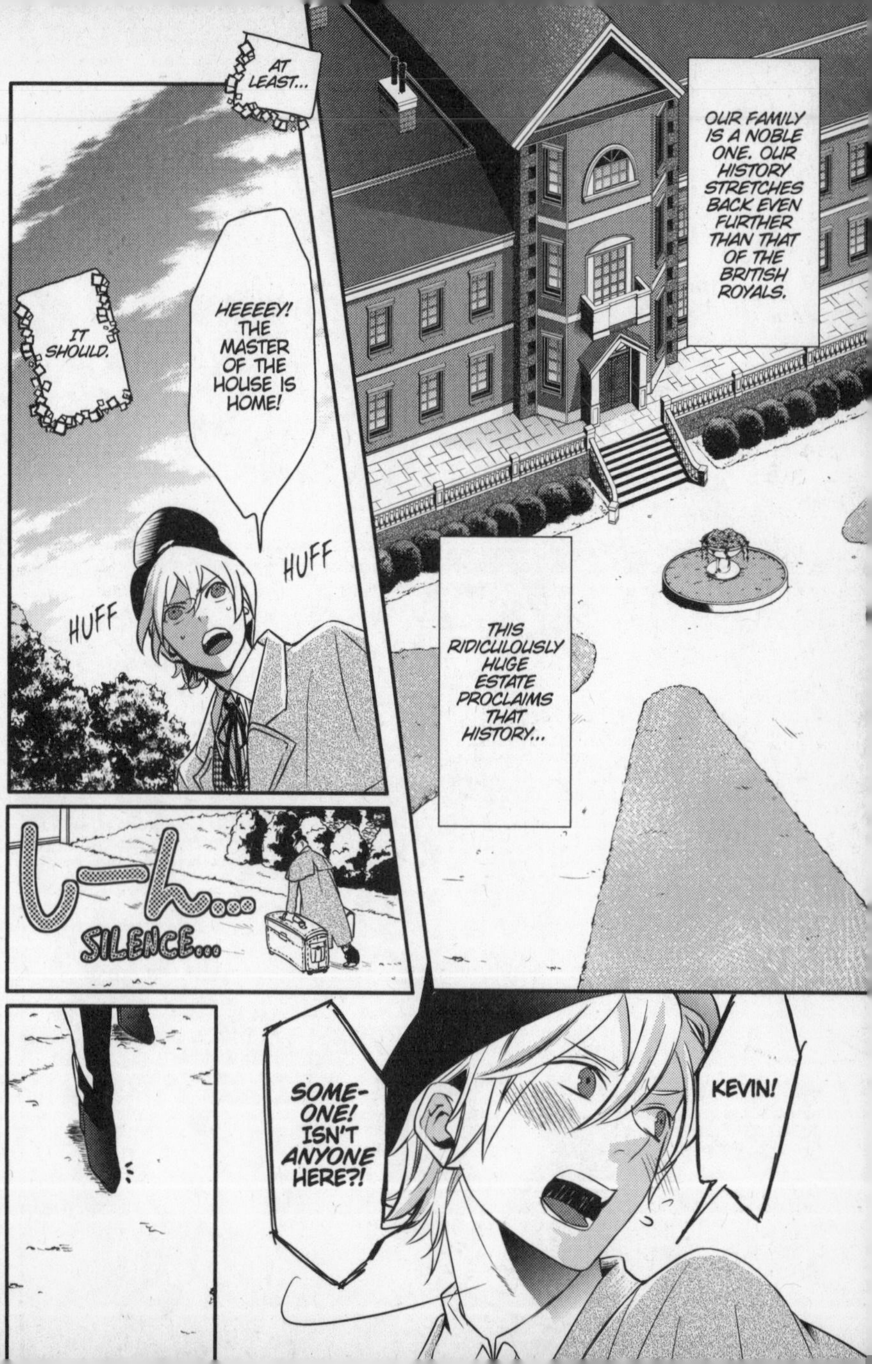
OUR FAMILY IS A NOBLE ONE. OUR HISTORY STRETCHES BACK EVEN FURTHER THAN THAT OF THE BRITISH ROYALS.
THIS RIDICULOUSLY HUGE ESTATE PROCLAIMS THAT HISTORY...
AT LEAST...
IT SHOULD.
HEEEEY! THE MASTER OF THE HOUSE IS HOME!
HUFF
HUFF
しーん…
SILENCE...
KEVIN!
SOME-ONE! ISN'T ANYONE HERE?!

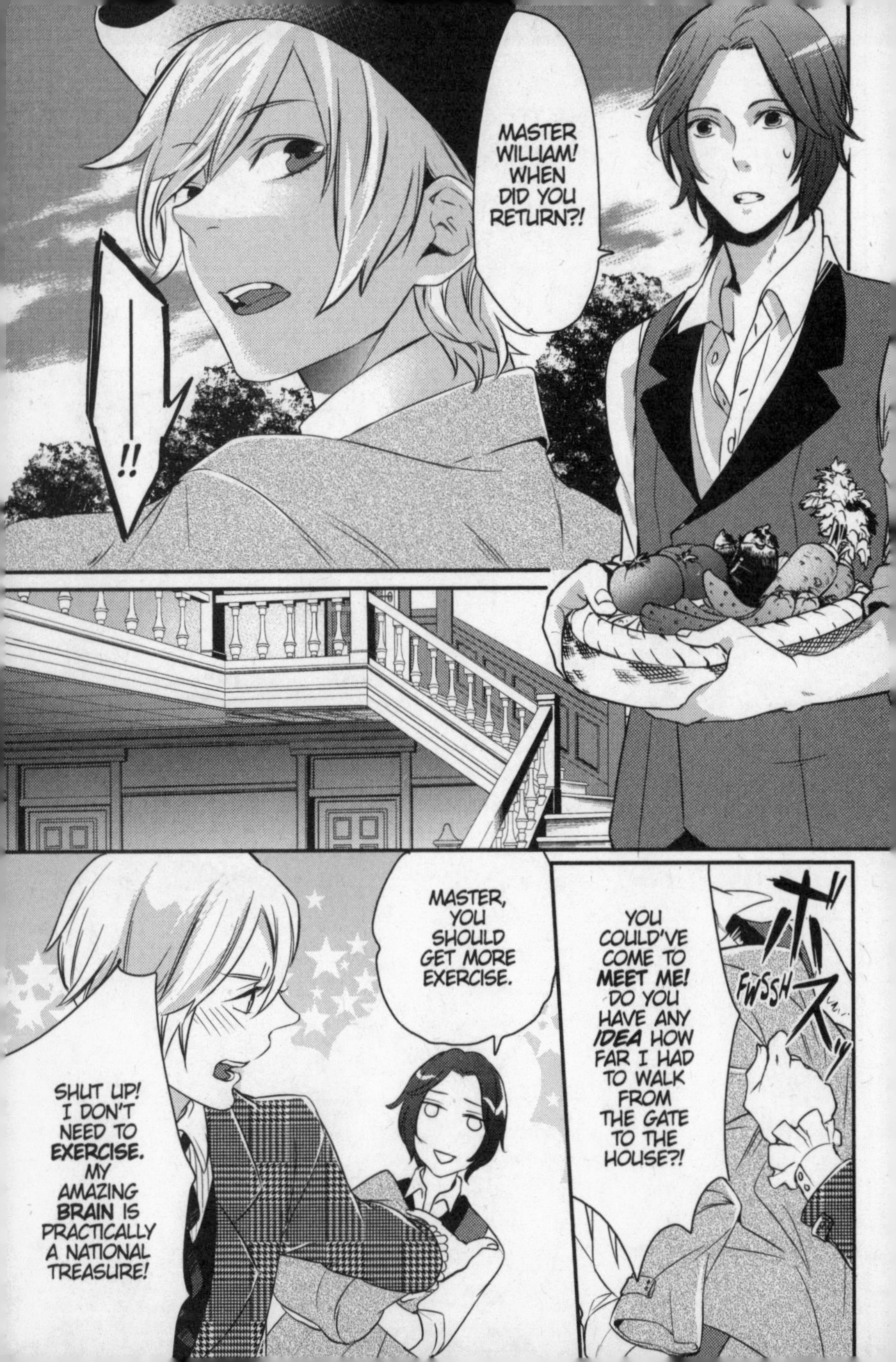
MASTER WILLIAM! WHEN DID YOU RETURN?!
!!
YOU COULD'VE COME TO MEET ME! DO YOU HAVE ANY *IDEA* HOW FAR I HAD TO WALK FROM THE GATE TO THE HOUSE?!
FWSSH
MASTER, YOU SHOULD GET MORE EXERCISE.
SHUT UP! I DON'T NEED TO **EXERCISE**. MY AMAZING **BRAIN** IS PRACTICALLY A NATIONAL TREASURE!

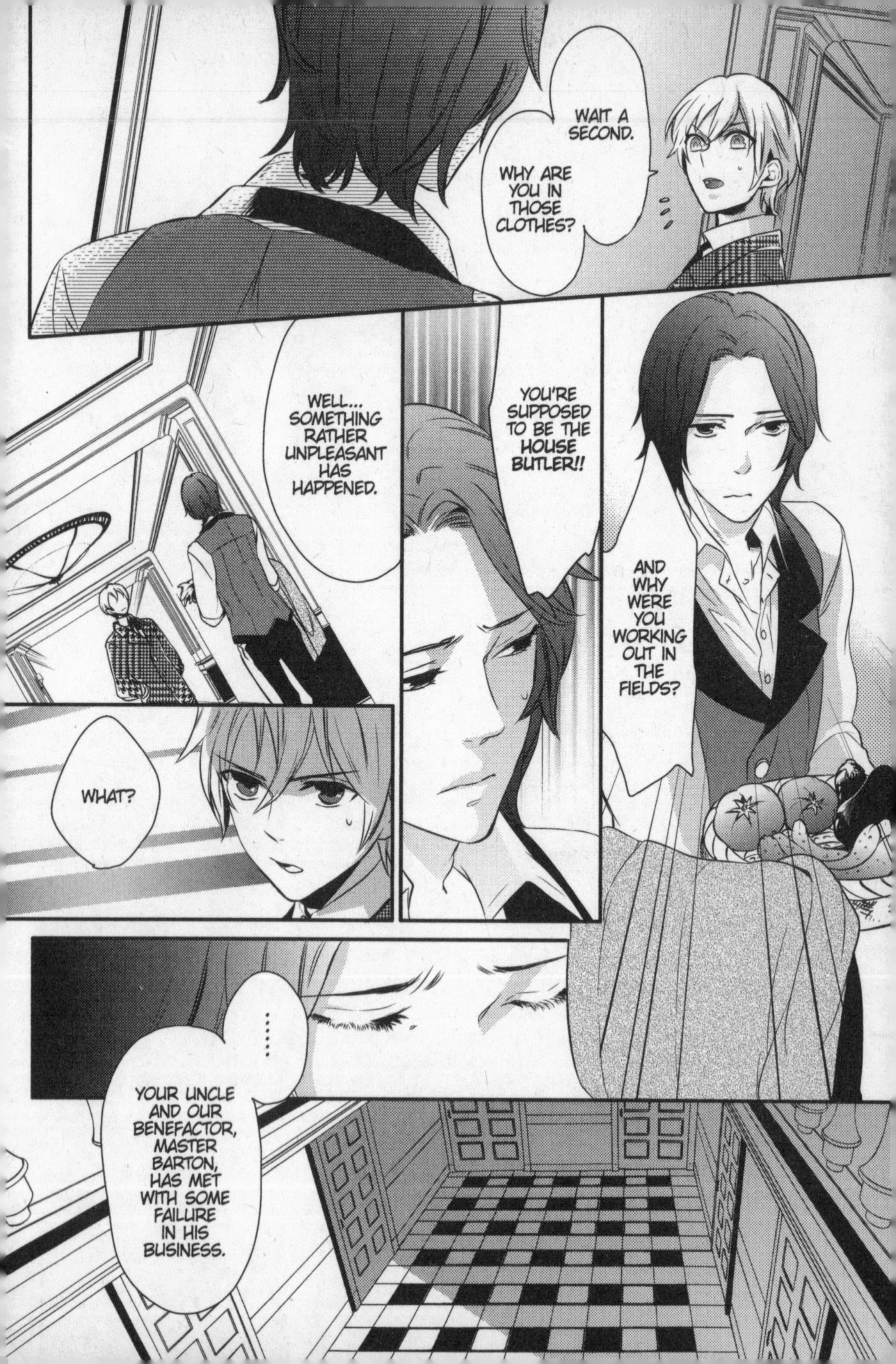
WAIT A SECOND.
WHY ARE YOU IN THOSE CLOTHES?
YOU'RE SUPPOSED TO BE THE HOUSE BUTLER!!
AND WHY WERE YOU WORKING OUT IN THE FIELDS?
WELL... SOMETHING RATHER UNPLEASANT HAS HAPPENED.
WHAT?
......
YOUR UNCLE AND OUR BENEFACTOR, MASTER BARTON, HAS MET WITH SOME FAILURE IN HIS BUSINESS.

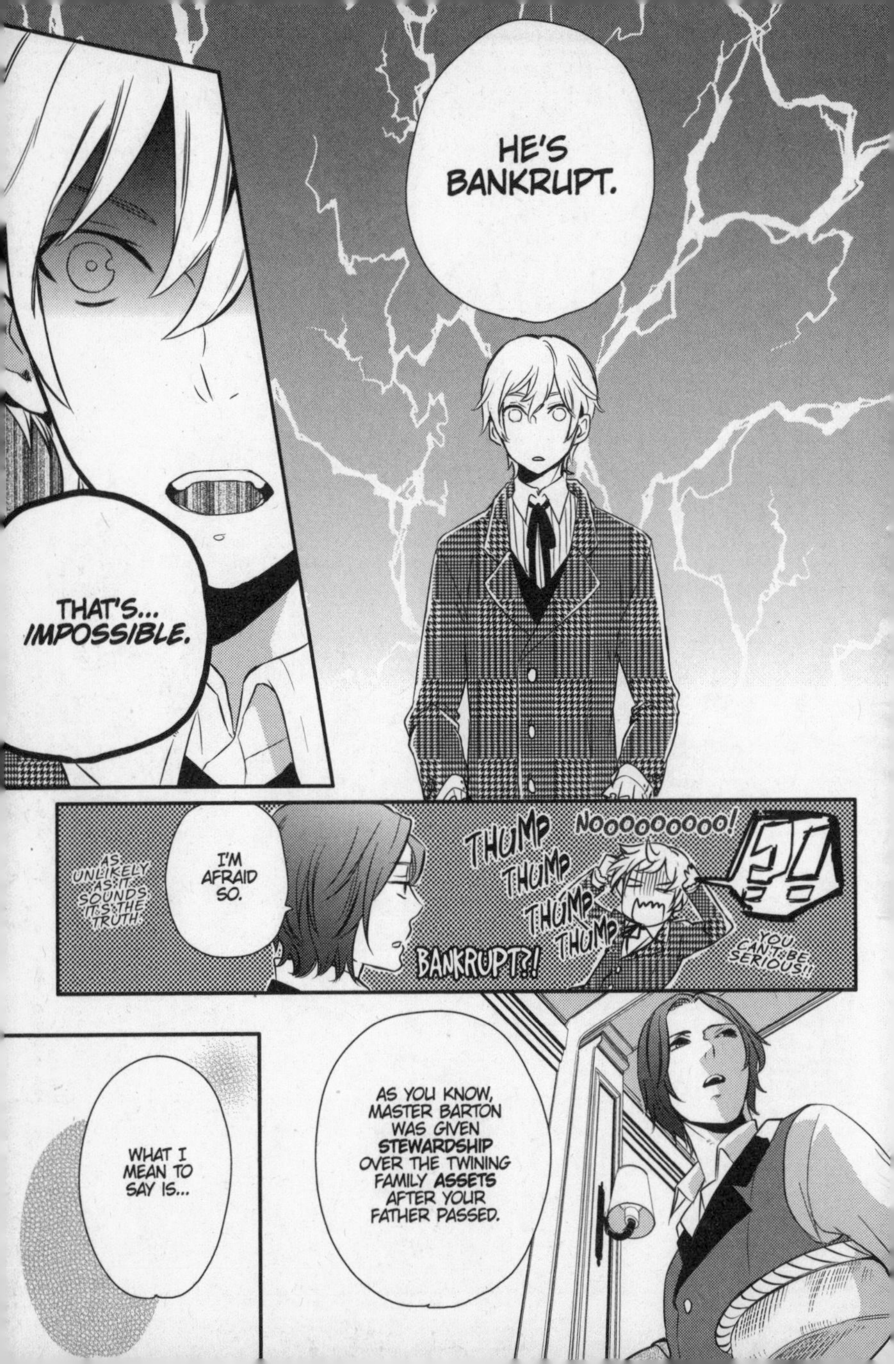
HE'S BANKRUPT.
THAT'S... IMPOSSIBLE.
NOOOOOOOOO!
YOU CAN'T BE SERIOUS!!
THUMP THUMP THUMP THUMP
BANKRUPT?!
I'M AFRAID SO.
AS UNLIKELY AS IT SOUNDS, IT'S THE TRUTH.
AS YOU KNOW, MASTER BARTON WAS GIVEN STEWARDSHIP OVER THE TWINING FAMILY ASSETS AFTER YOUR FATHER PASSED.
WHAT I MEAN TO SAY IS...

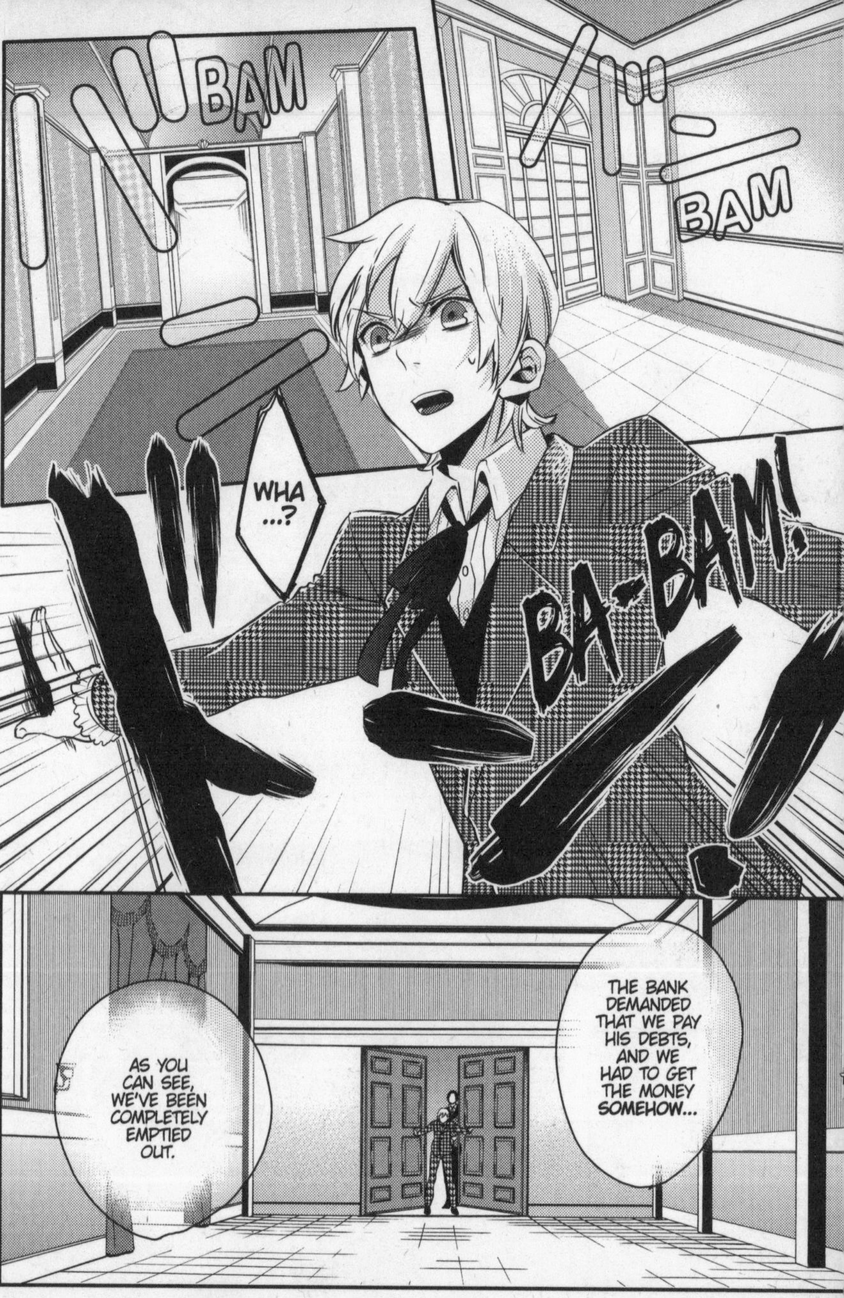
BAM
BAM
BA-BAM!
WHA ...?
THE BANK DEMANDED THAT WE PAY HIS DEBTS, AND WE HAD TO GET THE MONEY SOMEHOW...
AS YOU CAN SEE, WE'VE BEEN COMPLETELY EMPTIED OUT.

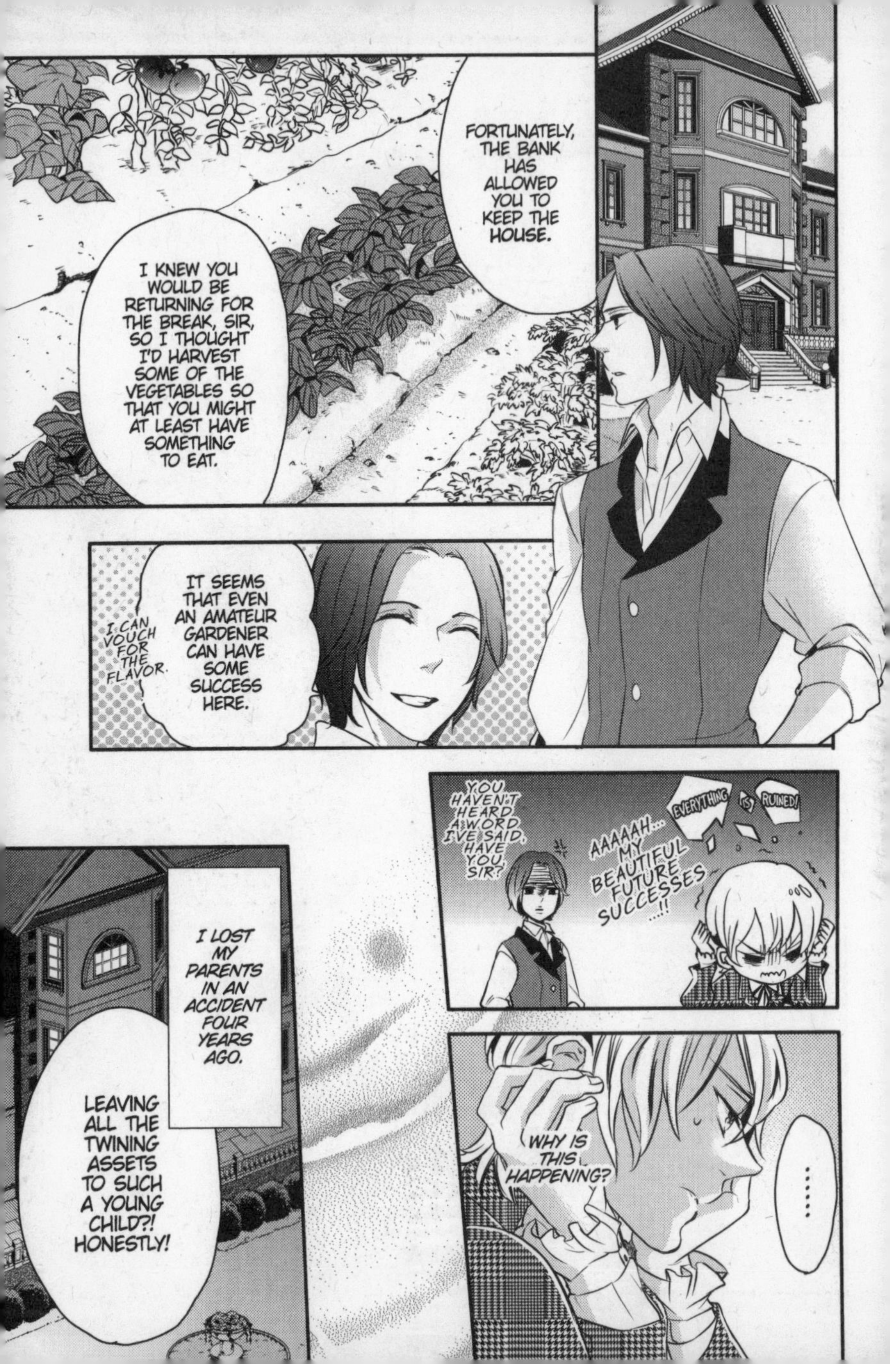
FORTUNATELY, THE BANK HAS ALLOWED YOU TO KEEP THE HOUSE.
I KNEW YOU WOULD BE RETURNING FOR THE BREAK, SIR, SO I THOUGHT I'D HARVEST SOME OF THE VEGETABLES SO THAT YOU MIGHT AT LEAST HAVE SOMETHING TO EAT.
IT SEEMS THAT EVEN AN AMATEUR GARDENER CAN HAVE SOME SUCCESS HERE.
I CAN VOUCH FOR THE FLAVOR.
EVERYTHING IS RUINED!
AAAAAH... MY BEAUTIFUL FUTURE SUCCESSES ...!!
YOU HAVEN'T HEARD A WORD I'VE SAID, HAVE YOU, SIR?
......
WHY IS THIS HAPPENING?
I LOST MY PARENTS IN AN ACCIDENT FOUR YEARS AGO.
LEAVING ALL THE TWINING ASSETS TO SUCH A YOUNG CHILD?! HONESTLY!

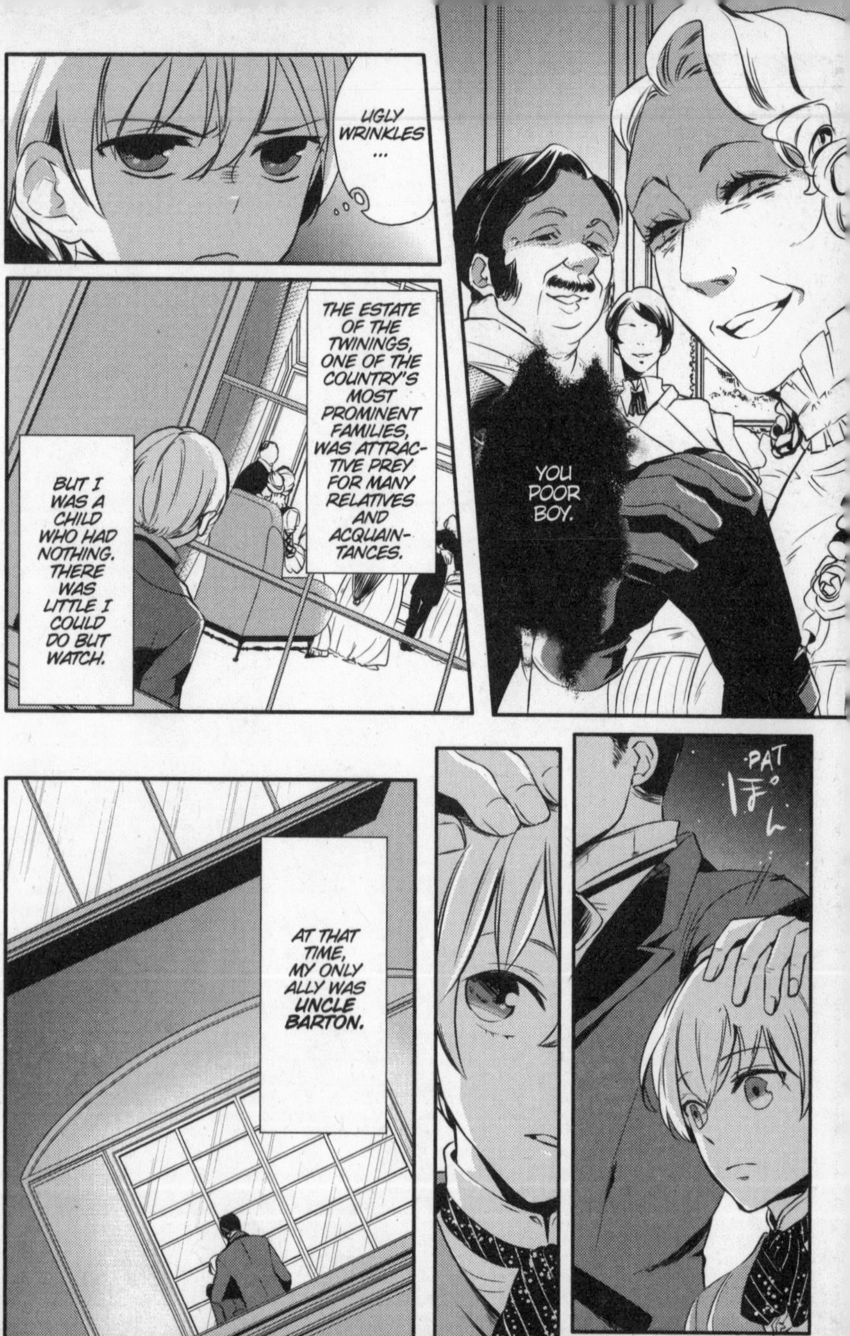
YOU POOR BOY.
UGLY WRINKLES ...
THE ESTATE OF THE TWININGS, ONE OF THE COUNTRY'S MOST PROMINENT FAMILIES, WAS ATTRACTIVE PREY FOR MANY RELATIVES AND ACQUAINTANCES.
BUT I WAS A CHILD WHO HAD NOTHING. THERE WAS LITTLE I COULD DO BUT WATCH.
PAT
ぽん
AT THAT TIME, MY ONLY ALLY WAS UNCLE BARTON.

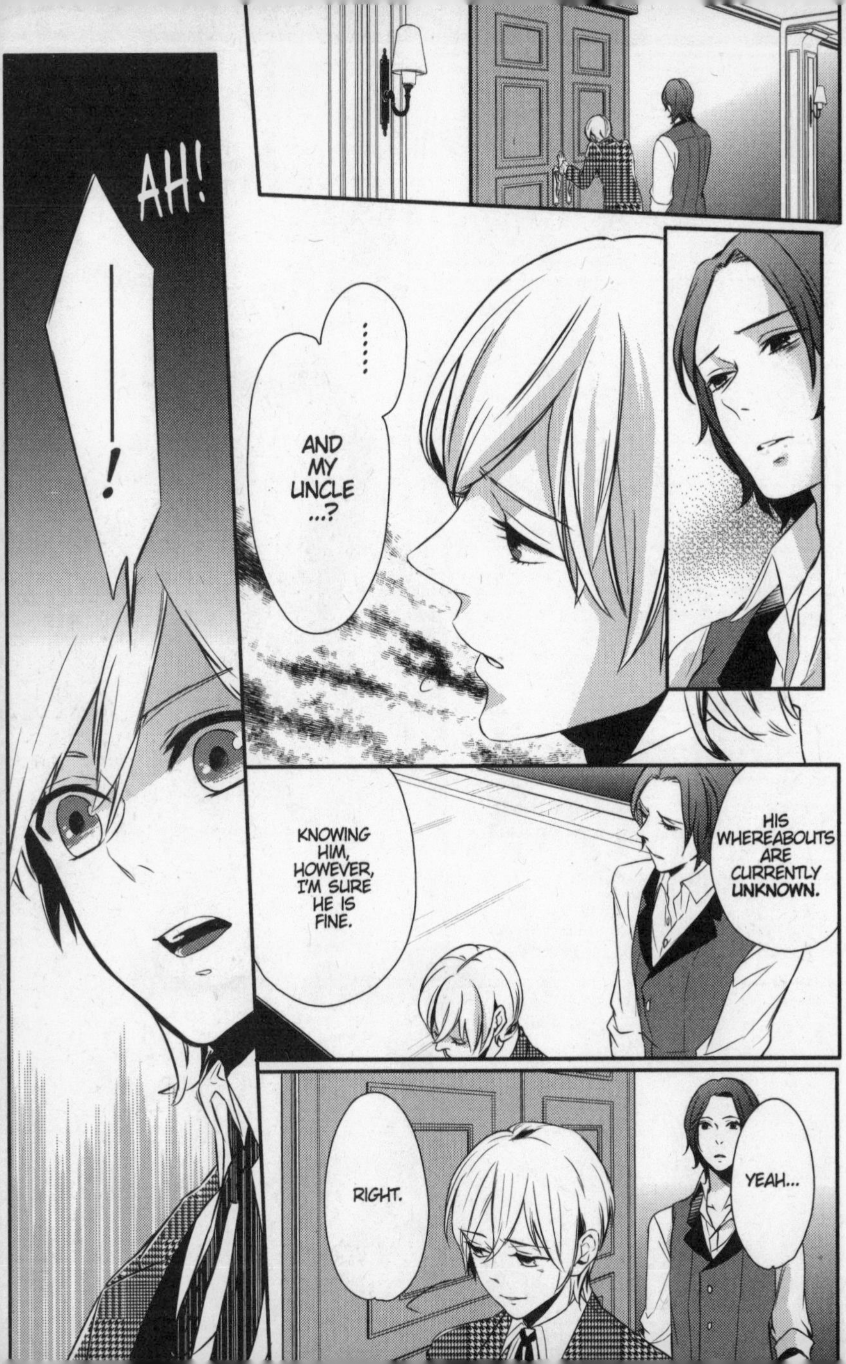

.....
AND MY UNCLE ...?
HIS WHEREABOUTS ARE CURRENTLY UNKNOWN.
KNOWING HIM, HOWEVER, I'M SURE HE IS FINE.
YEAH...
RIGHT.
AH!
!

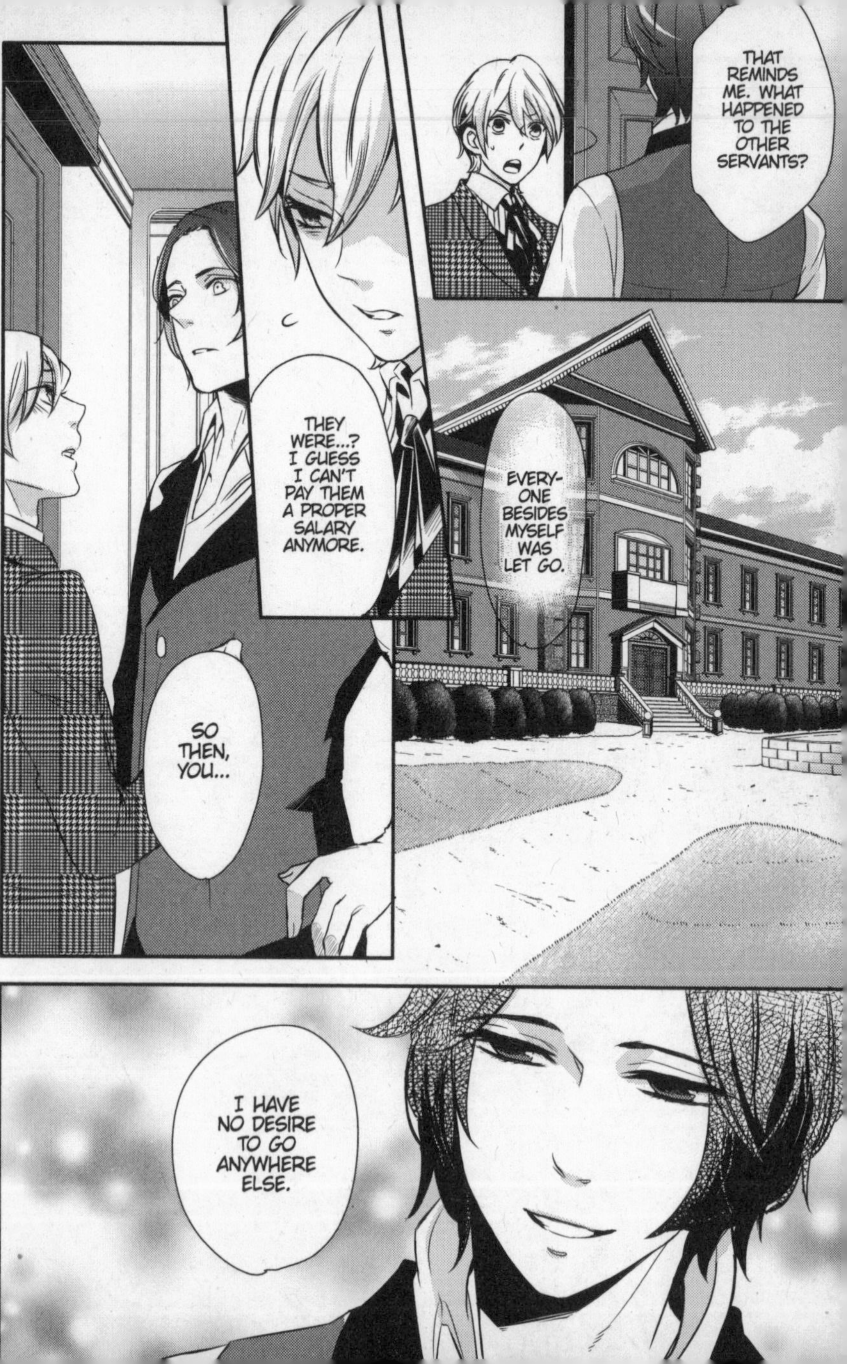
THAT REMINDS ME. WHAT HAPPENED TO THE OTHER SERVANTS?
EVERYONE BESIDES MYSELF WAS LET GO.
THEY WERE...? I GUESS I CAN'T PAY THEM A PROPER SALARY ANYMORE.
SO THEN, YOU...
I HAVE NO DESIRE TO GO ANYWHERE ELSE.

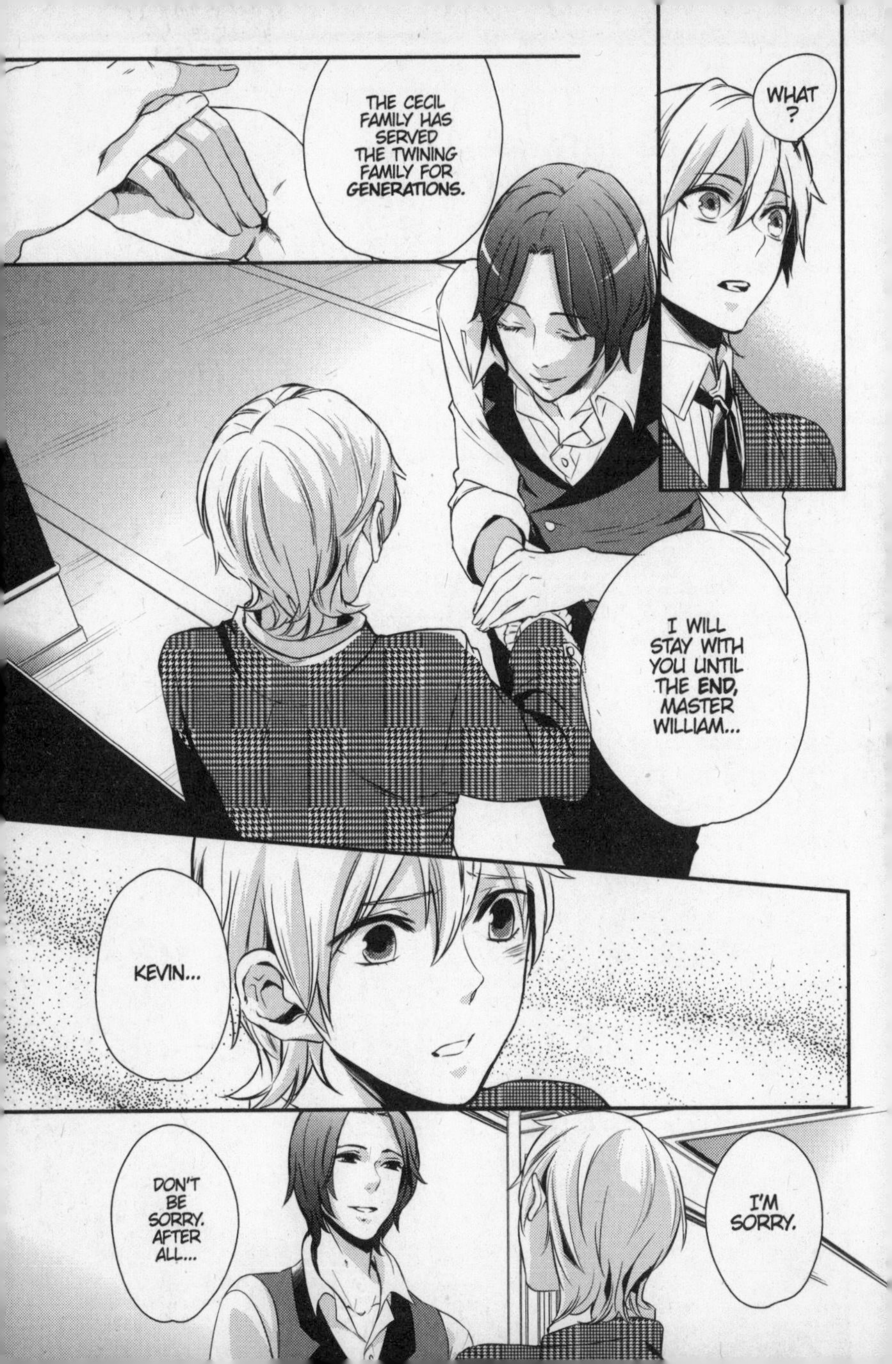
WHAT?
THE CECIL FAMILY HAS SERVED THE TWINING FAMILY FOR GENERATIONS.
I WILL STAY WITH YOU UNTIL THE END, MASTER WILLIAM...
KEVIN...
I'M SORRY.
DON'T BE SORRY. AFTER ALL...

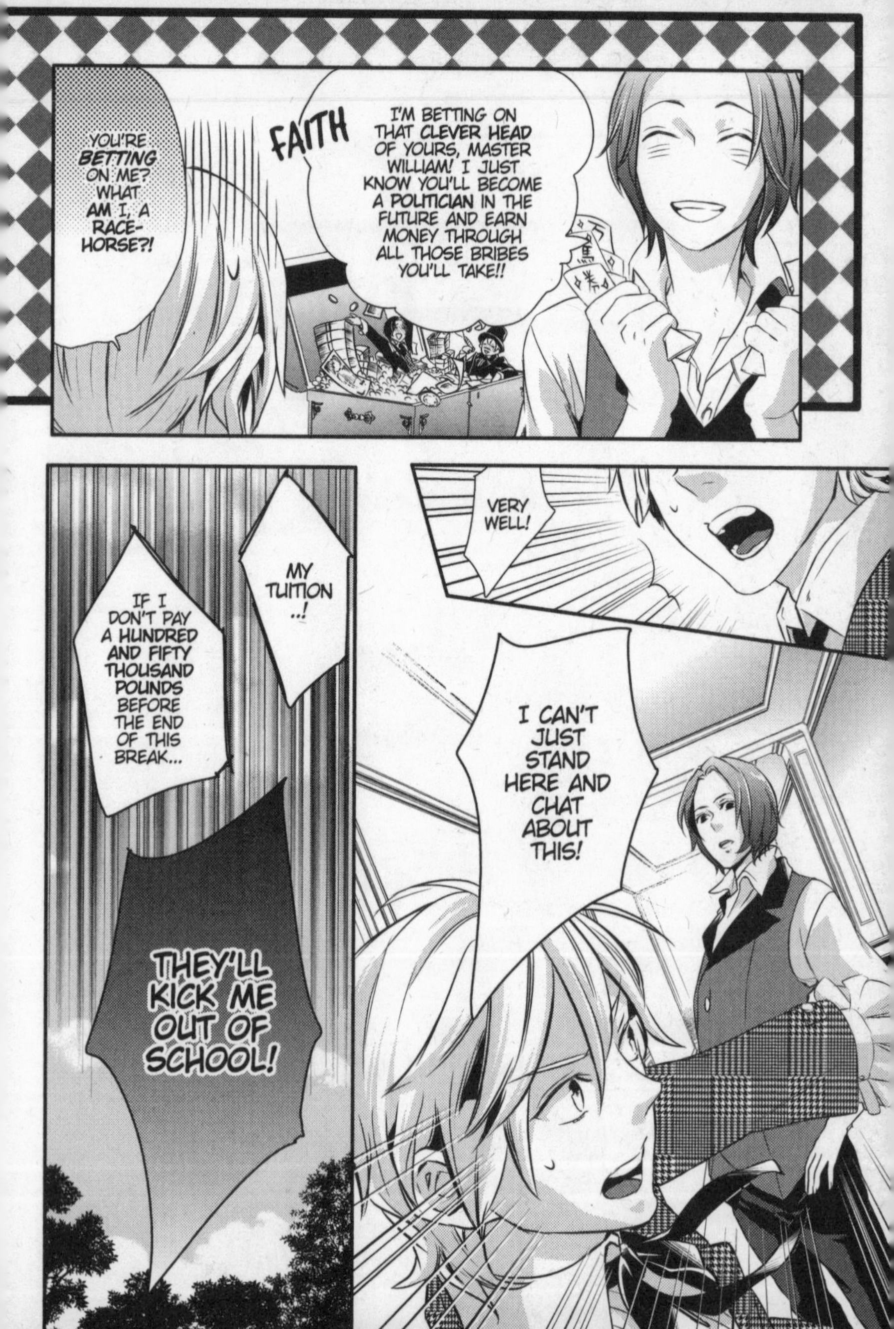
I'M BETTING ON THAT CLEVER HEAD OF YOURS, MASTER WILLIAM! I JUST KNOW YOU'LL BECOME A POLITICIAN IN THE FUTURE AND EARN MONEY THROUGH ALL THOSE BRIBES YOU'LL TAKE!!
FAITH
YOU'RE BETTING ON ME? WHAT AM I, A RACE-HORSE?!
VERY WELL!
I CAN'T JUST STAND HERE AND CHAT ABOUT THIS!
MY TUITION..!
IF I DON'T PAY A HUNDRED AND FIFTY THOUSAND POUNDS BEFORE THE END OF THIS BREAK...
THEY'LL KICK ME OUT OF SCHOOL!

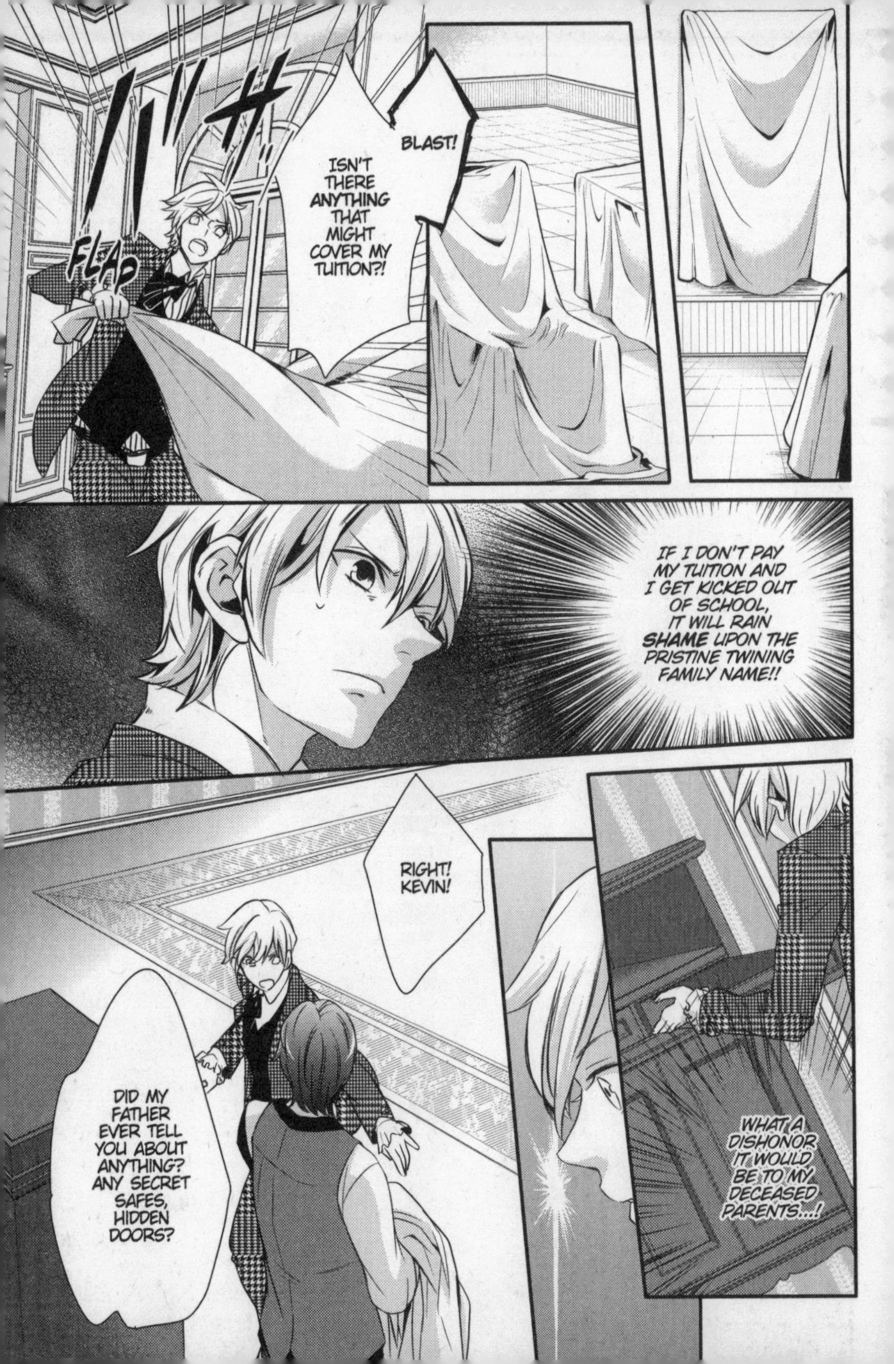
BLAST!
ISN'T THERE ANYTHING THAT MIGHT COVER MY TUITION?!
バサッ
FLAP
IF I DON'T PAY MY TUITION AND I GET KICKED OUT OF SCHOOL, IT WILL RAIN SHAME UPON THE PRISTINE TWINING FAMILY NAME!!
WHAT A DISHONOR IT WOULD BE TO MY DECEASED PARENTS...!
RIGHT! KEVIN!
DID MY FATHER EVER TELL YOU ABOUT ANYTHING? ANY SECRET SAFES, HIDDEN DOORS?

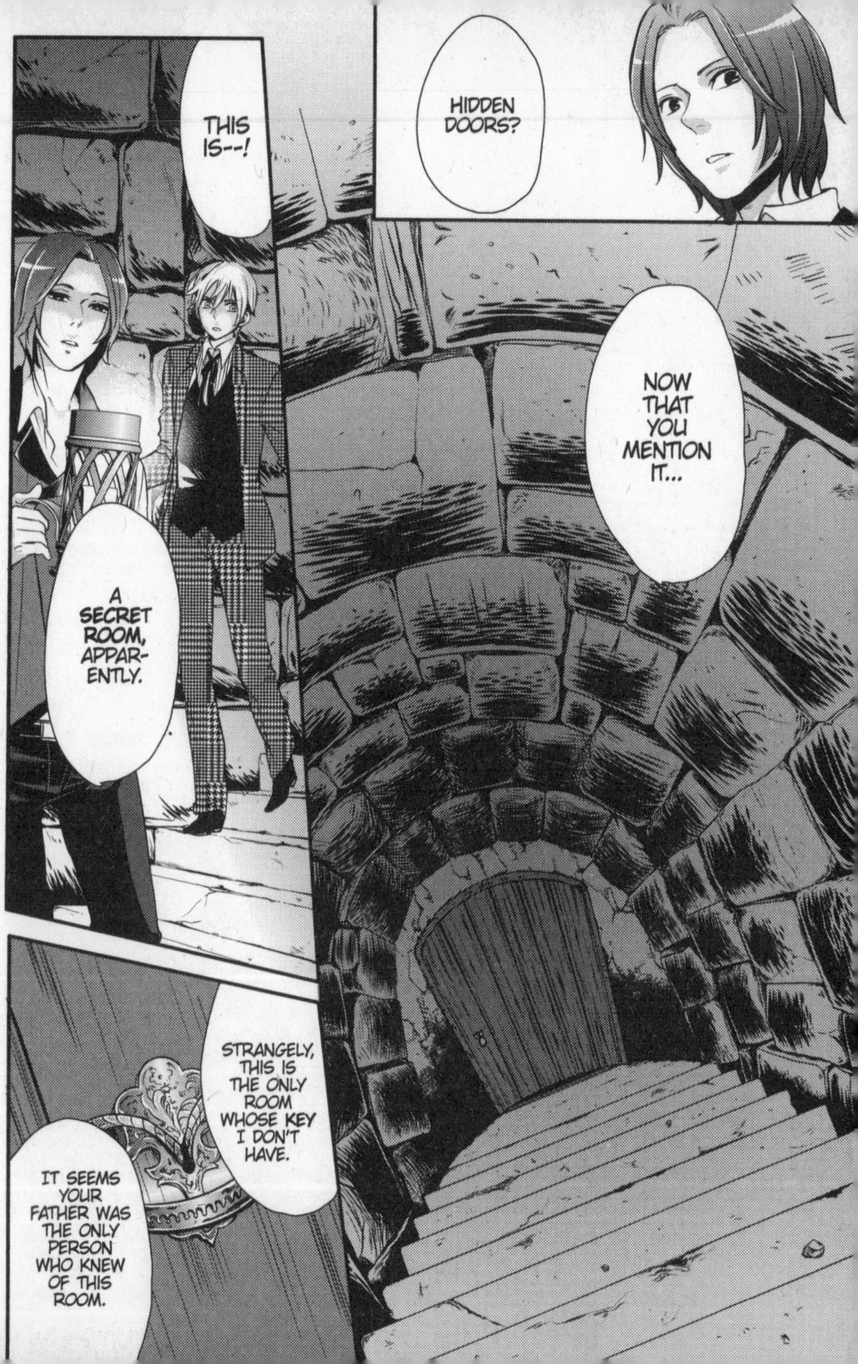
HIDDEN DOORS?
NOW THAT YOU MENTION IT...
THIS IS--!
A SECRET ROOM, APPARENTLY.
STRANGELY, THIS IS THE ONLY ROOM WHOSE KEY I DON'T HAVE.
IT SEEMS YOUR FATHER WAS THE ONLY PERSON WHO KNEW OF THIS ROOM.

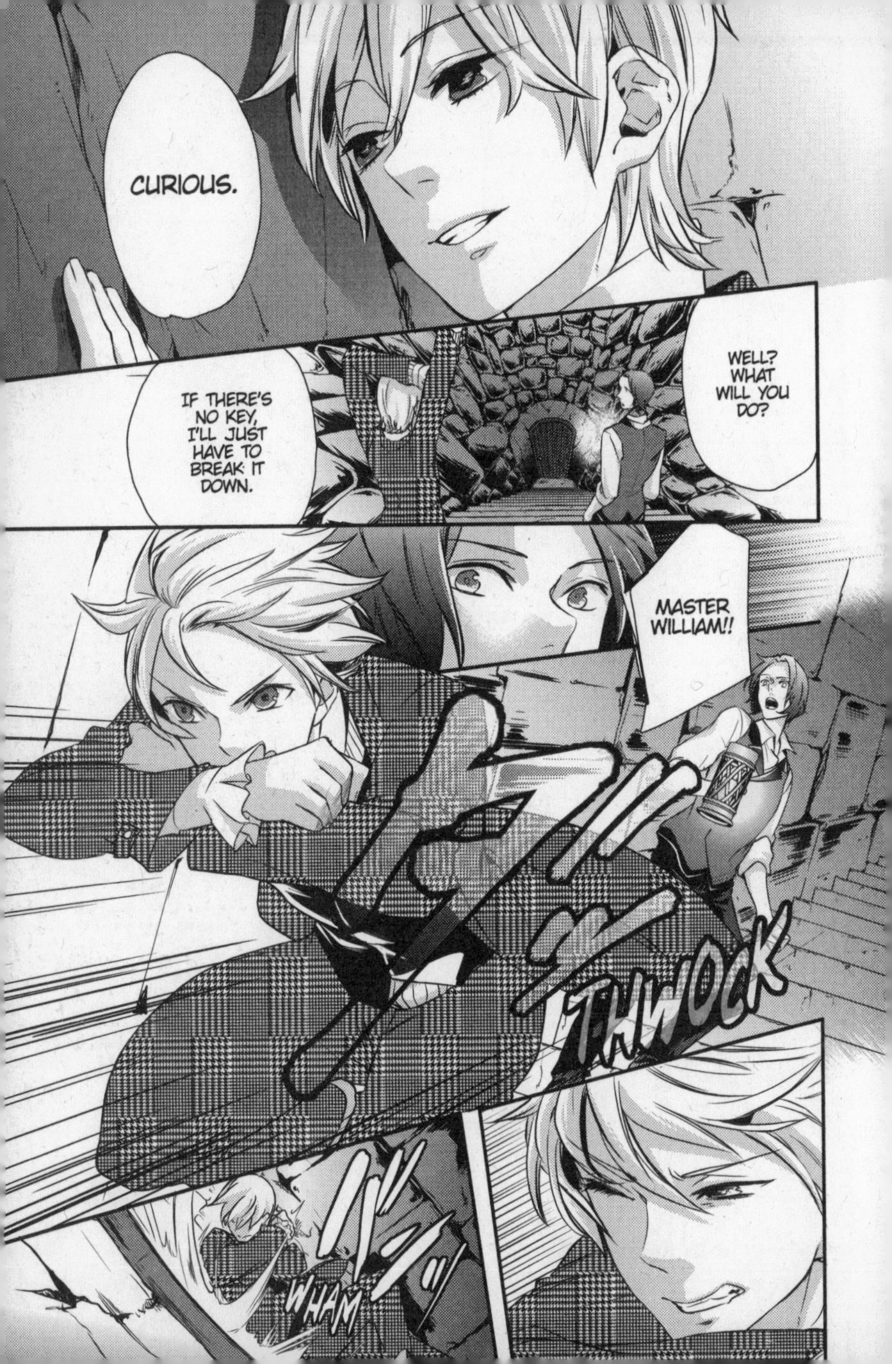
CURIOUS.
WELL? WHAT WILL YOU DO?
IF THERE'S NO KEY, I'LL JUST HAVE TO BREAK IT DOWN.
MASTER WILLIAM!!
THWOCK
WHAM

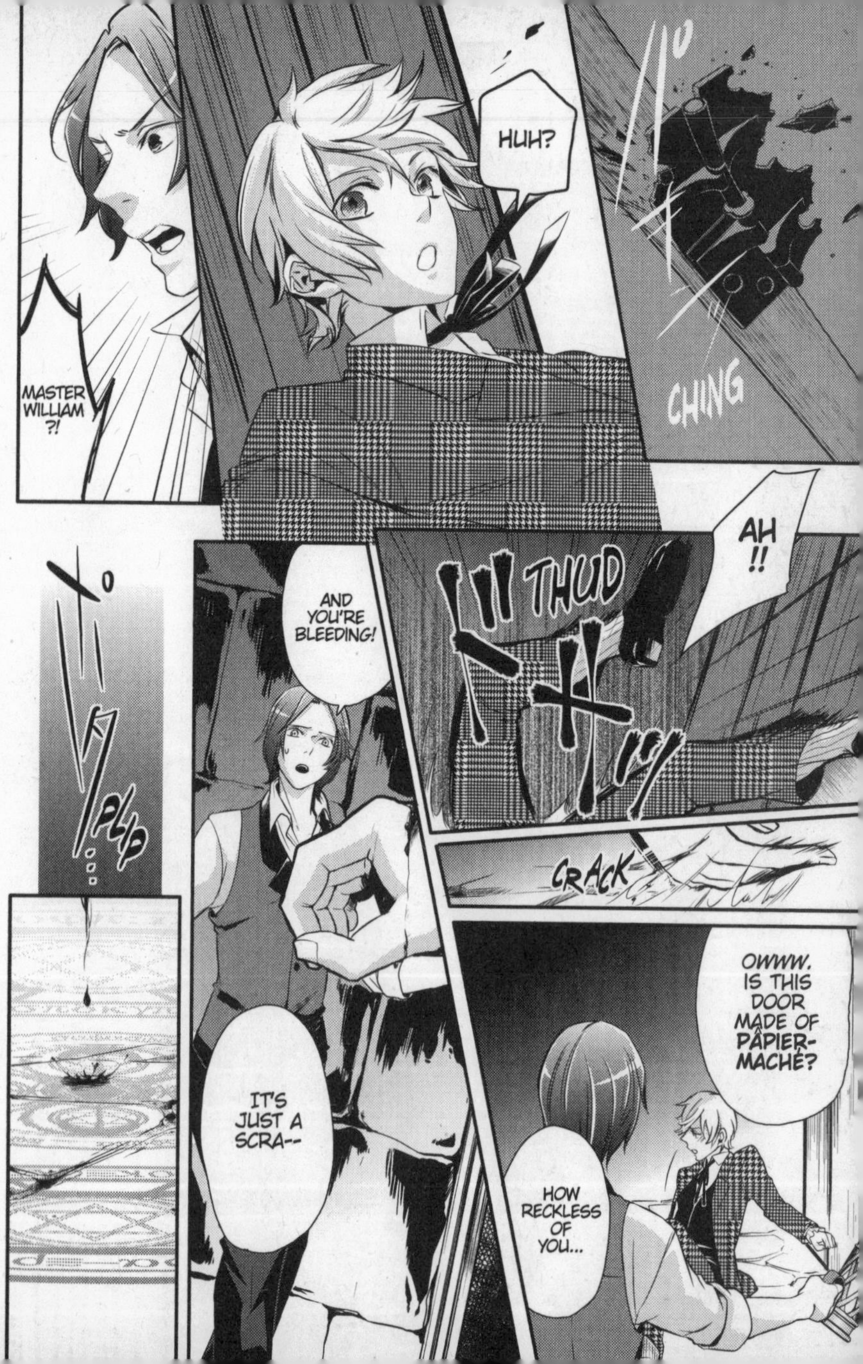
CHING
HUH?
MASTER WILLIAM ?!
AH !!
THUD
CRACK
OWWW. IS THIS DOOR MADE OF PÂPIER-MACHÉ?
HOW RECKLESS OF YOU...
AND YOU'RE BLEEDING!
IT'S JUST A SCRA--
PLIP...

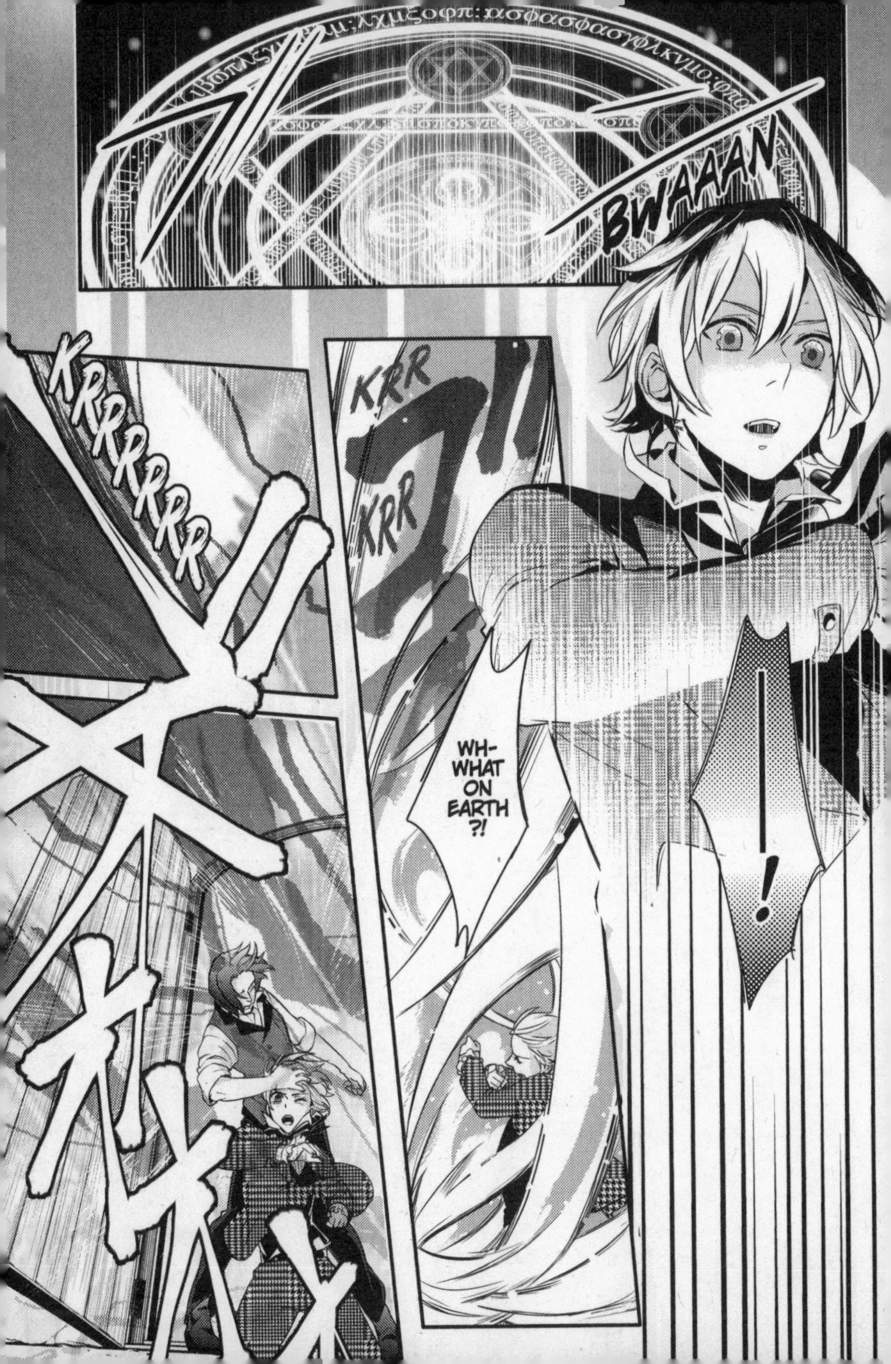
BWAAAN
!
KRR
KRR
WH-WHAT ON EARTH?!
KRRRRRRR

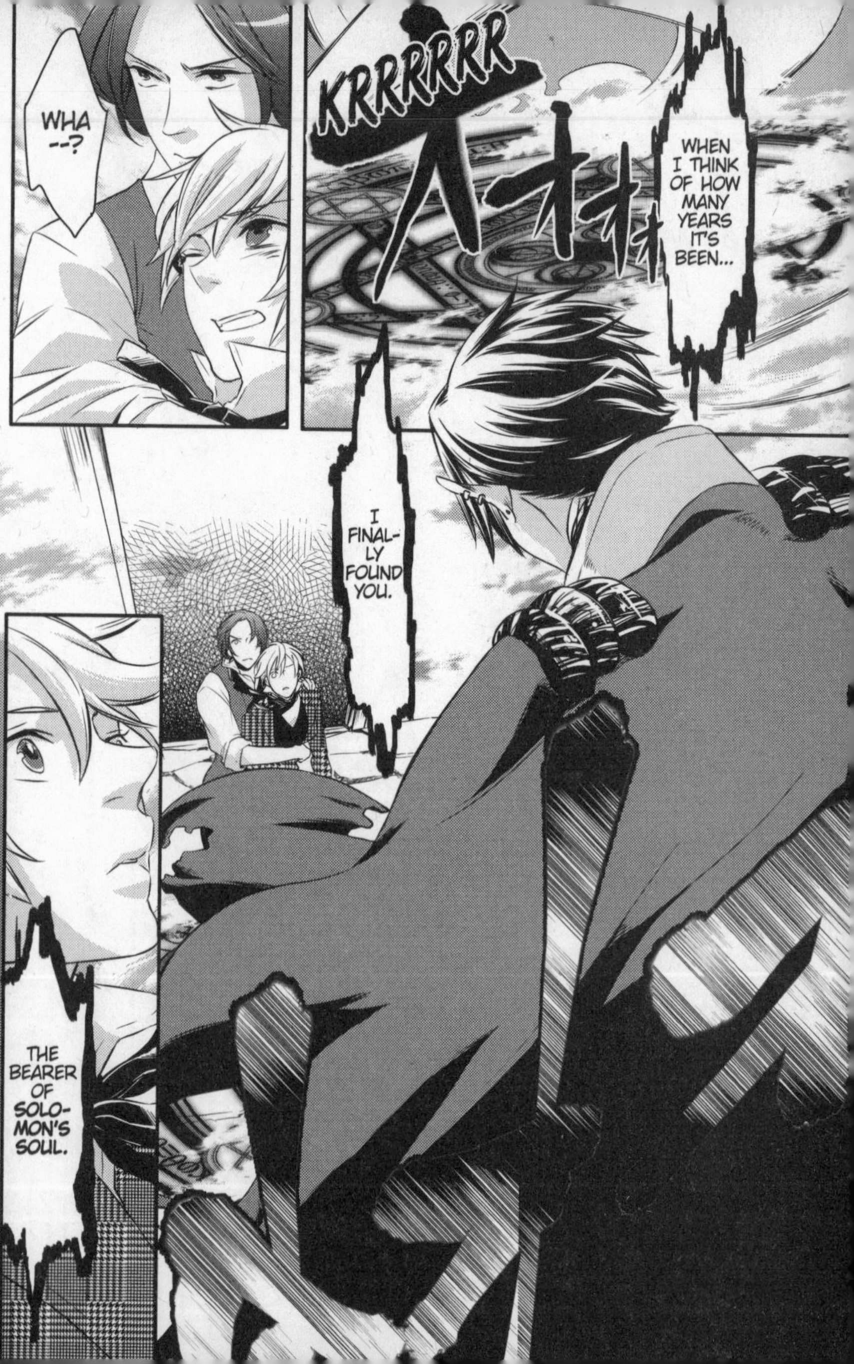
KRRRRRR
WHEN I THINK OF HOW MANY YEARS IT'S BEEN...
WHA--?
I FINAL-LY FOUND YOU.
THE BEARER OF SOLO-MON'S SOUL.

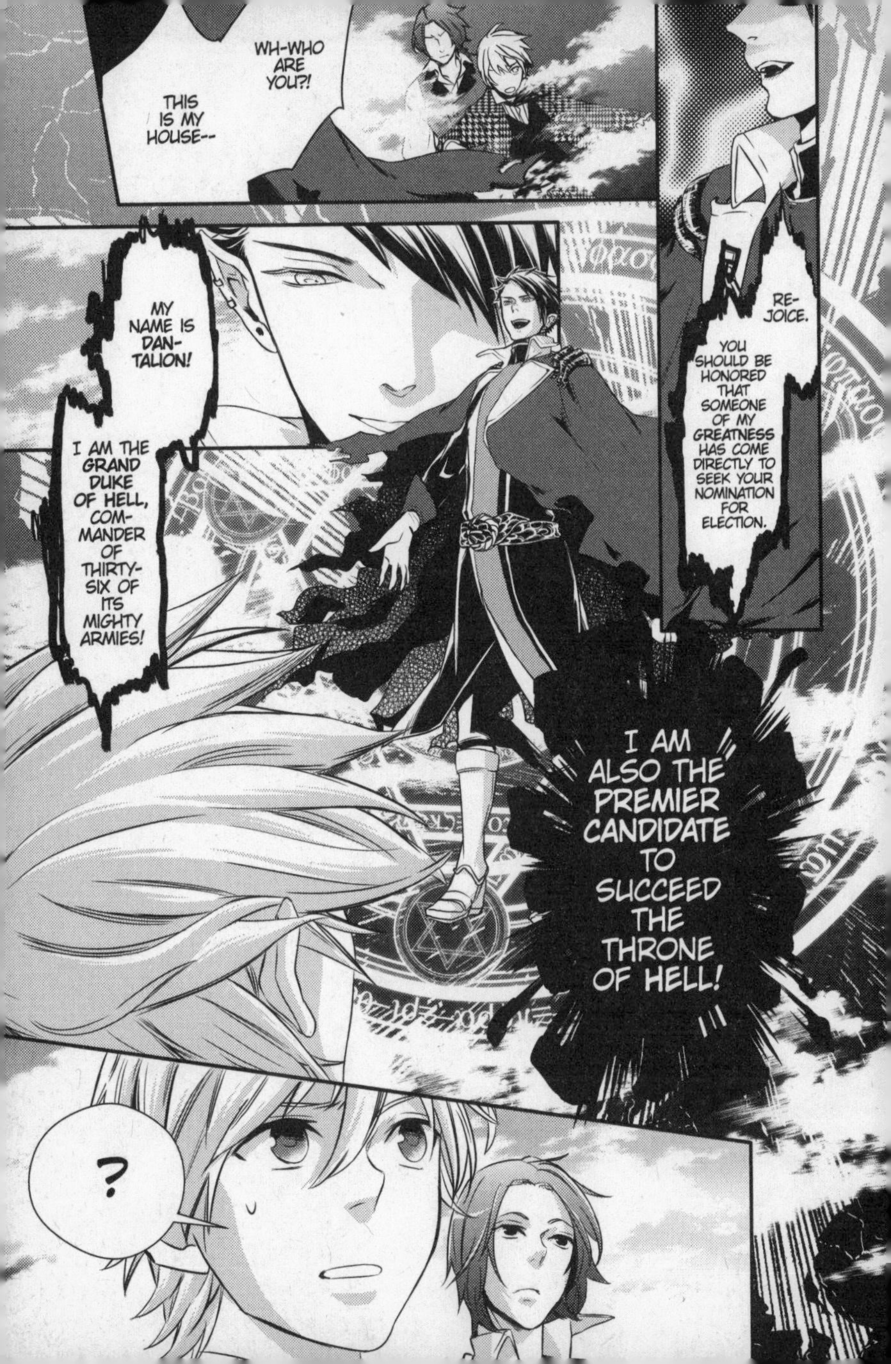
REJOICE.
YOU SHOULD BE HONORED THAT SOMEONE OF MY GREATNESS HAS COME DIRECTLY TO SEEK YOUR NOMINATION FOR ELECTION.
WH-WHO ARE YOU?!
THIS IS MY HOUSE--
MY NAME IS DANTALION!
I AM THE GRAND DUKE OF HELL, COMMANDER OF THIRTY-SIX OF ITS MIGHTY ARMIES!
I AM ALSO THE PREMIER CANDIDATE TO SUCCEED THE THRONE OF HELL!
?

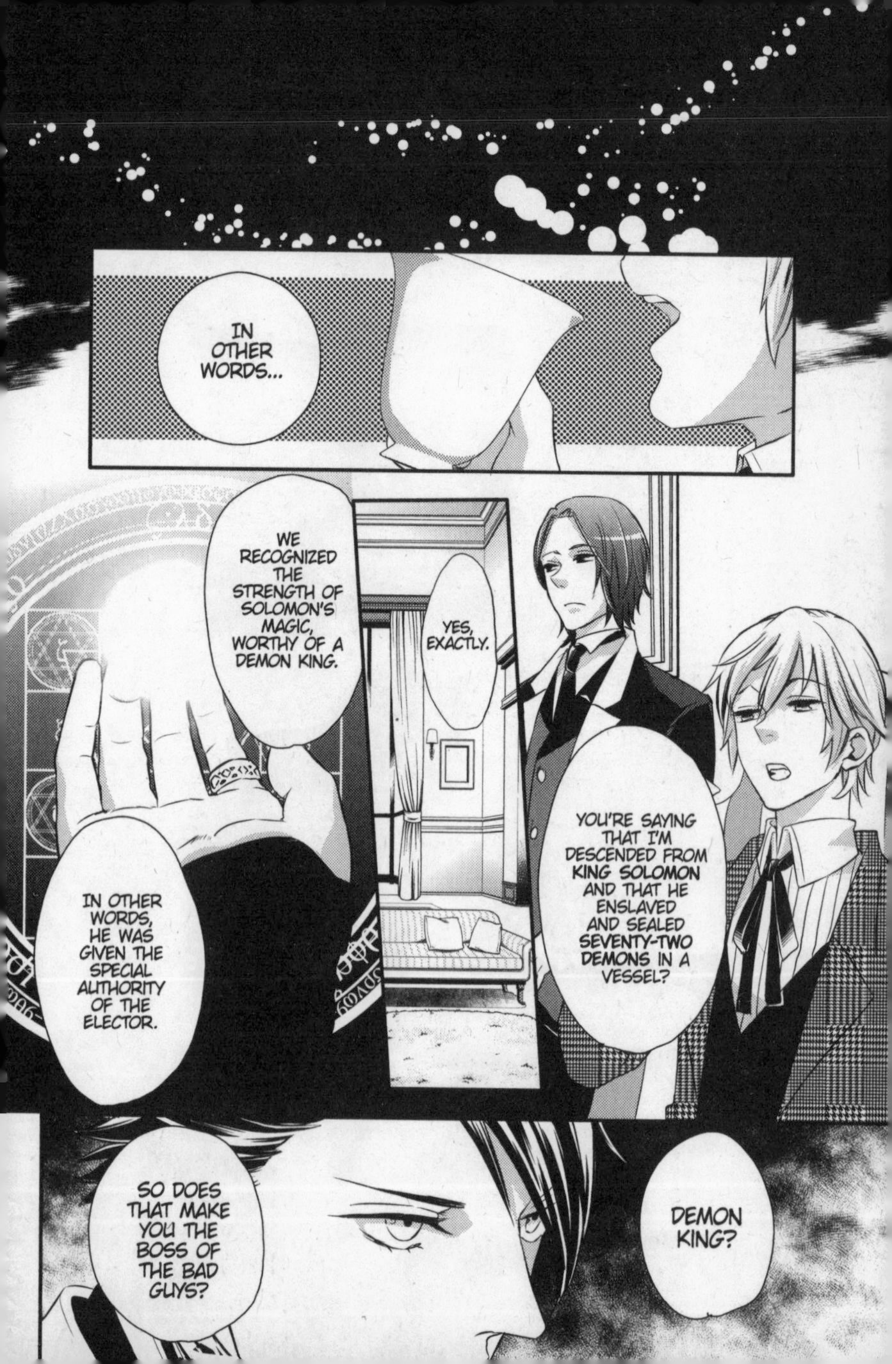
IN OTHER WORDS...
YOU'RE SAYING THAT I'M DESCENDED FROM KING SOLOMON AND THAT HE ENSLAVED AND SEALED SEVENTY-TWO DEMONS IN A VESSEL?
YES, EXACTLY.
WE RECOGNIZED THE STRENGTH OF SOLOMON'S MAGIC, WORTHY OF A DEMON KING.
IN OTHER WORDS, HE WAS GIVEN THE SPECIAL AUTHORITY OF THE ELECTOR.
DEMON KING?
SO DOES THAT MAKE YOU THE BOSS OF THE BAD GUYS?

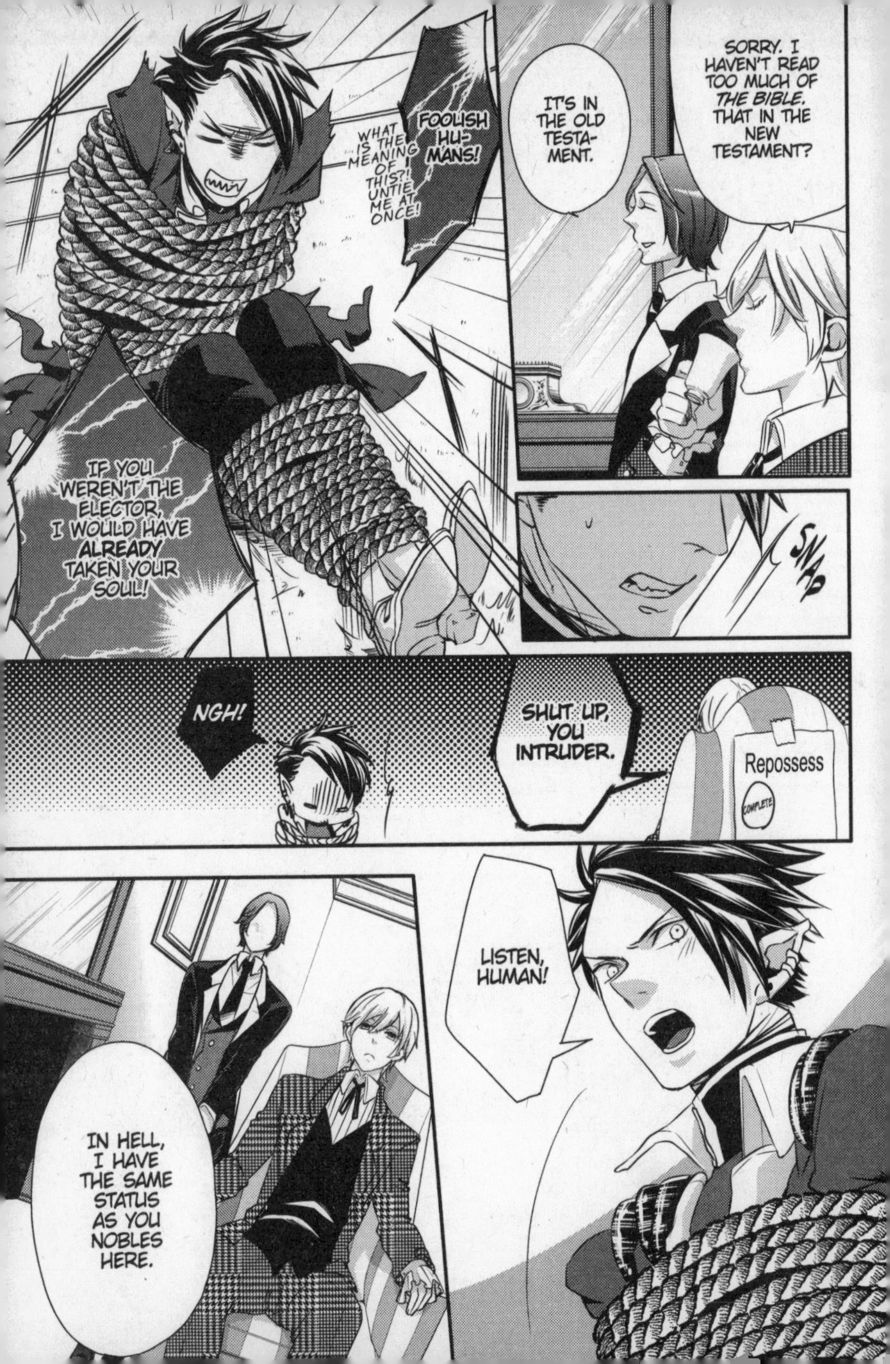
SORRY. I HAVEN'T READ TOO MUCH OF *THE BIBLE*. THAT IN THE NEW TESTAMENT?
IT'S IN THE OLD TESTAMENT.
SNAP
FOOLISH HUMANS!
WHAT IS THE MEANING OF THIS?! UNTIE ME AT ONCE!
IF YOU WEREN'T THE ELECTOR, I WOULD HAVE **ALREADY** TAKEN YOUR SOUL!
Repossess
COMPLETE
SHUT UP, YOU INTRUDER.
NGH!
LISTEN, HUMAN!
IN HELL, I HAVE THE SAME STATUS AS YOU NOBLES HERE.

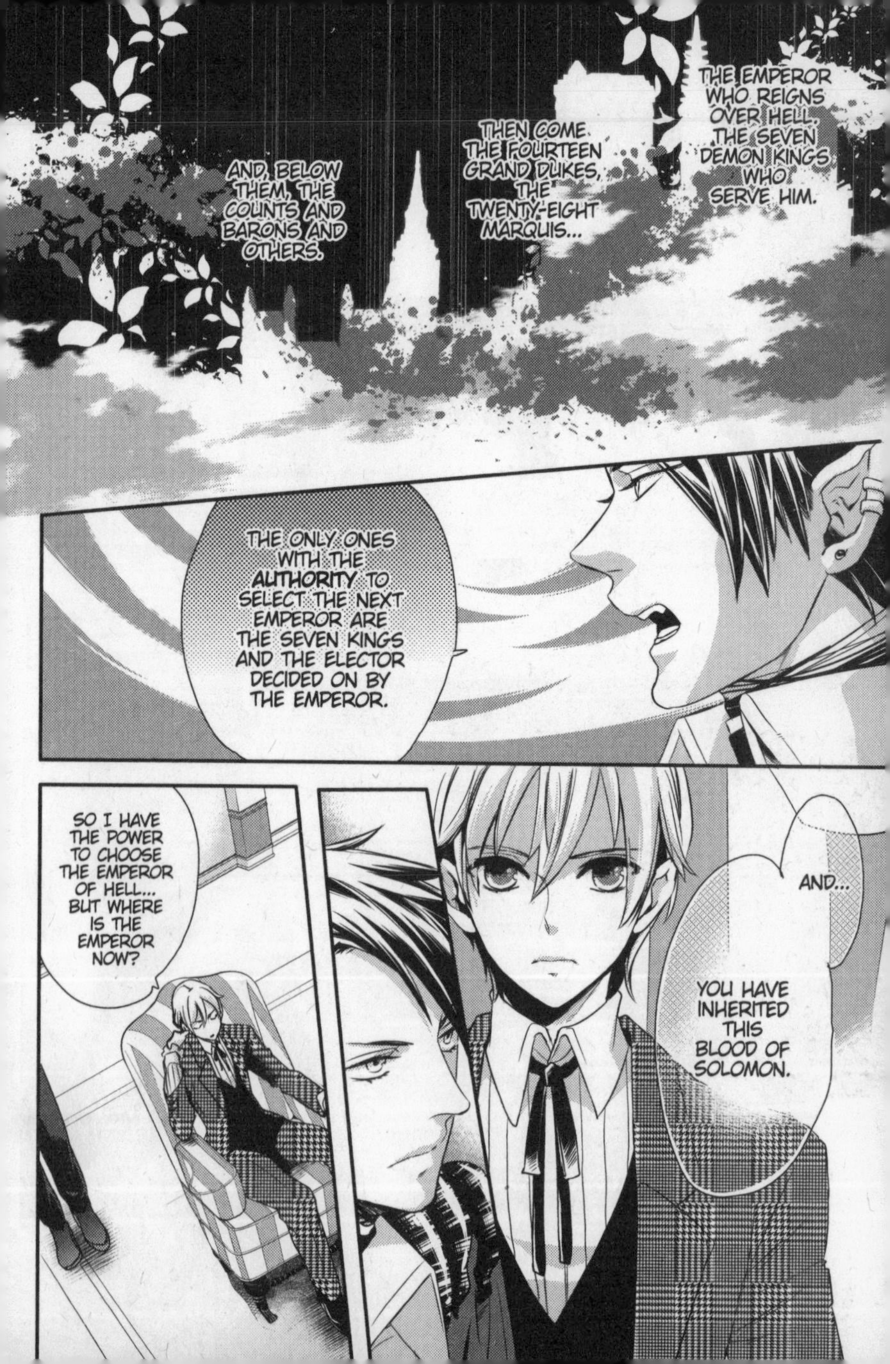
THE EMPEROR WHO REIGNS OVER HELL. THE SEVEN DEMON KINGS WHO SERVE HIM.
THEN COME THE FOURTEEN GRAND DUKES, THE TWENTY-EIGHT MARQUIS...
AND, BELOW THEM, THE COUNTS AND BARONS AND OTHERS.
THE ONLY ONES WITH THE **AUTHORITY** TO SELECT THE NEXT EMPEROR ARE THE SEVEN KINGS AND THE ELECTOR DECIDED ON BY THE EMPEROR.
AND...
YOU HAVE INHERITED THIS BLOOD OF SOLOMON.
SO I HAVE THE POWER TO CHOOSE THE EMPEROR OF HELL... BUT WHERE IS THE EMPEROR NOW?

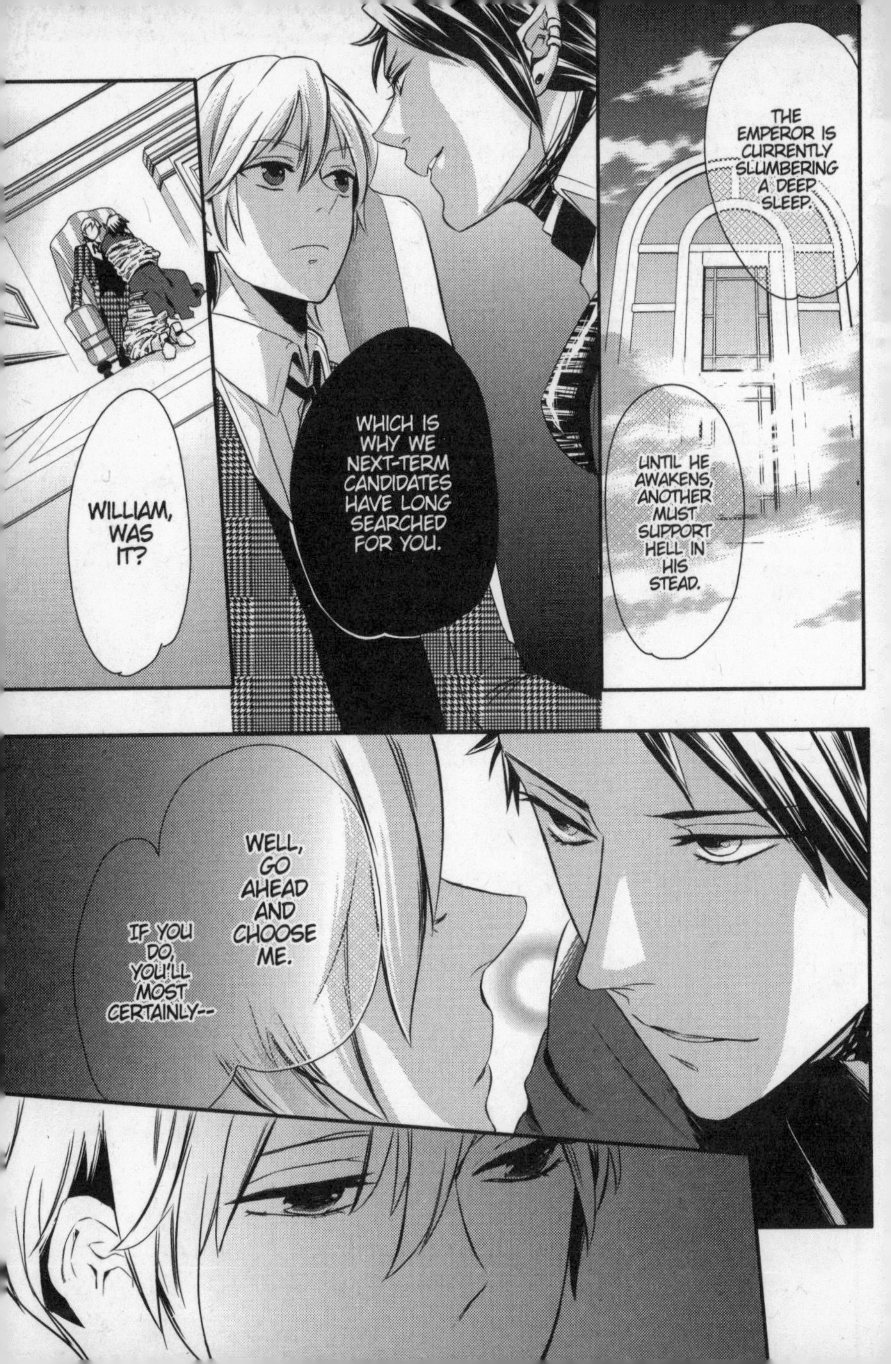
THE EMPEROR IS CURRENTLY SLUMBERING A DEEP SLEEP.
UNTIL HE AWAKENS, ANOTHER MUST SUPPORT HELL IN HIS STEAD.
WHICH IS WHY WE NEXT-TERM CANDIDATES HAVE LONG SEARCHED FOR YOU.
WILLIAM, WAS IT?
WELL, GO AHEAD AND CHOOSE ME.
IF YOU DO, YOU'LL MOST CERTAINLY--

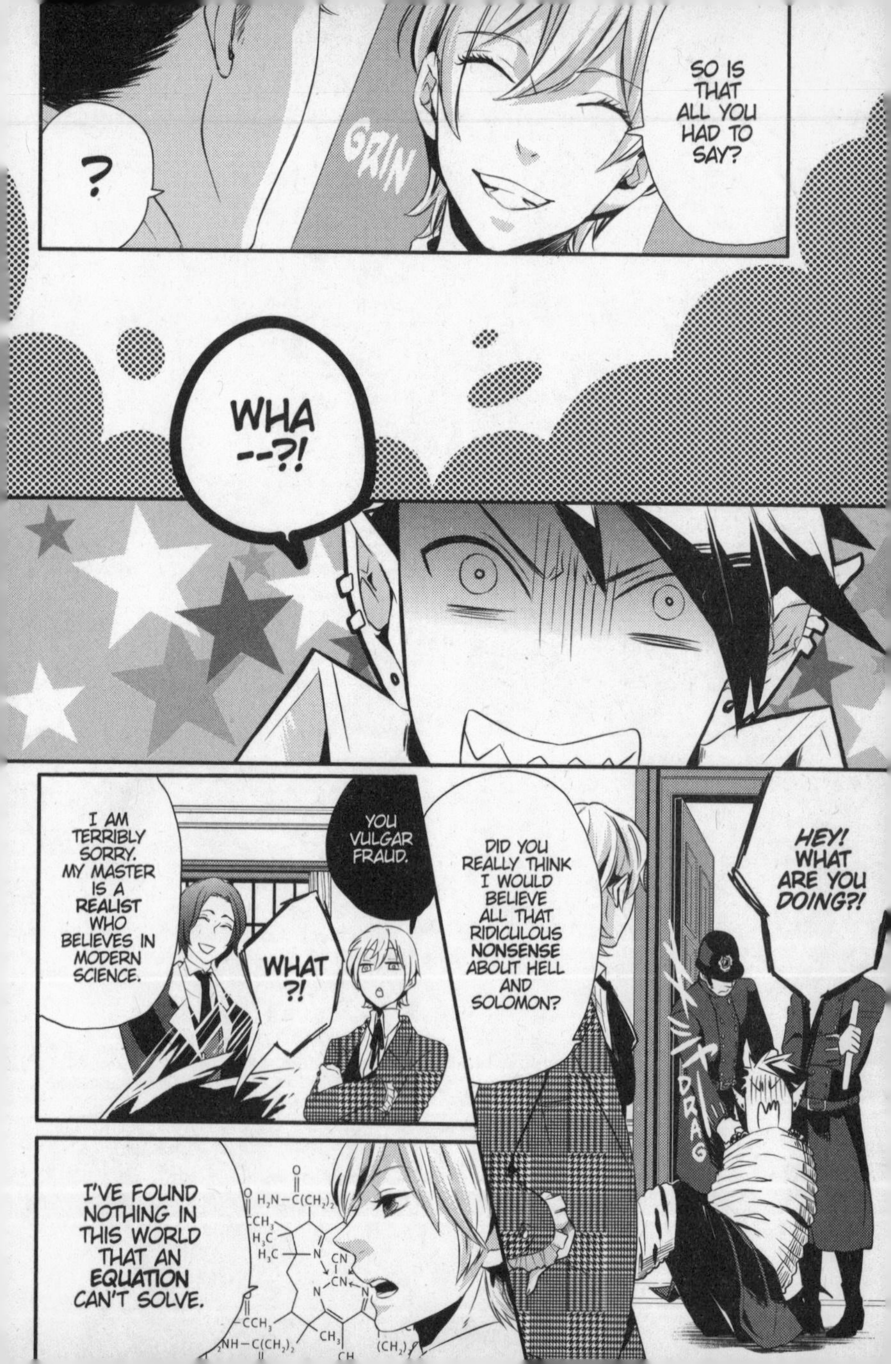
SO IS THAT ALL YOU HAD TO SAY?
GRIN
?
WHA--?!
HEY! WHAT ARE YOU DOING?!
DRAG
DID YOU REALLY THINK I WOULD BELIEVE ALL THAT RIDICULOUS NONSENSE ABOUT HELL AND SOLOMON?
YOU VULGAR FRAUD.
WHAT?!
I AM TERRIBLY SORRY. MY MASTER IS A REALIST WHO BELIEVES IN MODERN SCIENCE.
I'VE FOUND NOTHING IN THIS WORLD THAT AN EQUATION CAN'T SOLVE.

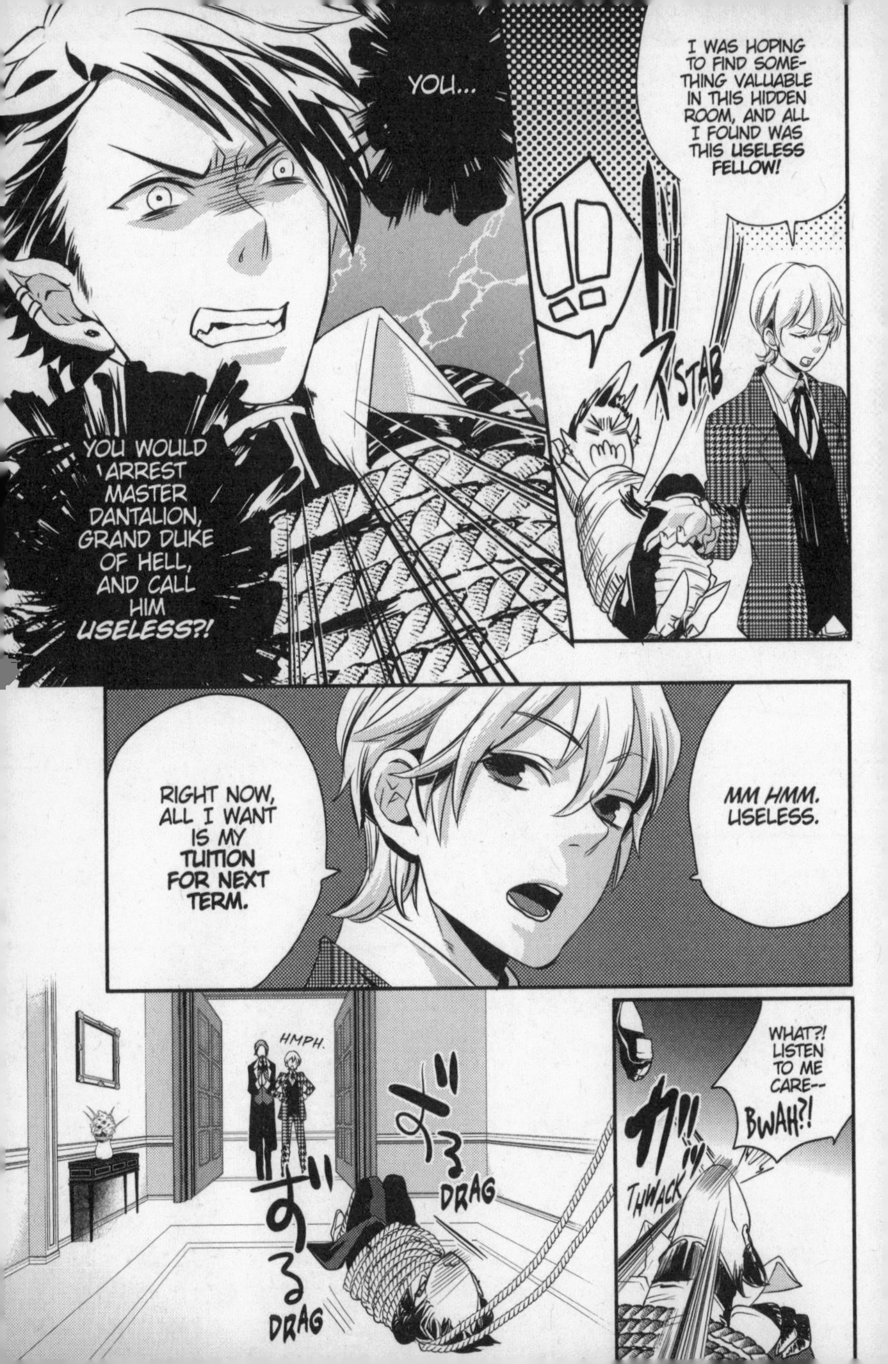
I WAS HOPING TO FIND SOMETHING VALUABLE IN THIS HIDDEN ROOM, AND ALL I FOUND WAS THIS USELESS FELLOW!
!!
STAB
YOU...
YOU WOULD ARREST MASTER DANTALION, GRAND DUKE OF HELL, AND CALL HIM USELESS?!
MM HMM. USELESS.
RIGHT NOW, ALL I WANT IS MY TUITION FOR NEXT TERM.
WHAT?! LISTEN TO ME CARE--
BWAH?!
THWACK
HMPH.
DRAG
DRAG

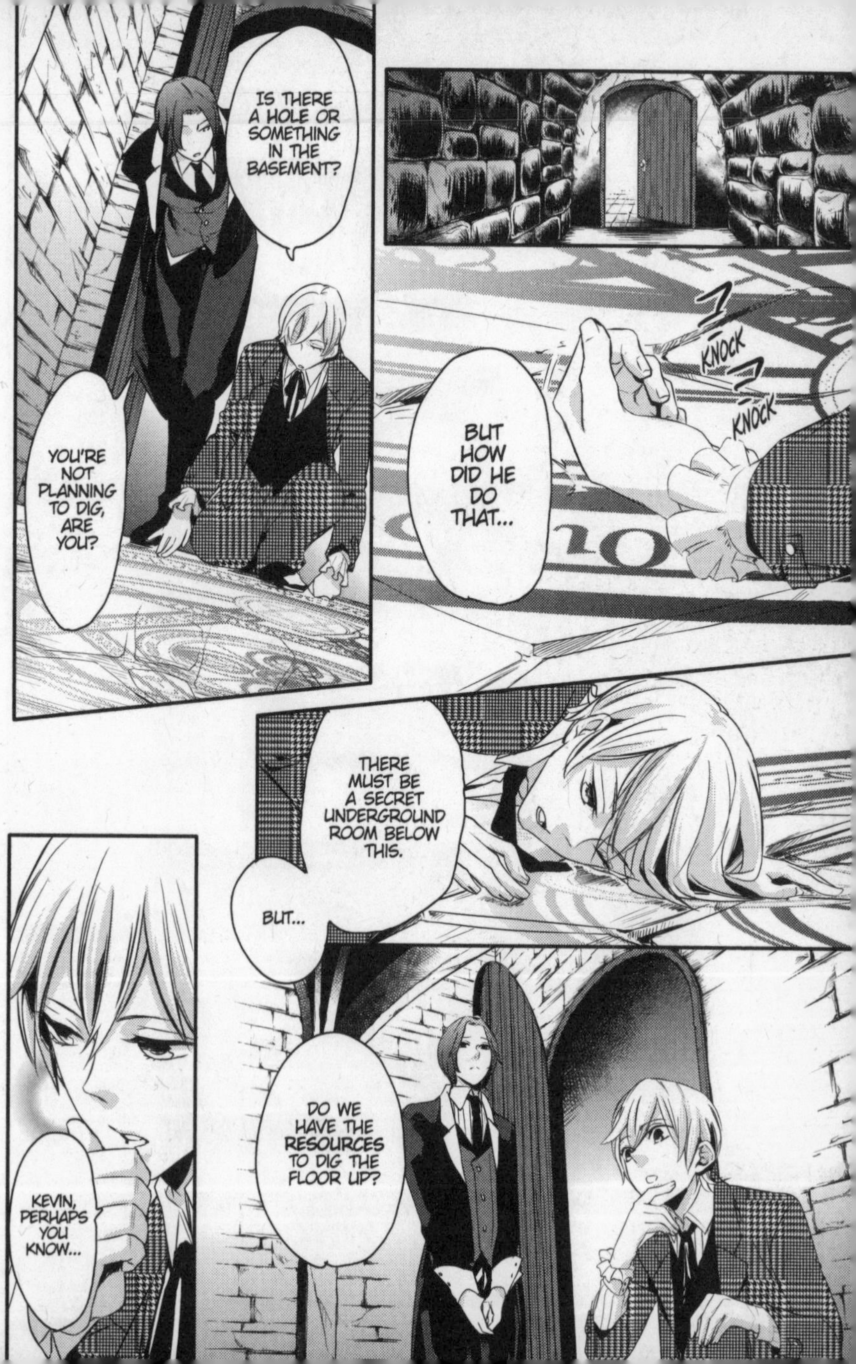
KNOCK
KNOCK
BUT HOW DID HE DO THAT...
IS THERE A HOLE OR SOMETHING IN THE BASEMENT?
YOU'RE NOT PLANNING TO DIG, ARE YOU?
THERE MUST BE A SECRET UNDERGROUND ROOM BELOW THIS.
BUT...
DO WE HAVE THE RESOURCES TO DIG THE FLOOR UP?
KEVIN, PERHAPS YOU KNOW...

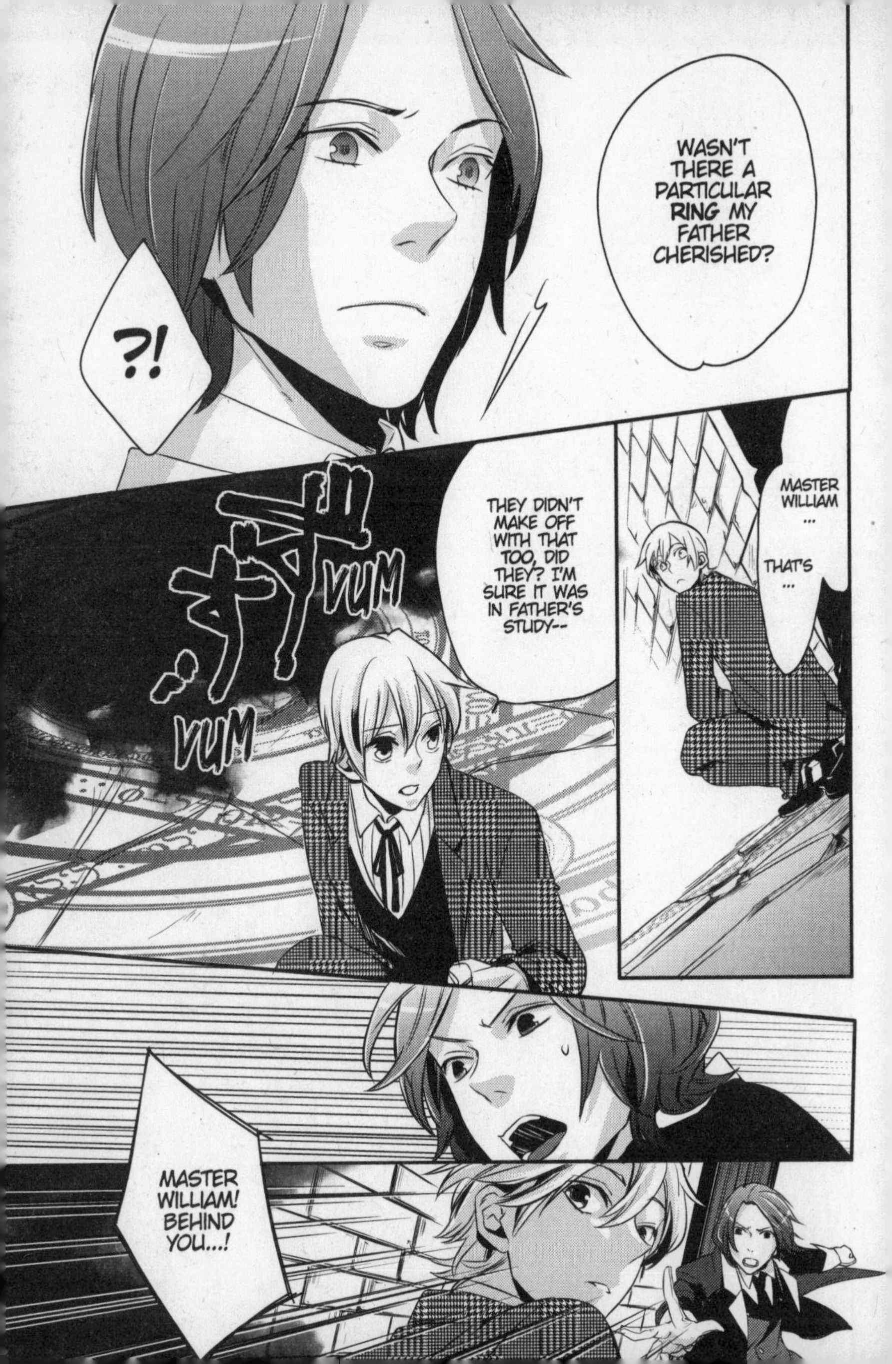
WASN'T THERE A PARTICULAR RING MY FATHER CHERISHED?
?!
MASTER WILLIAM ...
THAT'S ...
THEY DIDN'T MAKE OFF WITH THAT TOO, DID THEY? I'M SURE IT WAS IN FATHER'S STUDY--
VUM
VUM
MASTER WILLIAM! BEHIND YOU...!

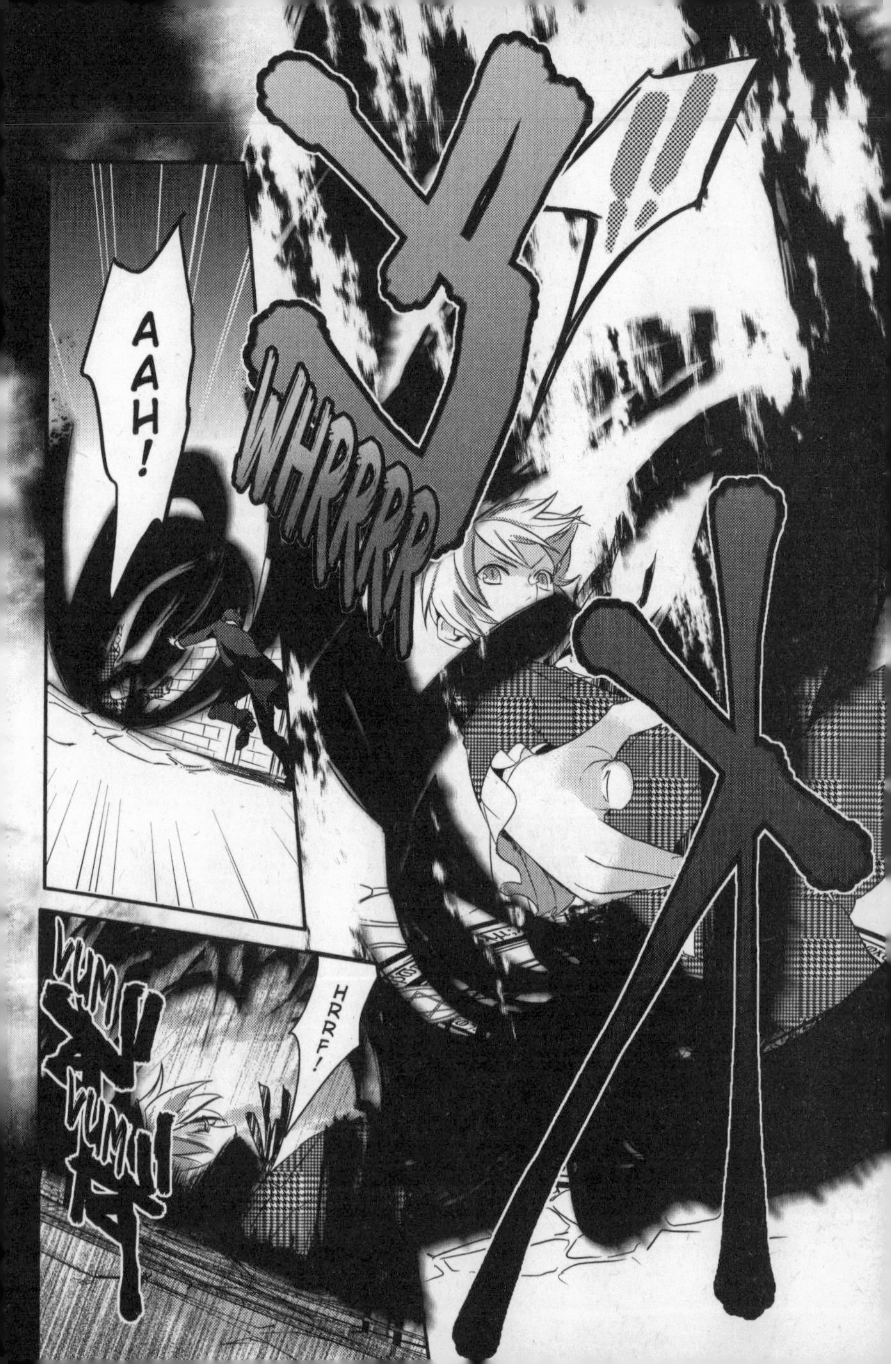
!!
WHRRRR
AAH!
HRRF!
VUM! VUM!

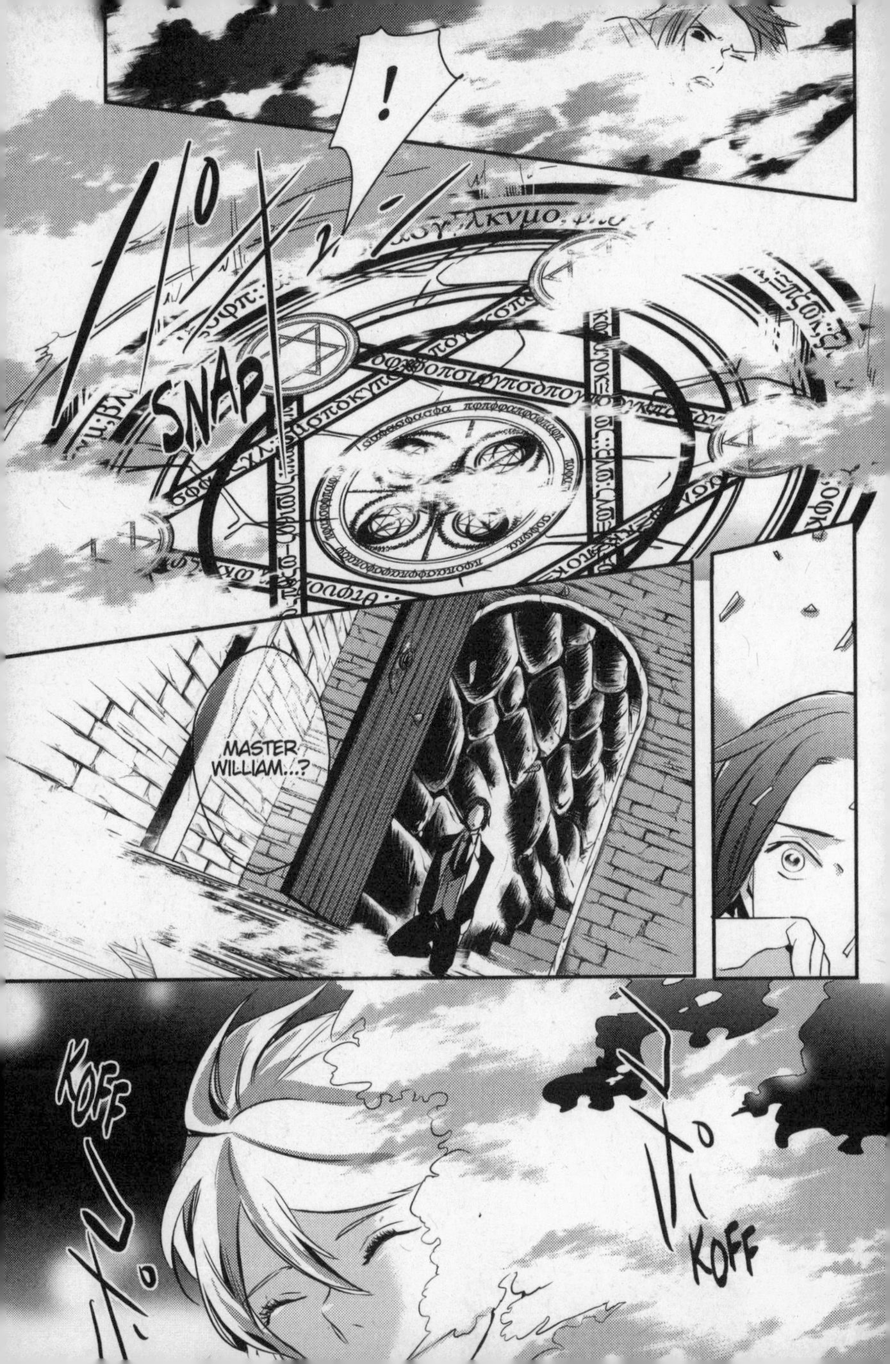
!
SNAP
MASTER WILLIAM...?
KOFF
KOFF

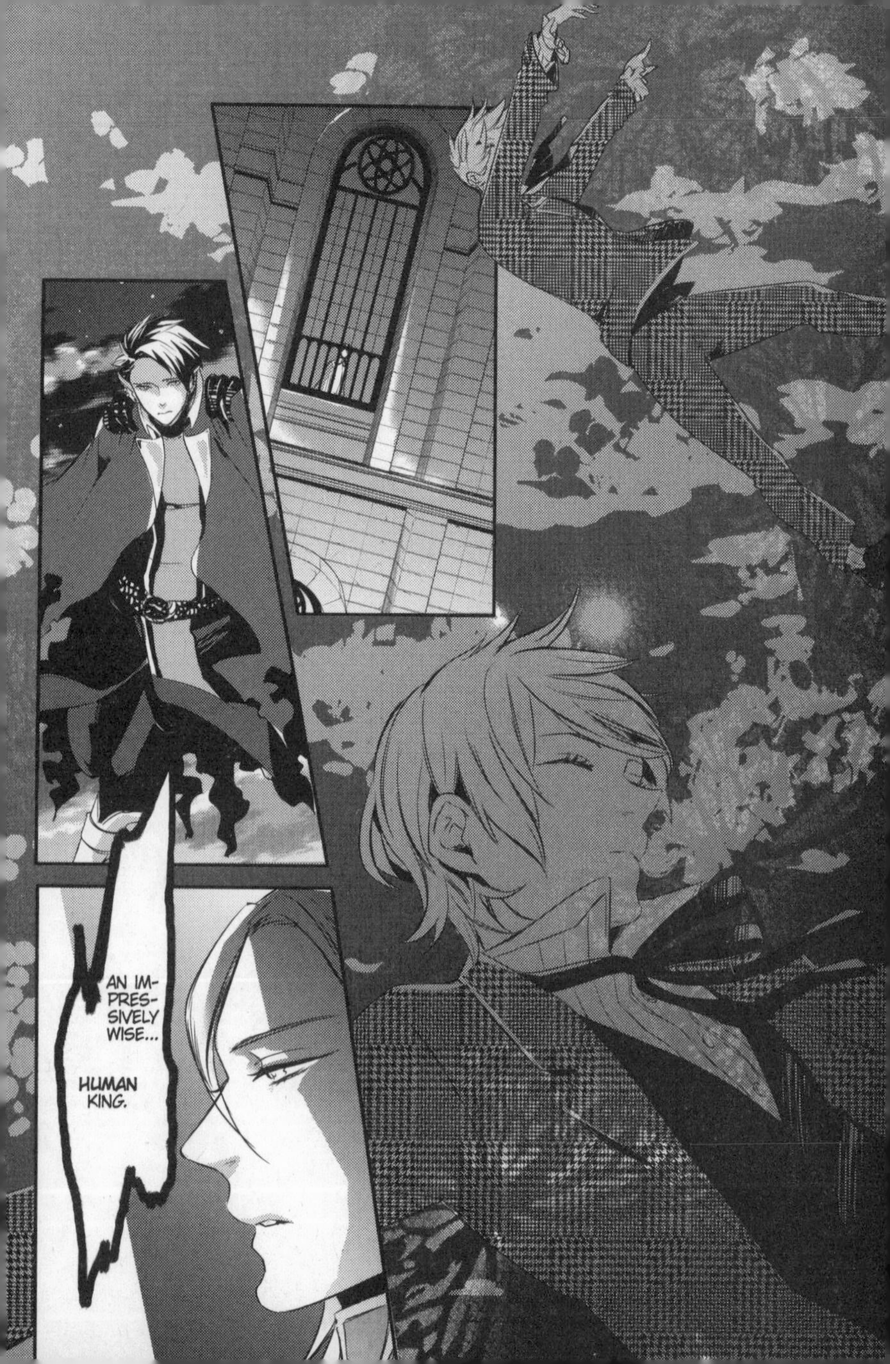
AN IMPRESSIVELY WISE...
HUMAN KING.

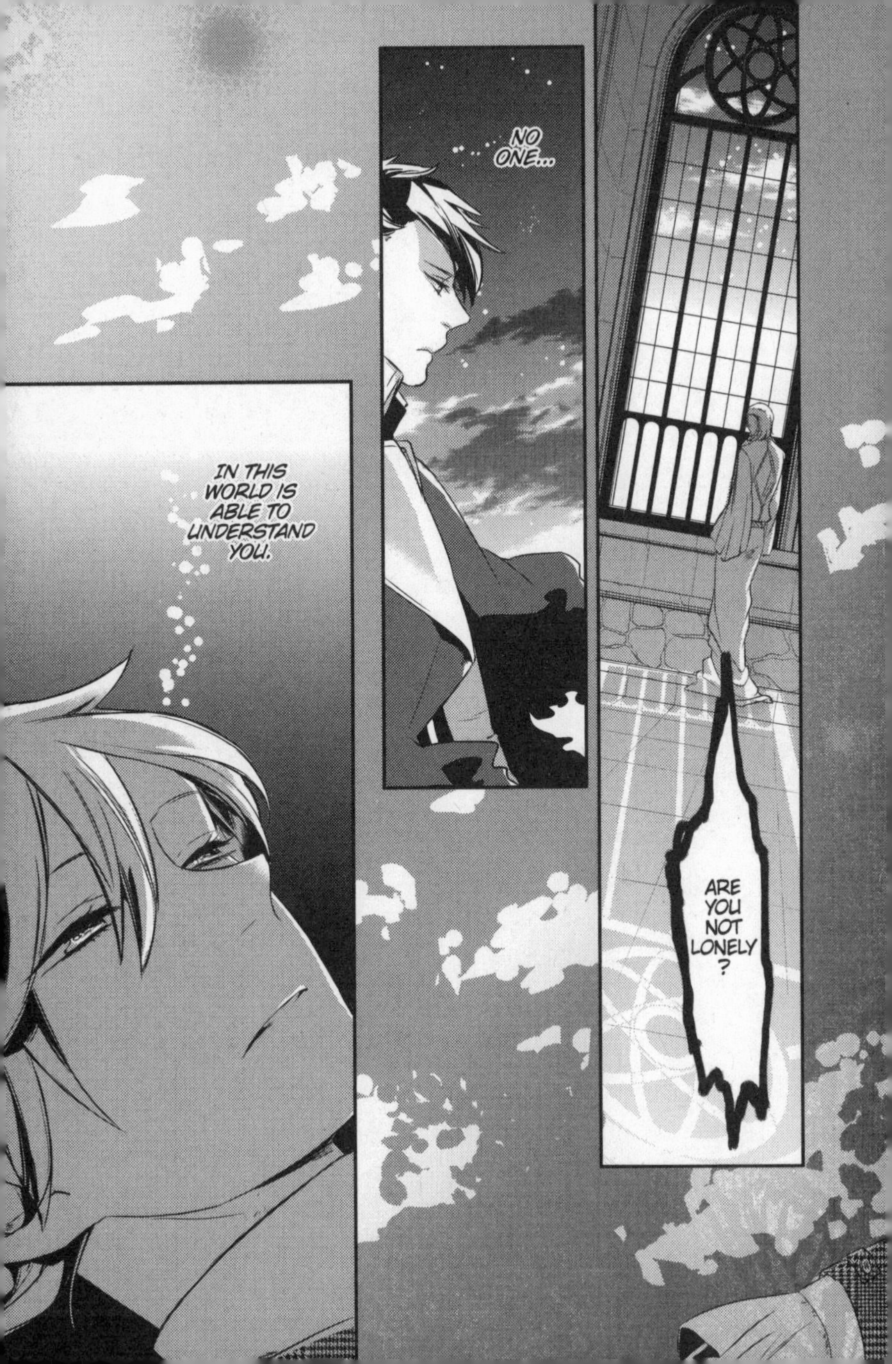
ARE YOU NOT LONELY?
NO ONE...
IN THIS WORLD IS ABLE TO UNDERSTAND YOU.

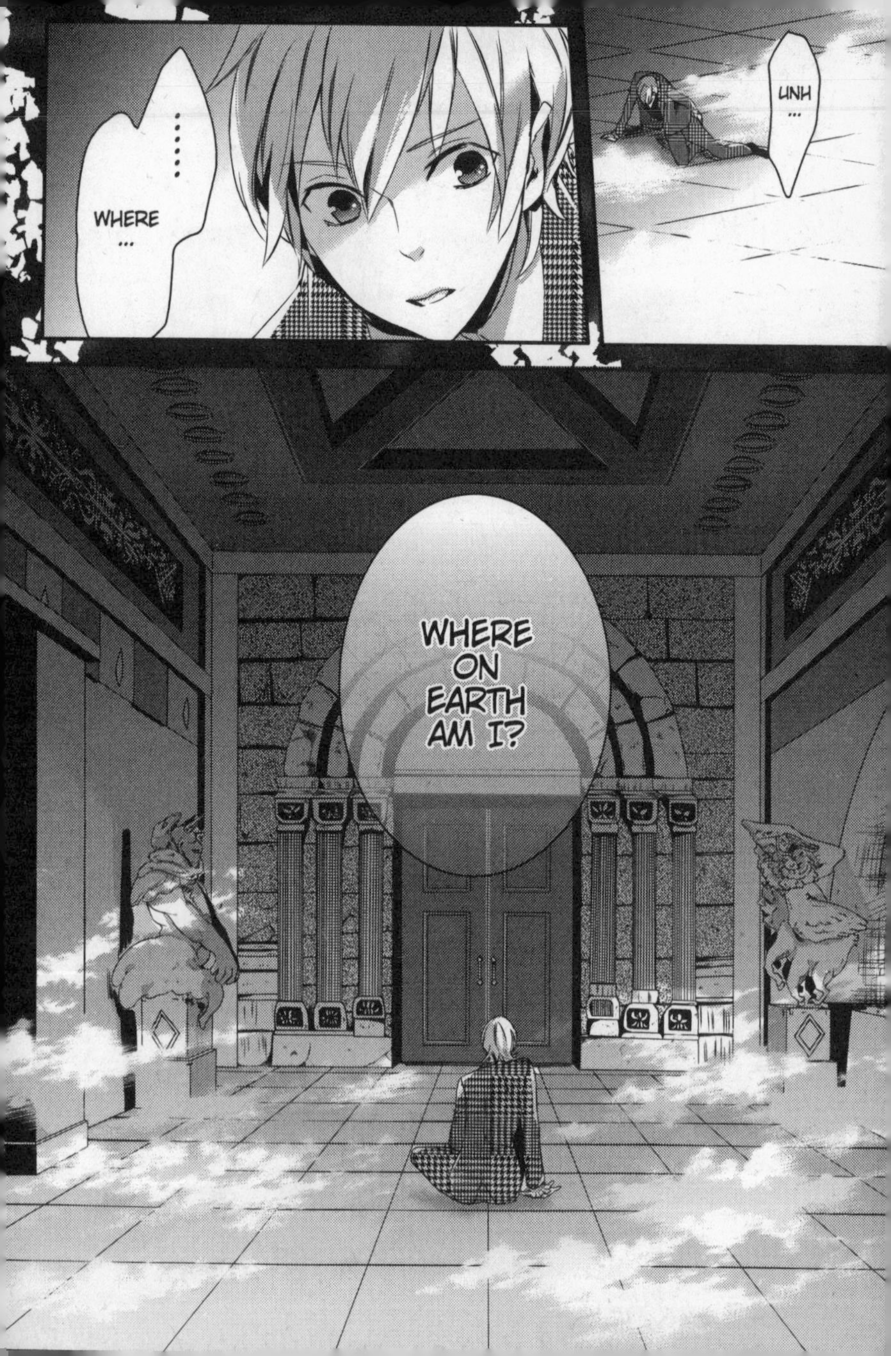
UNH ...
...... WHERE ...
WHERE ON EARTH AM I?

Pillar 2

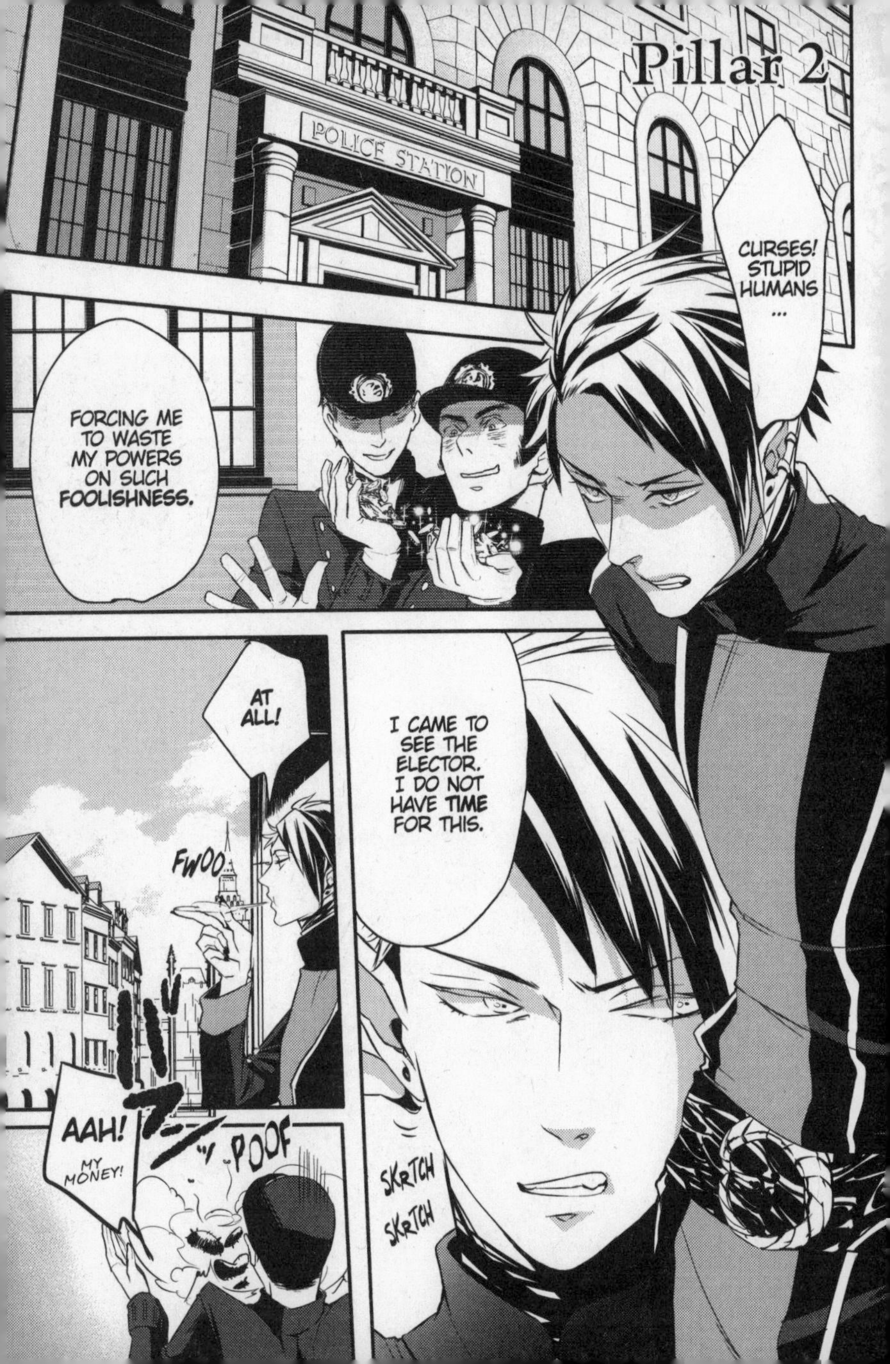

POLICE STATION
CURSES! STUPID HUMANS ...
FORCING ME TO WASTE MY POWERS ON SUCH FOOLISHNESS.
I CAME TO SEE THE ELECTOR. I DO NOT HAVE TIME FOR THIS.
SKRTCH SKRTCH
AT ALL!
FWOO
AAH! MY MONEY!
POOF

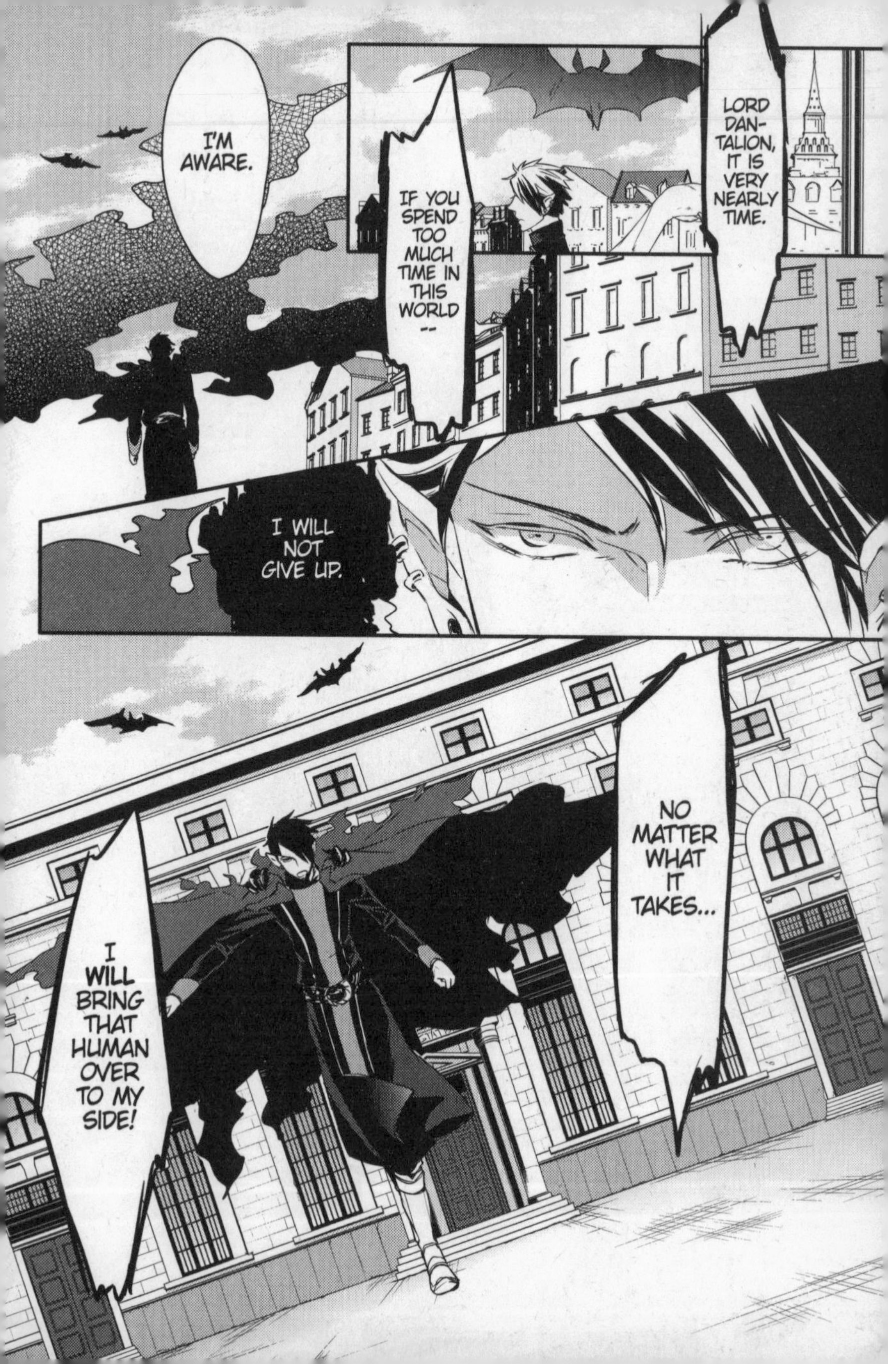
LORD DANTALION, IT IS VERY NEARLY TIME.
IF YOU SPEND TOO MUCH TIME IN THIS WORLD --
I'M AWARE.
I WILL NOT GIVE UP.
NO MATTER WHAT IT TAKES...
I WILL BRING THAT HUMAN OVER TO MY SIDE!

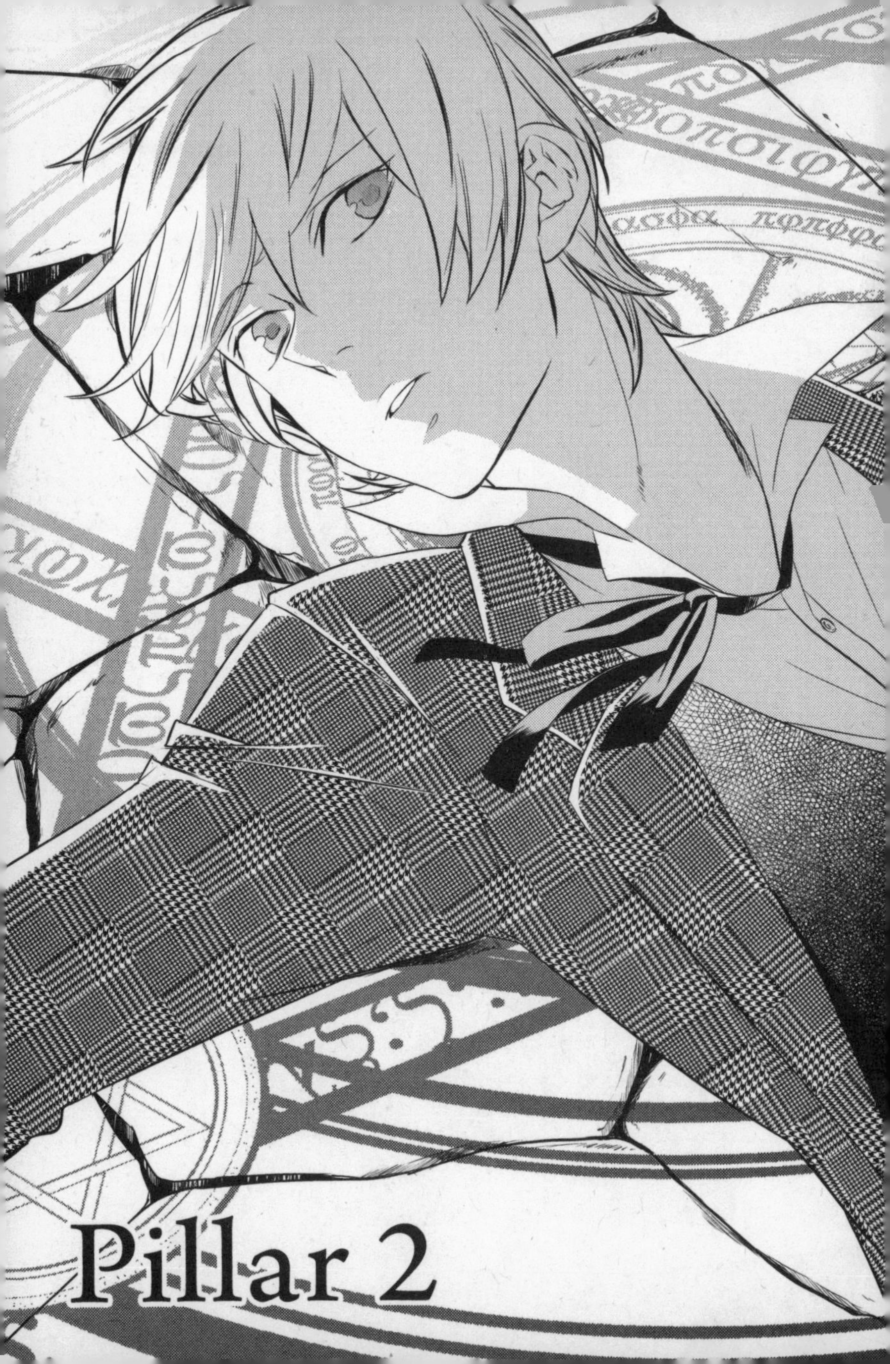
Pillar 2

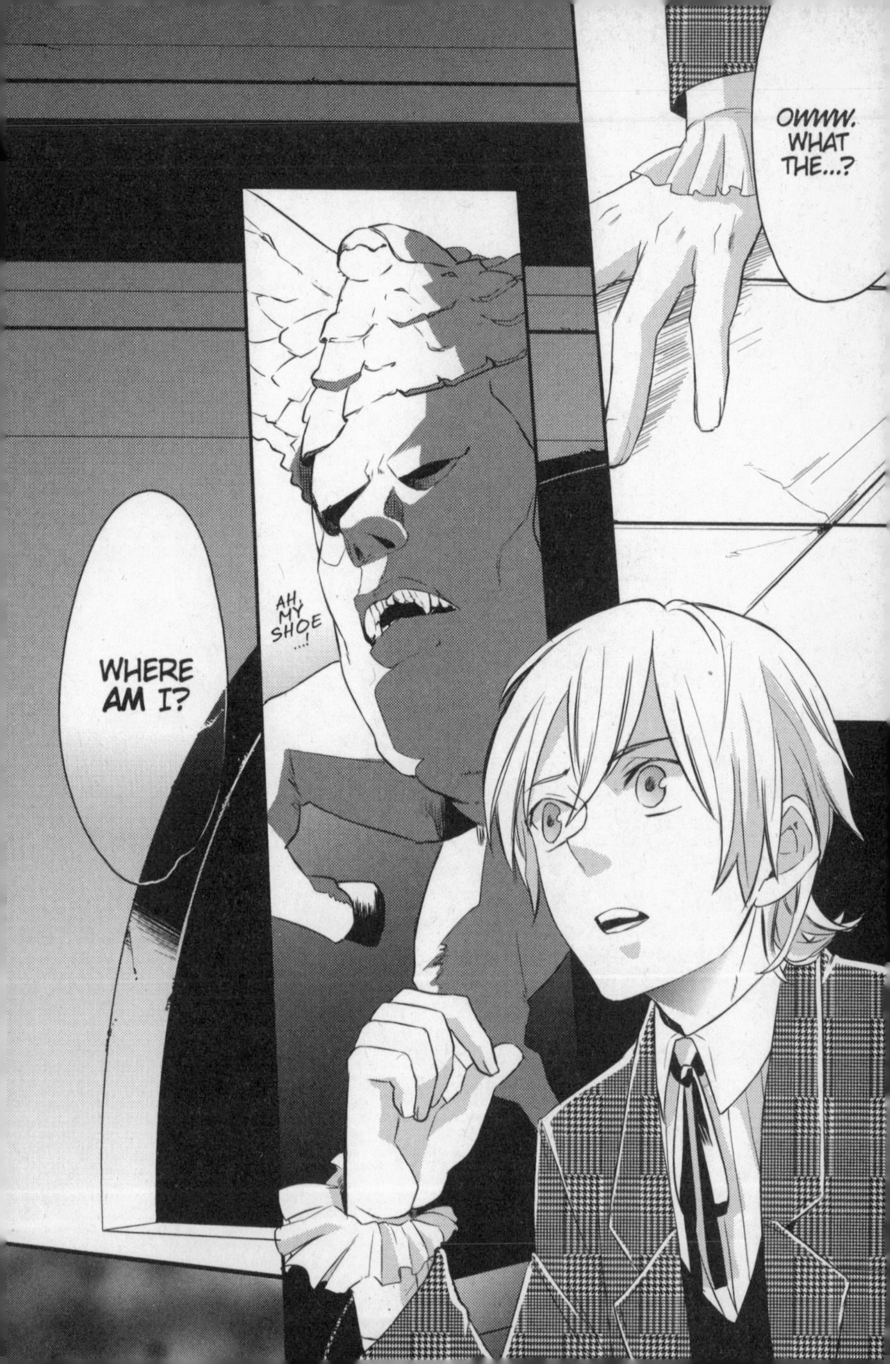
OWWW. WHAT THE...?
AH, MY SHOE...!
WHERE AM I?

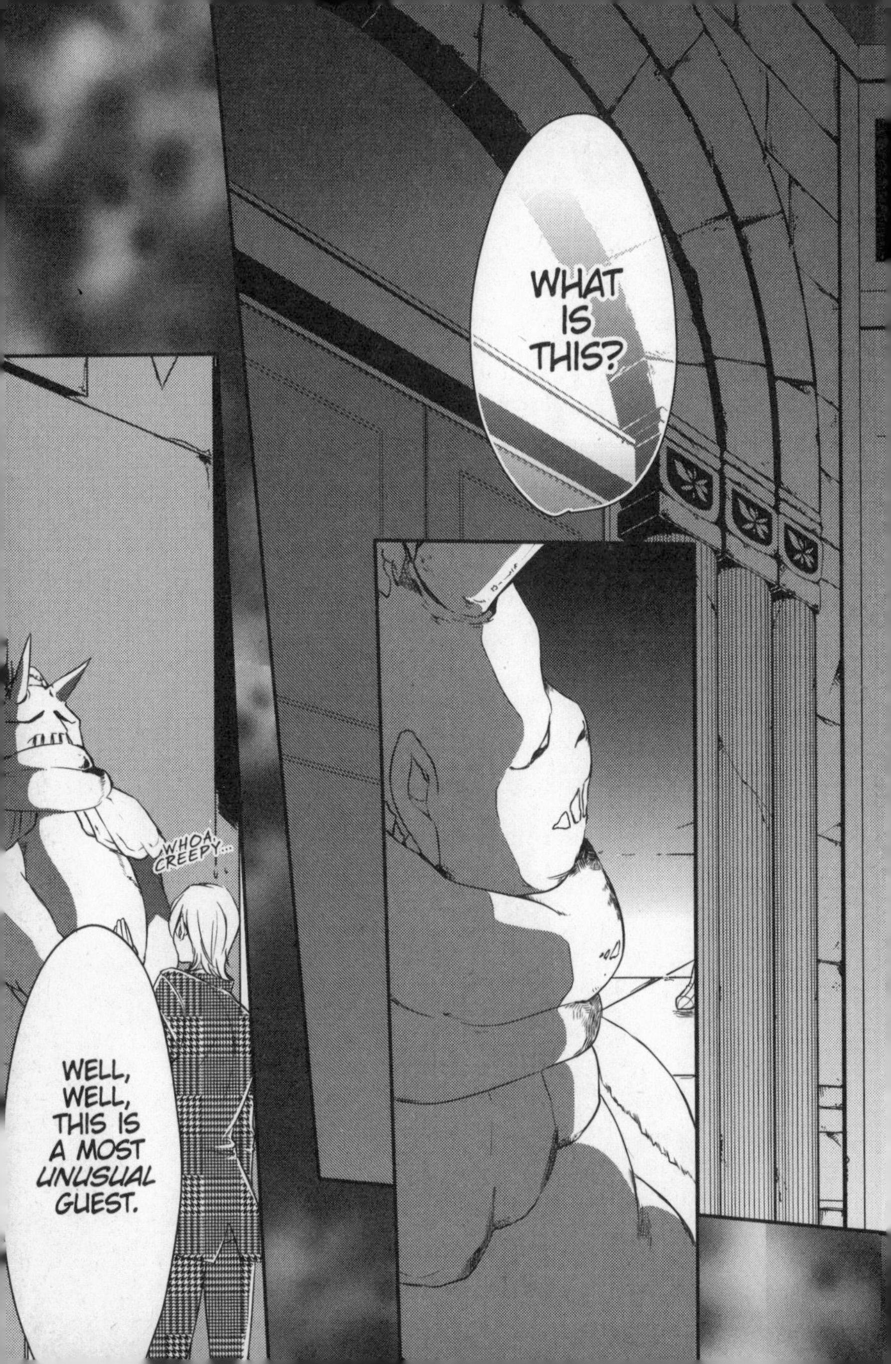
WHAT IS THIS?
WHOA, CREEPY...
WELL, WELL, THIS IS A MOST *UNUSUAL* GUEST.

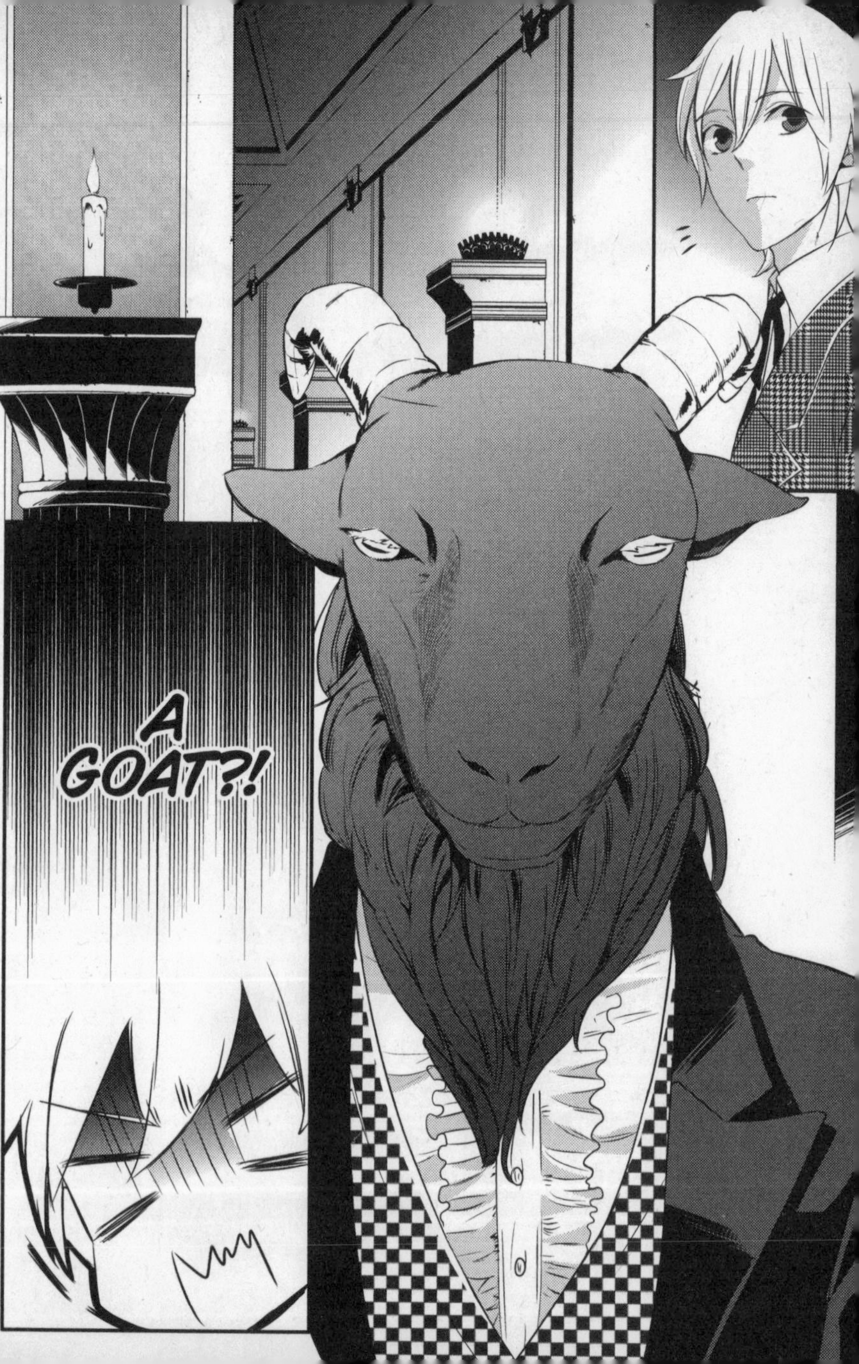
A GOAT?!

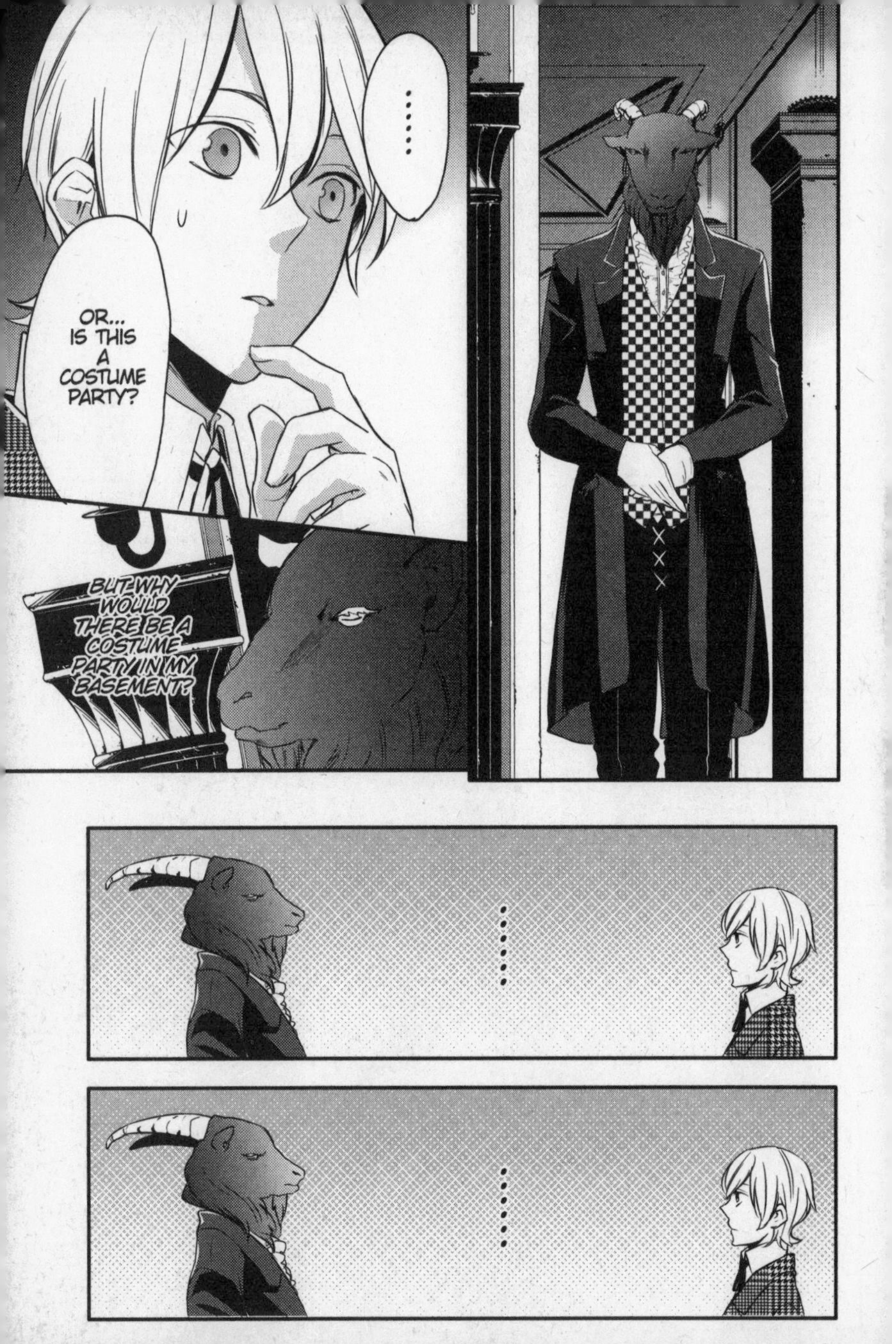
......
OR... IS THIS A COSTUME PARTY?
BUT WHY WOULD THERE BE A COSTUME PARTY IN MY BASEMENT?
......
......

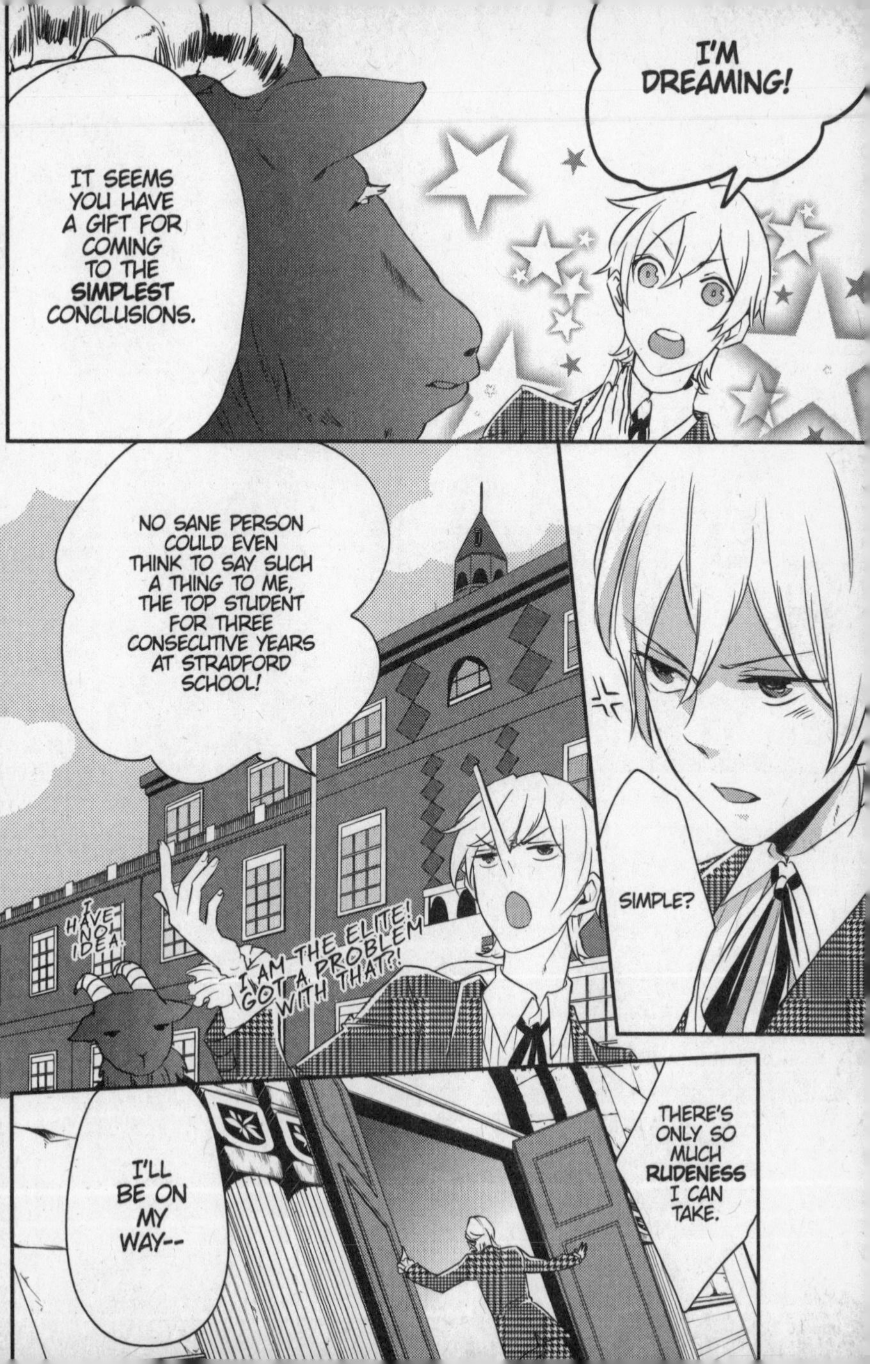
I'M DREAMING!
IT SEEMS YOU HAVE A GIFT FOR COMING TO THE SIMPLEST CONCLUSIONS.
SIMPLE?
NO SANE PERSON COULD EVEN THINK TO SAY SUCH A THING TO ME, THE TOP STUDENT FOR THREE CONSECUTIVE YEARS AT STRADFORD SCHOOL!
I AM THE ELITE! GOT A PROBLEM WITH THAT?!
I HAVE NO IDEA.
THERE'S ONLY SO MUCH RUDENESS I CAN TAKE.
I'LL BE ON MY WAY--

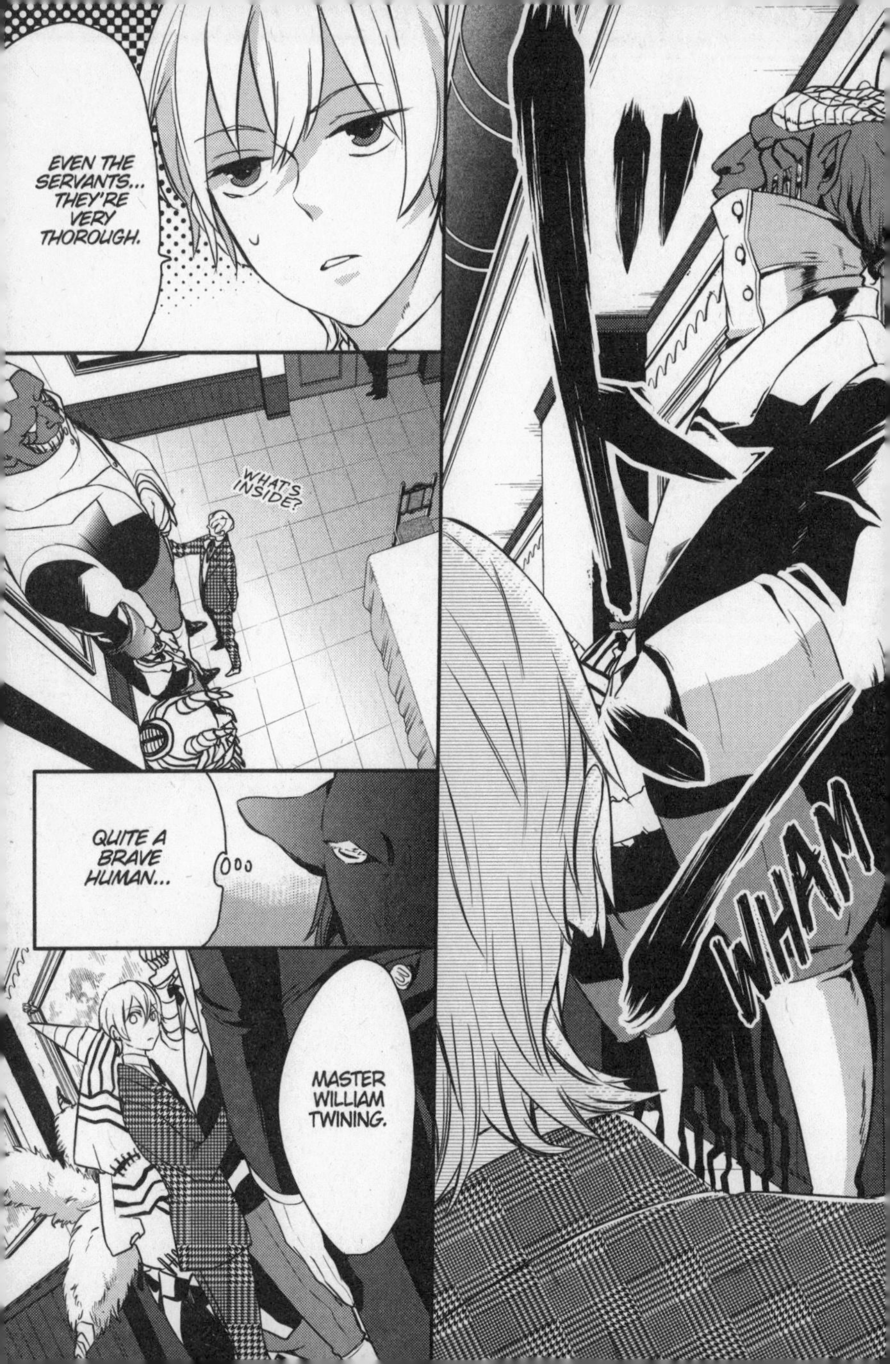
WHAM
EVEN THE SERVANTS... THEY'RE VERY THOROUGH.
WHAT'S INSIDE?
QUITE A BRAVE HUMAN...
MASTER WILLIAM TWINING.

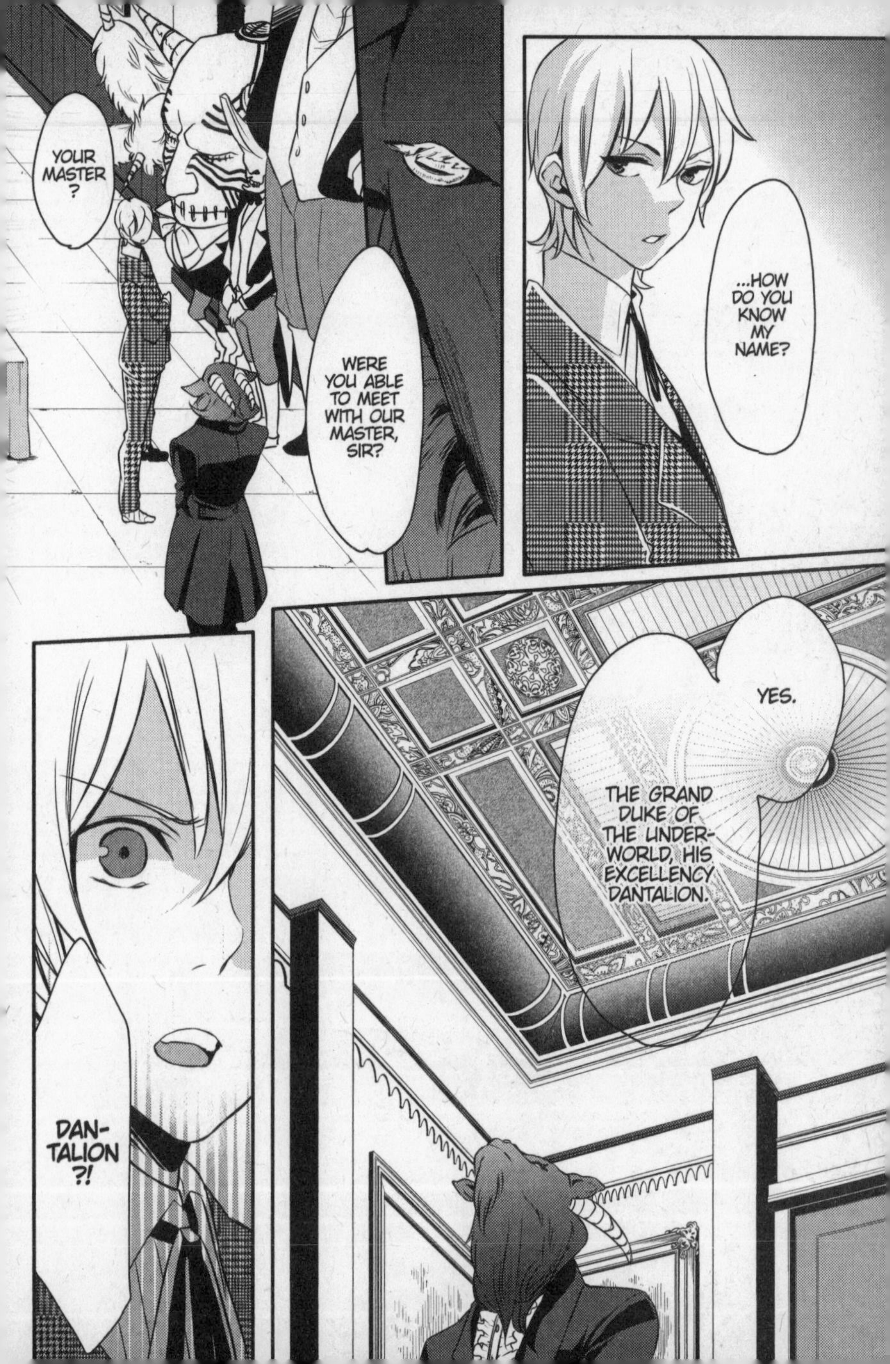

...HOW DO YOU KNOW MY NAME?
WERE YOU ABLE TO MEET WITH OUR MASTER, SIR?
YOUR MASTER?
YES.
THE GRAND DUKE OF THE UNDER-WORLD, HIS EXCELLENCY DANTALION.
DAN-TALION?!

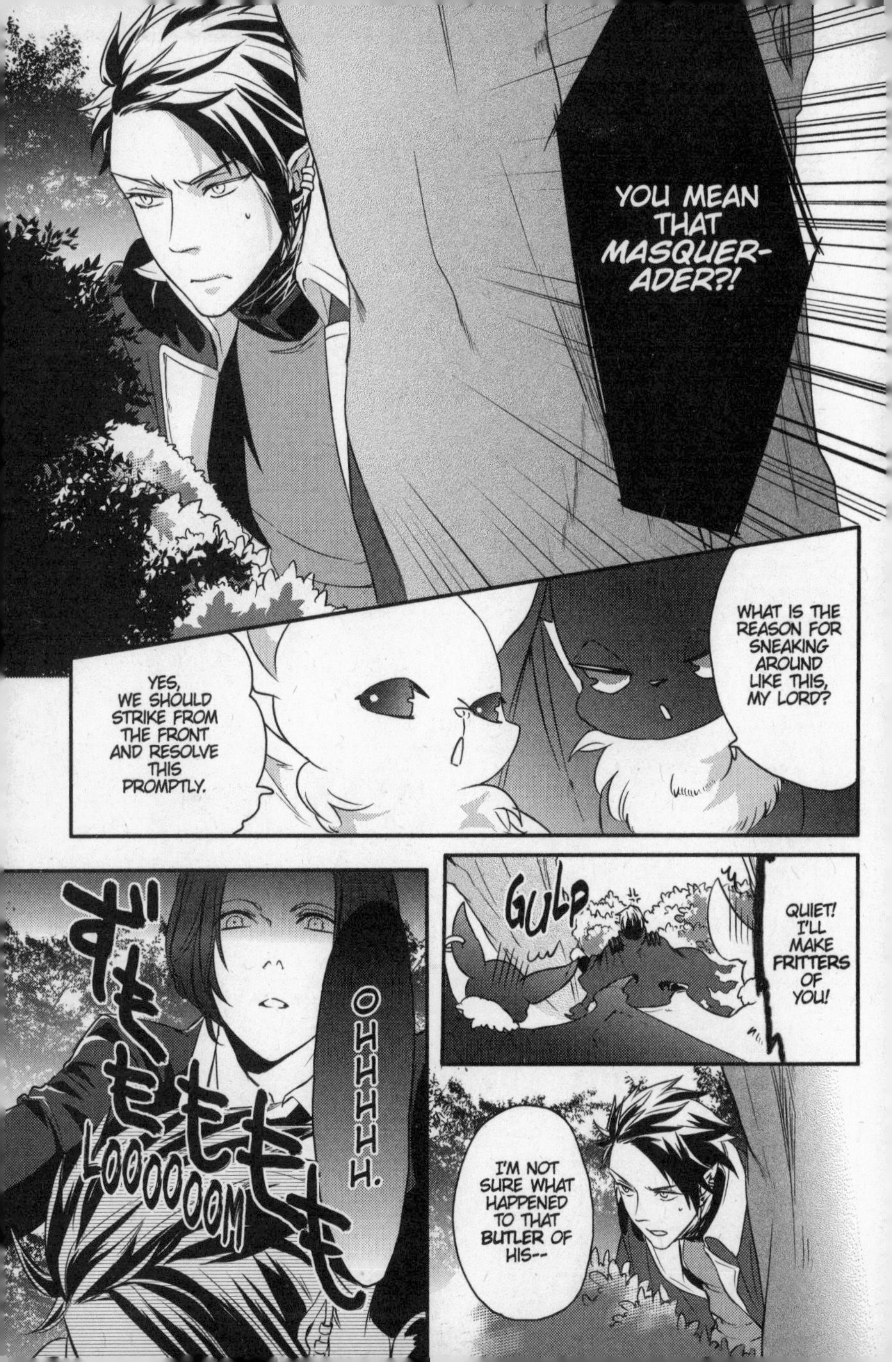
YOU MEAN THAT MASQUERADER?!
WHAT IS THE REASON FOR SNEAKING AROUND LIKE THIS, MY LORD?
YES, WE SHOULD STRIKE FROM THE FRONT AND RESOLVE THIS PROMPTLY.
QUIET! I'LL MAKE FRITTERS OF YOU!
GULP
I'M NOT SURE WHAT HAPPENED TO THAT BUTLER OF HIS--
OHHHHHH.
LOOOOOOM

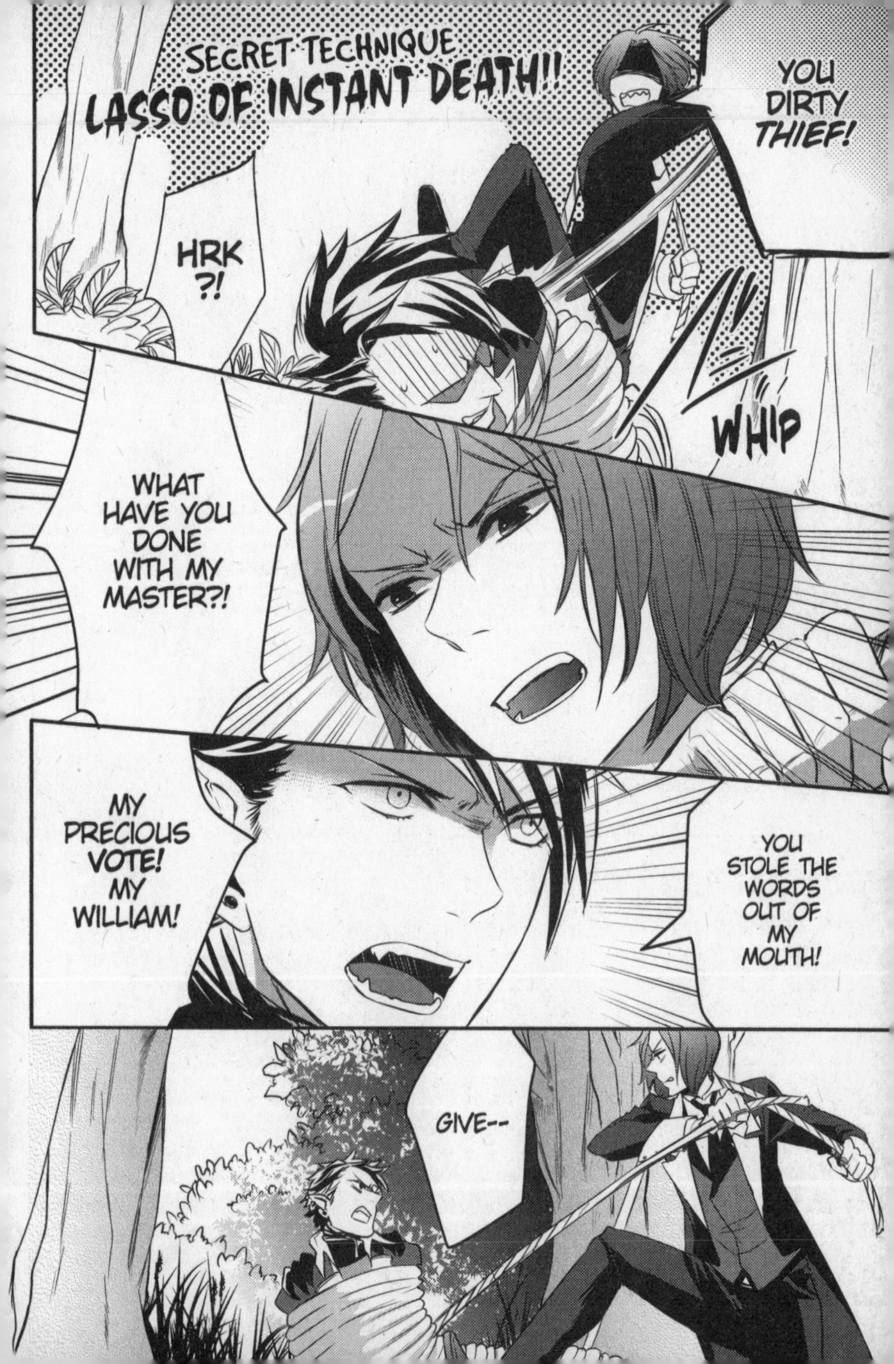
YOU DIRTY THIEF!
SECRET TECHNIQUE LASSO OF INSTANT DEATH!!
HRK ?!
WHIP
WHAT HAVE YOU DONE WITH MY MASTER?!
YOU STOLE THE WORDS OUT OF MY MOUTH!
MY PRECIOUS VOTE! MY WILLIAM!
GIVE--

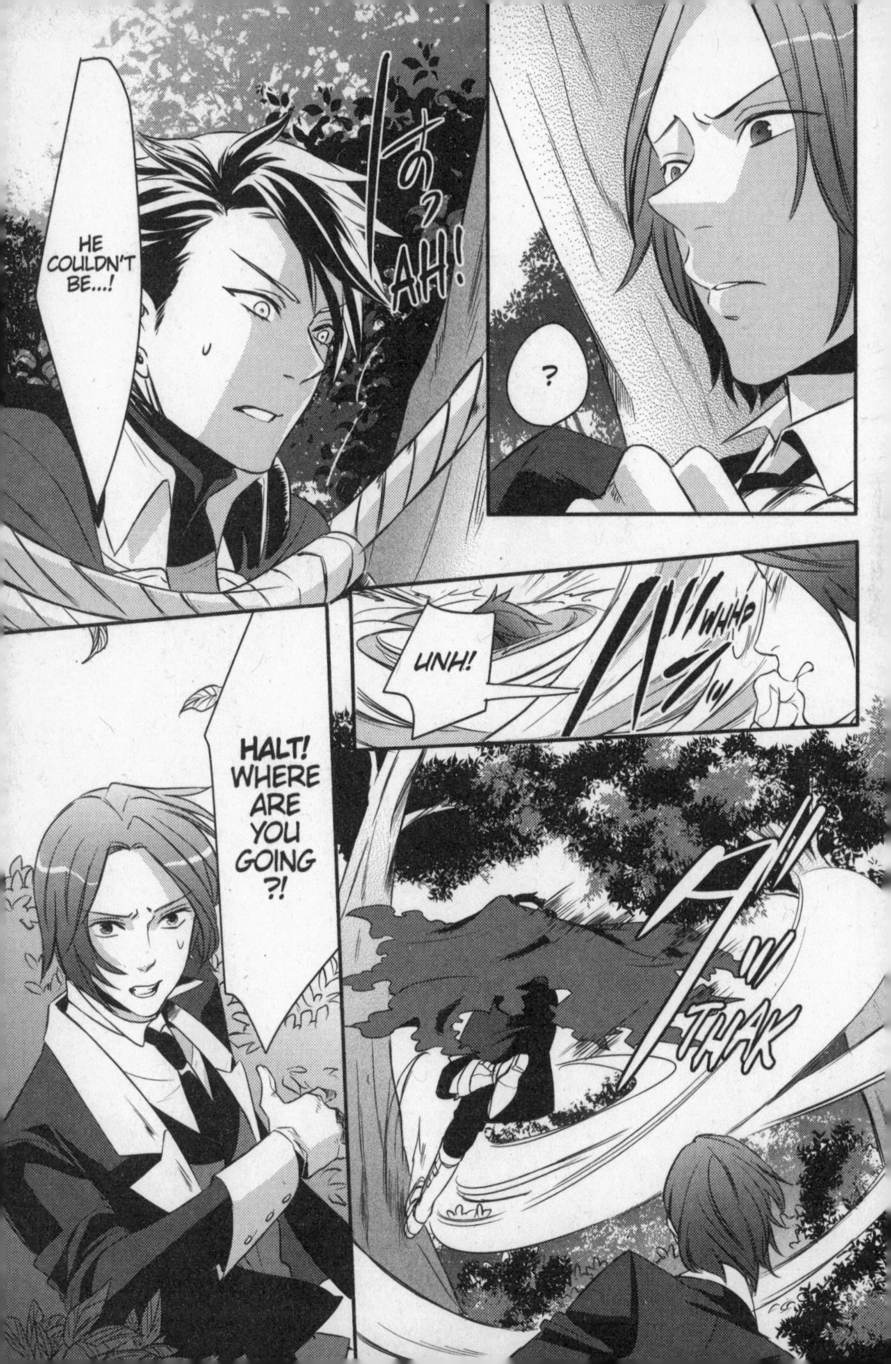

?
HE COULDN'T BE...!
あっ
AH!
UNH!
WHHP
THAK
HALT! WHERE ARE YOU GOING?!

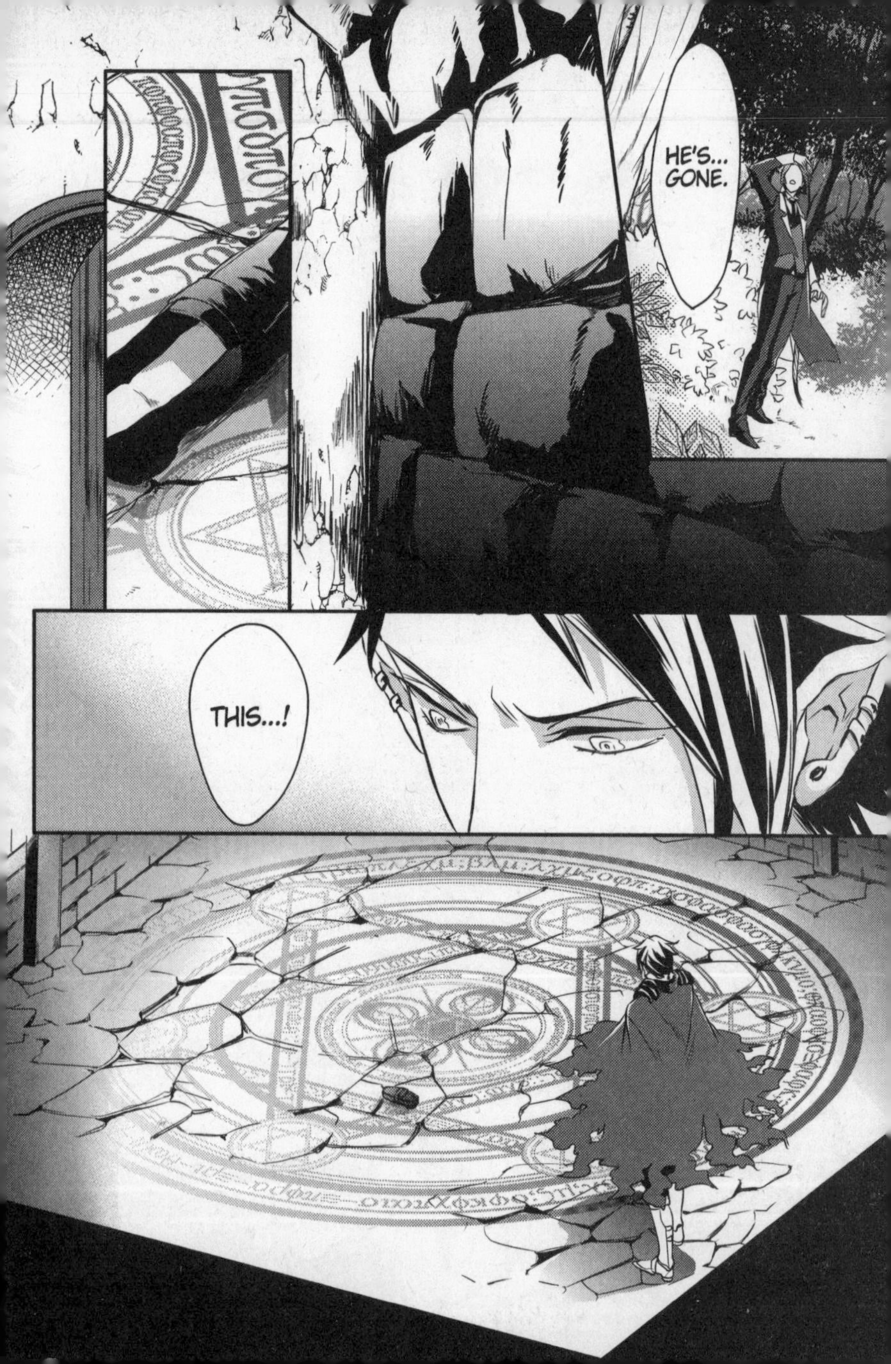
HE'S... GONE.
THIS...!

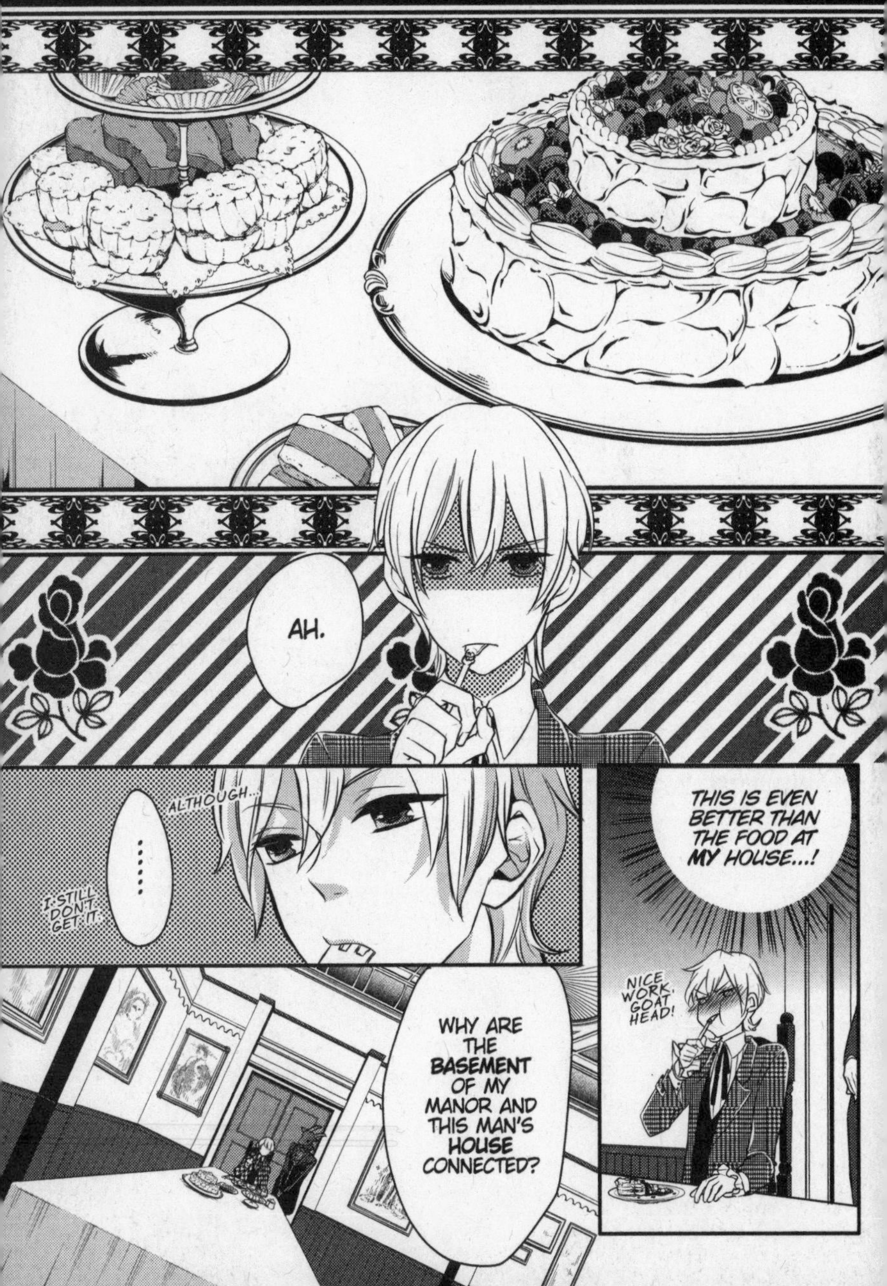
AH.
THIS IS EVEN BETTER THAN THE FOOD AT MY HOUSE...!
NICE WORK, GOAT HEAD!
ALTHOUGH...
......
I STILL DON'T GET IT.
WHY ARE THE BASEMENT OF MY MANOR AND THIS MAN'S HOUSE CONNECTED?

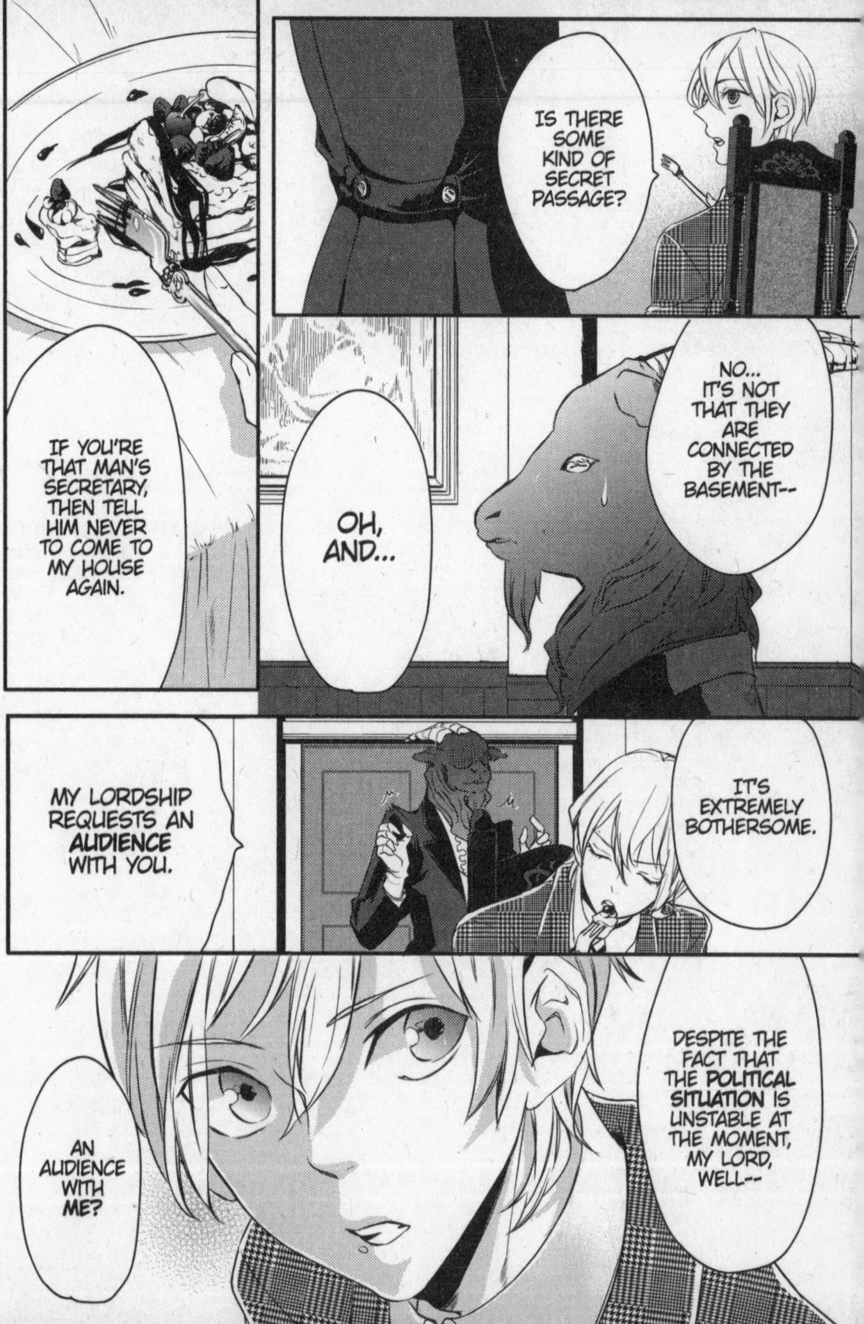
IS THERE SOME KIND OF SECRET PASSAGE?
NO... IT'S NOT THAT THEY ARE CONNECTED BY THE BASEMENT--
OH, AND...
IF YOU'RE THAT MAN'S SECRETARY, THEN TELL HIM NEVER TO COME TO MY HOUSE AGAIN.
IT'S EXTREMELY BOTHERSOME.
MY LORDSHIP REQUESTS AN **AUDIENCE** WITH YOU.
DESPITE THE FACT THAT THE **POLITICAL SITUATION** IS UNSTABLE AT THE MOMENT, MY LORD, WELL--
AN AUDIENCE WITH **ME?**

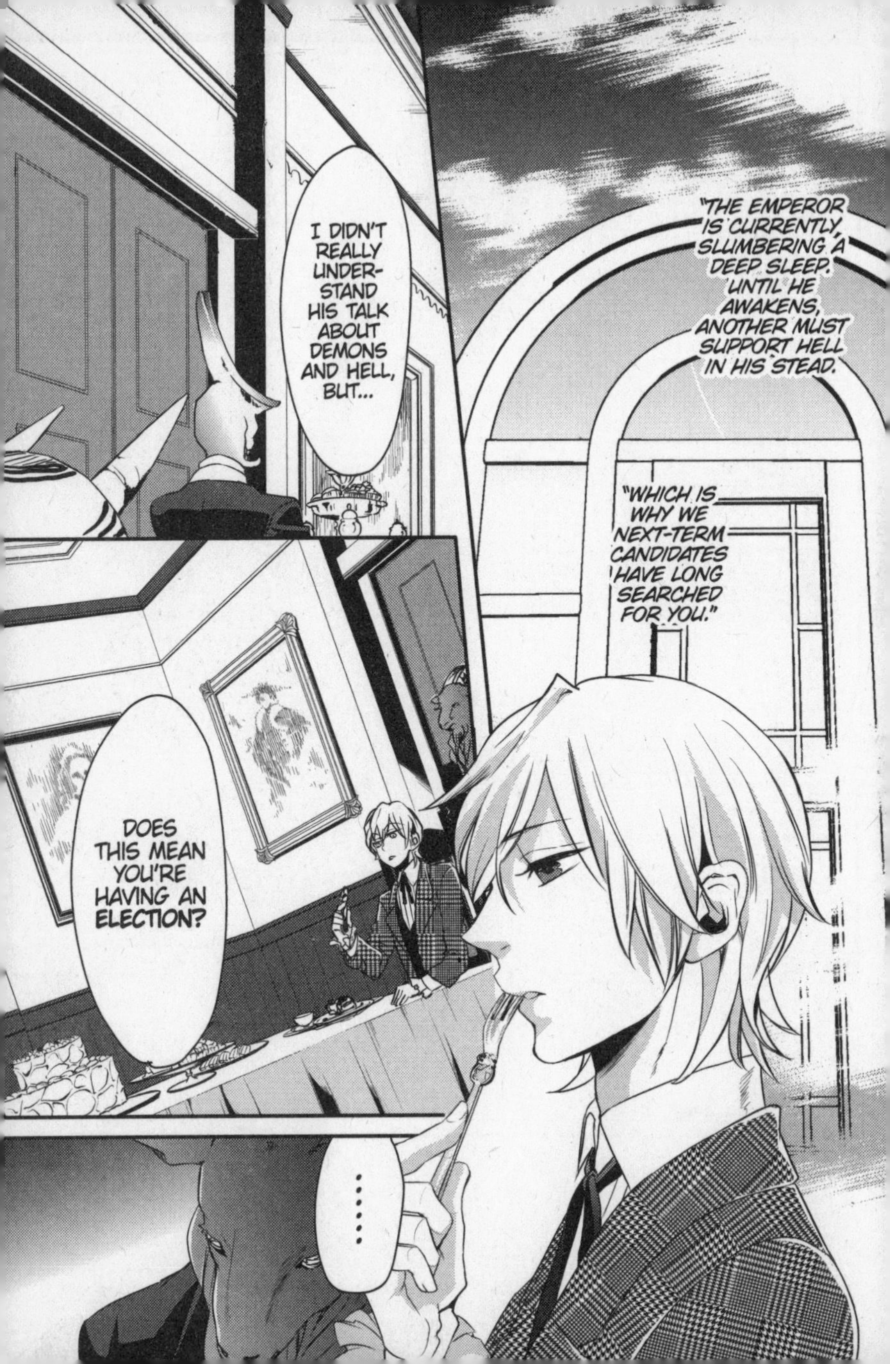
"THE EMPEROR IS CURRENTLY SLUMBERING A DEEP SLEEP. UNTIL HE AWAKENS, ANOTHER MUST SUPPORT HELL IN HIS STEAD.
"WHICH IS WHY WE NEXT-TERM CANDIDATES HAVE LONG SEARCHED FOR YOU."
I DIDN'T REALLY UNDER-STAND HIS TALK ABOUT DEMONS AND HELL, BUT...
DOES THIS MEAN YOU'RE HAVING AN ELECTION?
......

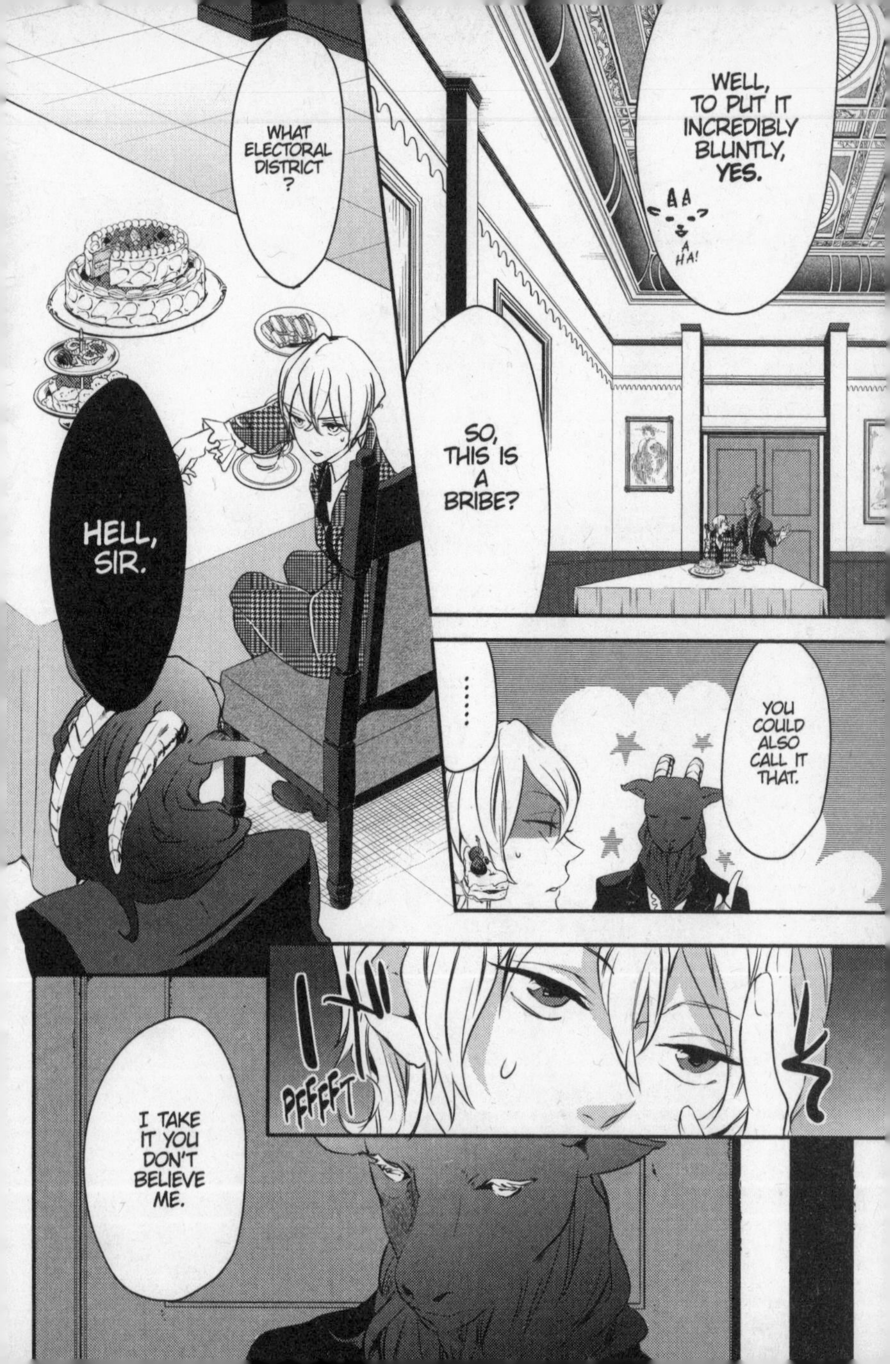
WELL, TO PUT IT INCREDIBLY BLUNTLY, YES.
A HA!
SO, THIS IS A BRIBE?
YOU COULD ALSO CALL IT THAT.
......
WHAT ELECTORAL DISTRICT ?
HELL, SIR.
PFFFFT
I TAKE IT YOU DON'T BELIEVE ME.

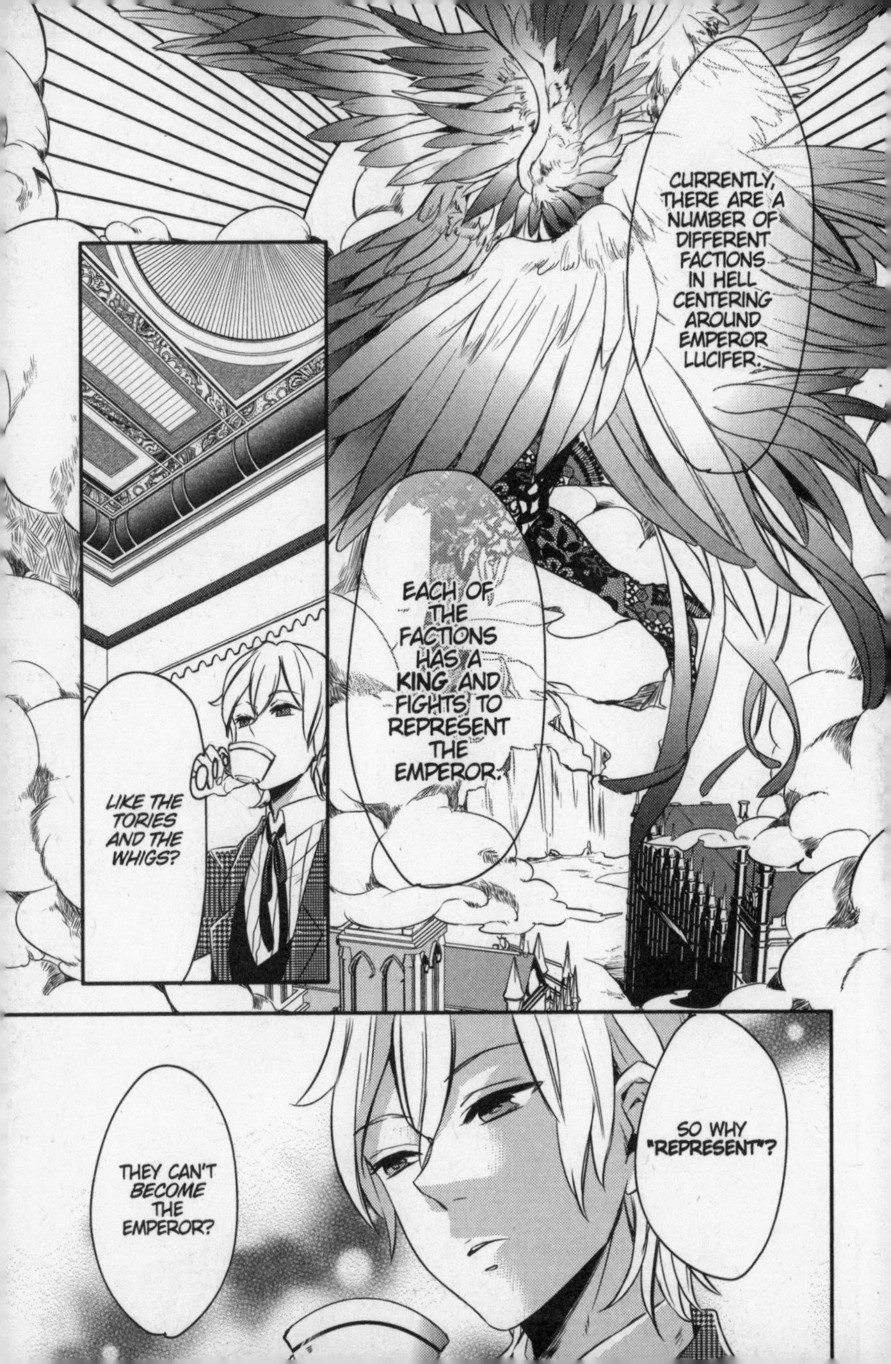
CURRENTLY, THERE ARE A NUMBER OF DIFFERENT FACTIONS IN HELL CENTERING AROUND EMPEROR LUCIFER.
EACH OF THE FACTIONS HAS A KING AND FIGHTS TO REPRESENT THE EMPEROR.
LIKE THE TORIES AND THE WHIGS?
SO WHY "REPRESENT"?
THEY CAN'T *BECOME* THE EMPEROR?

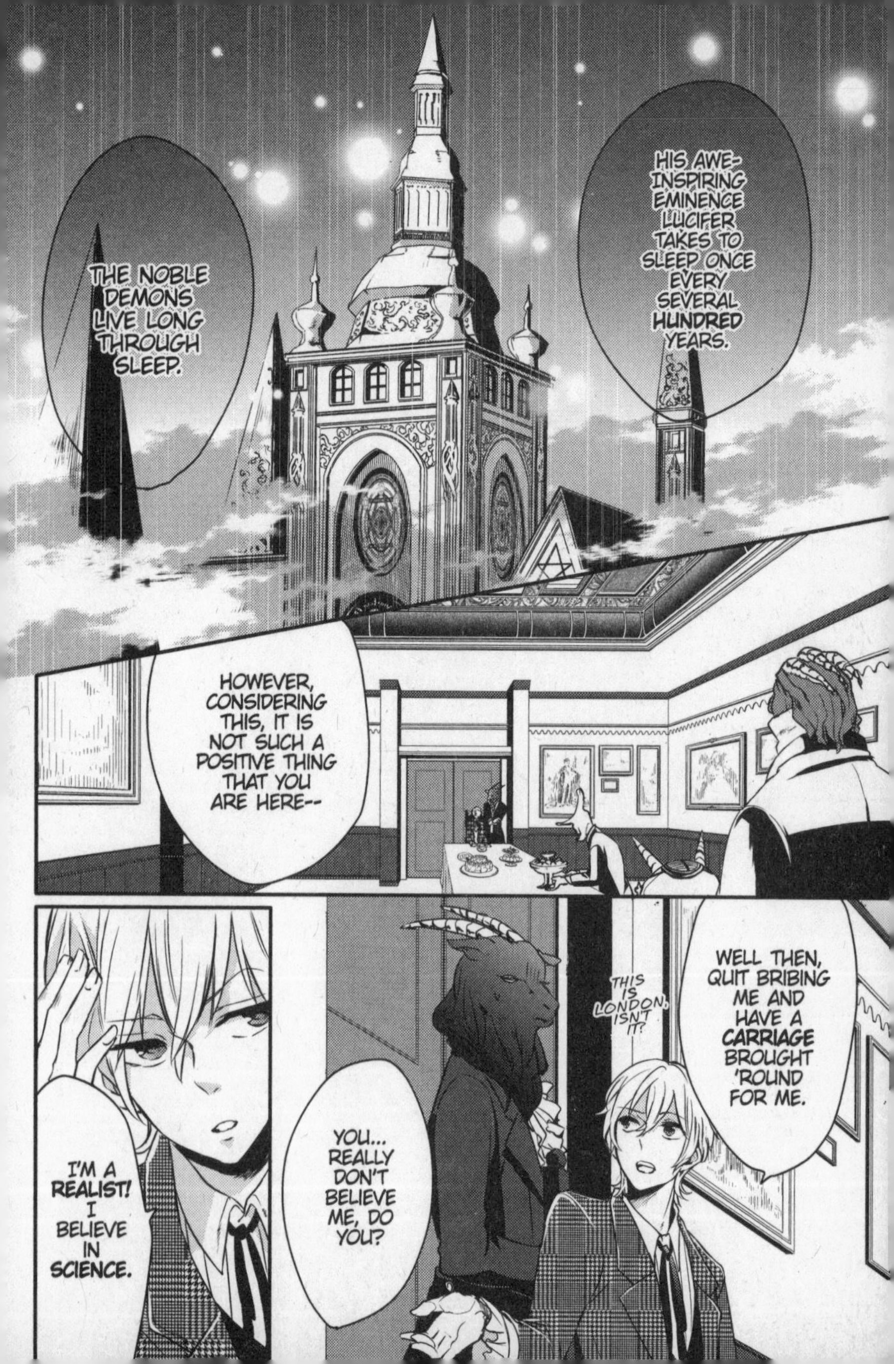
HIS AWE-INSPIRING EMINENCE LUCIFER TAKES TO SLEEP ONCE EVERY SEVERAL HUNDRED YEARS.
THE NOBLE DEMONS LIVE LONG THROUGH SLEEP.
HOWEVER, CONSIDERING THIS, IT IS NOT SUCH A POSITIVE THING THAT YOU ARE HERE--
WELL THEN, QUIT BRIBING ME AND HAVE A CARRIAGE BROUGHT 'ROUND FOR ME.
THIS IS LONDON, ISN'T IT?
YOU... REALLY DON'T BELIEVE ME, DO YOU?
I'M A REALIST! I BELIEVE IN SCIENCE.

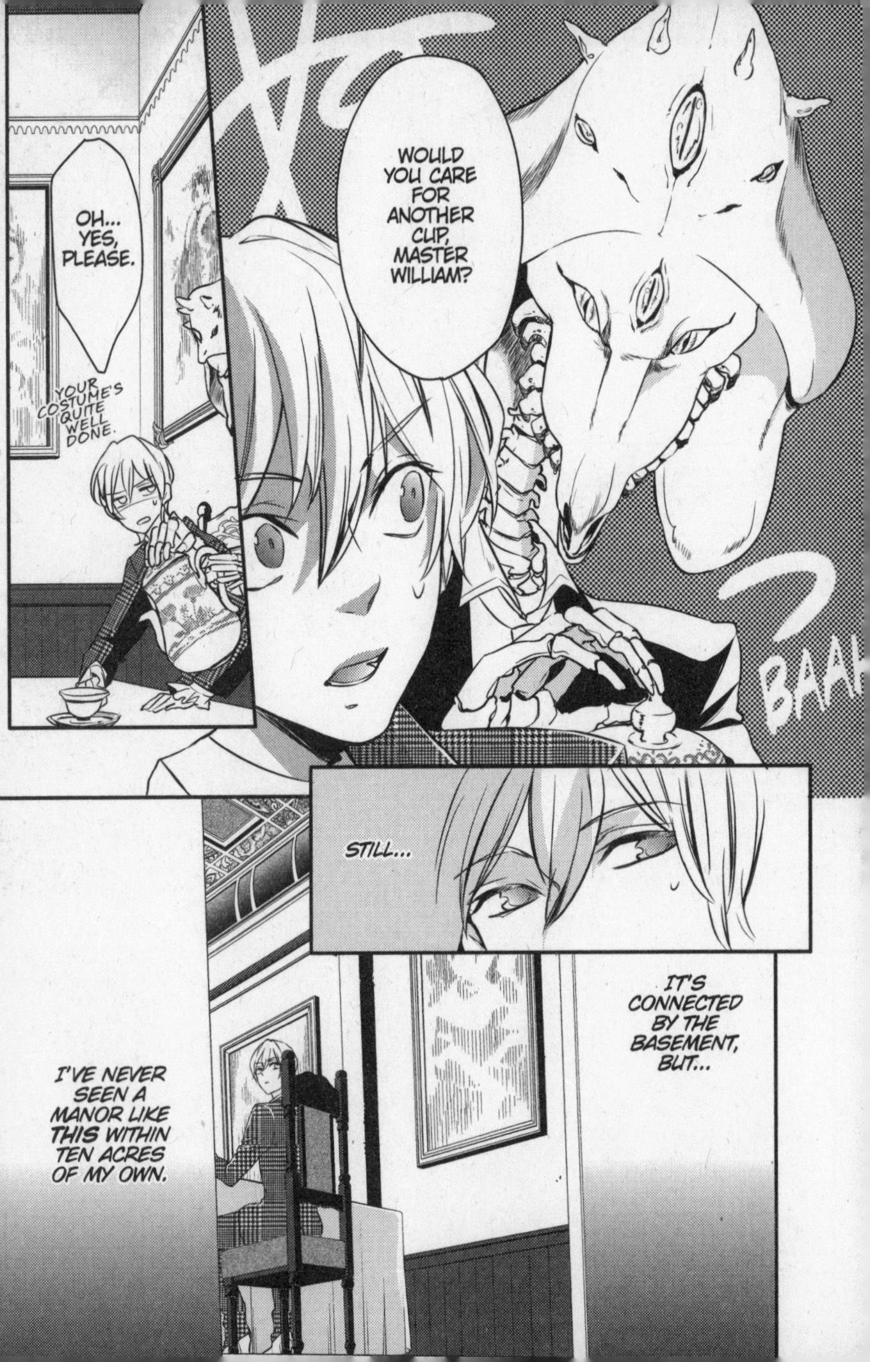
WOULD YOU CARE FOR ANOTHER CUP, MASTER WILLIAM?
BAAH
OH... YES, PLEASE.
YOUR COSTUME'S QUITE WELL DONE.
STILL...
IT'S CONNECTED BY THE BASEMENT, BUT...
I'VE NEVER SEEN A MANOR LIKE THIS WITHIN TEN ACRES OF MY OWN.

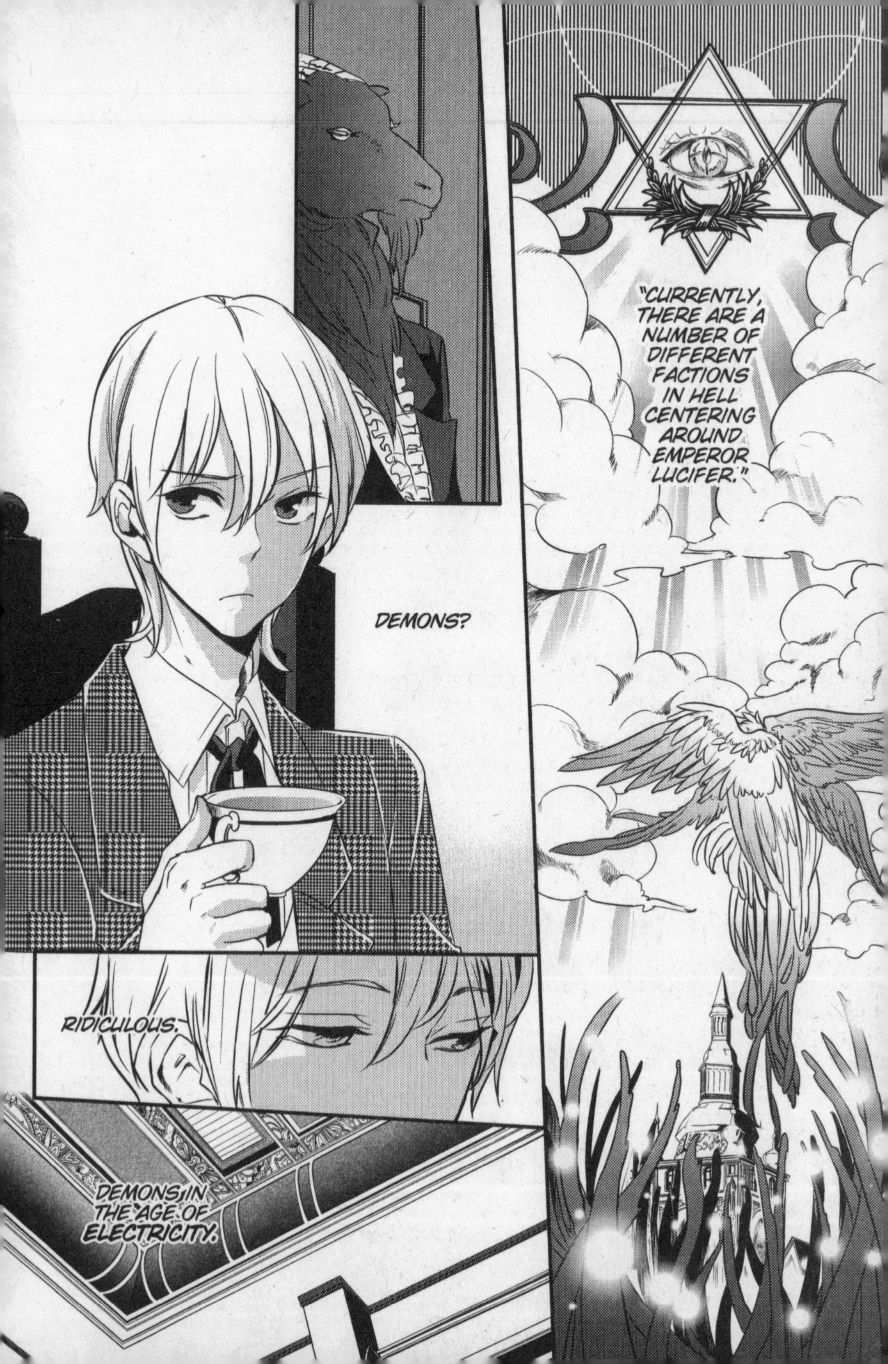
"CURRENTLY, THERE ARE A NUMBER OF DIFFERENT FACTIONS IN HELL CENTERING AROUND EMPEROR LUCIFER."
DEMONS?
RIDICULOUS.
DEMONS IN THE AGE OF ELECTRICITY.

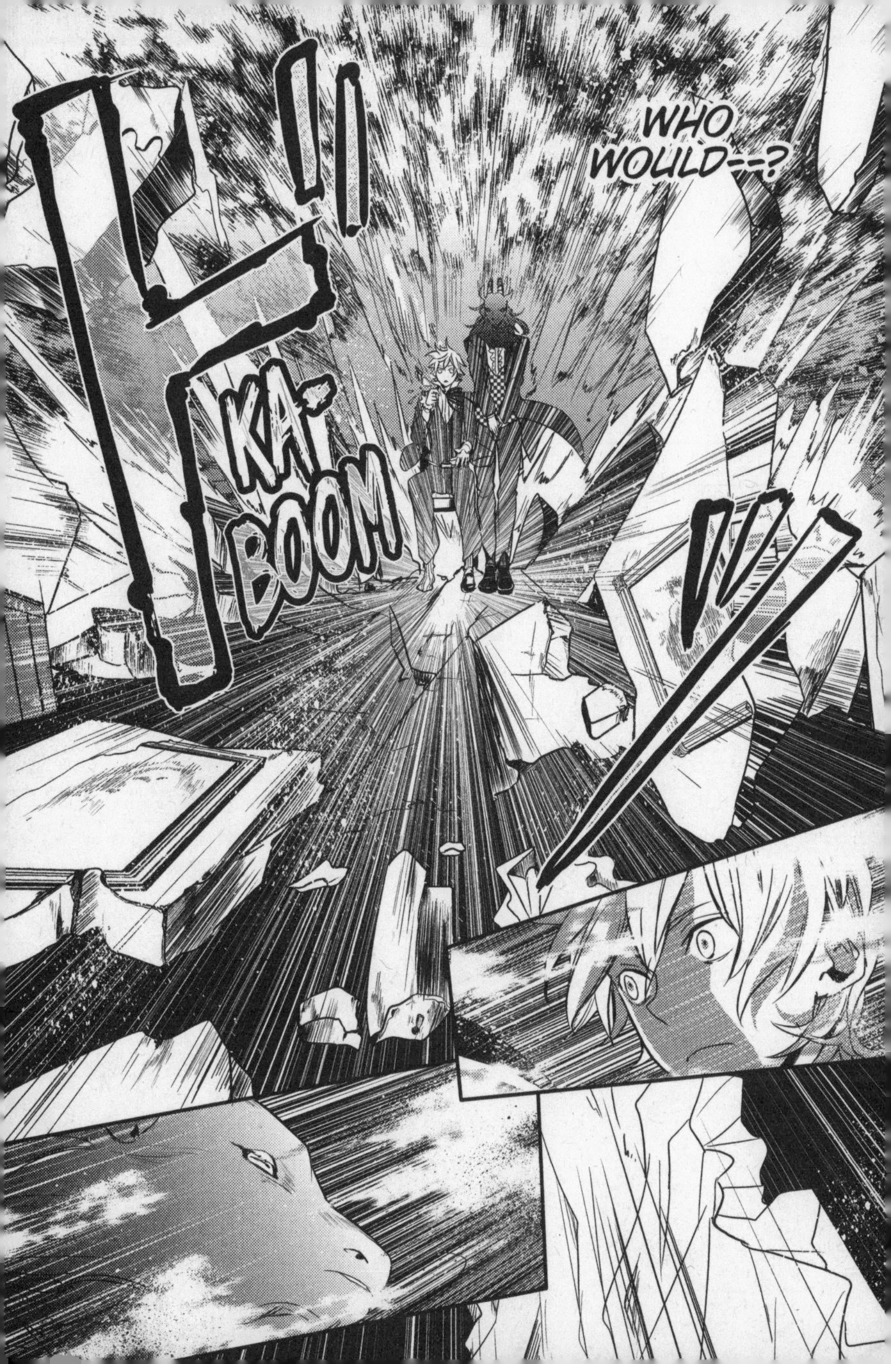
WHO WOULD---?
KA-BOOM

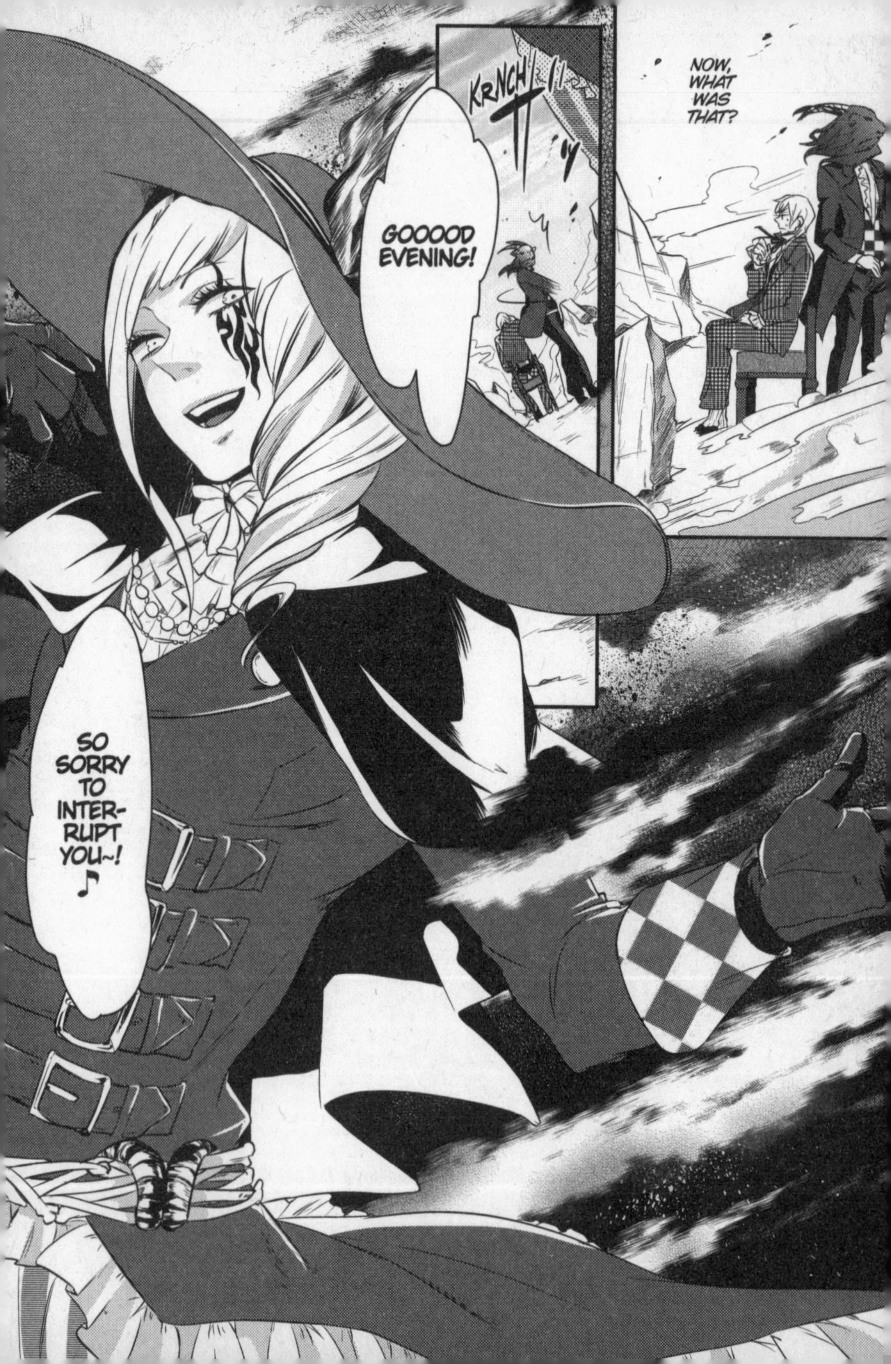
NOW, WHAT WAS THAT?
KRNCH
GOOOOD EVENING!
SO SORRY TO INTERRUPT YOU~! ♪

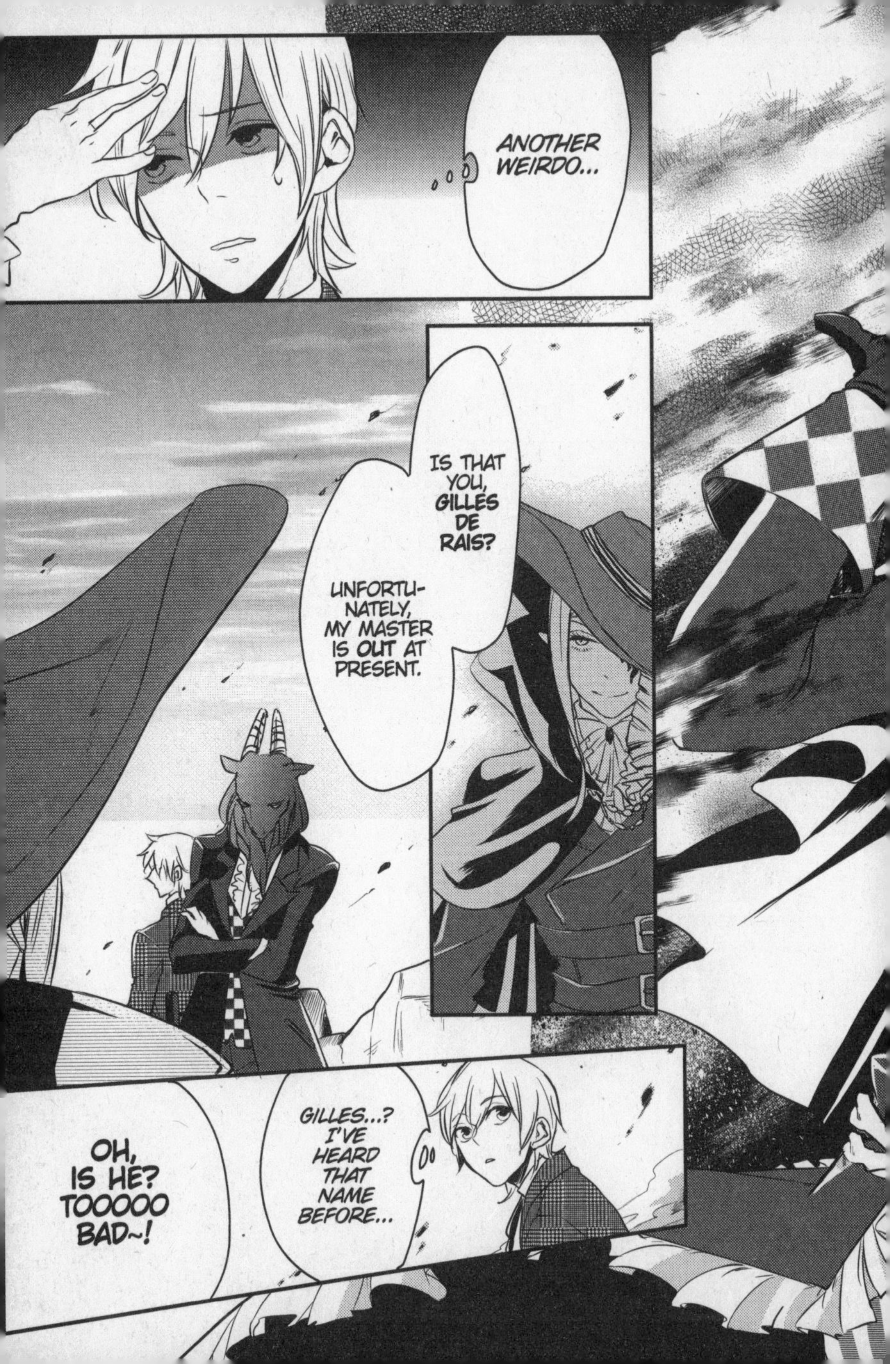
ANOTHER WEIRDO...
IS THAT YOU, GILLES DE RAIS?
UNFORTU-NATELY, MY MASTER IS OUT AT PRESENT.
GILLES...? I'VE HEARD THAT NAME BEFORE...
OH, IS HE? TOOOOO BAD~!

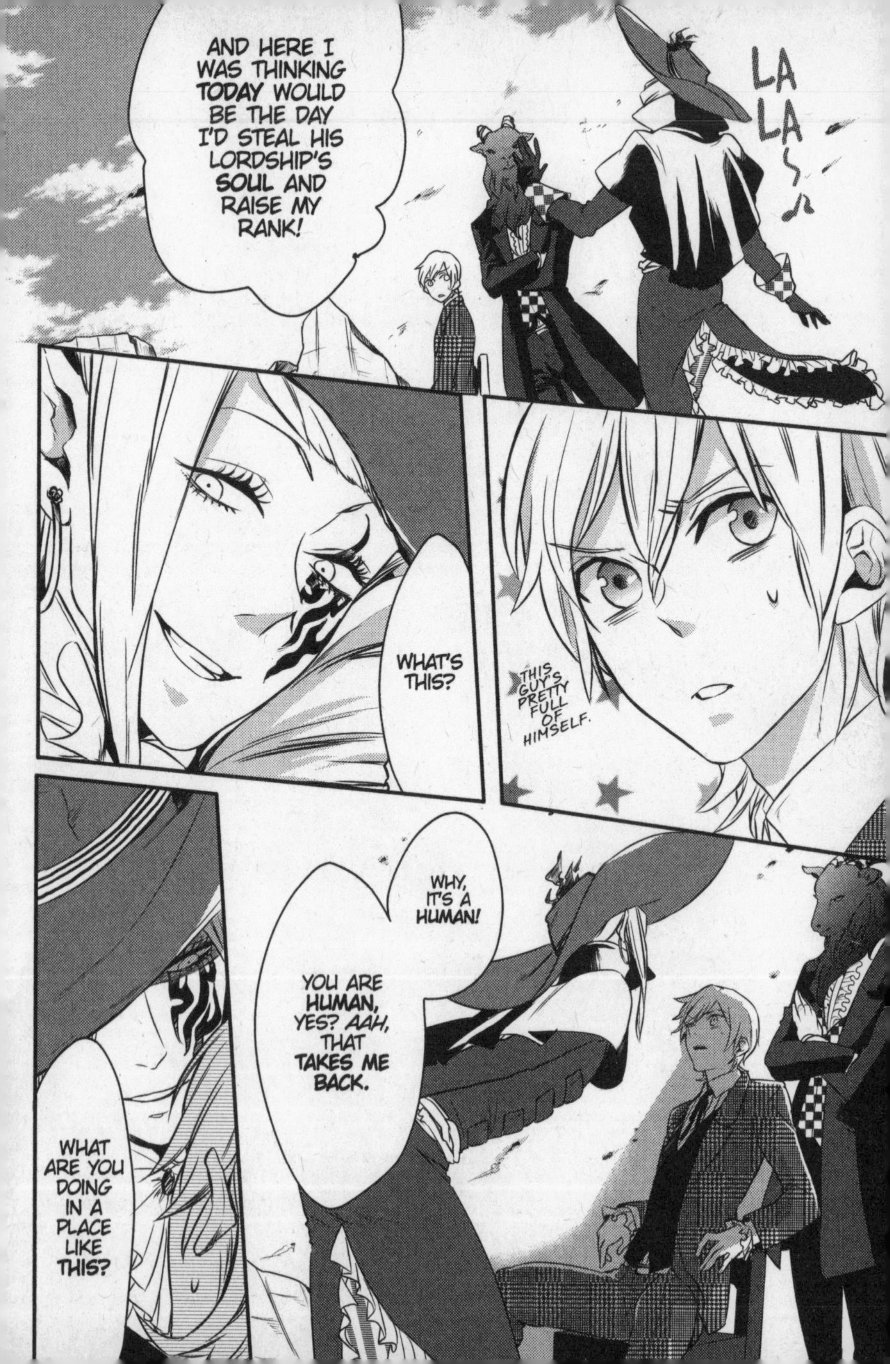
LA LA~♪
AND HERE I WAS THINKING TODAY WOULD BE THE DAY I'D STEAL HIS LORDSHIP'S SOUL AND RAISE MY RANK!
THIS GUY'S PRETTY FULL OF HIMSELF.
WHAT'S THIS?
WHY, IT'S A HUMAN!
YOU ARE HUMAN, YES? AAH, THAT TAKES ME BACK.
WHAT ARE YOU DOING IN A PLACE LIKE THIS?

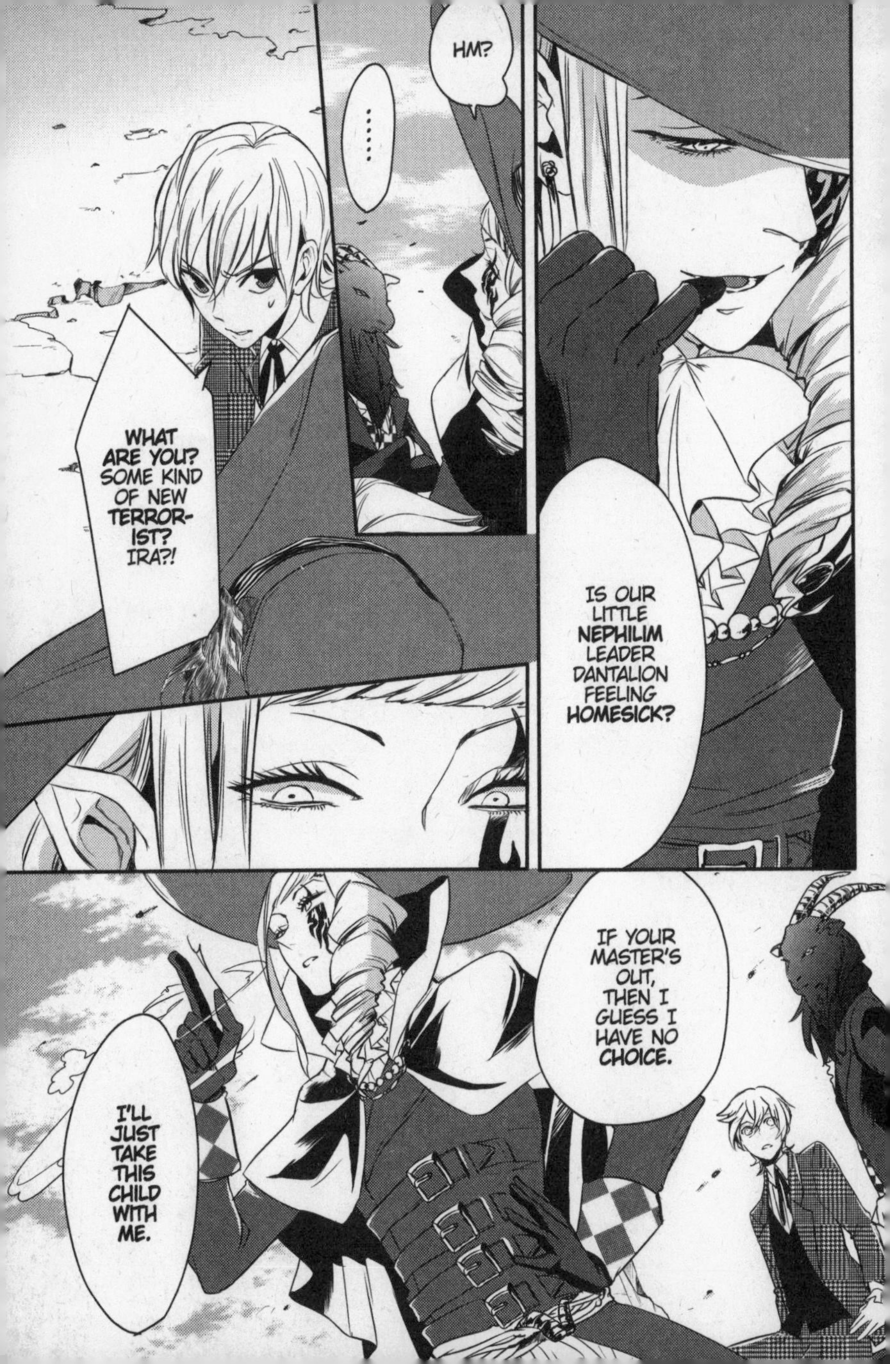
HM?
......
WHAT ARE YOU? SOME KIND OF NEW TERROR-IST? IRA?!
IS OUR LITTLE NEPHILIM LEADER DANTALION FEELING HOMESICK?
IF YOUR MASTER'S OUT, THEN I GUESS I HAVE NO CHOICE.
I'LL JUST TAKE THIS CHILD WITH ME.

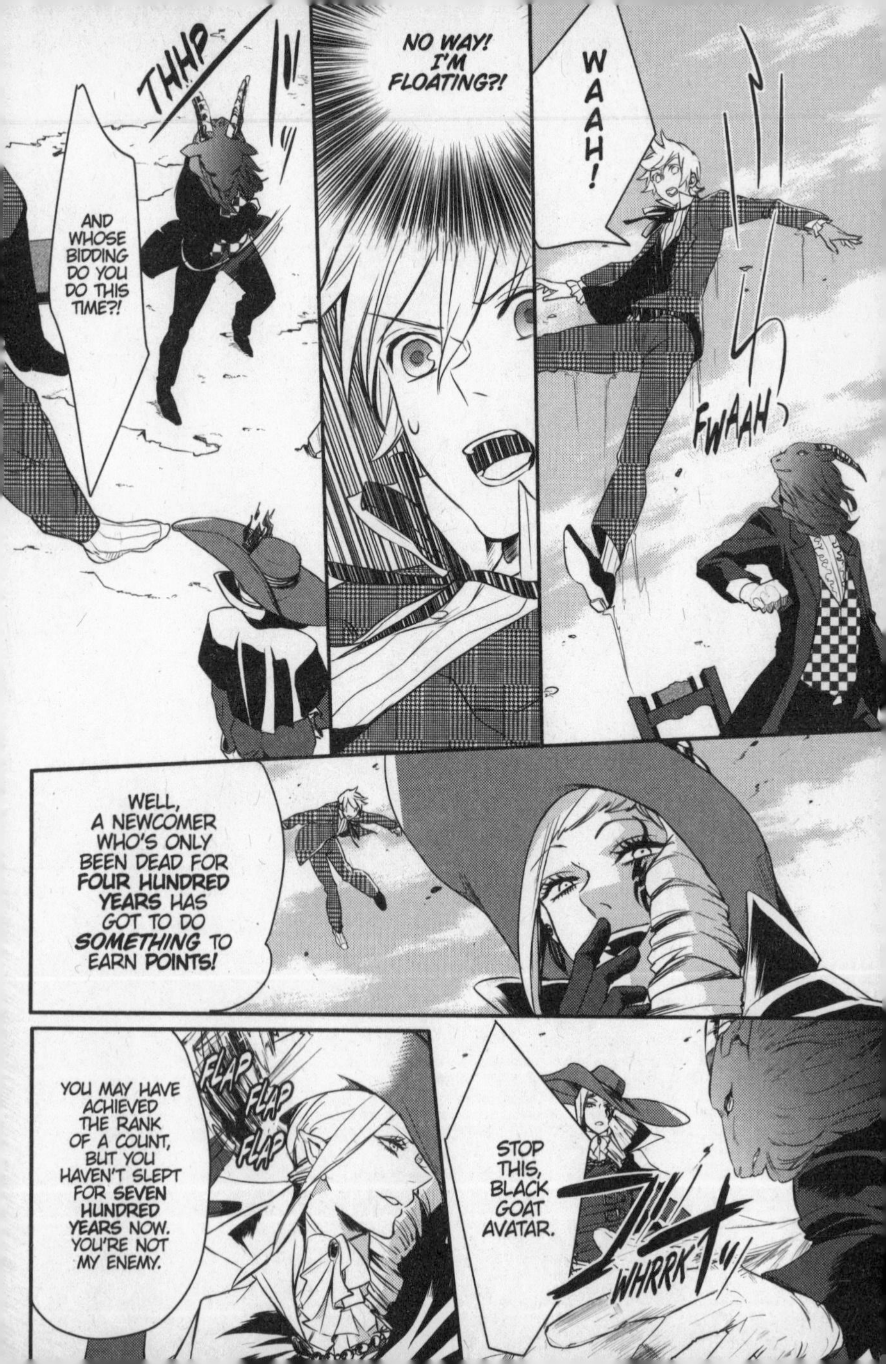

WAAH!
FWAAH
NO WAY! I'M FLOATING?!
THHP
AND WHOSE BIDDING DO YOU DO THIS TIME?!
WELL, A NEWCOMER WHO'S ONLY BEEN DEAD FOR FOUR HUNDRED YEARS HAS GOT TO DO SOMETHING TO EARN POINTS!
STOP THIS, BLACK GOAT AVATAR.
WHRRK
FLAP FLAP FLAP
YOU MAY HAVE ACHIEVED THE RANK OF A COUNT, BUT YOU HAVEN'T SLEPT FOR SEVEN HUNDRED YEARS NOW. YOU'RE NOT MY ENEMY.

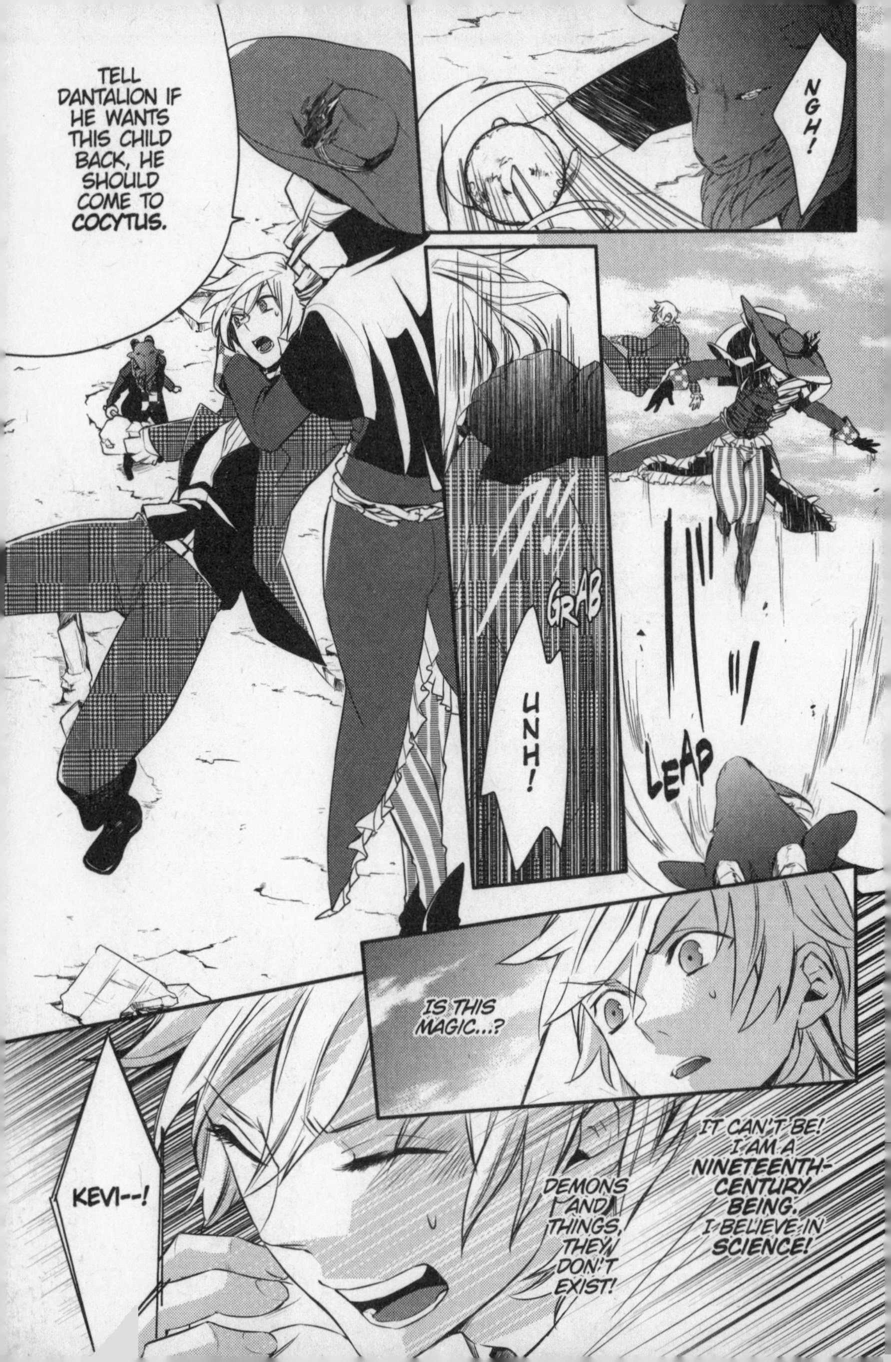
NGH!
TELL DANTALION IF HE WANTS THIS CHILD BACK, HE SHOULD COME TO COCYTUS.
LEAP
GRAB
UNH!
IS THIS MAGIC...?
IT CAN'T BE! I AM A NINETEENTH-CENTURY BEING. I BELIEVE IN SCIENCE!
DEMONS AND THINGS, THEY DON'T EXIST!
KEVI--!

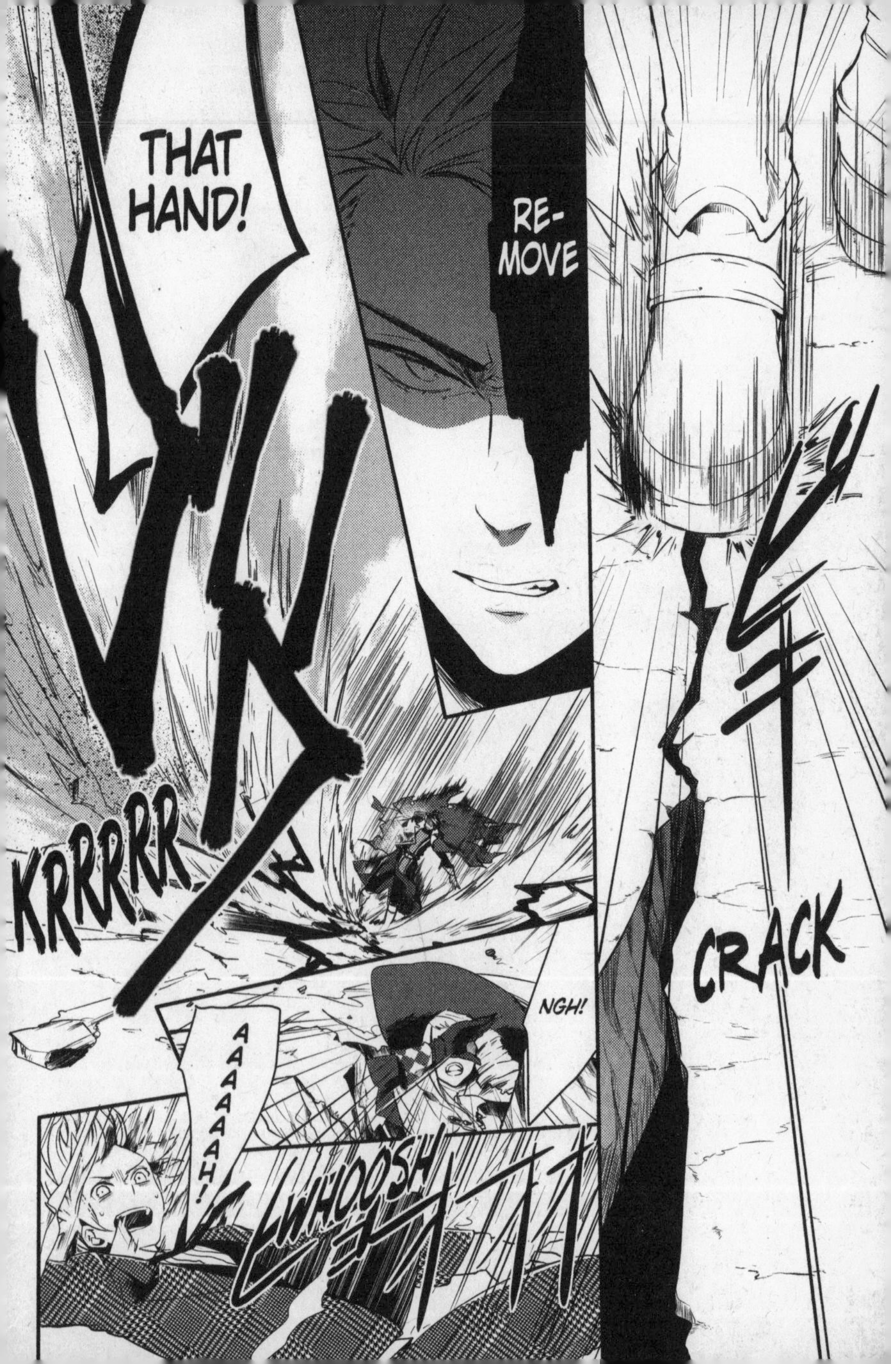
CRACK
RE-MOVE
THAT HAND!
KRRRRR
NGH!
AAAAAAAH!
WHOOSH

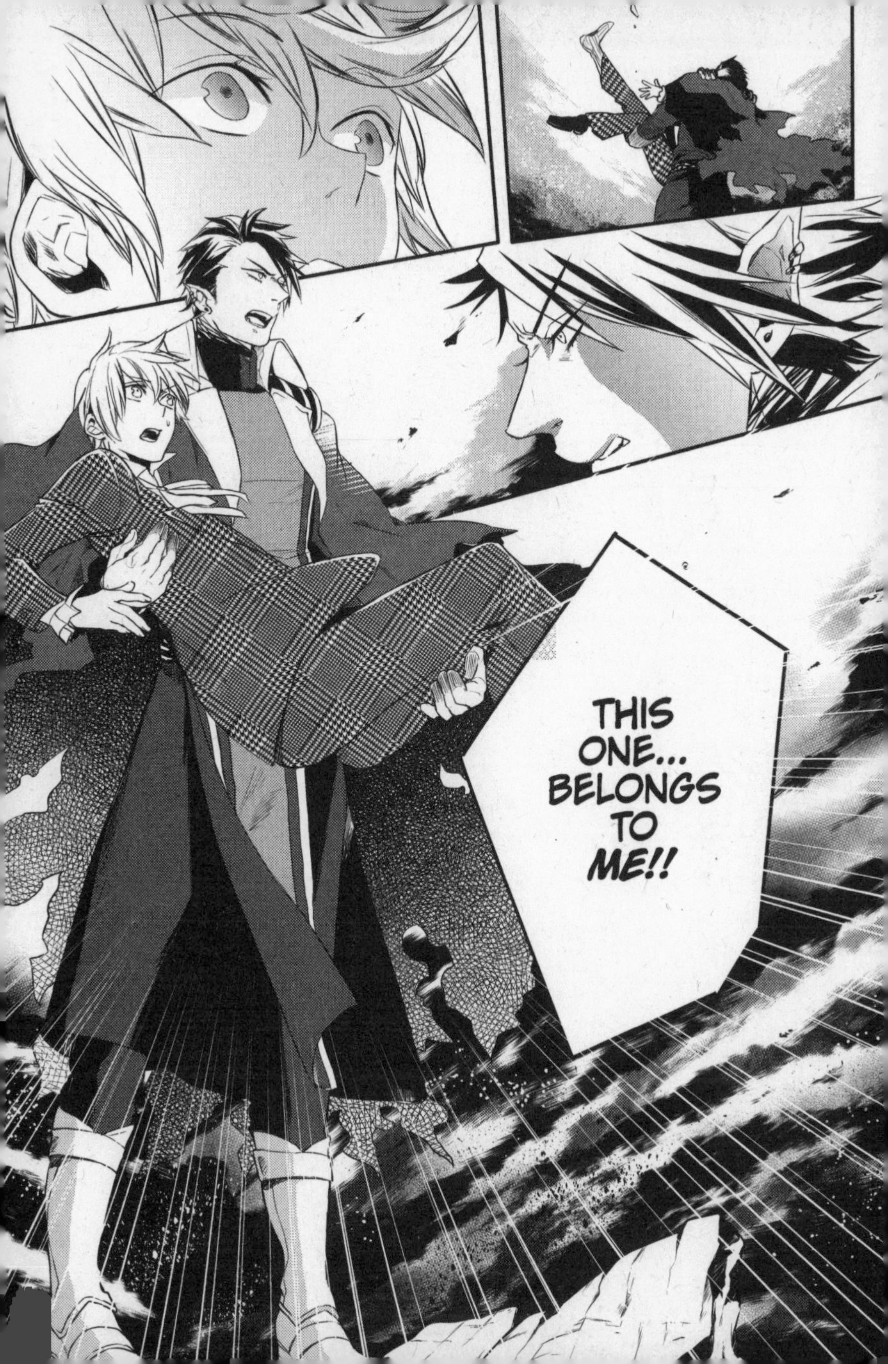
THIS ONE... BELONGS TO *ME!!*

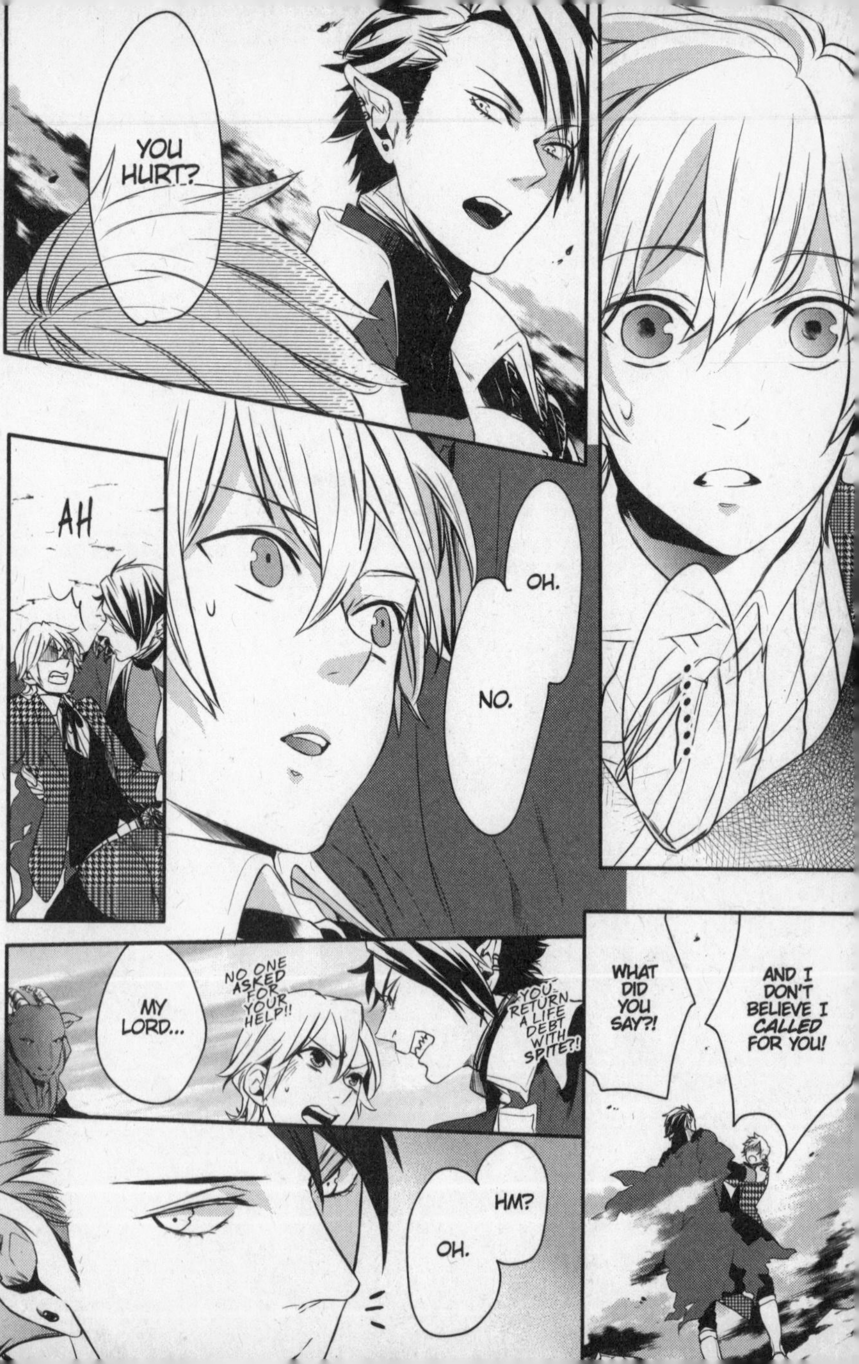
YOU HURT?
OH.
NO.
AH
AND I DON'T BELIEVE I CALLED FOR YOU!
WHAT DID YOU SAY?!
YOU RETURN A LIFE DEBT WITH SPITE?!
NO ONE ASKED FOR YOUR HELP!!
MY LORD...
HM?
OH.

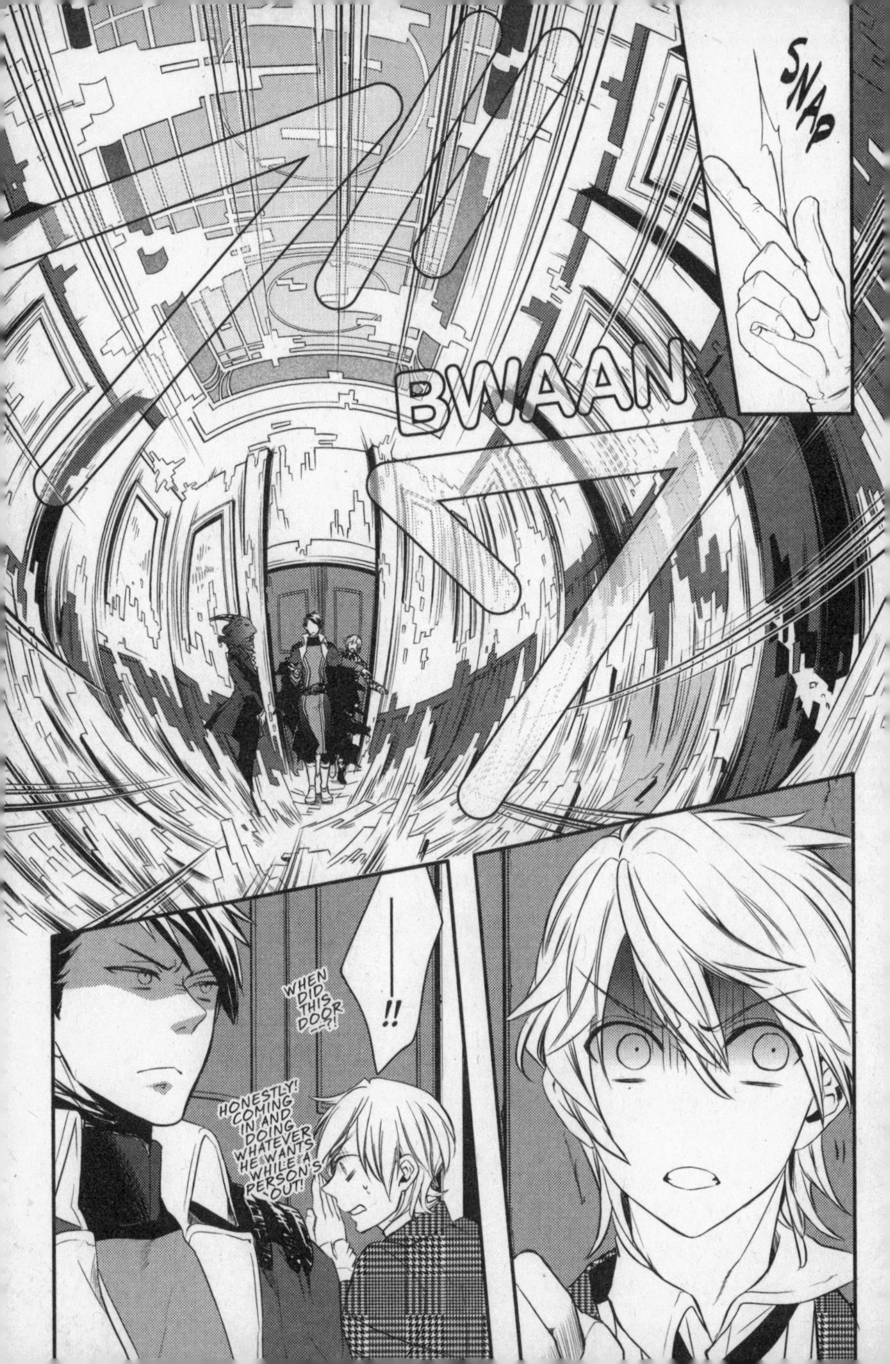
SNAP
BWAAN
—!!
WHEN DID THIS DOOR—?!
HONESTLY! COMING IN AND DOING WHATEVER HE WANTS WHILE A PERSON'S OUT!

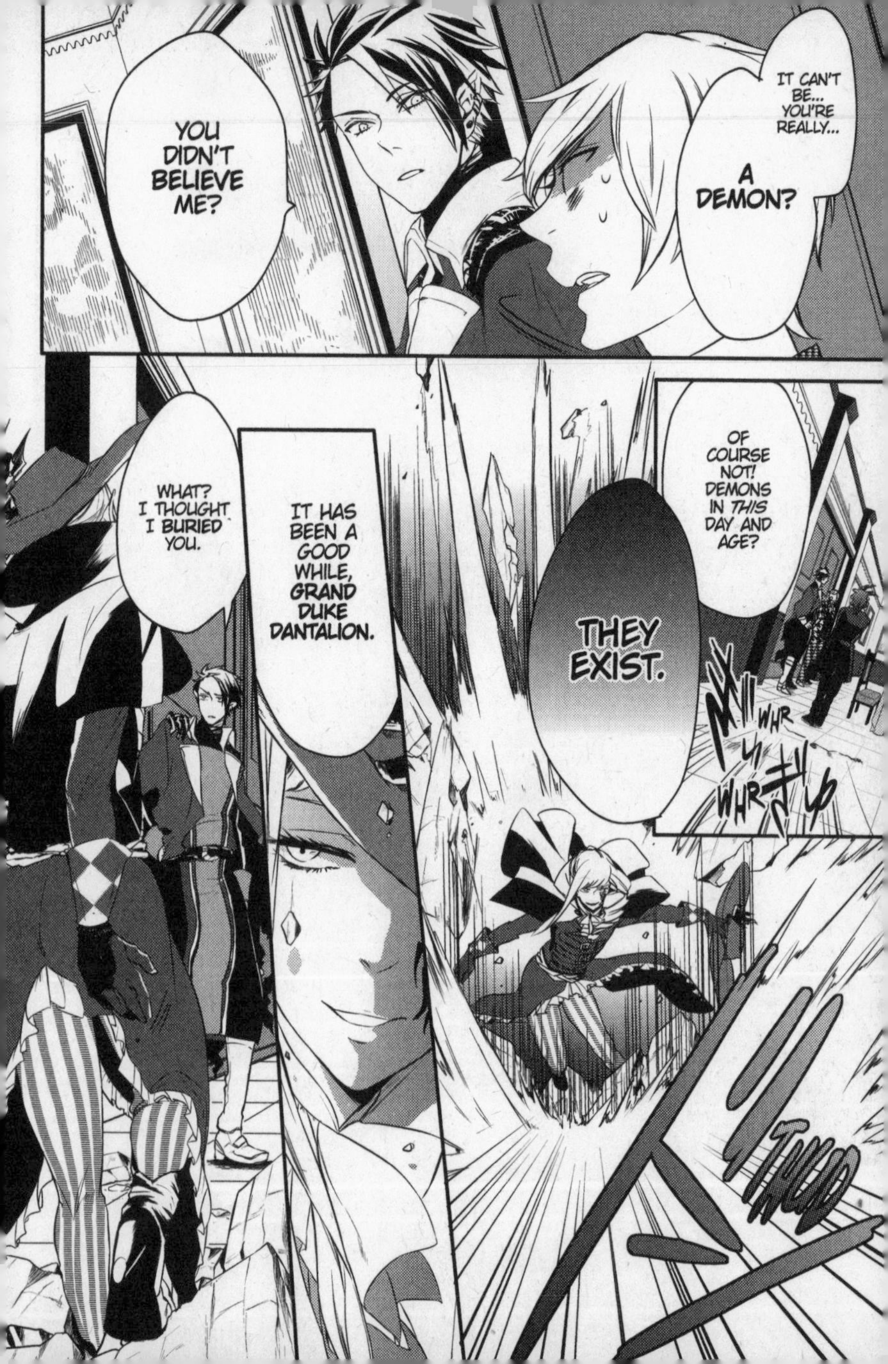
IT CAN'T BE... YOU'RE REALLY...
A DEMON?
YOU DIDN'T BELIEVE ME?
OF COURSE NOT! DEMONS IN *THIS* DAY AND AGE?
THEY EXIST.
WHR
WHR
THUD
IT HAS BEEN A GOOD WHILE, GRAND DUKE DANTALION.
WHAT? I THOUGHT I BURIED YOU.

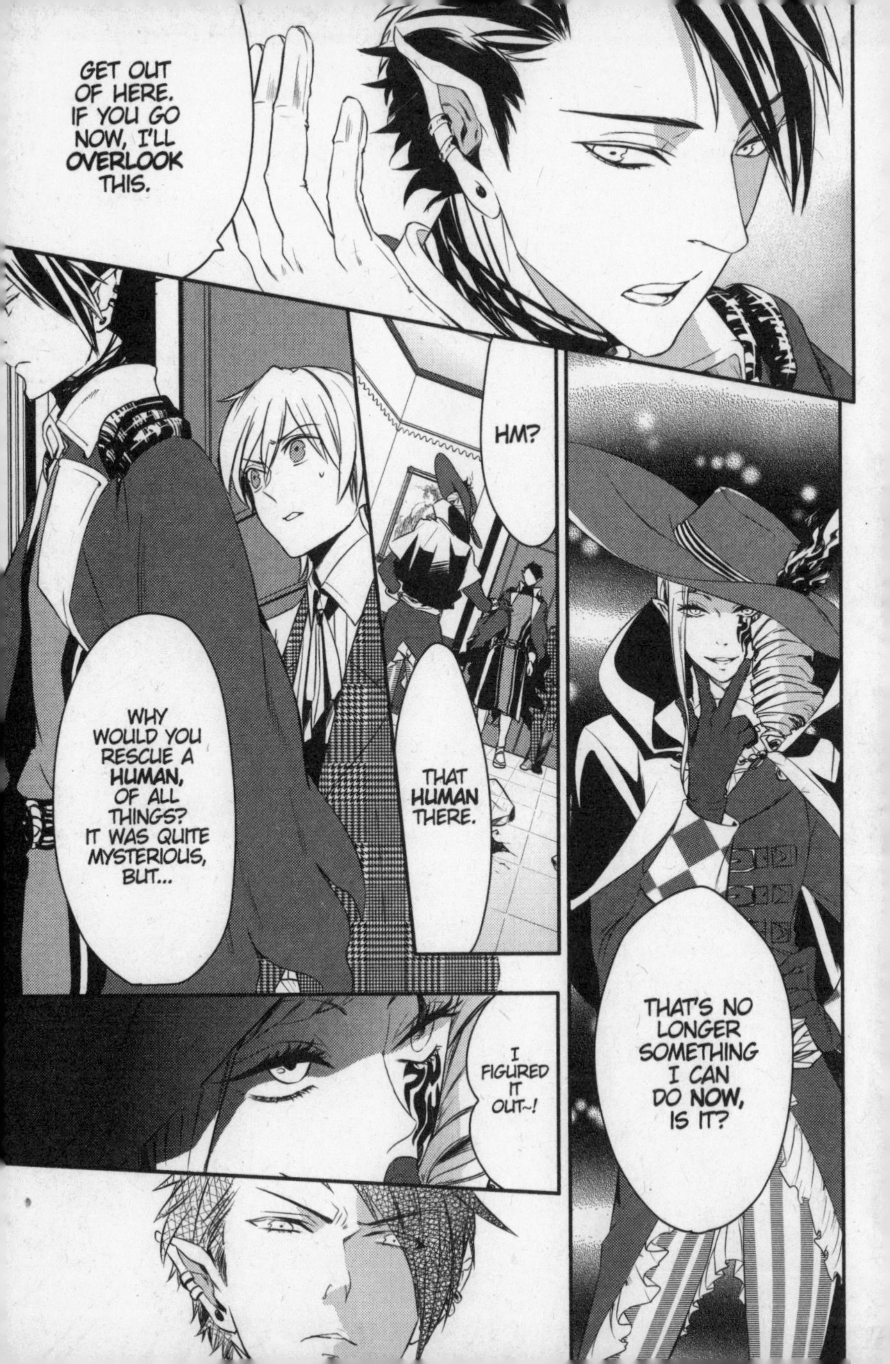
GET OUT OF HERE. IF YOU GO NOW, I'LL OVERLOOK THIS.
HM?
THAT'S NO LONGER SOMETHING I CAN DO NOW, IS IT?
THAT HUMAN THERE.
WHY WOULD YOU RESCUE A HUMAN, OF ALL THINGS? IT WAS QUITE MYSTERIOUS, BUT...
I FIGURED IT OUT~!

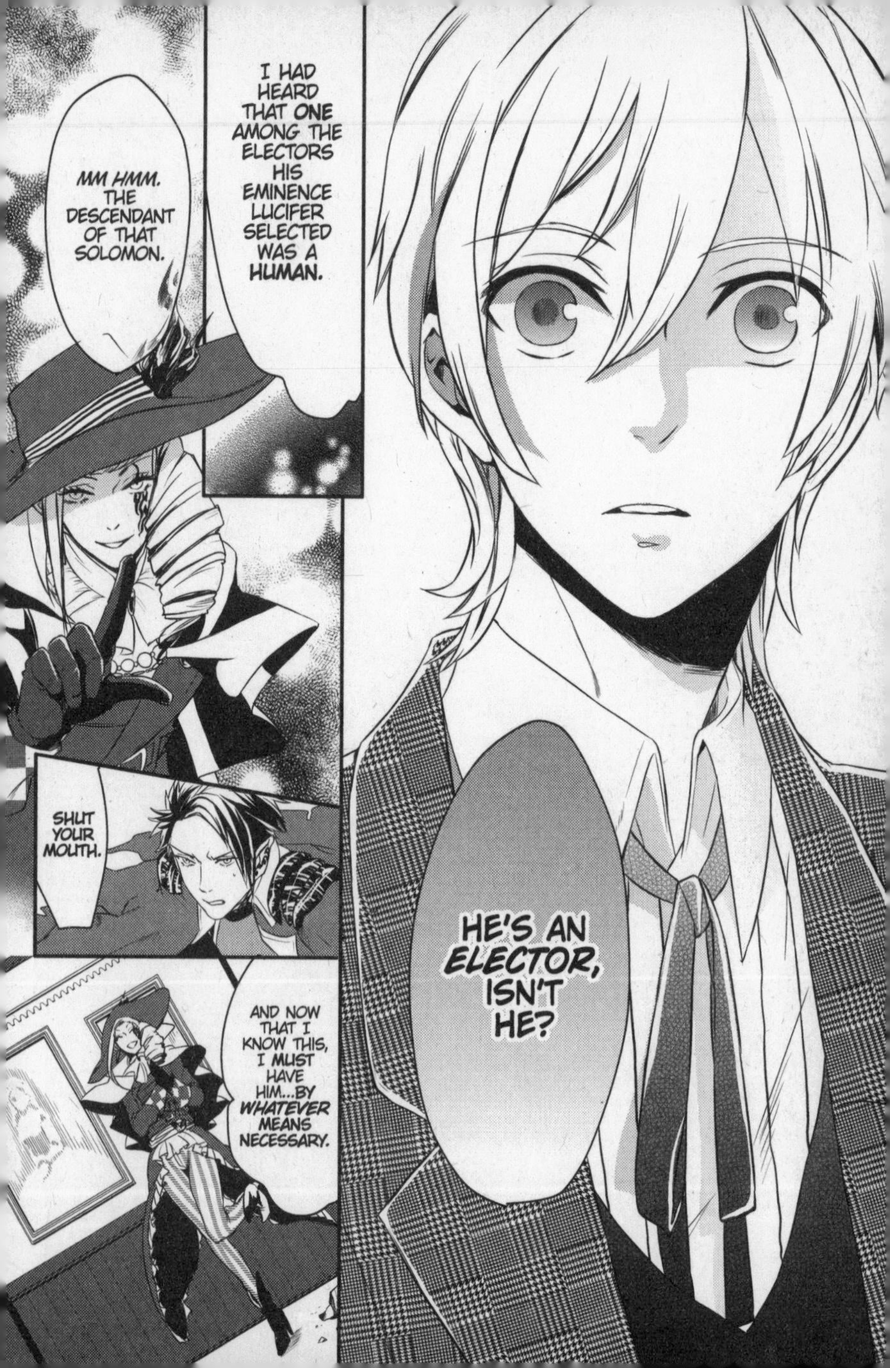
HE'S AN ELECTOR, ISN'T HE?
I HAD HEARD THAT ONE AMONG THE ELECTORS HIS EMINENCE LUCIFER SELECTED WAS A HUMAN.
MM HMM. THE DESCENDANT OF THAT SOLOMON.
SHUT YOUR MOUTH.
AND NOW THAT I KNOW THIS, I MUST HAVE HIM...BY WHATEVER MEANS NECESSARY.

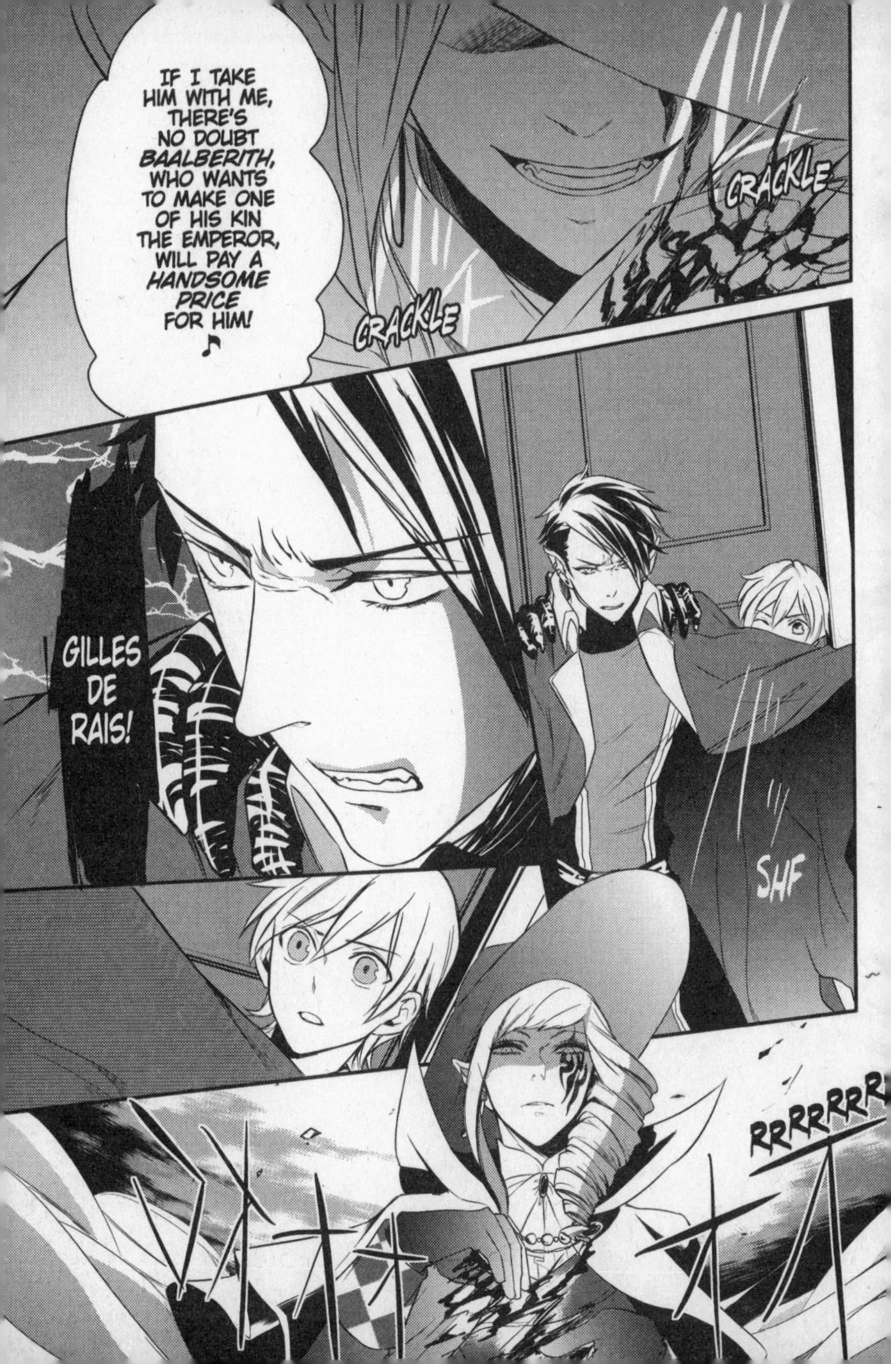
CRACKLE
IF I TAKE HIM WITH ME, THERE'S NO DOUBT *BAALBERITH*, WHO WANTS TO MAKE ONE OF HIS KIN THE EMPEROR, WILL PAY A *HANDSOME PRICE* FOR HIM! ♪
CRACKLE
SHF
GILLES DE RAIS!
RRRRRRR

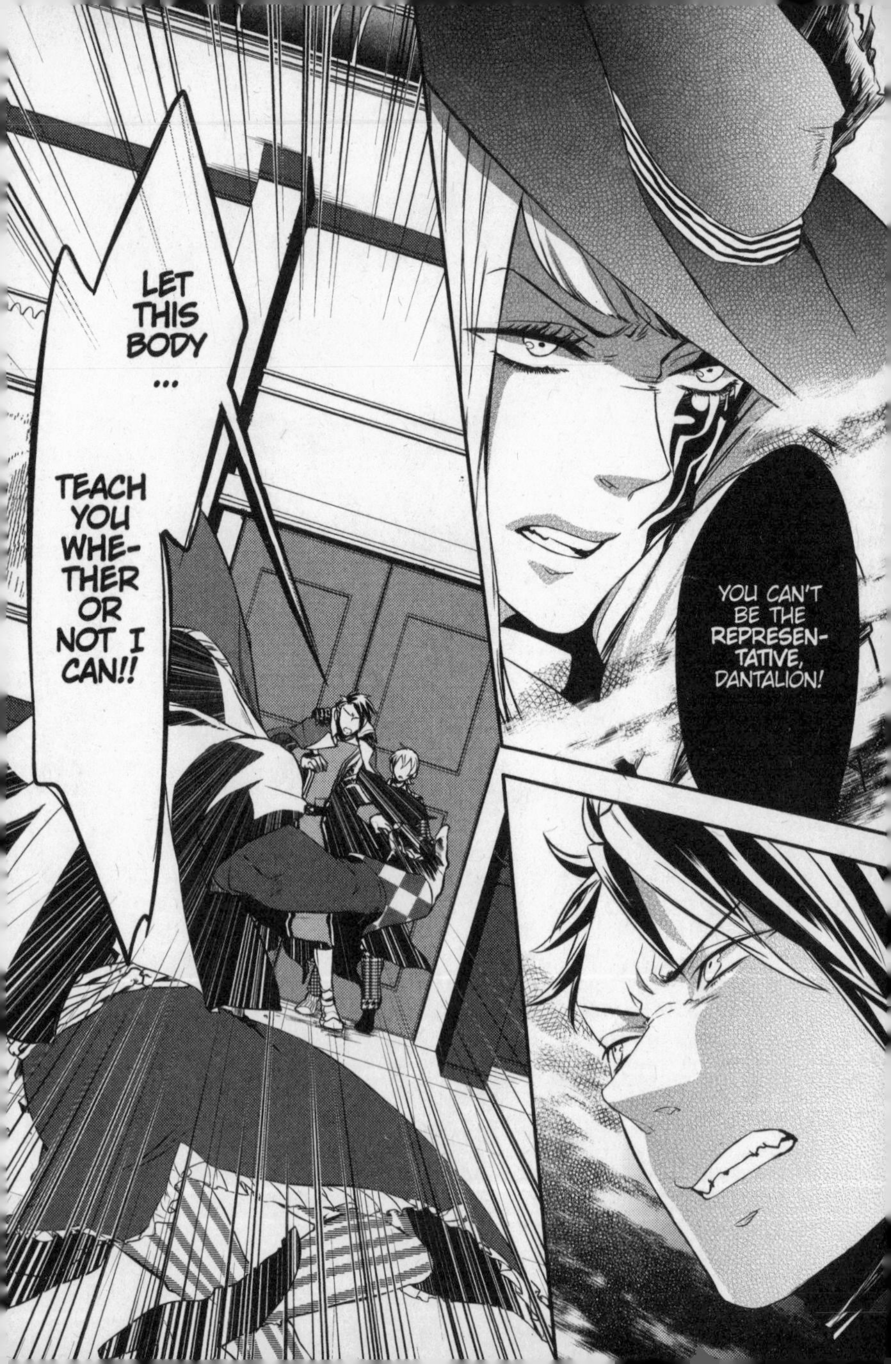
YOU CAN'T BE THE REPRESENTATIVE, DANTALION!
LET THIS BODY ...
TEACH YOU WHETHER OR NOT I CAN!!

Pillar 3

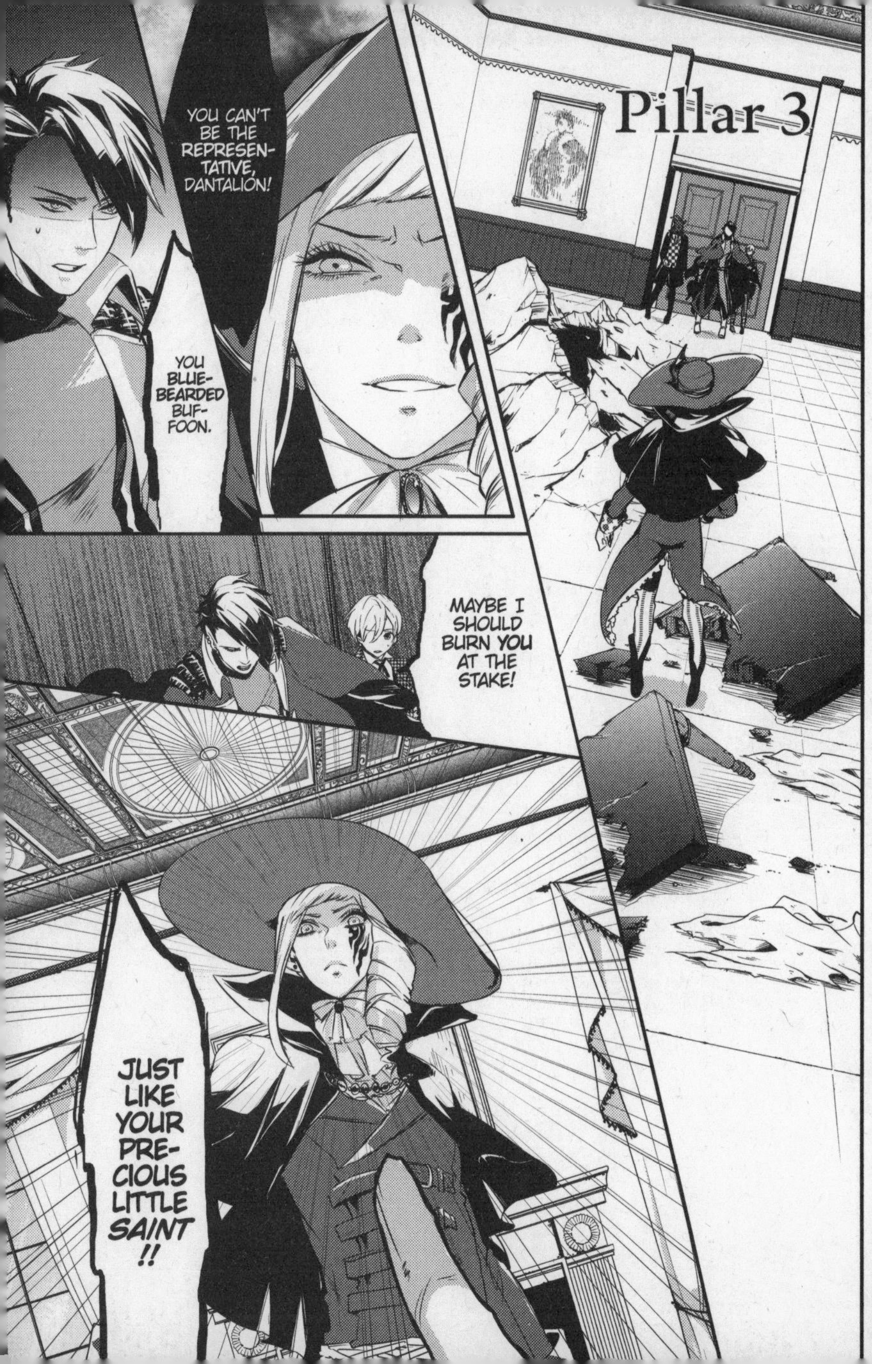

YOU CAN'T BE THE REPRESEN-TATIVE, DANTALION!
YOU BLUE-BEARDED BUF-FOON.
MAYBE I SHOULD BURN YOU AT THE STAKE!
JUST LIKE YOUR PRE-CIOUS LITTLE SAINT!!

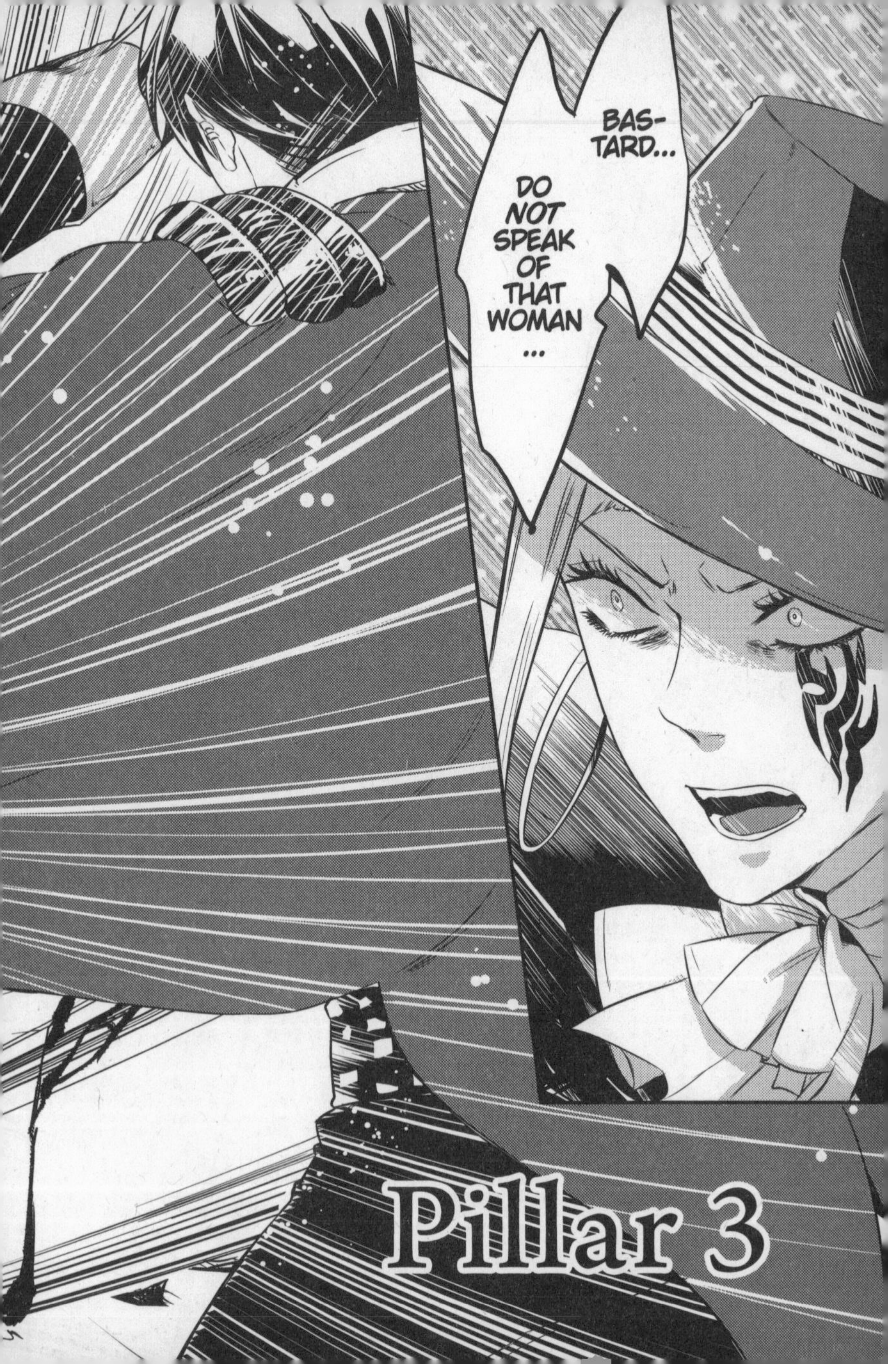
BAS-
TARD...
DO NOT SPEAK OF THAT WOMAN ...
Pillar 3

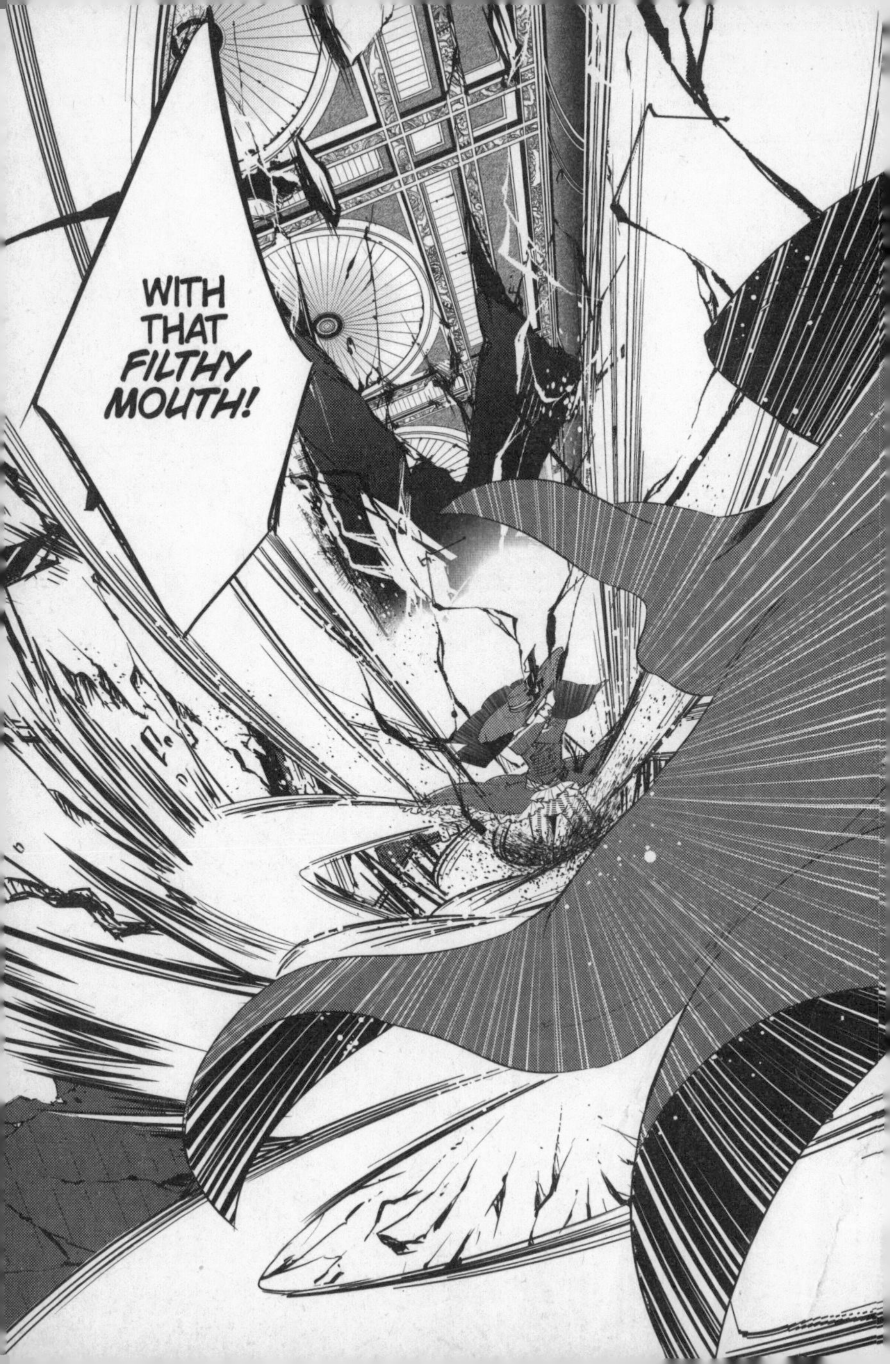
WITH THAT FILTHY MOUTH!

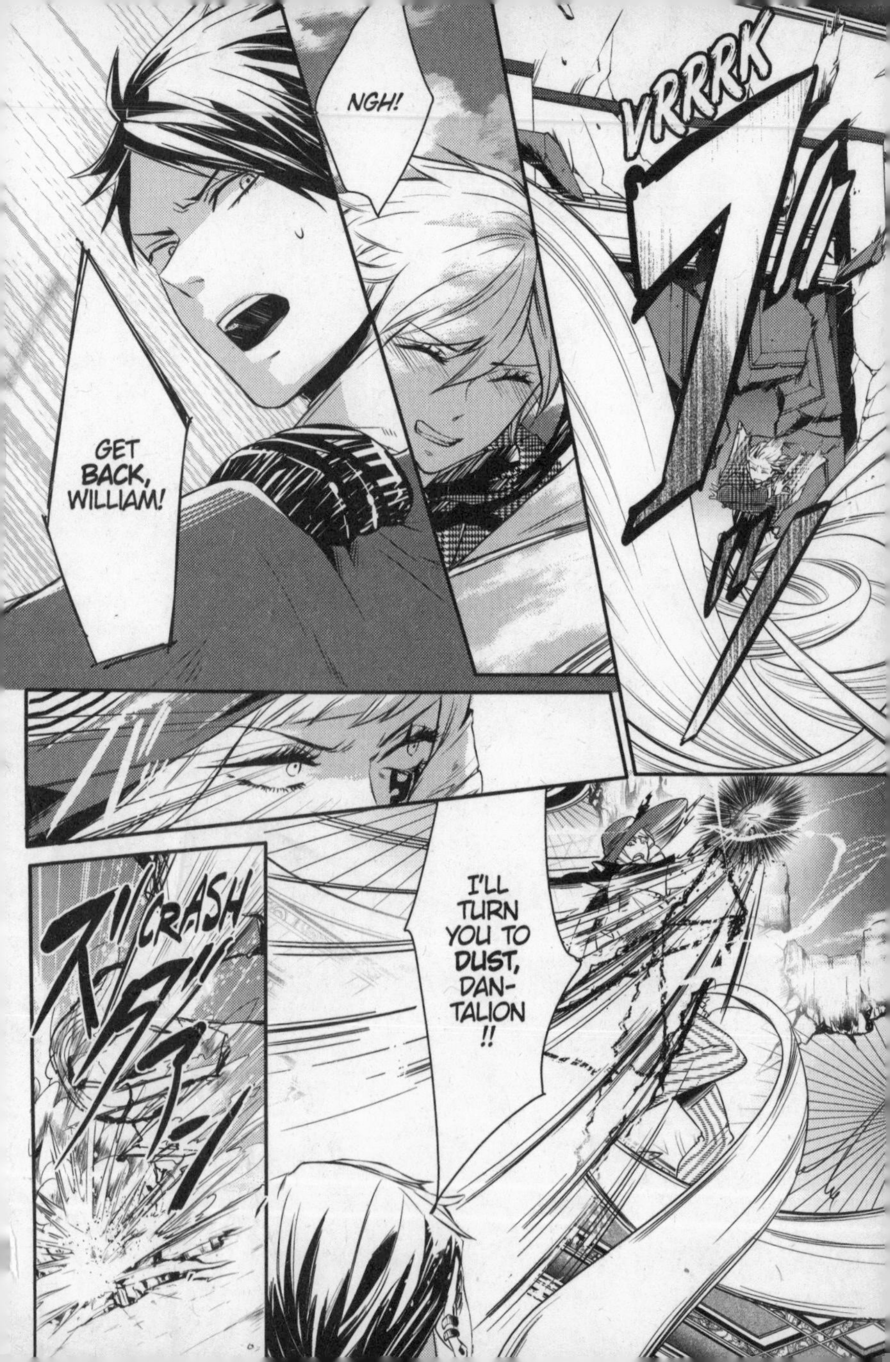
VRRRK
NGH!
GET BACK, WILLIAM!
I'LL TURN YOU TO DUST, DAN-TALION !!
CRASH

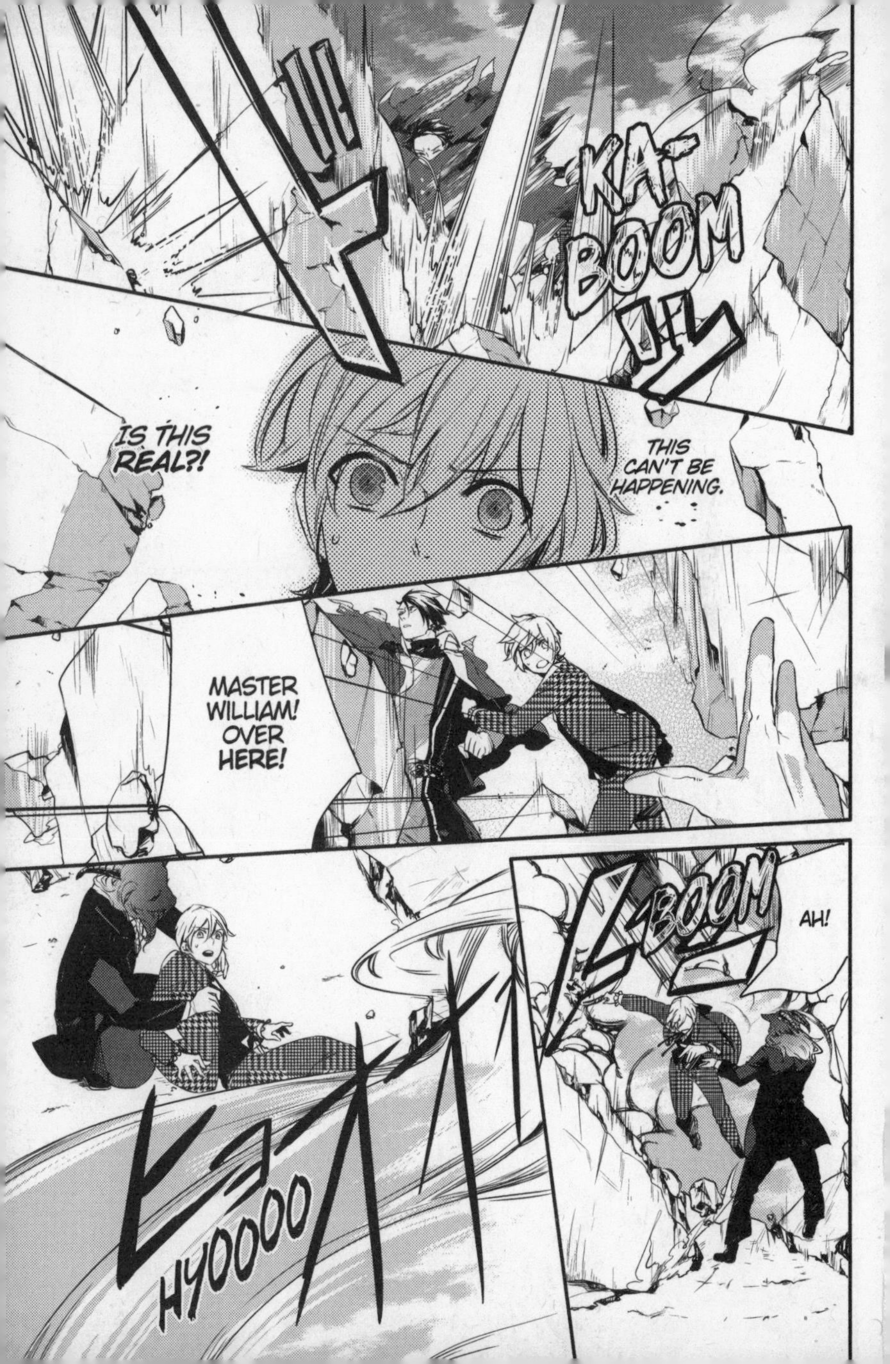
KA-BOOM
THIS CAN'T BE HAPPENING.
IS THIS REAL?!
MASTER WILLIAM! OVER HERE!
AH!
BOOM
HYOOOO

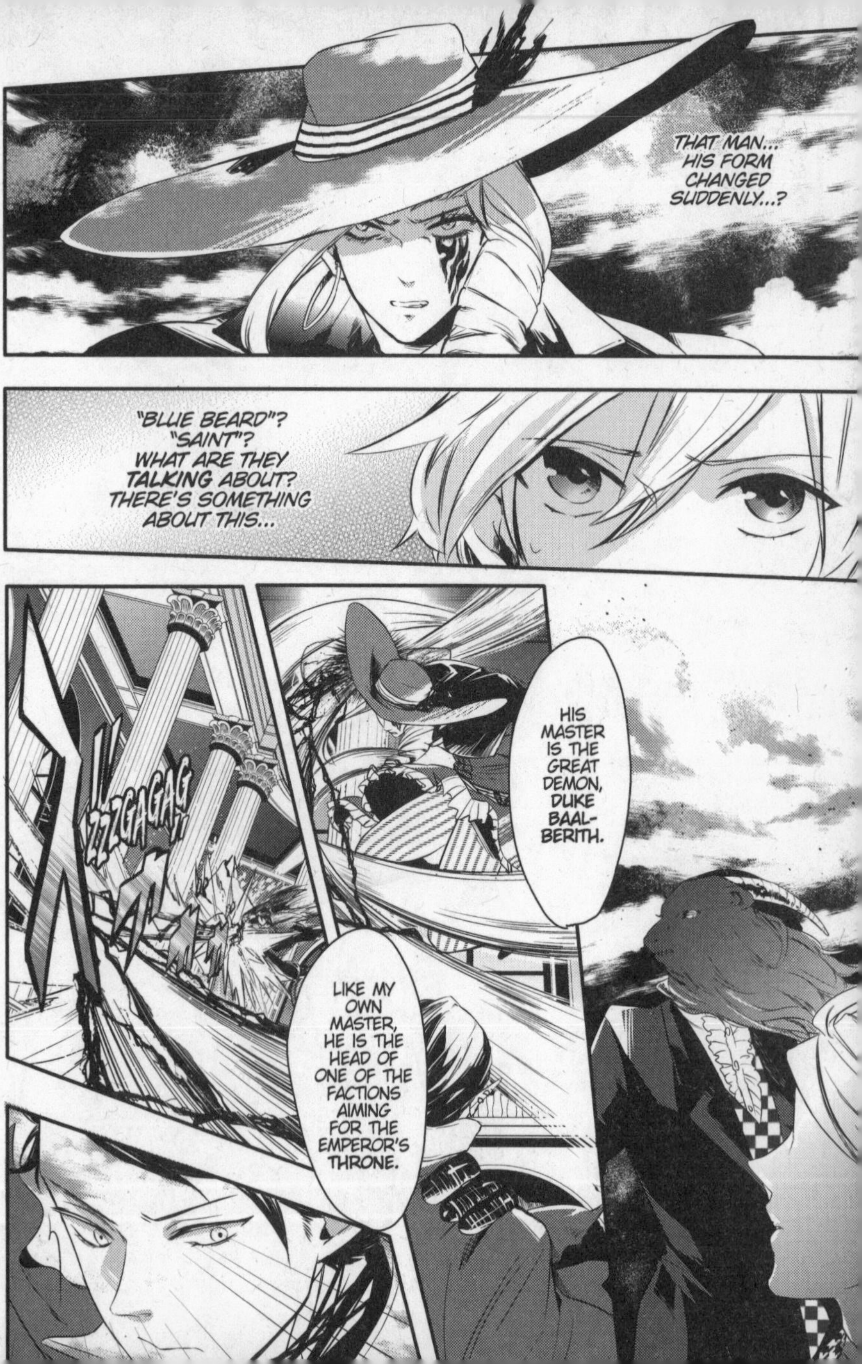
THAT MAN... HIS FORM CHANGED SUDDENLY...?
"BLUE BEARD"? "SAINT"? WHAT ARE THEY TALKING ABOUT? THERE'S SOMETHING ABOUT THIS...
HIS MASTER IS THE GREAT DEMON, DUKE BAAL-BERITH.
ZZZGAGAG
LIKE MY OWN MASTER, HE IS THE HEAD OF ONE OF THE FACTIONS AIMING FOR THE EMPEROR'S THRONE.

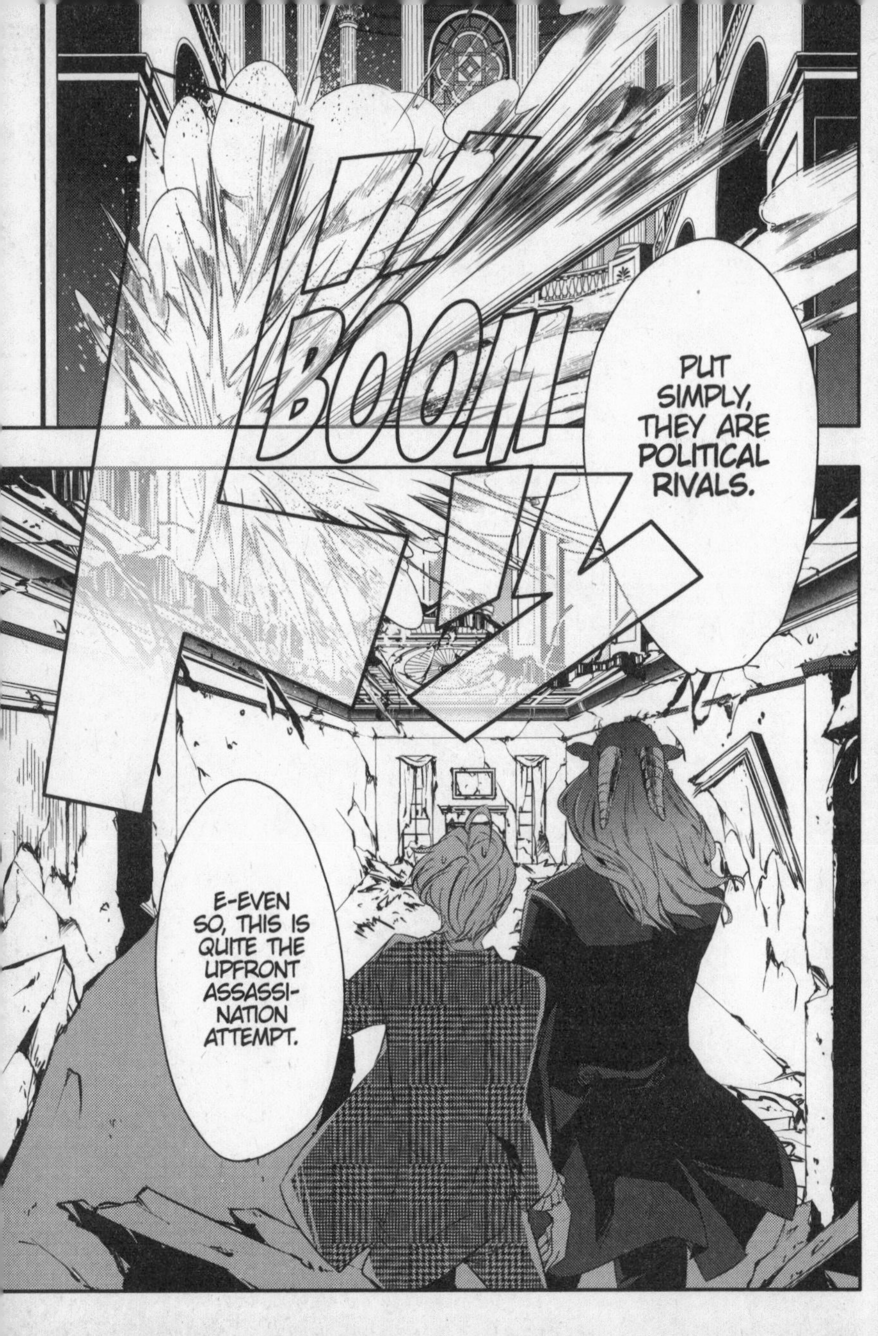
BOOM
PUT SIMPLY, THEY ARE POLITICAL RIVALS.
E-EVEN SO, THIS IS QUITE THE UPFRONT ASSASSI-NATION ATTEMPT.

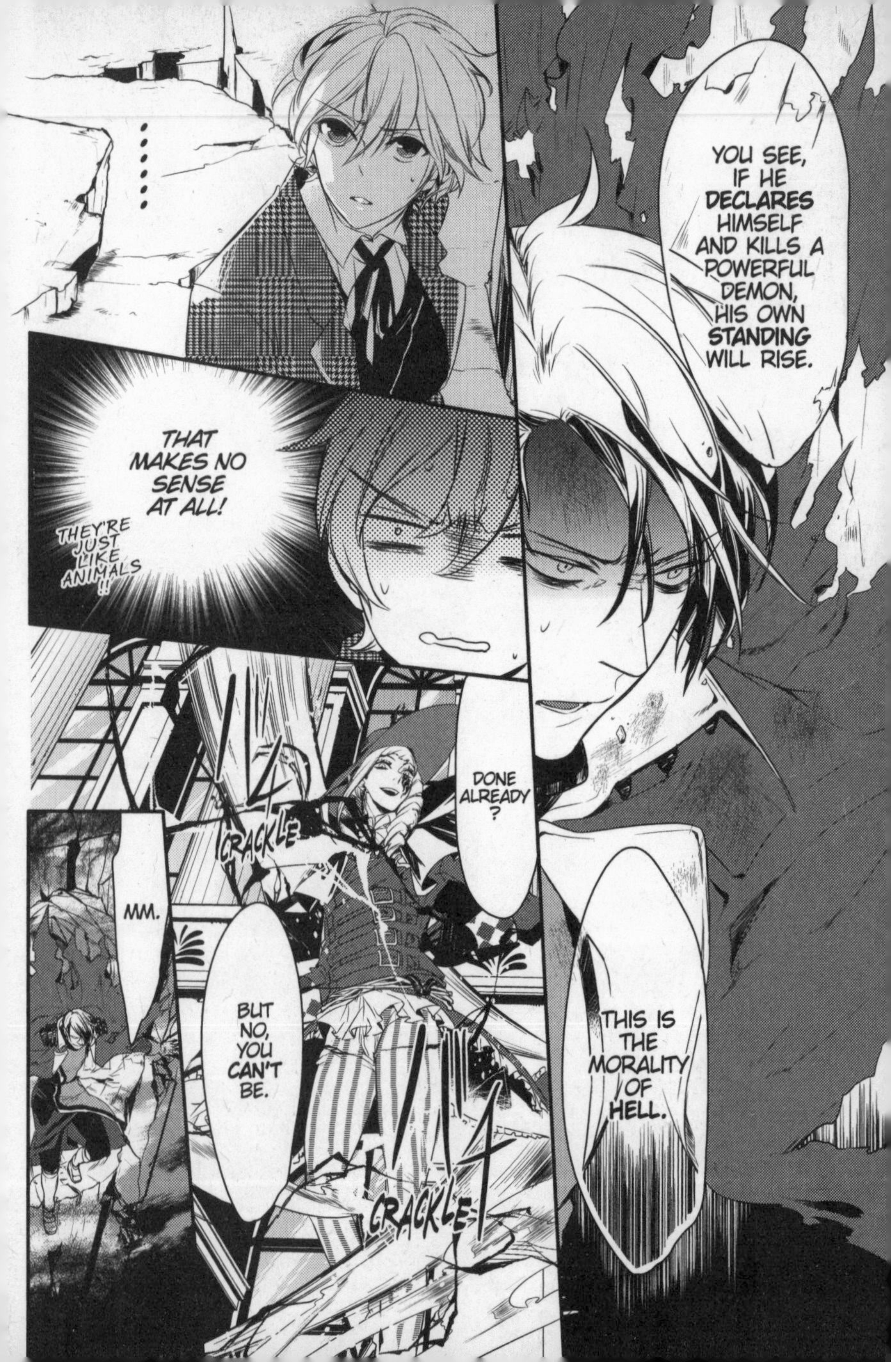
YOU SEE, IF HE DECLARES HIMSELF AND KILLS A POWERFUL DEMON, HIS OWN STANDING WILL RISE.
THIS IS THE MORALITY OF HELL.
......
THAT MAKES NO SENSE AT ALL!
THEY'RE JUST LIKE ANIMALS!!
DONE ALREADY?
CRACKLE
BUT NO, YOU CAN'T BE.
MM.
CRACKLE

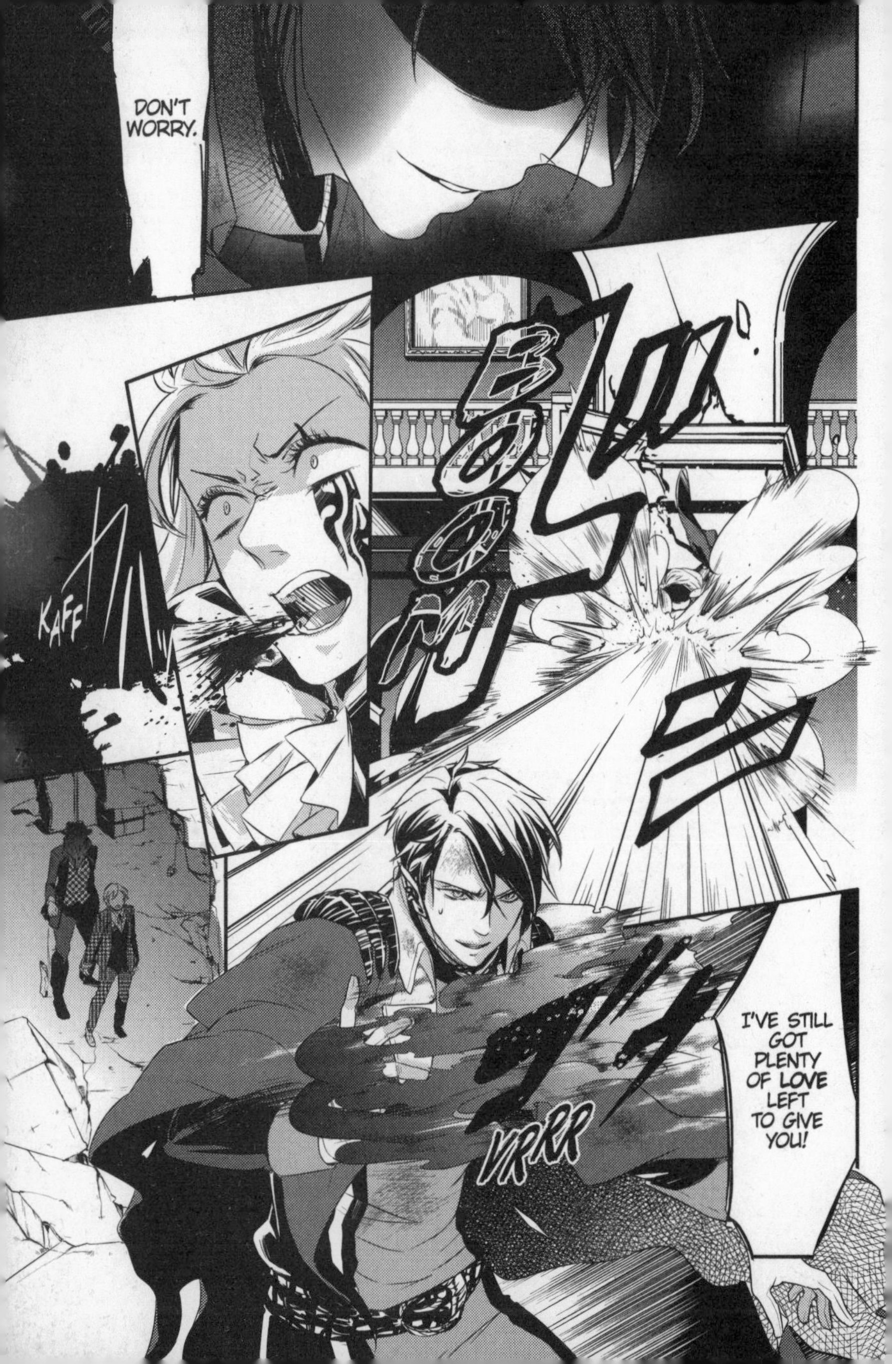
DON'T WORRY.
KAFF
I'VE STILL GOT PLENTY OF LOVE LEFT TO GIVE YOU!
VRRR

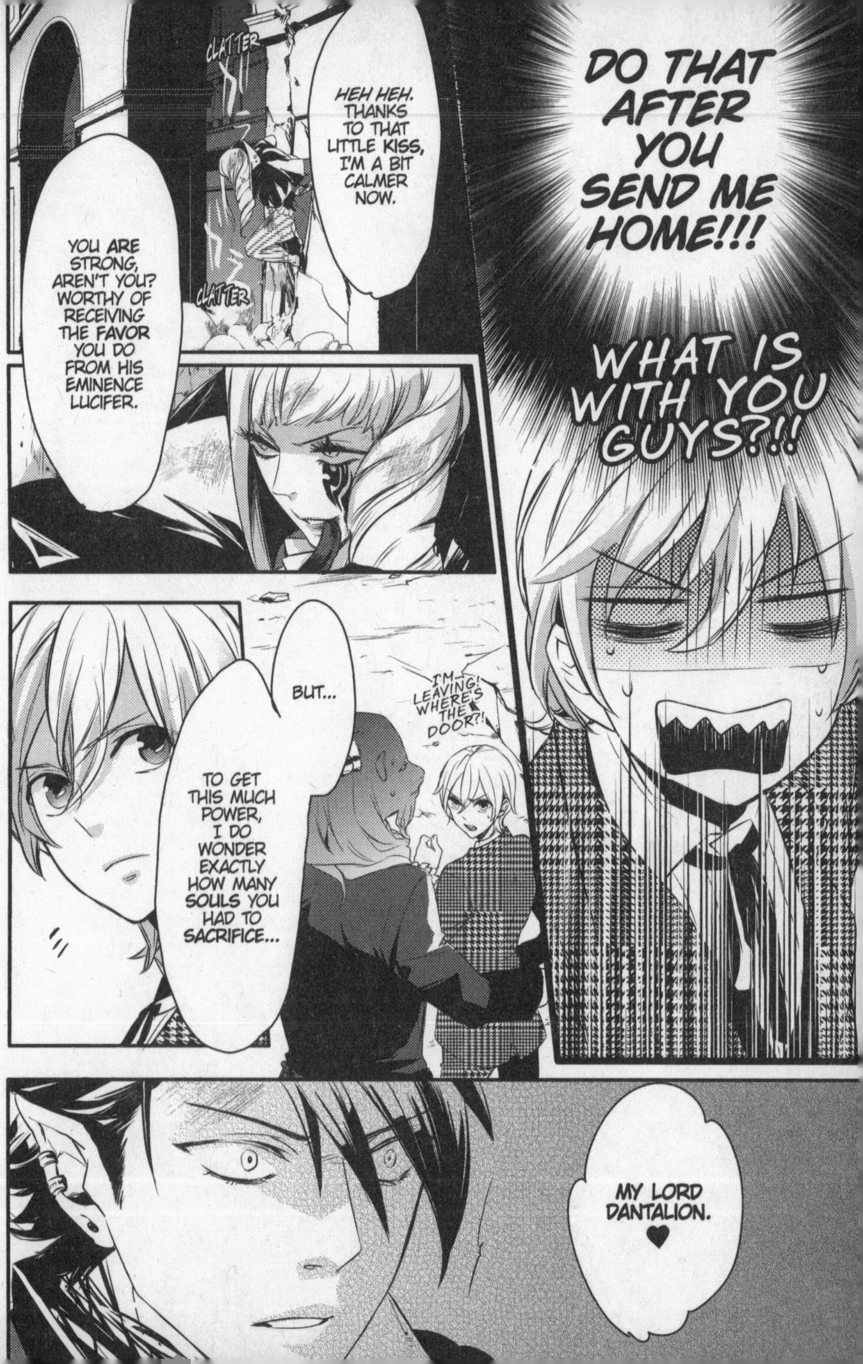
DO THAT AFTER YOU SEND ME HOME!!!
WHAT IS WITH YOU GUYS?!!
CLATTER
CLATTER
HEH HEH. THANKS TO THAT LITTLE KISS, I'M A BIT CALMER NOW.
YOU ARE STRONG, AREN'T YOU? WORTHY OF RECEIVING THE FAVOR YOU DO FROM HIS EMINENCE LUCIFER.
I'M LEAVING! WHERE'S THE DOOR?!
BUT...
TO GET THIS MUCH POWER, I DO WONDER EXACTLY HOW MANY SOULS YOU HAD TO SACRIFICE...
MY LORD DANTALION. ♥

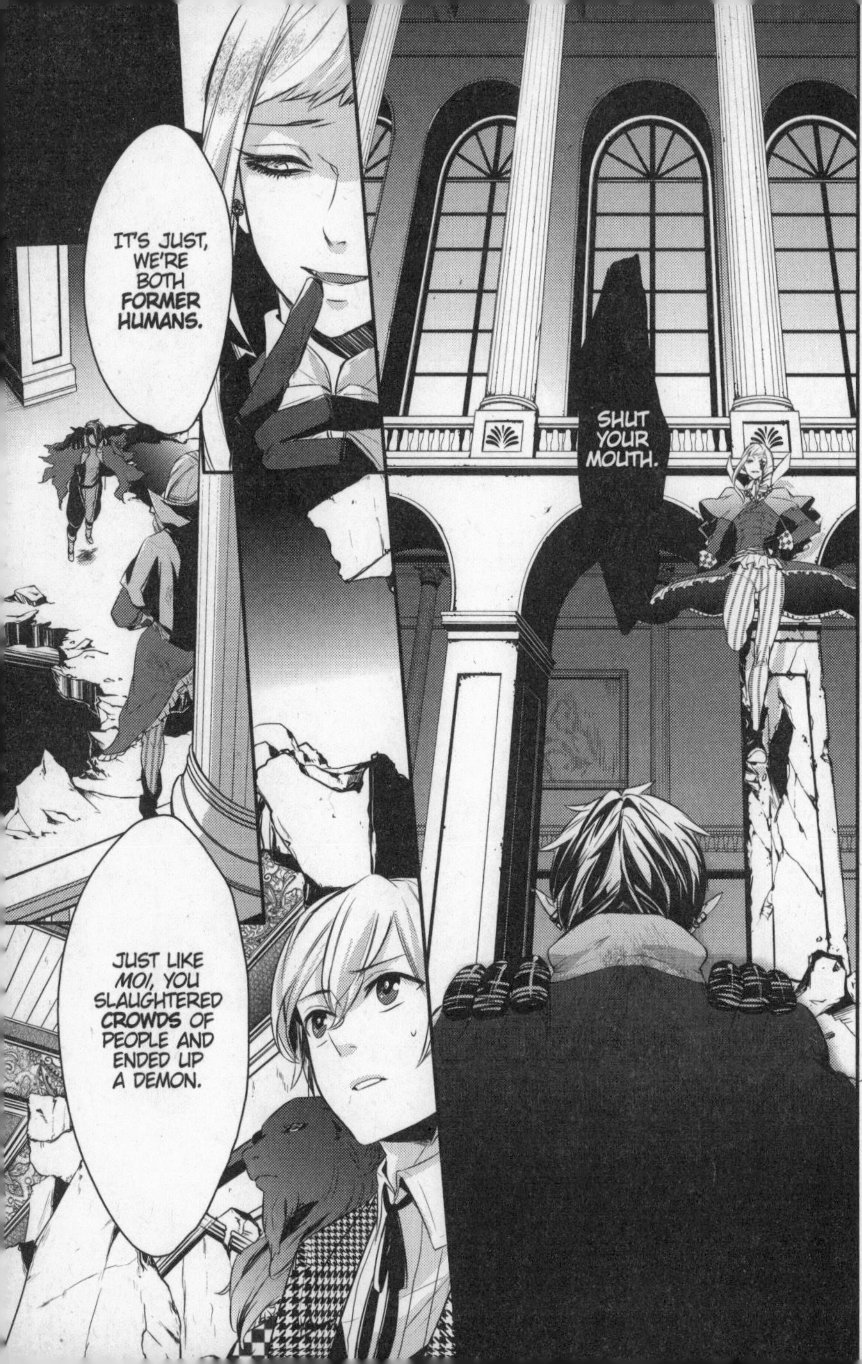
SHUT YOUR MOUTH.
IT'S JUST, WE'RE BOTH FORMER HUMANS.
JUST LIKE *MOI*, YOU SLAUGHTERED **CROWDS** OF PEOPLE AND ENDED UP A DEMON.

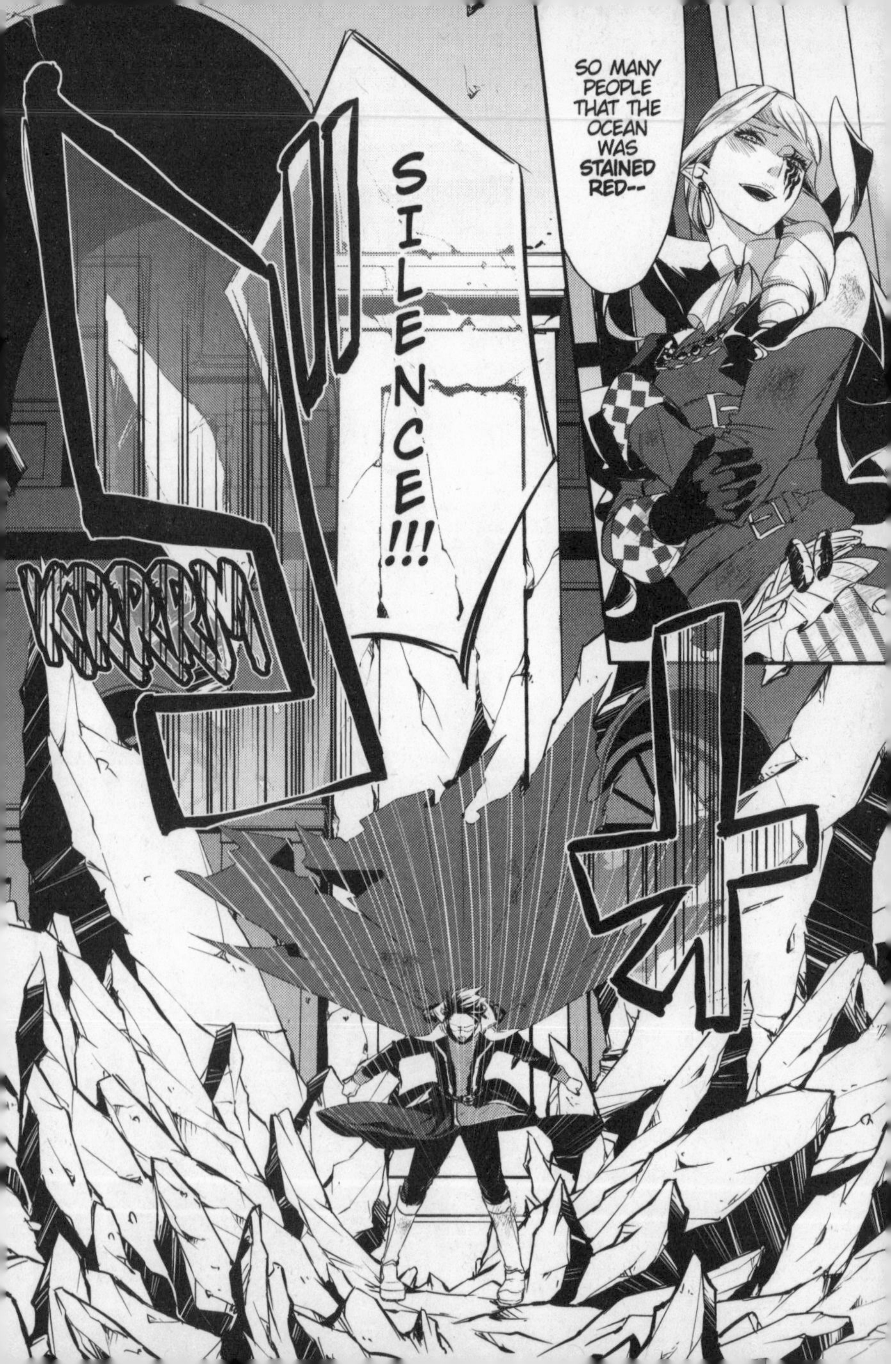
SO MANY PEOPLE THAT THE OCEAN WAS STAINED RED--
SILENCE!!!

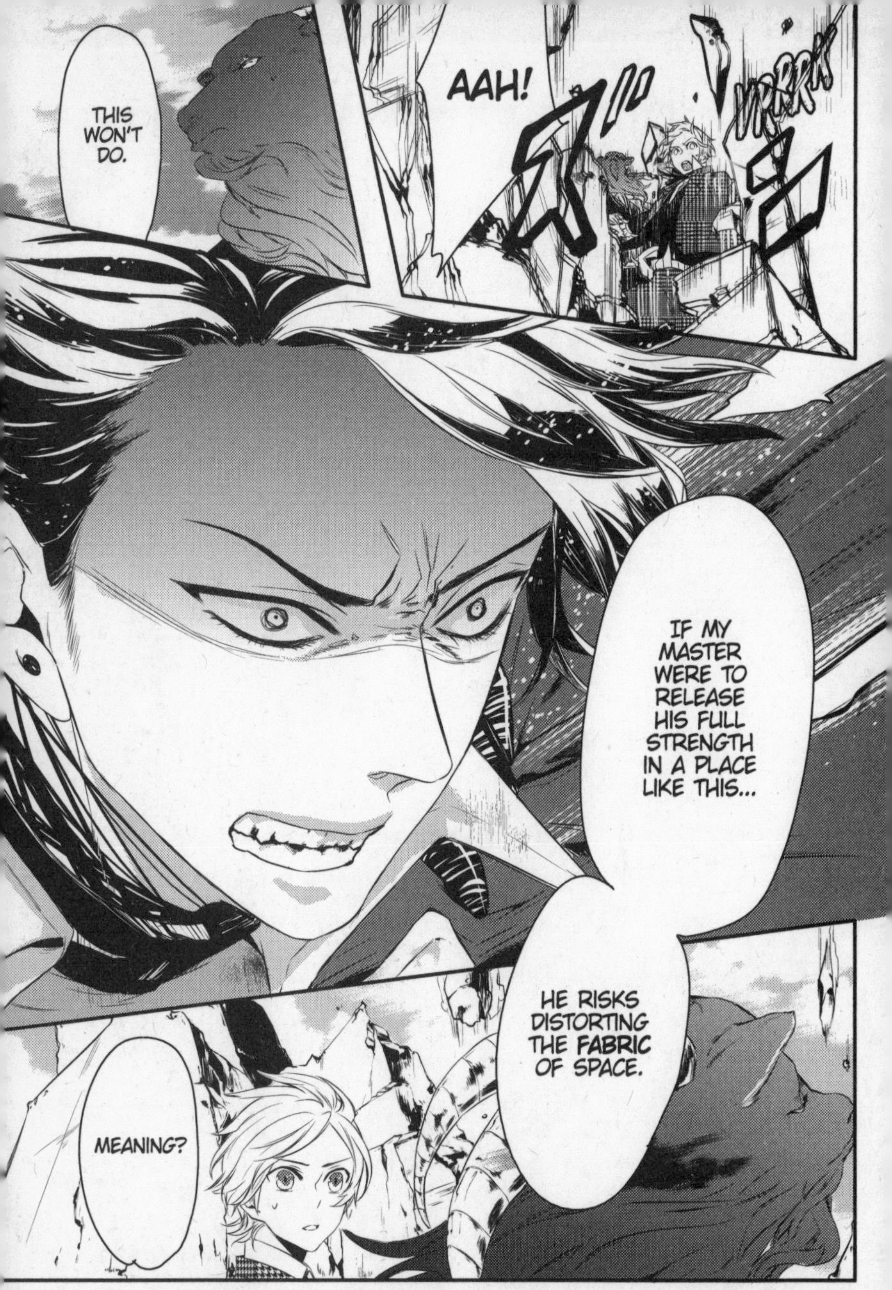
VRRRK
AAH!
THIS WON'T DO.
IF MY MASTER WERE TO RELEASE HIS FULL STRENGTH IN A PLACE LIKE THIS...
HE RISKS DISTORTING THE FABRIC OF SPACE.
MEANING?

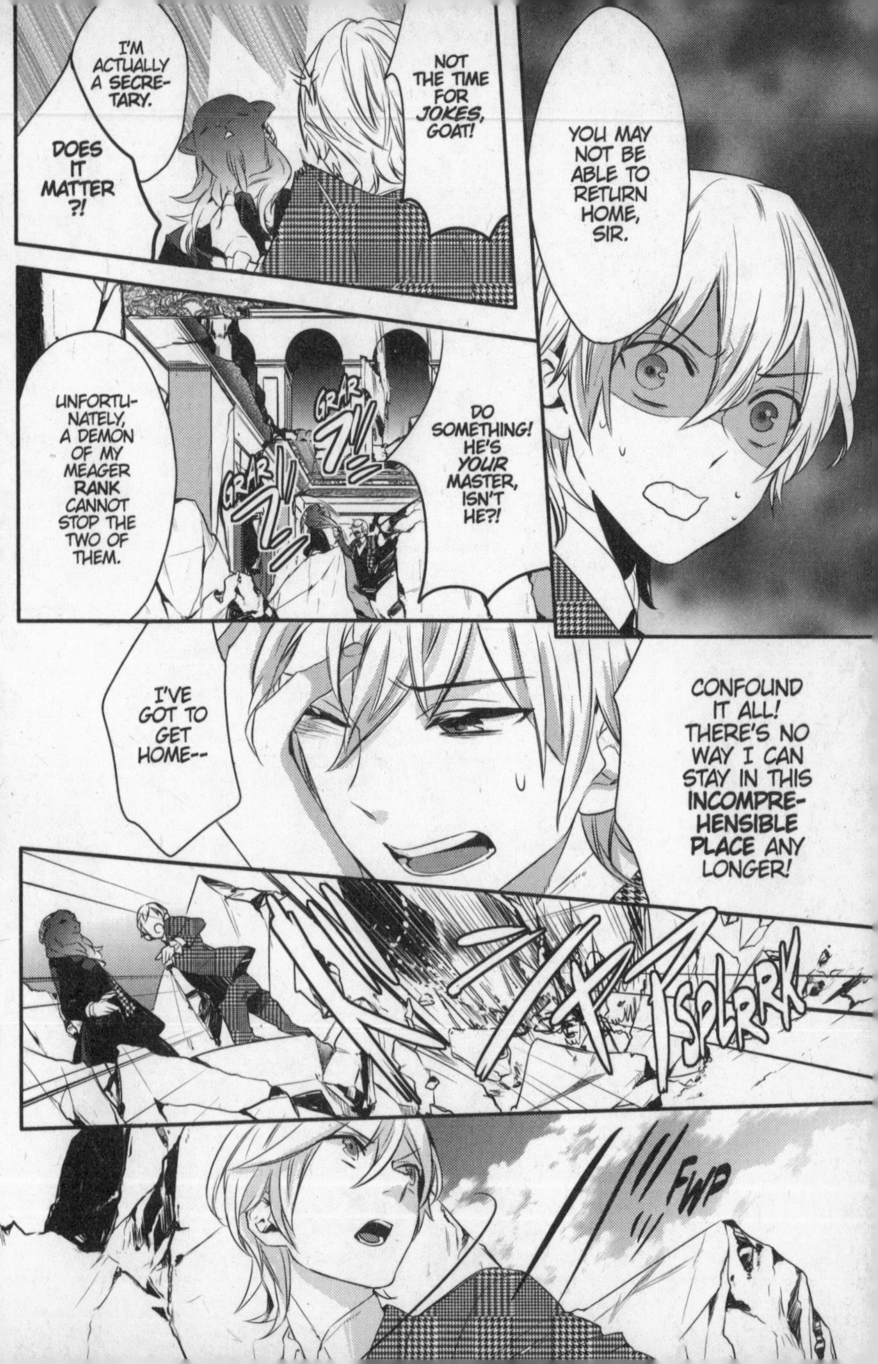
YOU MAY NOT BE ABLE TO RETURN HOME, SIR.
NOT THE TIME FOR JOKES, GOAT!
I'M ACTUALLY A SECRETARY.
DOES IT MATTER?!
DO SOMETHING! HE'S YOUR MASTER, ISN'T HE?!
GRAR
GRAR
UNFORTUNATELY, A DEMON OF MY MEAGER RANK CANNOT STOP THE TWO OF THEM.
CONFOUND IT ALL! THERE'S NO WAY I CAN STAY IN THIS INCOMPREHENSIBLE PLACE ANY LONGER!
I'VE GOT TO GET HOME--
SPLRRK
FWP

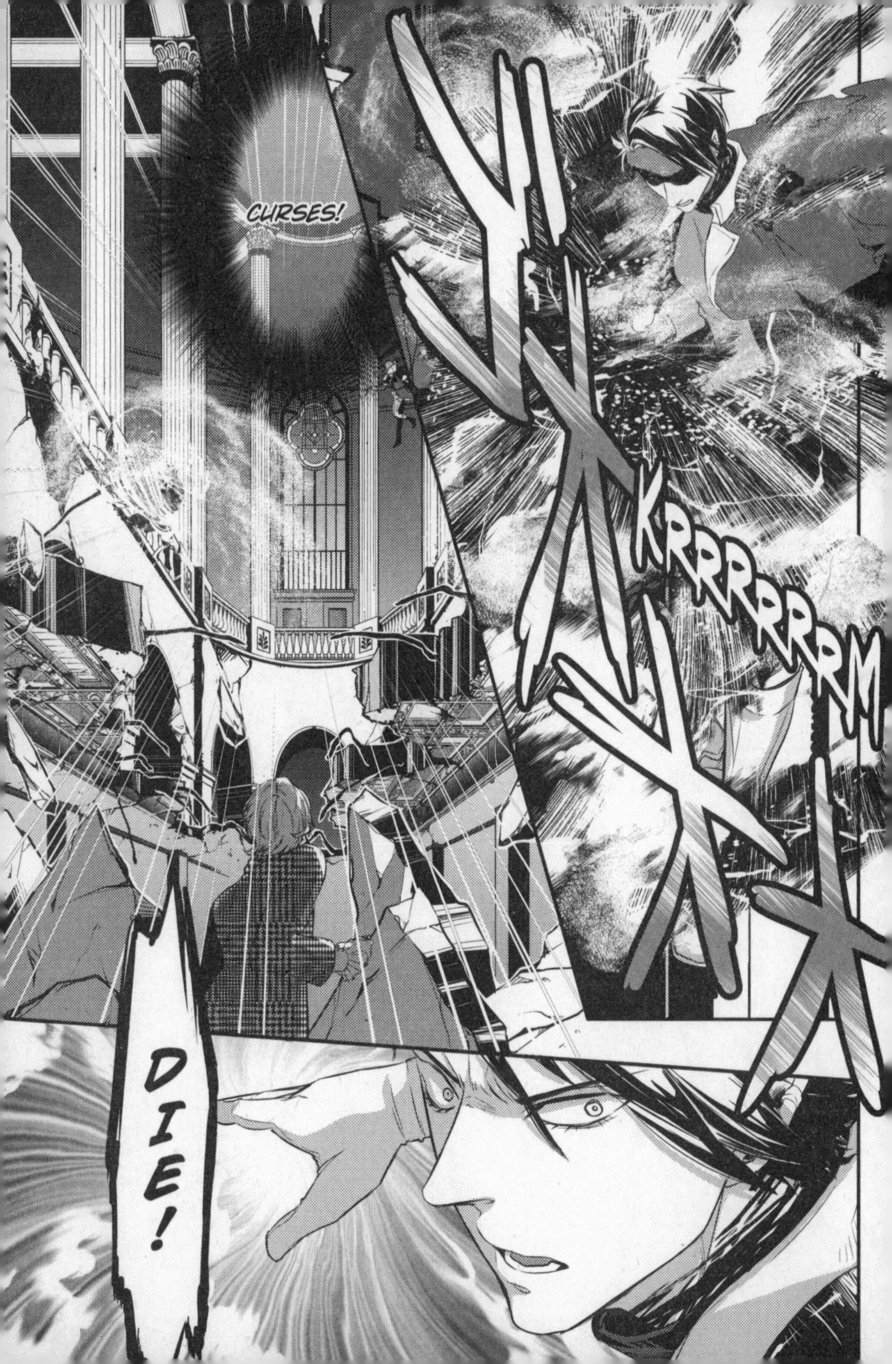
KRRRRRRRM
CURSES!
DIE!

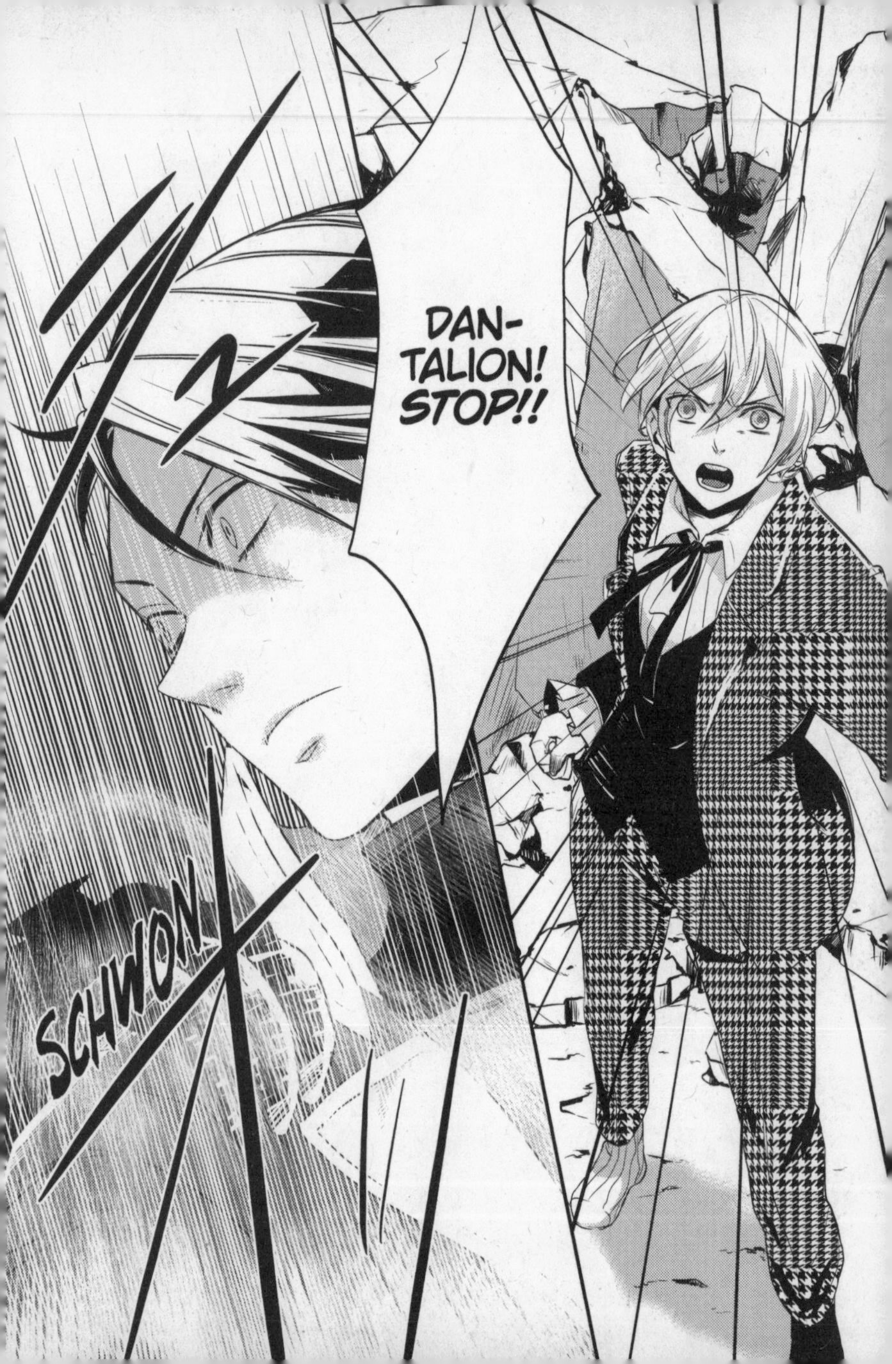
DAN-TALION! STOP!!
SCHWON

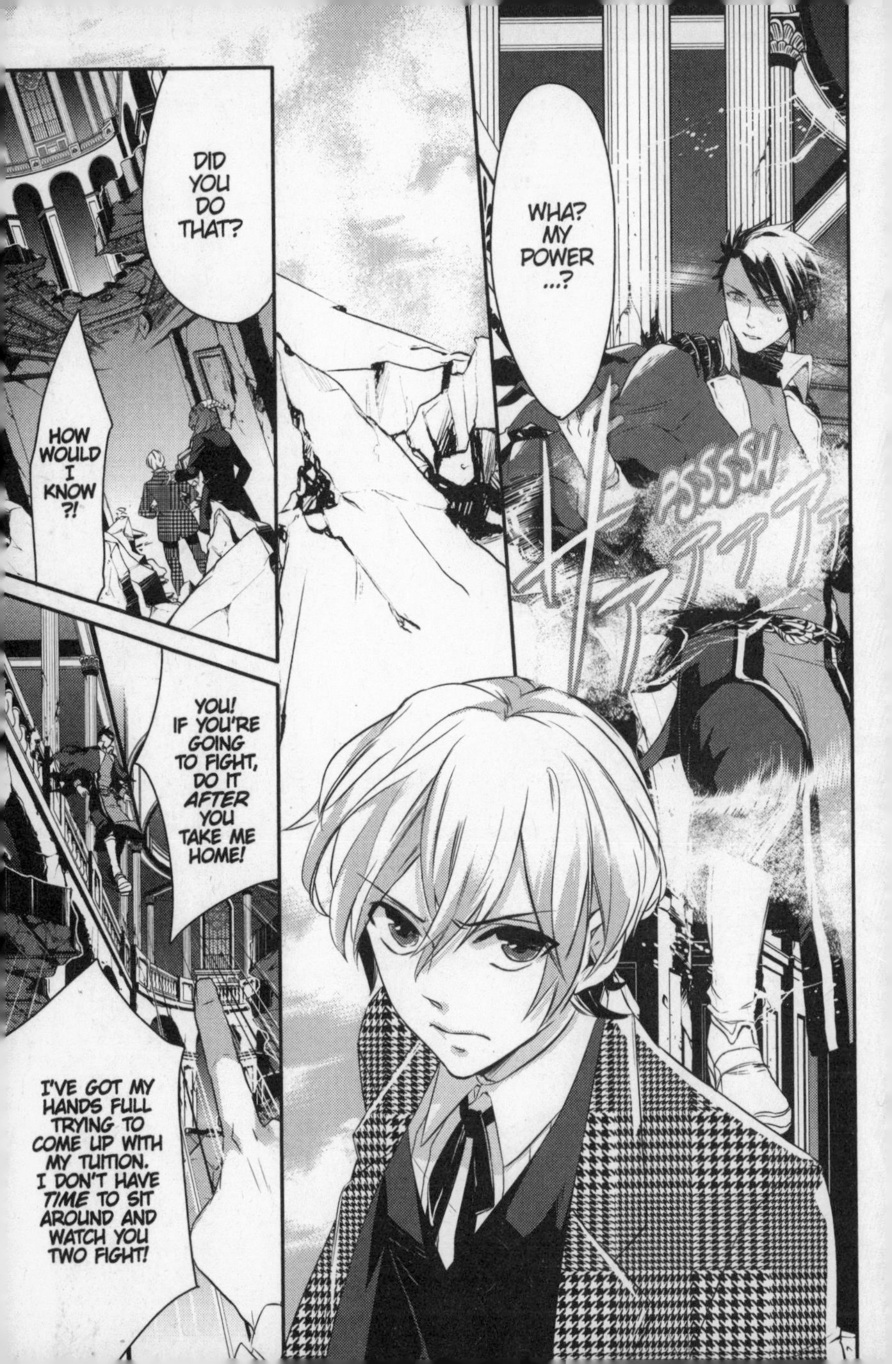
WHA? MY POWER ...?
PSSSSH
DID YOU DO THAT?
HOW WOULD I KNOW ?!
YOU! IF YOU'RE GOING TO FIGHT, DO IT *AFTER* YOU TAKE ME HOME!
I'VE GOT MY HANDS FULL TRYING TO COME UP WITH MY TUITION. I DON'T HAVE *TIME* TO SIT AROUND AND WATCH YOU TWO FIGHT!

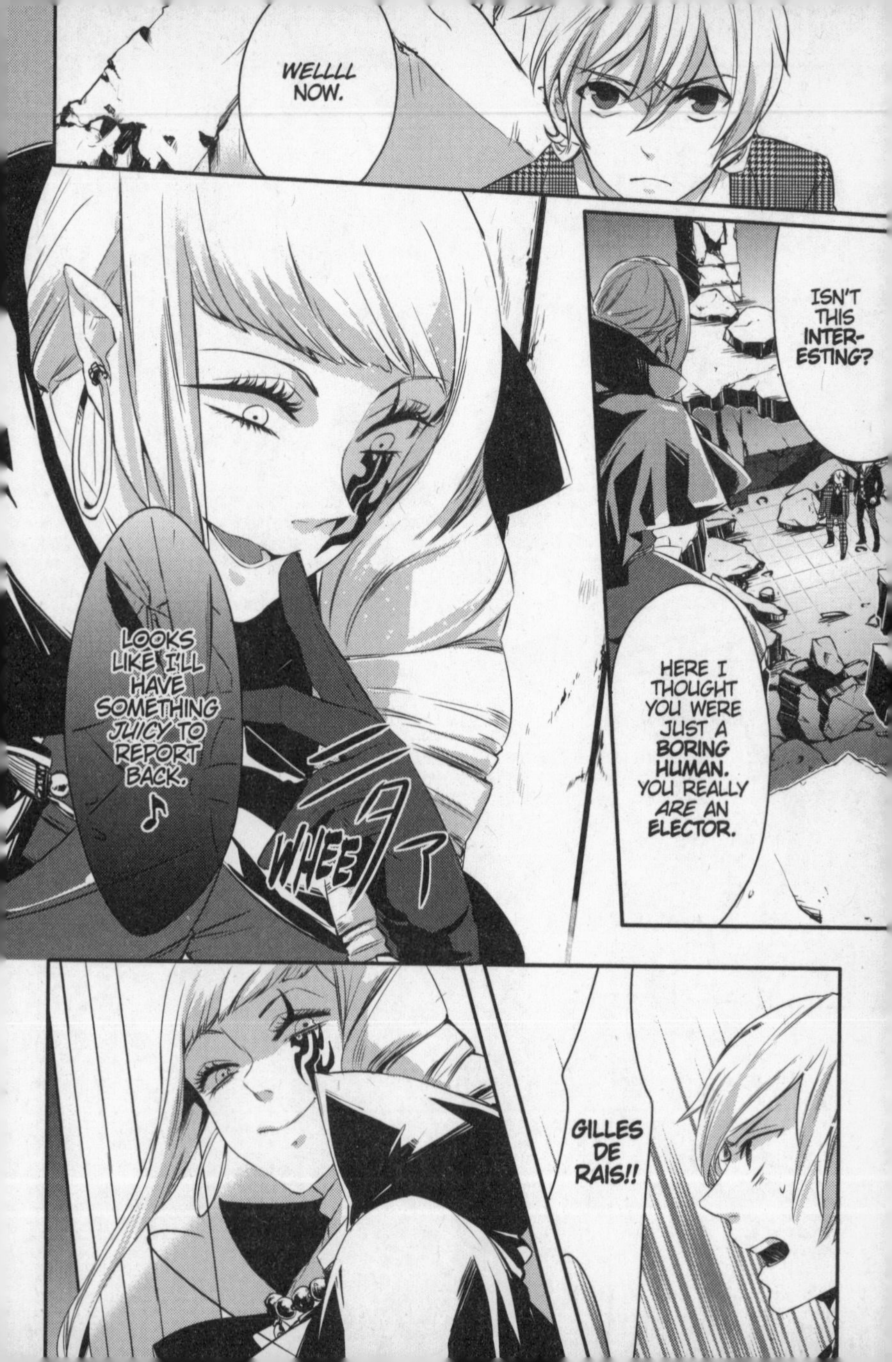
WELLLL NOW.
ISN'T THIS INTERESTING?
HERE I THOUGHT YOU WERE JUST A BORING HUMAN. YOU REALLY *ARE* AN ELECTOR.
LOOKS LIKE I'LL HAVE SOMETHING JUICY TO REPORT BACK. ♪
WHEE
GILLES DE RAIS!!

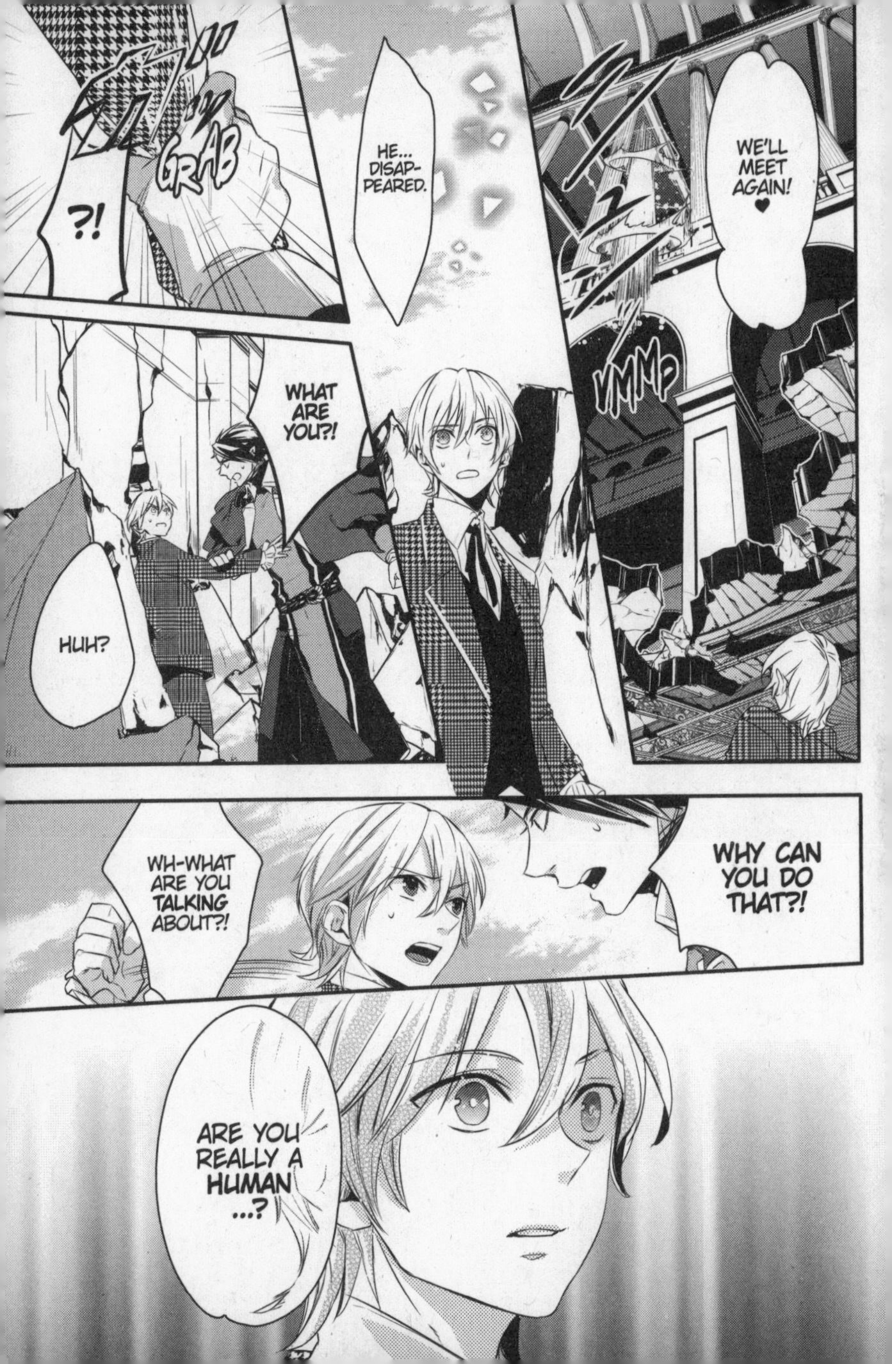

WE'LL MEET AGAIN! ♥
VMMP
HE... DISAP-PEARED.
GRAB
?!
WHAT ARE YOU?!
HUH?
WHY CAN YOU DO THAT?!
WH-WHAT ARE YOU TALKING ABOUT?!
ARE YOU REALLY A HUMAN ...?

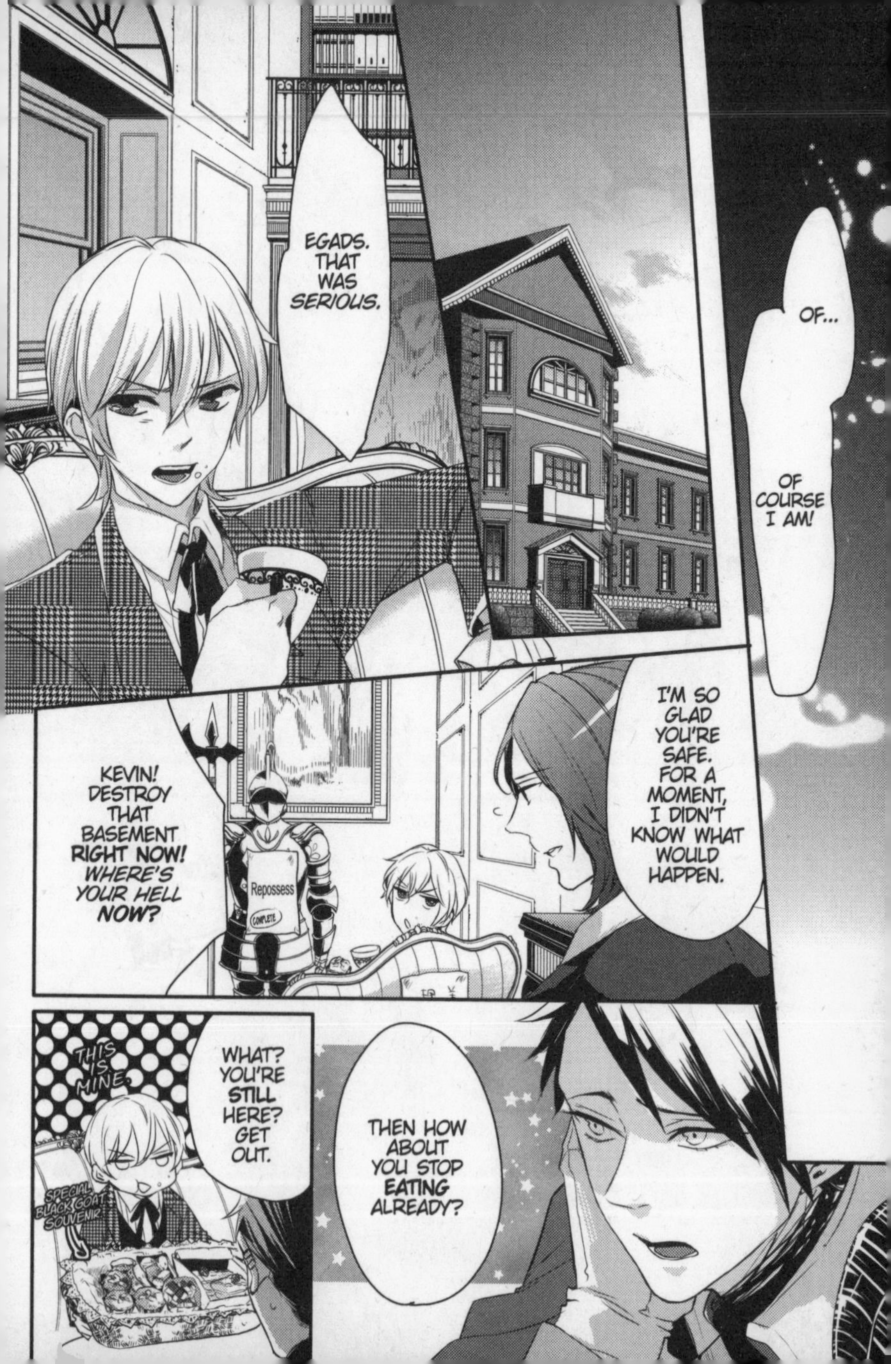
OF...
OF COURSE I AM!
EGADS. THAT WAS SERIOUS.
I'M SO GLAD YOU'RE SAFE. FOR A MOMENT, I DIDN'T KNOW WHAT WOULD HAPPEN.
KEVIN! DESTROY THAT BASEMENT RIGHT NOW! WHERE'S YOUR HELL NOW?
Repossess
COMPLETE
THEN HOW ABOUT YOU STOP EATING ALREADY?
WHAT? YOU'RE STILL HERE? GET OUT.
THIS IS MINE.
SPECIAL BLACK GOAT SOUVENIR

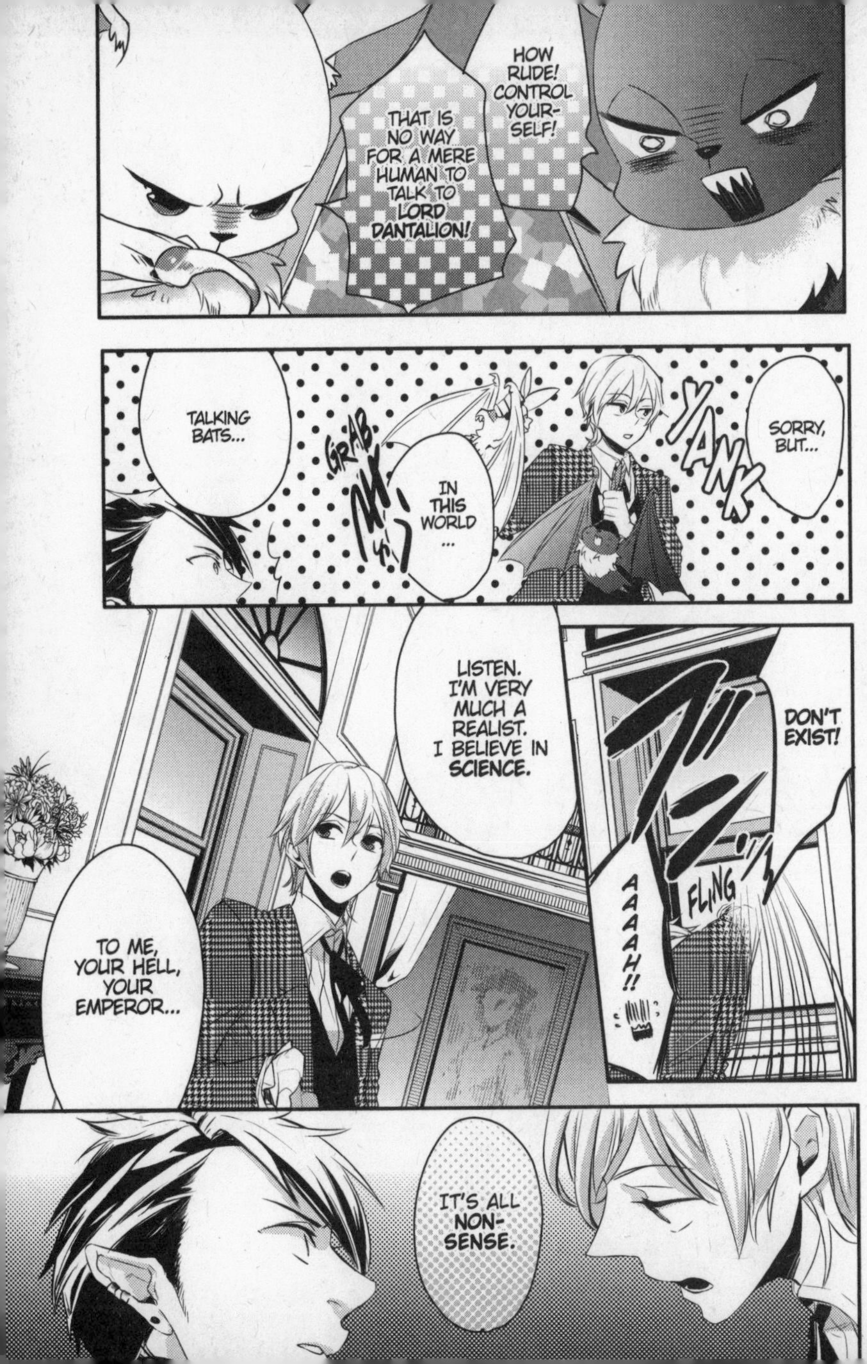
HOW RUDE! CONTROL YOURSELF!
THAT IS NO WAY FOR A MERE HUMAN TO TALK TO LORD DANTALION!
YANK
SORRY, BUT...
IN THIS WORLD...
GRAB
TALKING BATS...
DON'T EXIST!
FLING
AAAAAH!!
LISTEN. I'M VERY MUCH A REALIST. I BELIEVE IN SCIENCE.
TO ME, YOUR HELL, YOUR EMPEROR...
IT'S ALL NONSENSE.

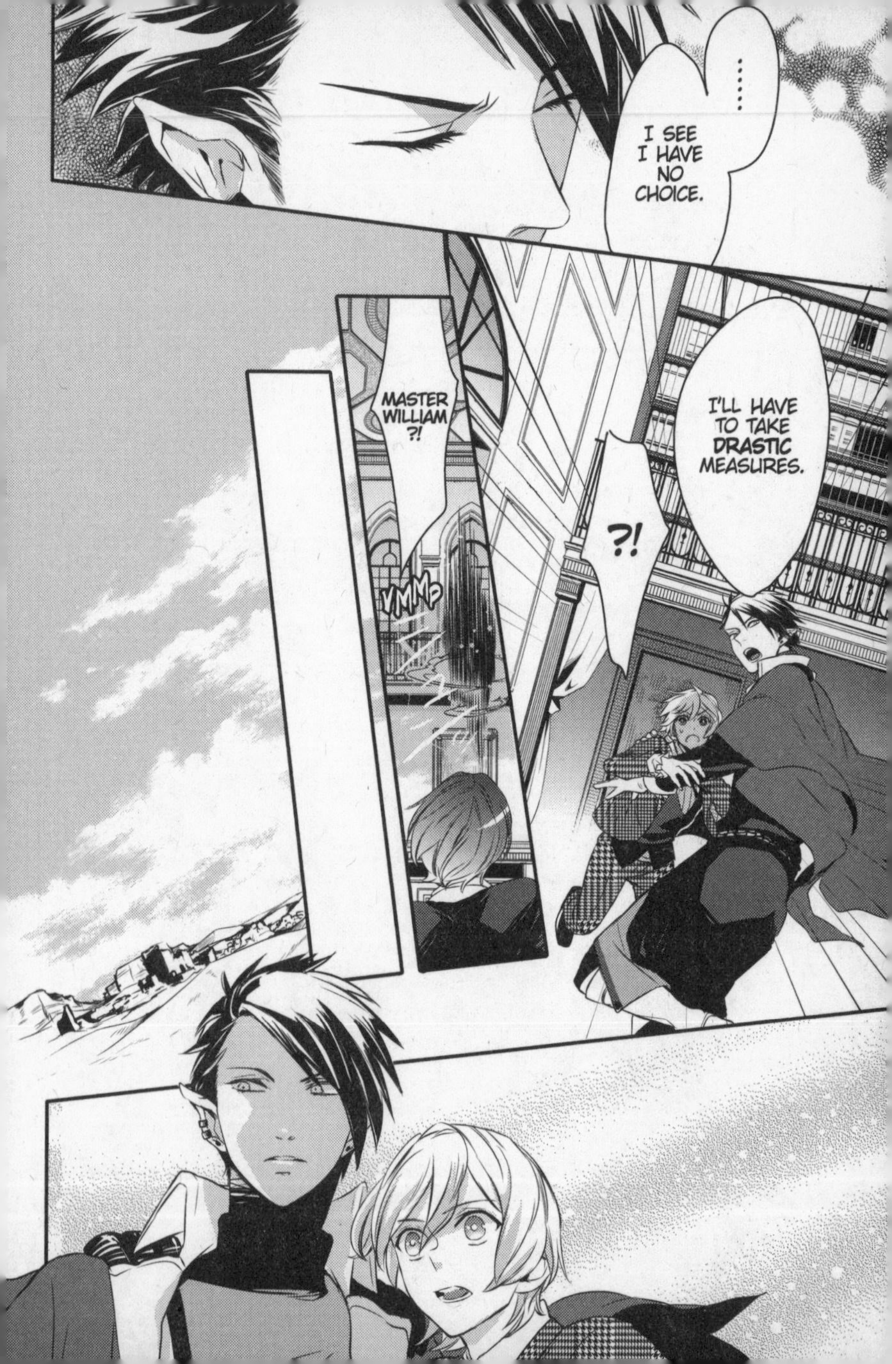
......
I SEE I HAVE NO CHOICE.
I'LL HAVE TO TAKE DRASTIC MEASURES.
?!
MASTER WILLIAM ?!
VMMP

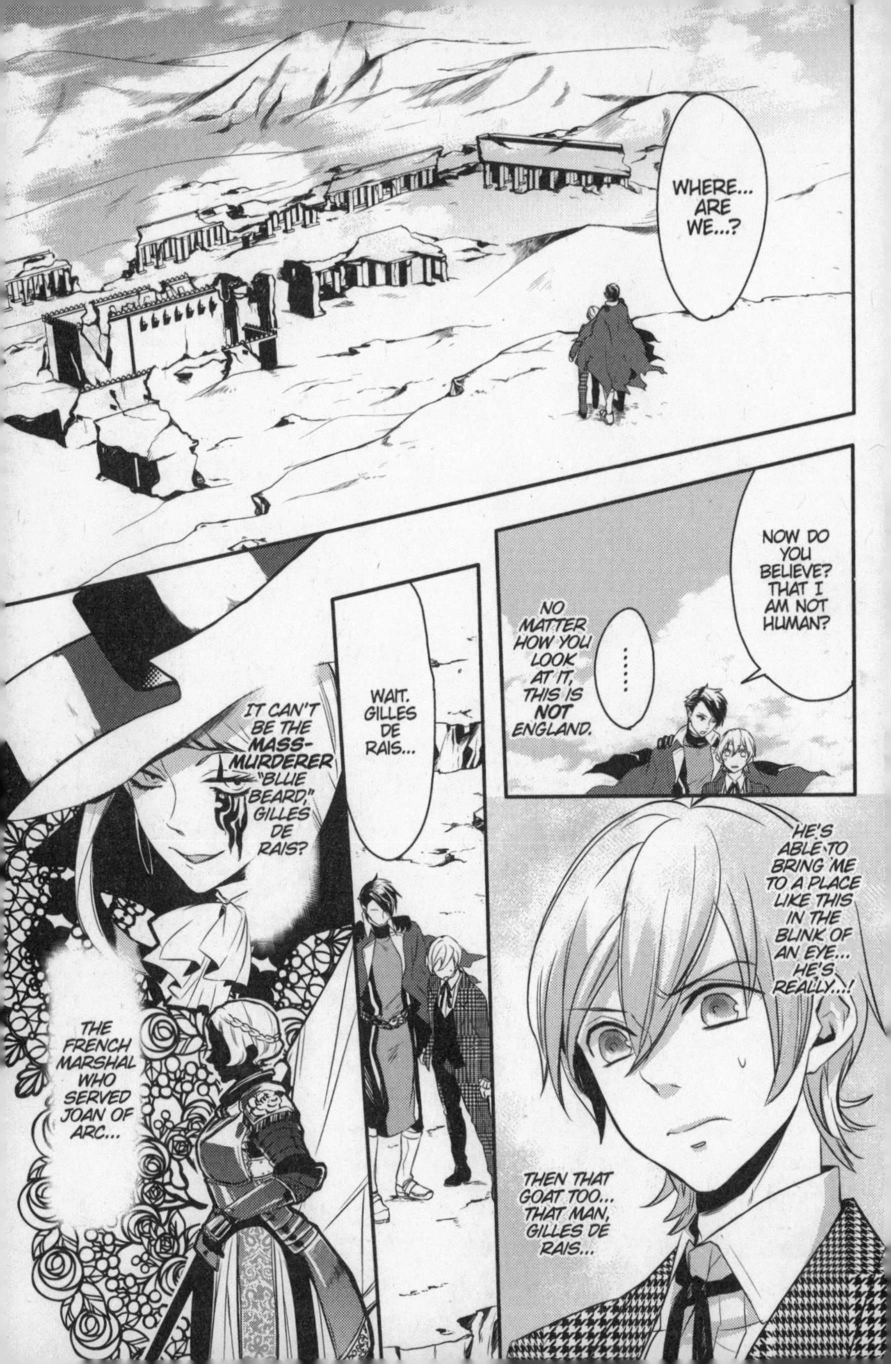

WHERE... ARE WE...?
NOW DO YOU BELIEVE? THAT I AM NOT HUMAN?
......
NO MATTER HOW YOU LOOK AT IT, THIS IS **NOT** ENGLAND.
HE'S ABLE TO BRING ME TO A PLACE LIKE THIS IN THE BLINK OF AN EYE... HE'S REALLY...!
THEN THAT GOAT TOO... THAT MAN, GILLES DE RAIS...
WAIT. GILLES DE RAIS...
IT CAN'T BE THE **MASS-MURDERER** "BLUE BEARD," GILLES DE RAIS?
THE FRENCH MARSHAL WHO SERVED JOAN OF ARC...

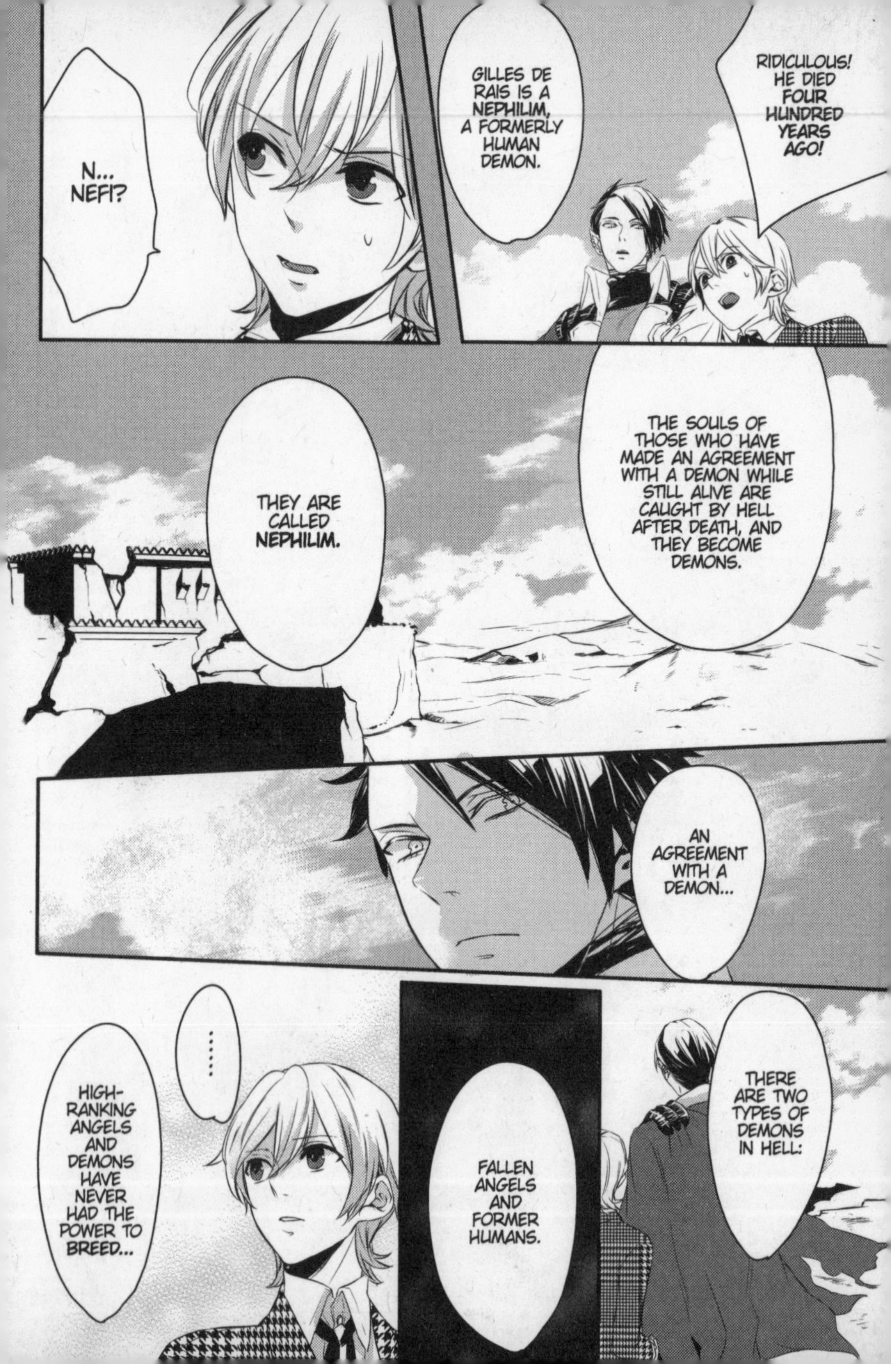
RIDICULOUS! HE DIED FOUR HUNDRED YEARS AGO!
GILLES DE RAIS IS A NEPHILIM, A FORMERLY HUMAN DEMON.
N... NEFI?
THE SOULS OF THOSE WHO HAVE MADE AN AGREEMENT WITH A DEMON WHILE STILL ALIVE ARE CAUGHT BY HELL AFTER DEATH, AND THEY BECOME DEMONS.
THEY ARE CALLED NEPHILIM.
AN AGREEMENT WITH A DEMON...
THERE ARE TWO TYPES OF DEMONS IN HELL:
FALLEN ANGELS AND FORMER HUMANS.
......
HIGH-RANKING ANGELS AND DEMONS HAVE NEVER HAD THE POWER TO BREED...

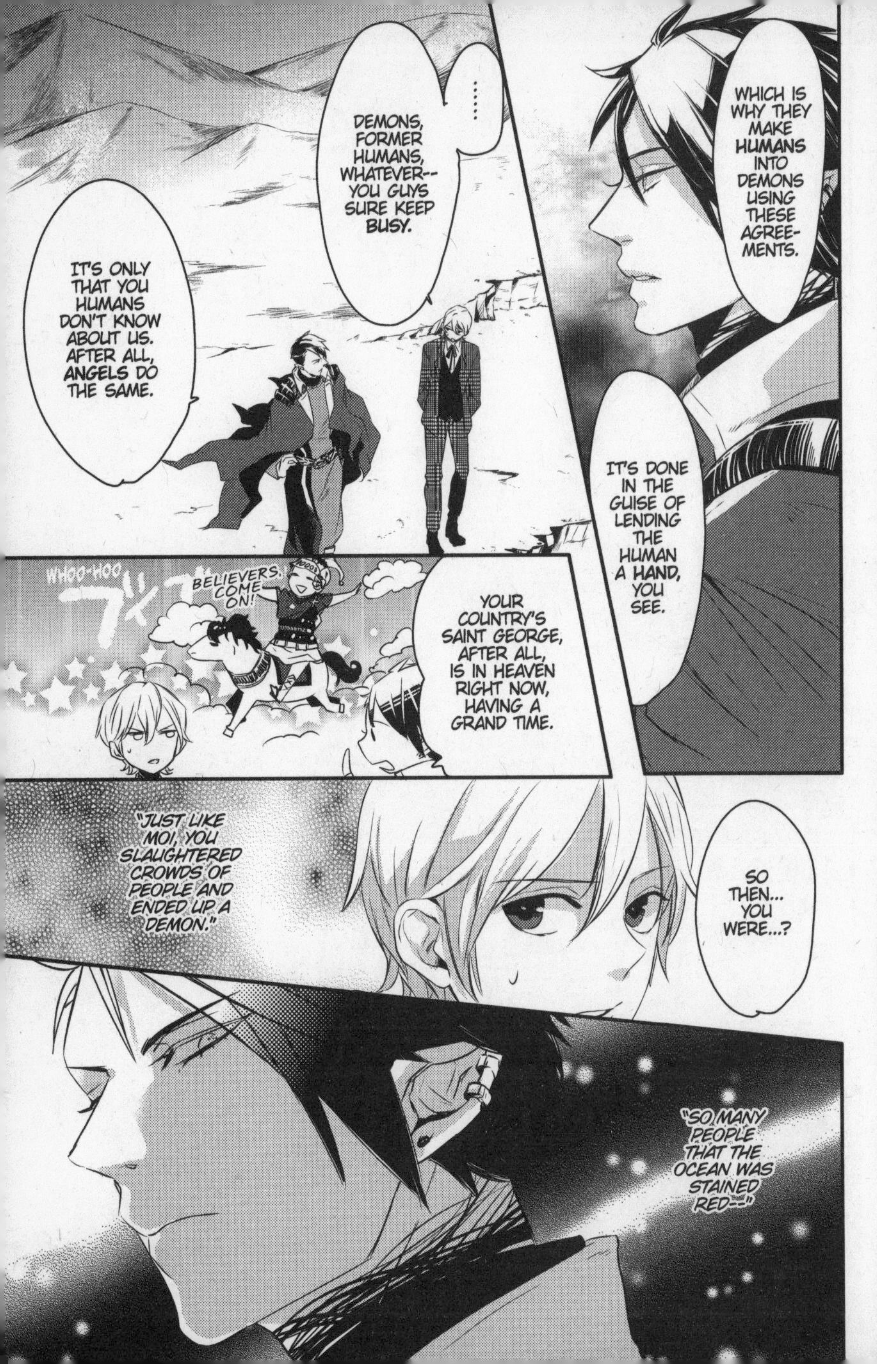
WHICH IS WHY THEY MAKE HUMANS INTO DEMONS USING THESE AGREEMENTS.
IT'S DONE IN THE GUISE OF LENDING THE HUMAN A HAND, YOU SEE.
......
DEMONS, FORMER HUMANS, WHATEVER-- YOU GUYS SURE KEEP BUSY.
IT'S ONLY THAT YOU HUMANS DON'T KNOW ABOUT US. AFTER ALL, ANGELS DO THE SAME.
YOUR COUNTRY'S SAINT GEORGE, AFTER ALL, IS IN HEAVEN RIGHT NOW, HAVING A GRAND TIME.
BELIEVERS, COME ON!
WHOO-HOO
SO THEN... YOU WERE...?
"JUST LIKE MOI, YOU SLAUGHTERED CROWDS OF PEOPLE AND ENDED UP A DEMON."
"SO MANY PEOPLE THAT THE OCEAN WAS STAINED RED--"

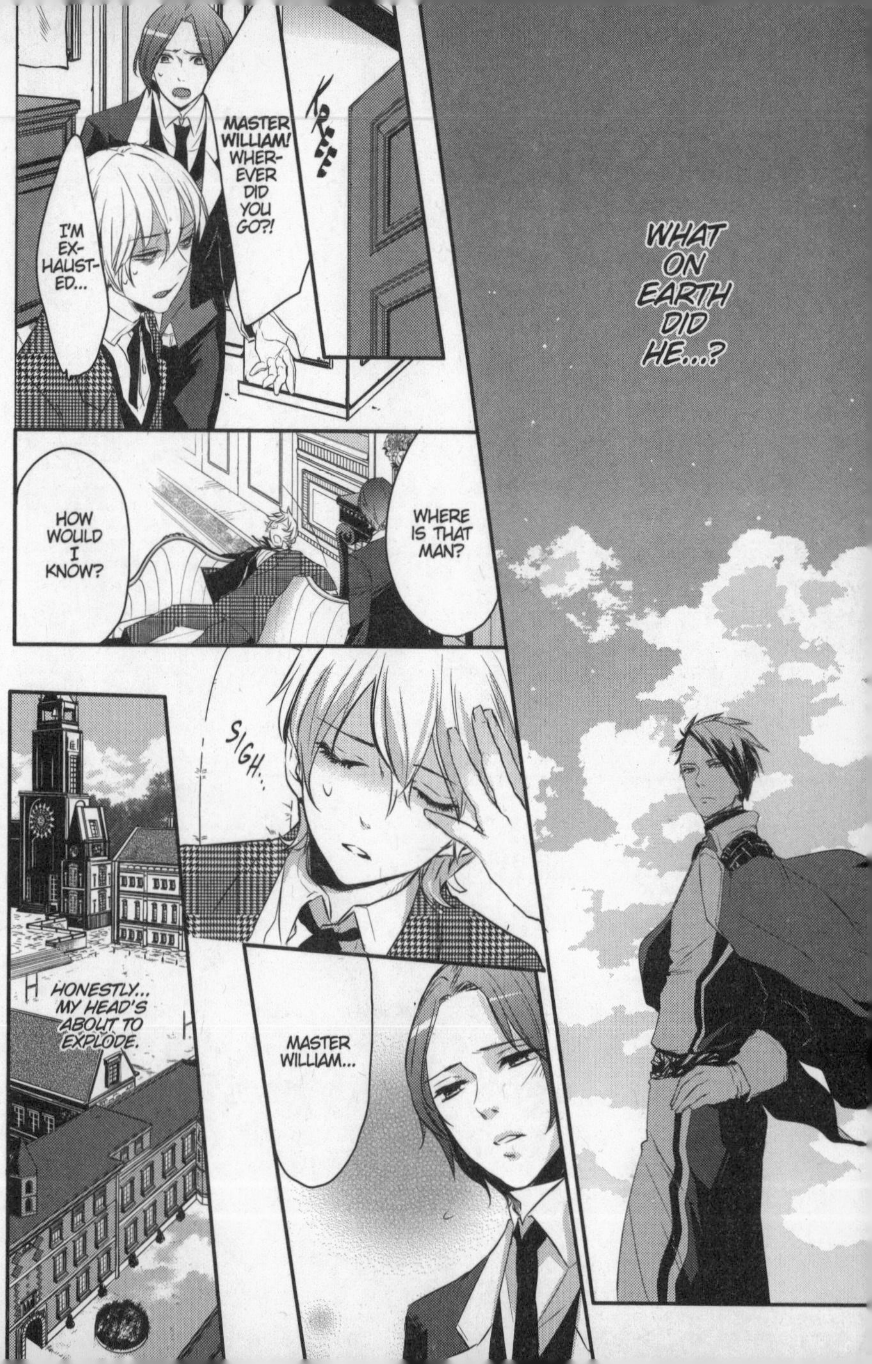
WHAT ON EARTH DID HE...?
MASTER WILLIAM! WHER-EVER DID YOU GO?!
KREE
I'M EX-HAUST-ED...
WHERE IS THAT MAN?
HOW WOULD I KNOW?
SIGH...
MASTER WILLIAM...
HONESTLY... MY HEAD'S ABOUT TO EXPLODE.

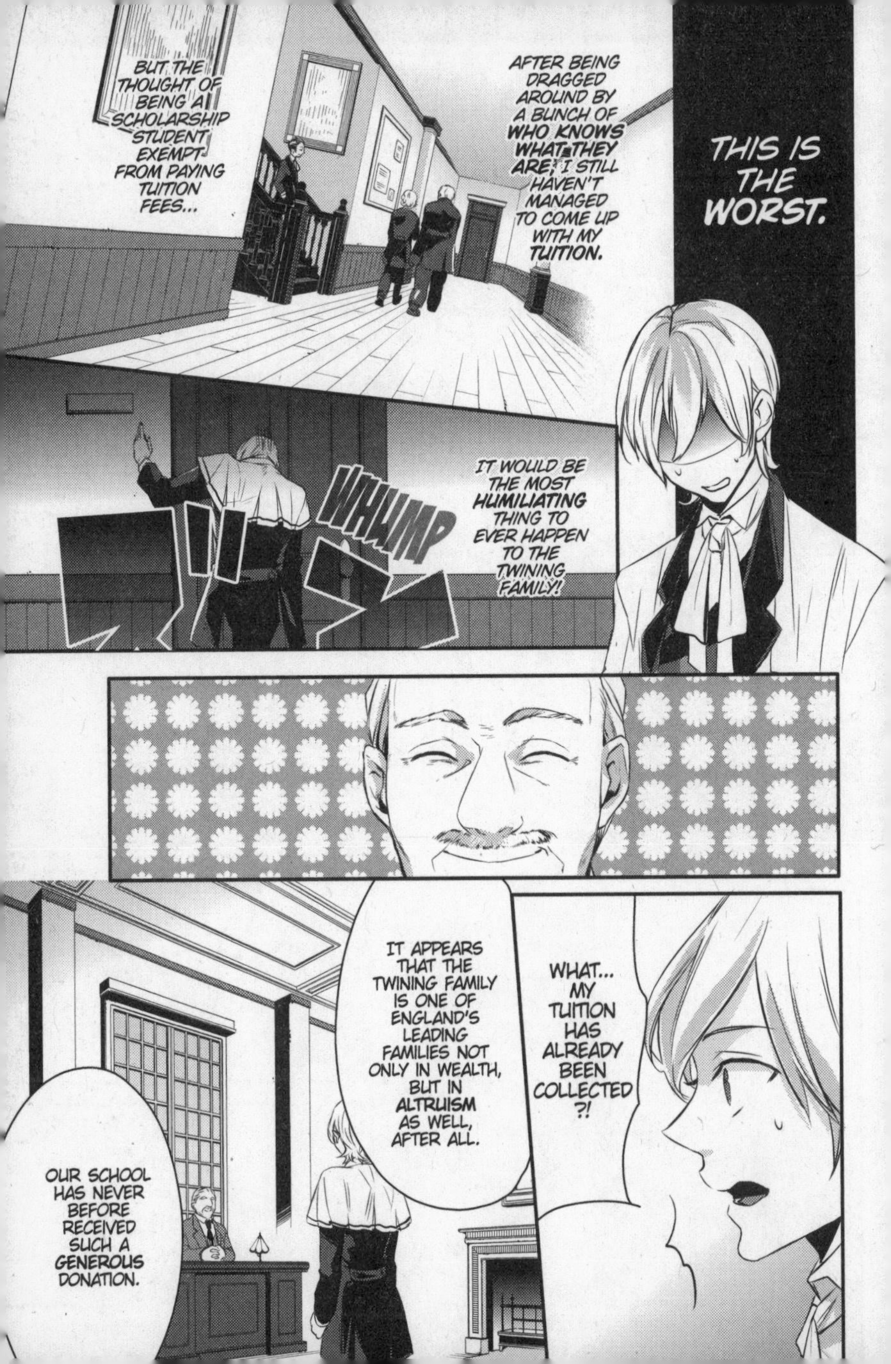

THIS IS THE WORST.
AFTER BEING DRAGGED AROUND BY A BUNCH OF WHO KNOWS WHAT THEY ARE, I STILL HAVEN'T MANAGED TO COME UP WITH MY TUITION.
BUT THE THOUGHT OF BEING A SCHOLARSHIP STUDENT EXEMPT FROM PAYING TUITION FEES...
IT WOULD BE THE MOST HUMILIATING THING TO EVER HAPPEN TO THE TWINING FAMILY!
WHUMP
WHAT... MY TUITION HAS ALREADY BEEN COLLECTED ?!
IT APPEARS THAT THE TWINING FAMILY IS ONE OF ENGLAND'S LEADING FAMILIES NOT ONLY IN WEALTH, BUT IN ALTRUISM AS WELL, AFTER ALL.
OUR SCHOOL HAS NEVER BEFORE RECEIVED SUCH A GENEROUS DONATION.

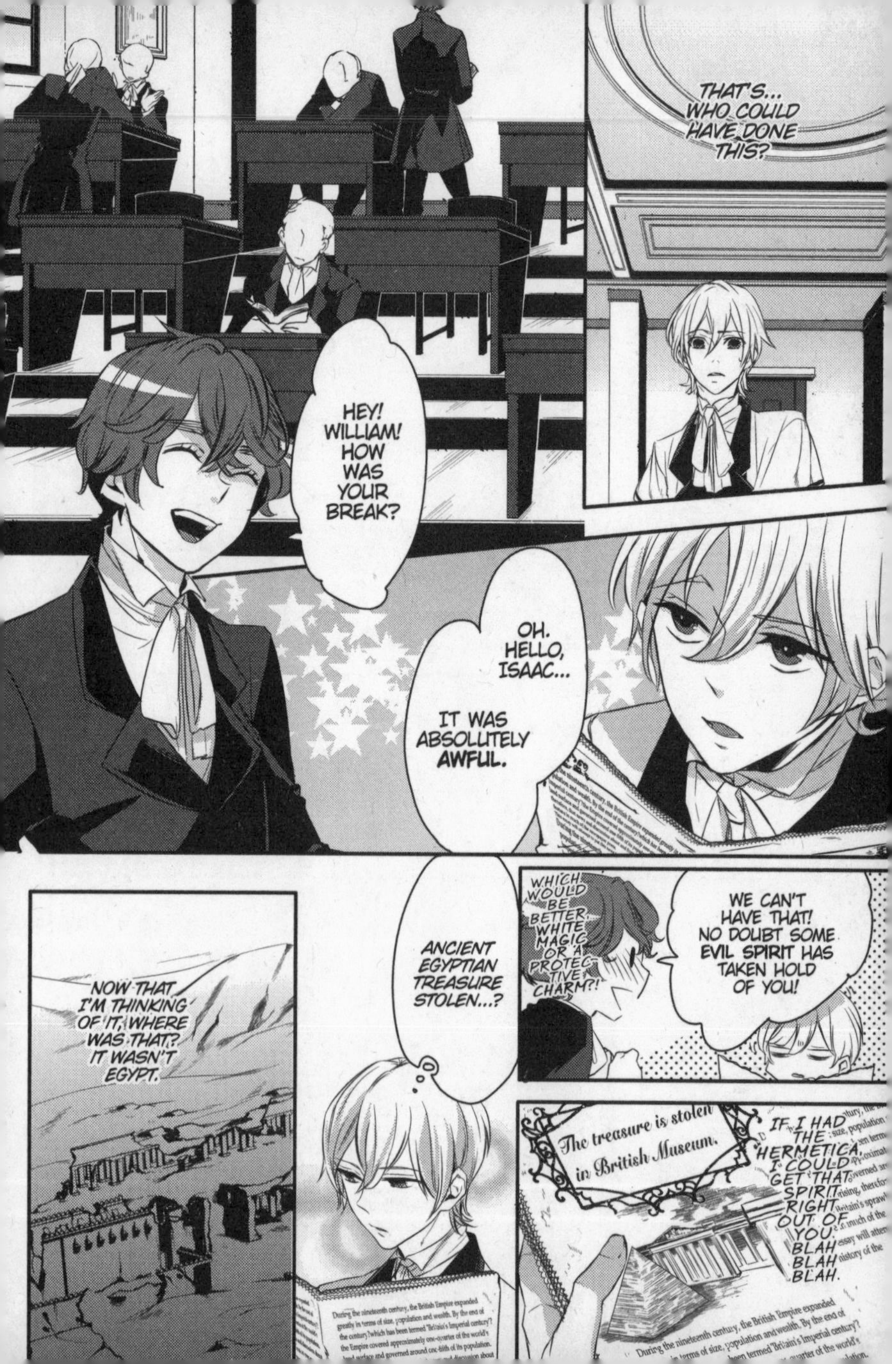
THAT'S... WHO COULD HAVE DONE THIS?
HEY! WILLIAM! HOW WAS YOUR BREAK?
OH. HELLO, ISAAC...
IT WAS ABSOLUTELY AWFUL.
WE CAN'T HAVE THAT! NO DOUBT SOME EVIL SPIRIT HAS TAKEN HOLD OF YOU!
WHICH WOULD BE BETTER, WHITE MAGIC OR A PROTECTIVE CHARM?!
The treasure is stolen in British Museum.
IF I HAD THE HERMETICA, I COULD GET THAT SPIRIT RIGHT OUT OF YOU. BLAH BLAH BLAH.
ANCIENT EGYPTIAN TREASURE STOLEN...?
NOW THAT I'M THINKING OF IT, WHERE WAS THAT? IT WASN'T EGYPT.

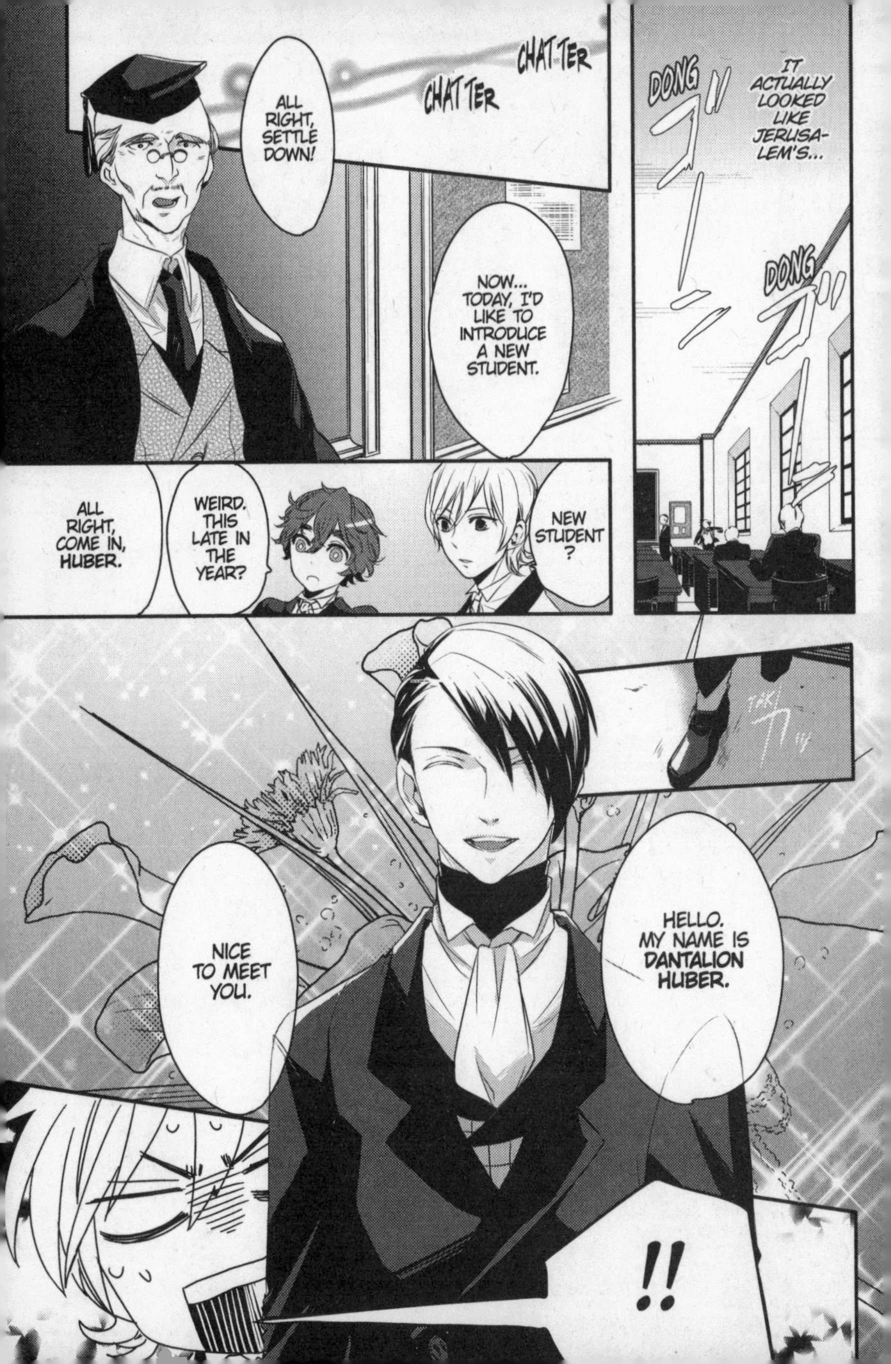
IT ACTUALLY LOOKED LIKE JERUSALEM'S...
DONG
DONG
CHATTER
CHATTER
ALL RIGHT, SETTLE DOWN!
NOW... TODAY, I'D LIKE TO INTRODUCE A NEW STUDENT.
NEW STUDENT?
WEIRD. THIS LATE IN THE YEAR?
ALL RIGHT, COME IN, HUBER.
TAK
HELLO. MY NAME IS DANTALION HUBER.
NICE TO MEET YOU.
!!

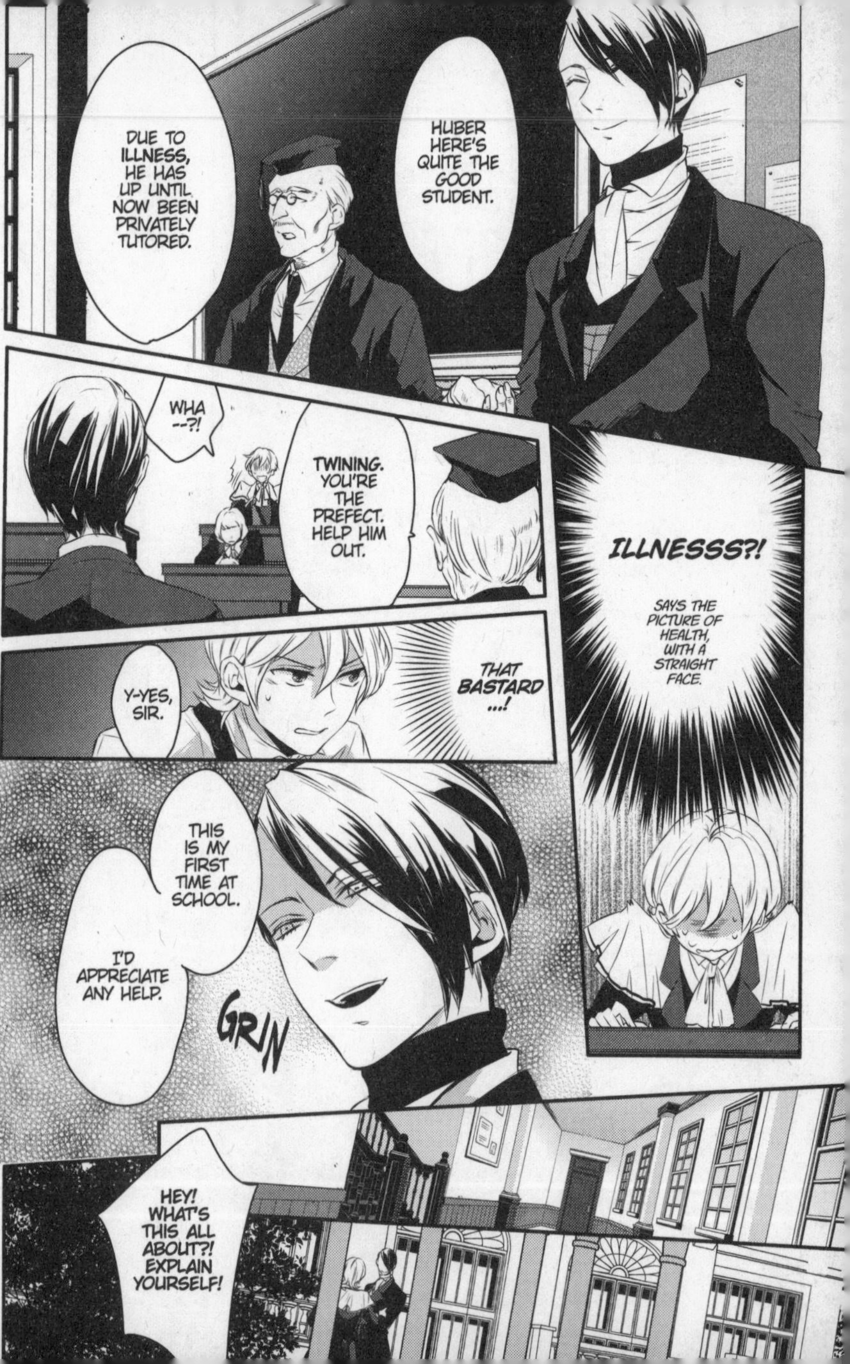
HUBER HERE'S QUITE THE GOOD STUDENT.
DUE TO ILLNESS, HE HAS UP UNTIL NOW BEEN PRIVATELY TUTORED.
ILLNESSS?!
SAYS THE PICTURE OF HEALTH, WITH A STRAIGHT FACE.
TWINING. YOU'RE THE PREFECT. HELP HIM OUT.
WHA--?!
THAT BASTARD...!
Y-YES, SIR.
THIS IS MY FIRST TIME AT SCHOOL.
I'D APPRECIATE ANY HELP.
GRIN
HEY! WHAT'S THIS ALL ABOUT?! EXPLAIN YOURSELF!

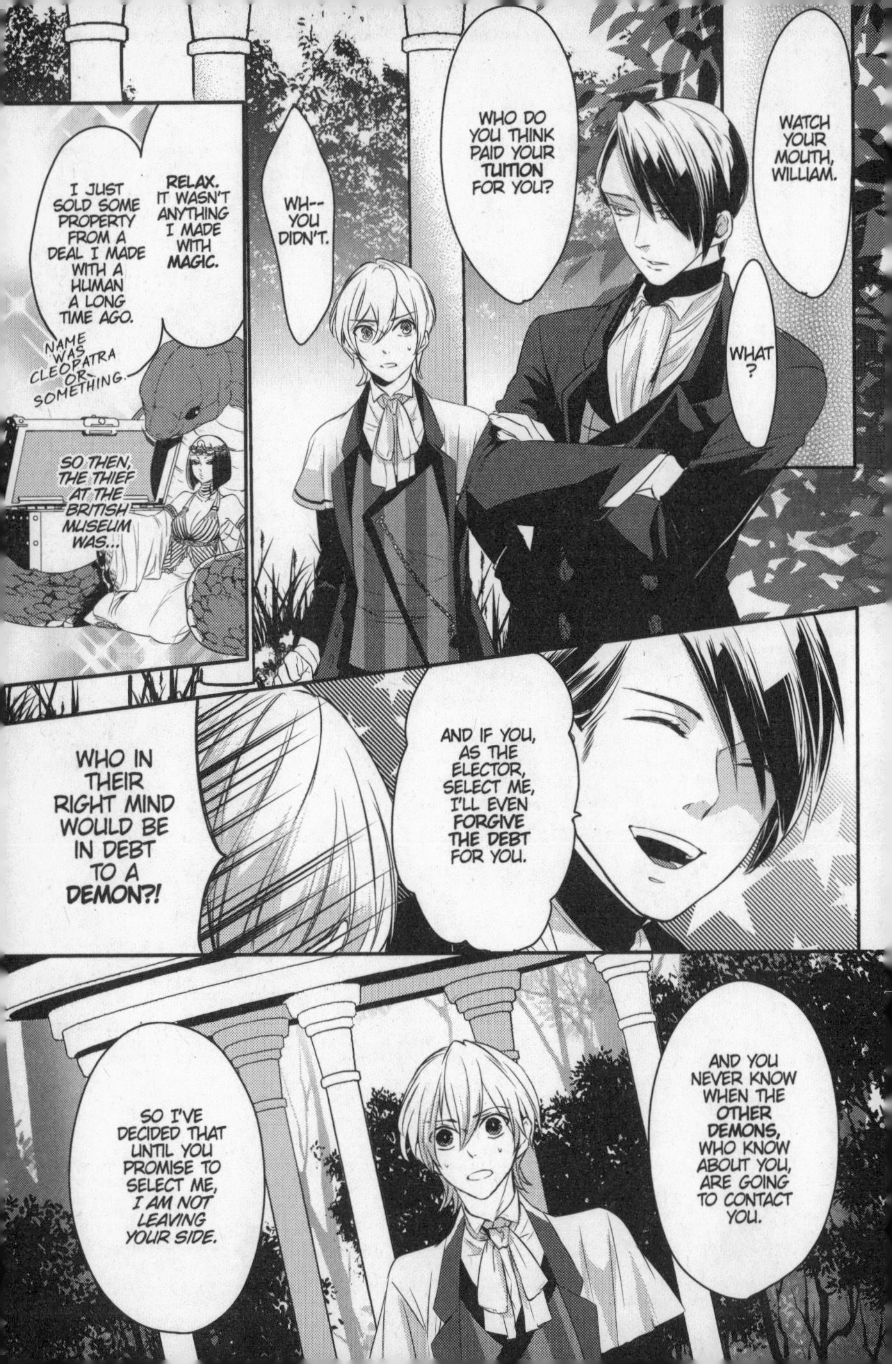
WATCH YOUR MOUTH, WILLIAM.
WHAT?
WHO DO YOU THINK PAID YOUR TUITION FOR YOU?
WH-- YOU DIDN'T.
RELAX. IT WASN'T ANYTHING I MADE WITH MAGIC.
I JUST SOLD SOME PROPERTY FROM A DEAL I MADE WITH A HUMAN A LONG TIME AGO.
NAME WAS CLEOPATRA OR SOMETHING.
SO THEN, THE THIEF AT THE BRITISH MUSEUM WAS...
AND IF YOU, AS THE ELECTOR, SELECT ME, I'LL EVEN FORGIVE THE DEBT FOR YOU.
WHO IN THEIR RIGHT MIND WOULD BE IN DEBT TO A DEMON?!
AND YOU NEVER KNOW WHEN THE OTHER DEMONS, WHO KNOW ABOUT YOU, ARE GOING TO CONTACT YOU.
SO I'VE DECIDED THAT UNTIL YOU PROMISE TO SELECT ME, I AM NOT LEAVING YOUR SIDE.

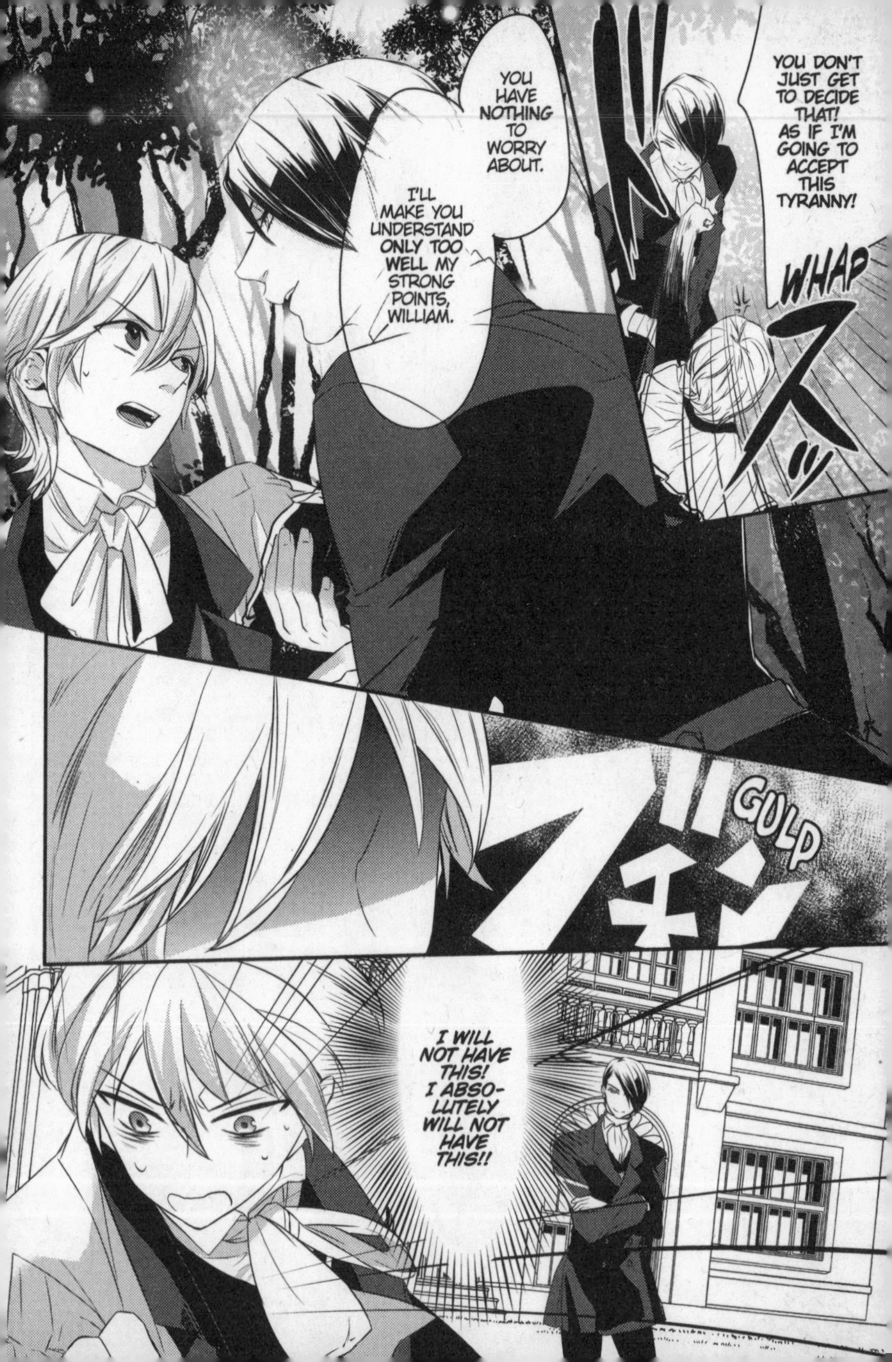
YOU DON'T JUST GET TO DECIDE THAT! AS IF I'M GOING TO ACCEPT THIS TYRANNY!
WHAP
YOU HAVE NOTHING TO WORRY ABOUT.
I'LL MAKE YOU UNDERSTAND ONLY TOO WELL MY STRONG POINTS, WILLIAM.
GULP
I WILL NOT HAVE THIS! I ABSO-LUTELY WILL NOT HAVE THIS!!

Pillar 4

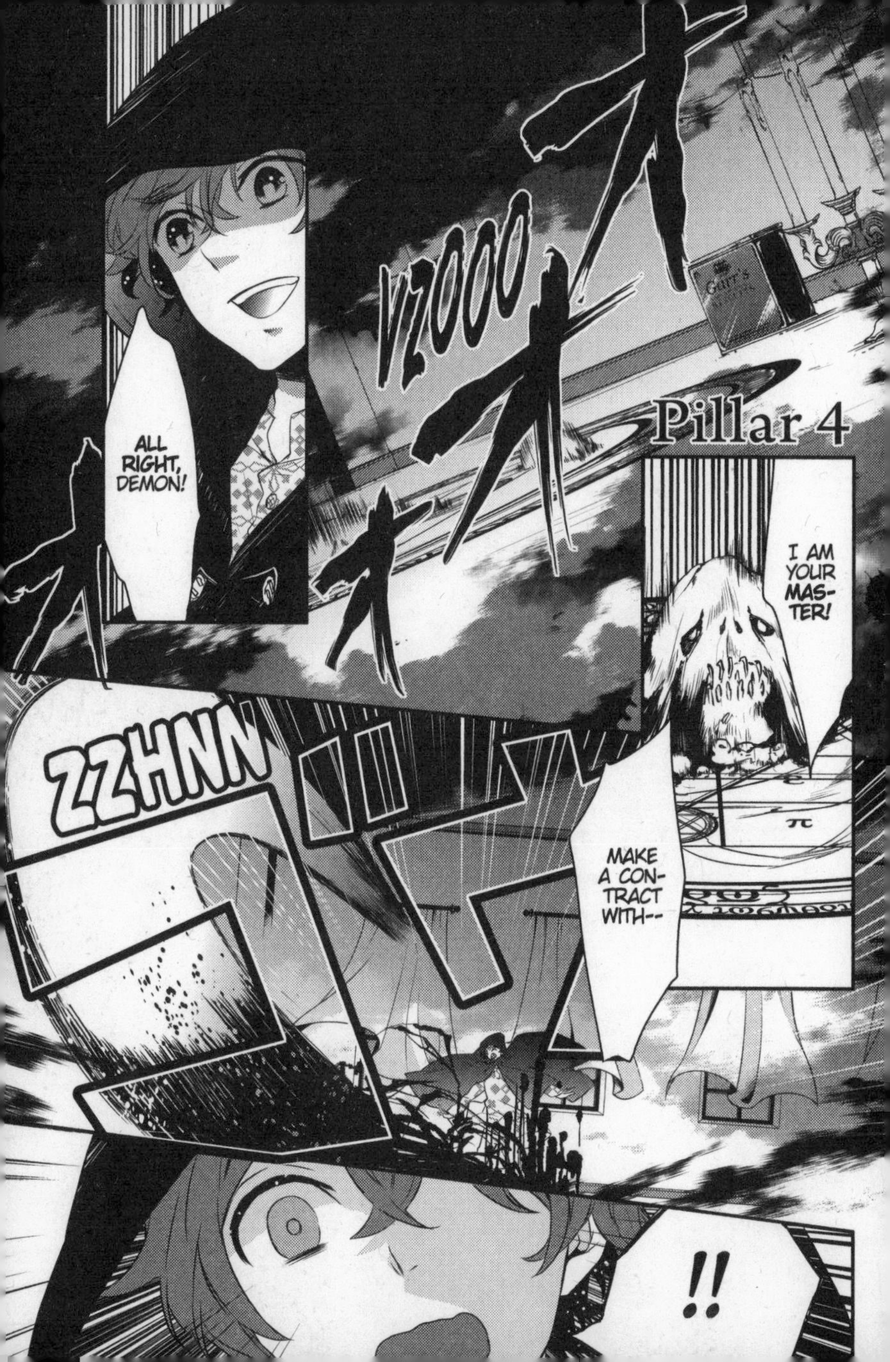
VZOOO
ALL RIGHT, DEMON!
I AM YOUR MASTER!
MAKE A CONTRACT WITH--
ZZHNN
!!

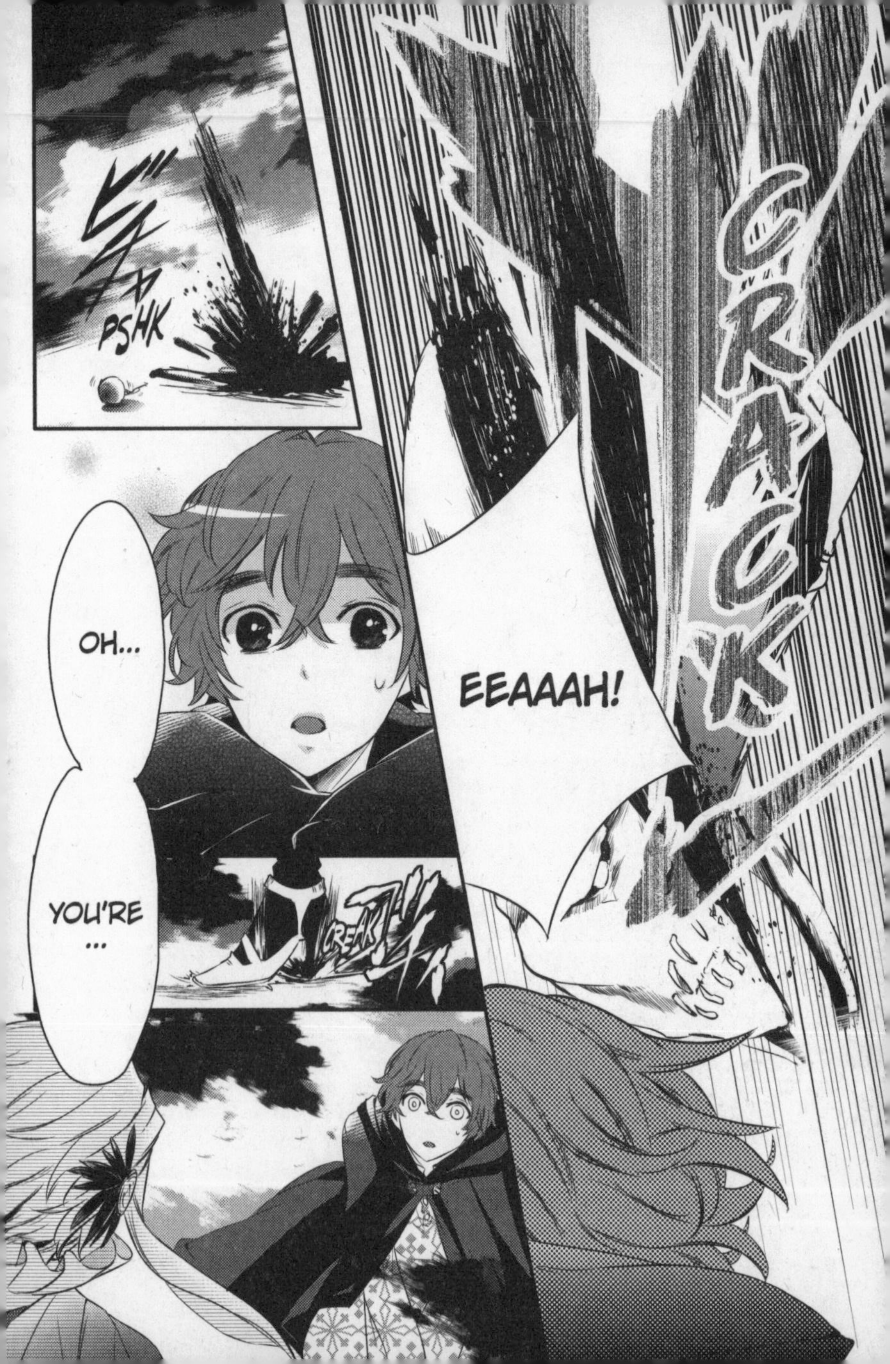
CRACK
EEAAAH!
PSHK
OH...
CREAK
YOU'RE ...

Pillar 4

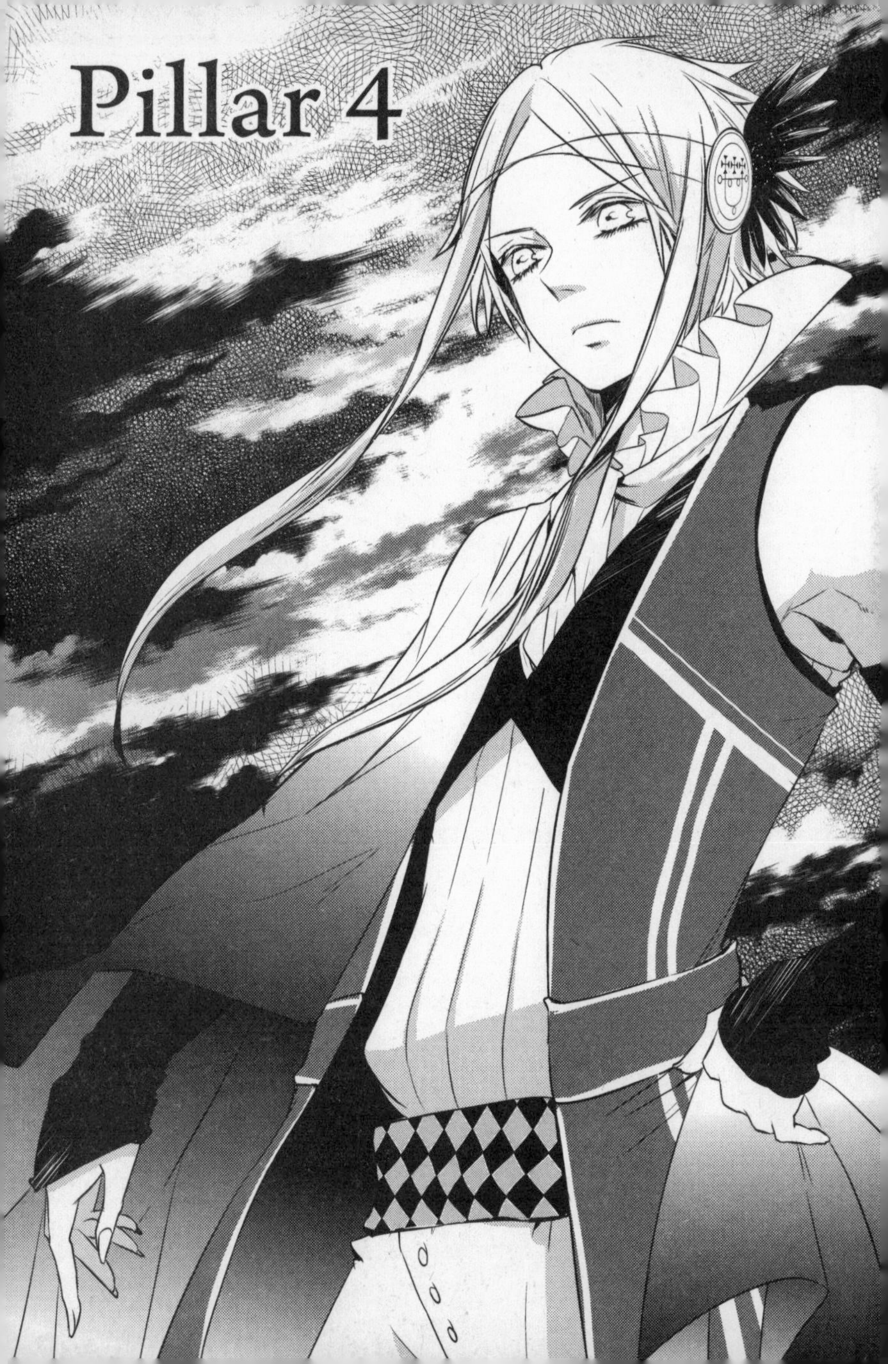

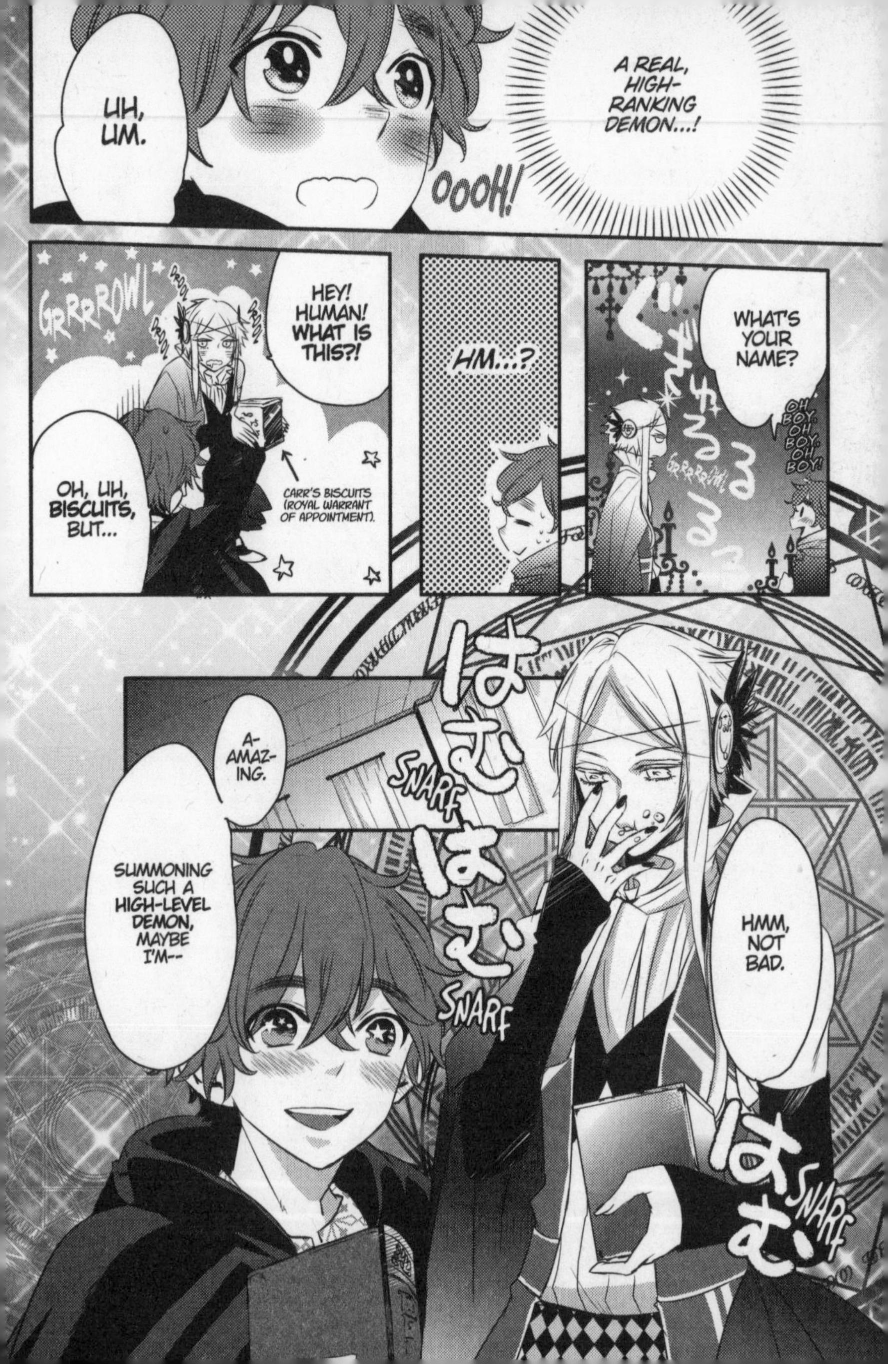
A REAL, HIGH-RANKING DEMON...!
OOOH!
UH, UM.
WHAT'S YOUR NAME?
OH BOY. OH BOY. OH BOY!
GRRRRWL!
HM...?
HEY! HUMAN! WHAT IS THIS?!
GRRRROWL
DROOL DROOL DROOL DROOL
OH, UH, BISCUITS, BUT...
CARR'S BISCUITS (ROYAL WARRANT OF APPOINTMENT).
HMM, NOT BAD.
SNARF
SNARF
SNARF
A-AMAZING.
SUMMONING SUCH A HIGH-LEVEL DEMON, MAYBE I'M--

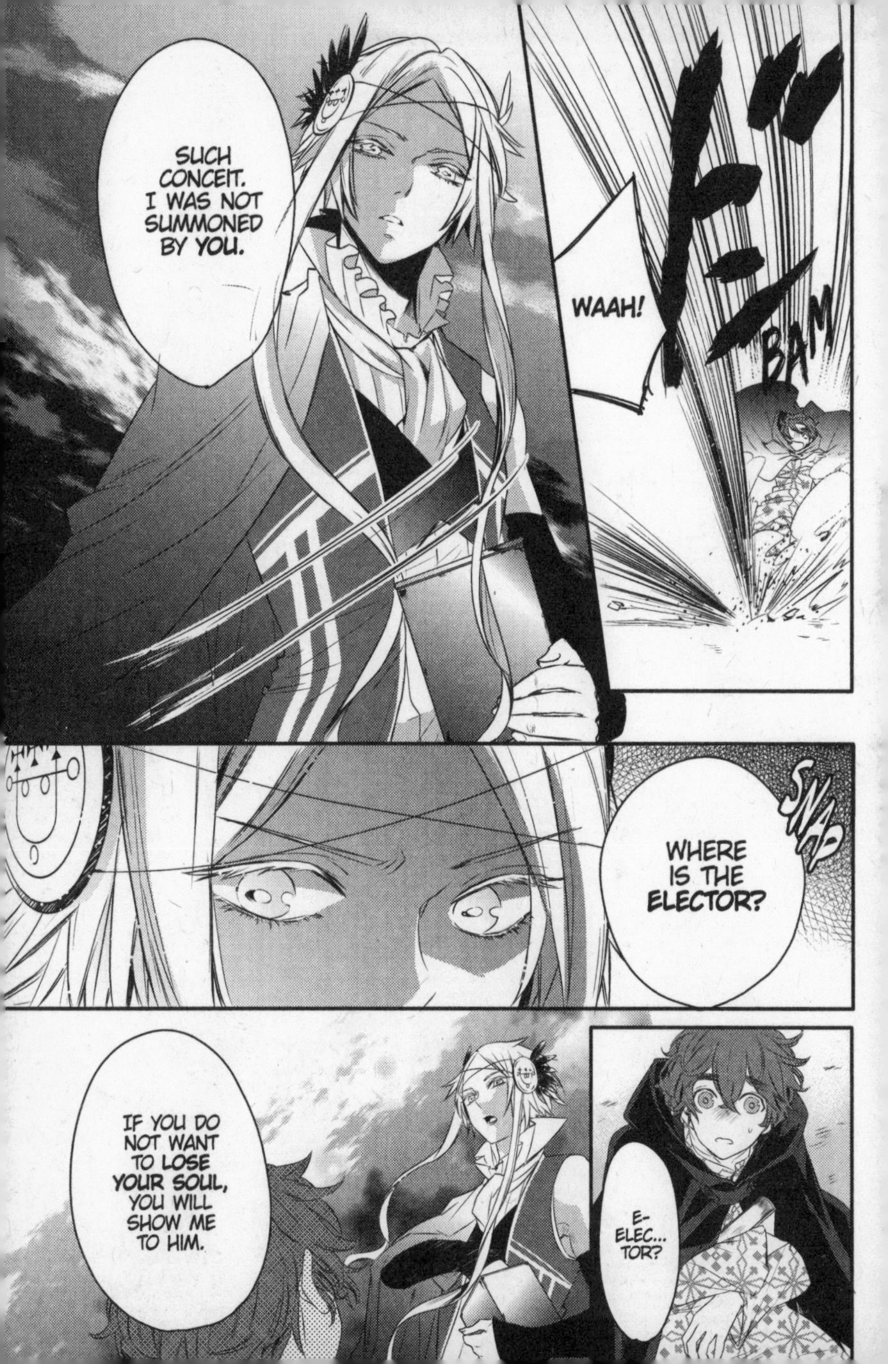
WAAH!
BAM
SUCH CONCEIT. I WAS NOT SUMMONED BY YOU.
SNAP
WHERE IS THE ELECTOR?
E-ELEC... TOR?
IF YOU DO NOT WANT TO LOSE YOUR SOUL, YOU WILL SHOW ME TO HIM.

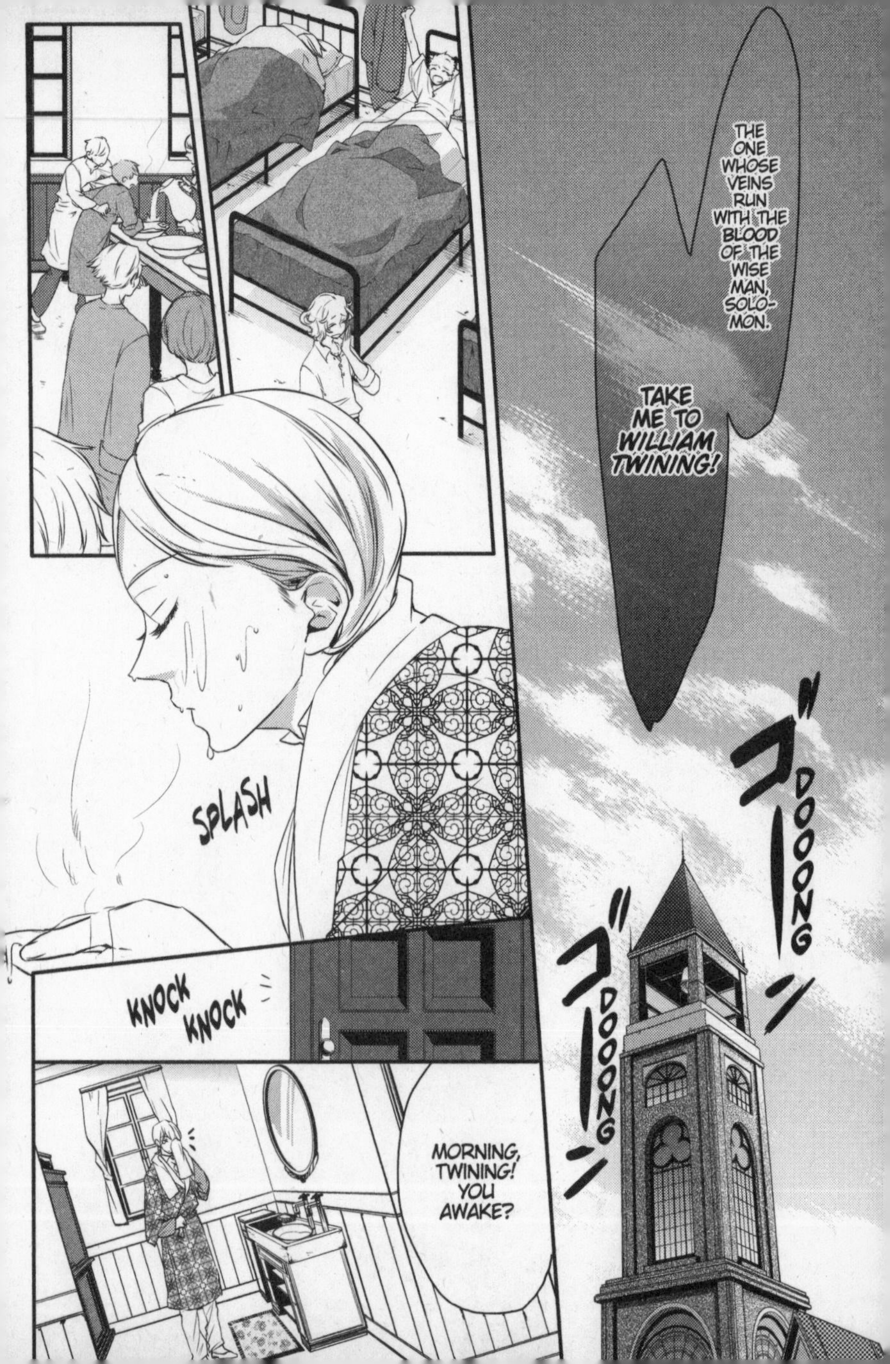
THE ONE WHOSE VEINS RUN WITH THE BLOOD OF THE WISE MAN, SOLOMON.
TAKE ME TO WILLIAM TWINING!
DOOOONG
DOOOONG
SPLASH
KNOCK KNOCK
MORNING, TWINING! YOU AWAKE?

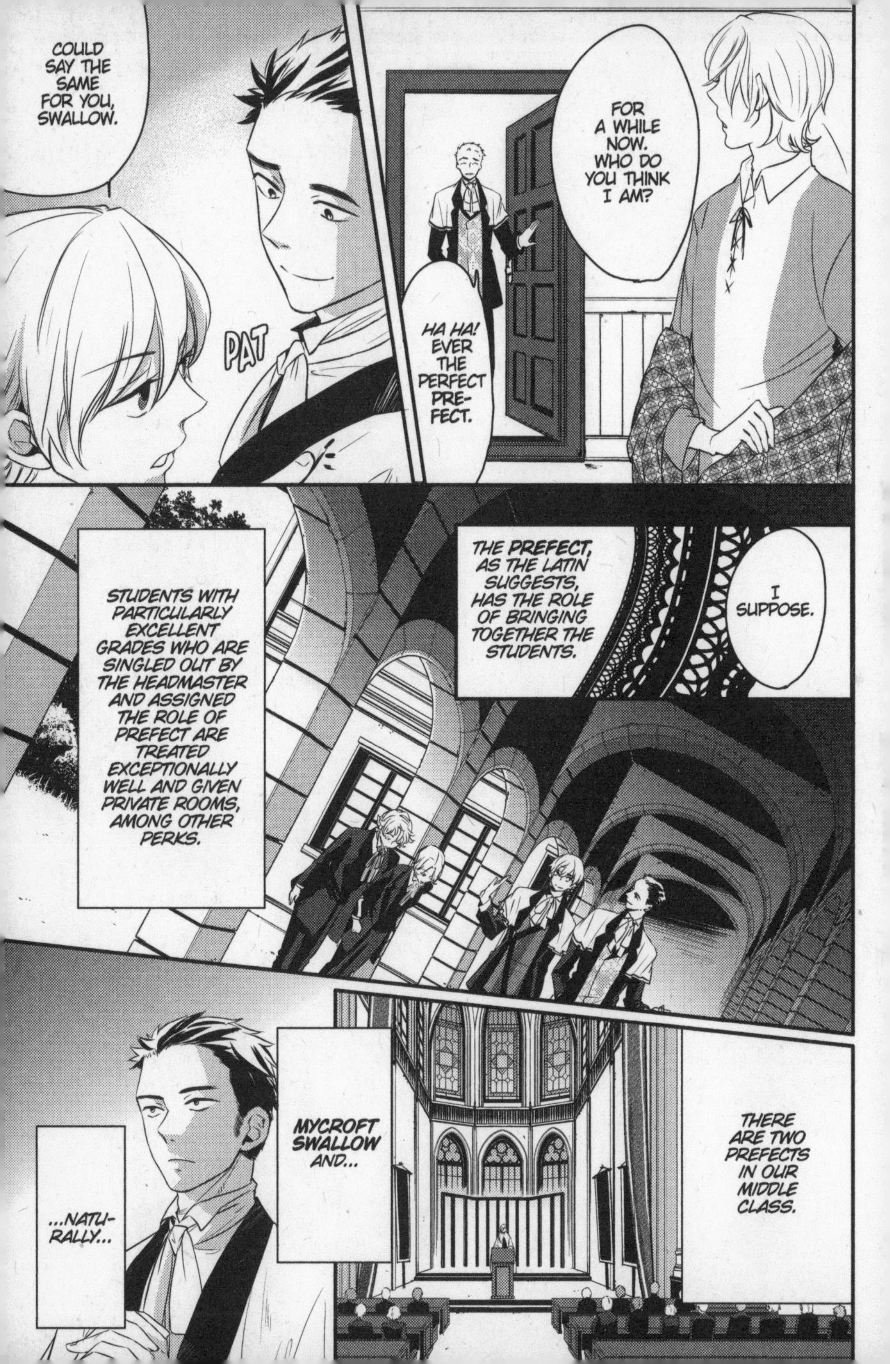
FOR A WHILE NOW. WHO DO YOU THINK I AM?
HA HA! EVER THE PERFECT PRE-FECT.
COULD SAY THE SAME FOR YOU, SWALLOW.
PAT
I SUPPOSE.
THE PREFECT, AS THE LATIN SUGGESTS, HAS THE ROLE OF BRINGING TOGETHER THE STUDENTS.
STUDENTS WITH PARTICULARLY EXCELLENT GRADES WHO ARE SINGLED OUT BY THE HEADMASTER AND ASSIGNED THE ROLE OF PREFECT ARE TREATED EXCEPTIONALLY WELL AND GIVEN PRIVATE ROOMS, AMONG OTHER PERKS.
THERE ARE TWO PREFECTS IN OUR MIDDLE CLASS.
MYCROFT SWALLOW AND...
...NATU-RALLY...

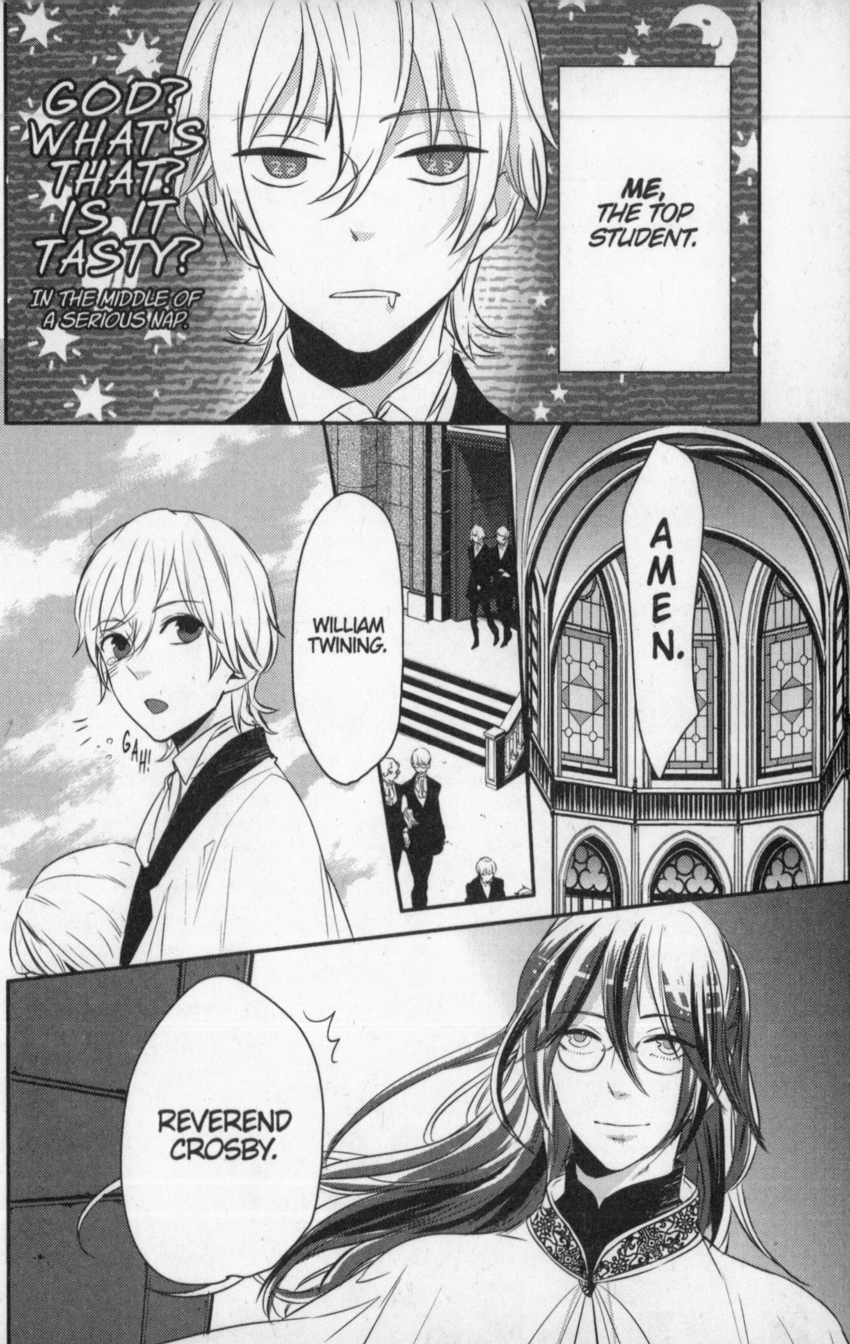
ME, THE TOP STUDENT.
GOD? WHAT'S THAT? IS IT TASTY?
IN THE MIDDLE OF A SERIOUS NAP.
AMEN.
WILLIAM TWINING.
GAH!
REVEREND CROSBY.

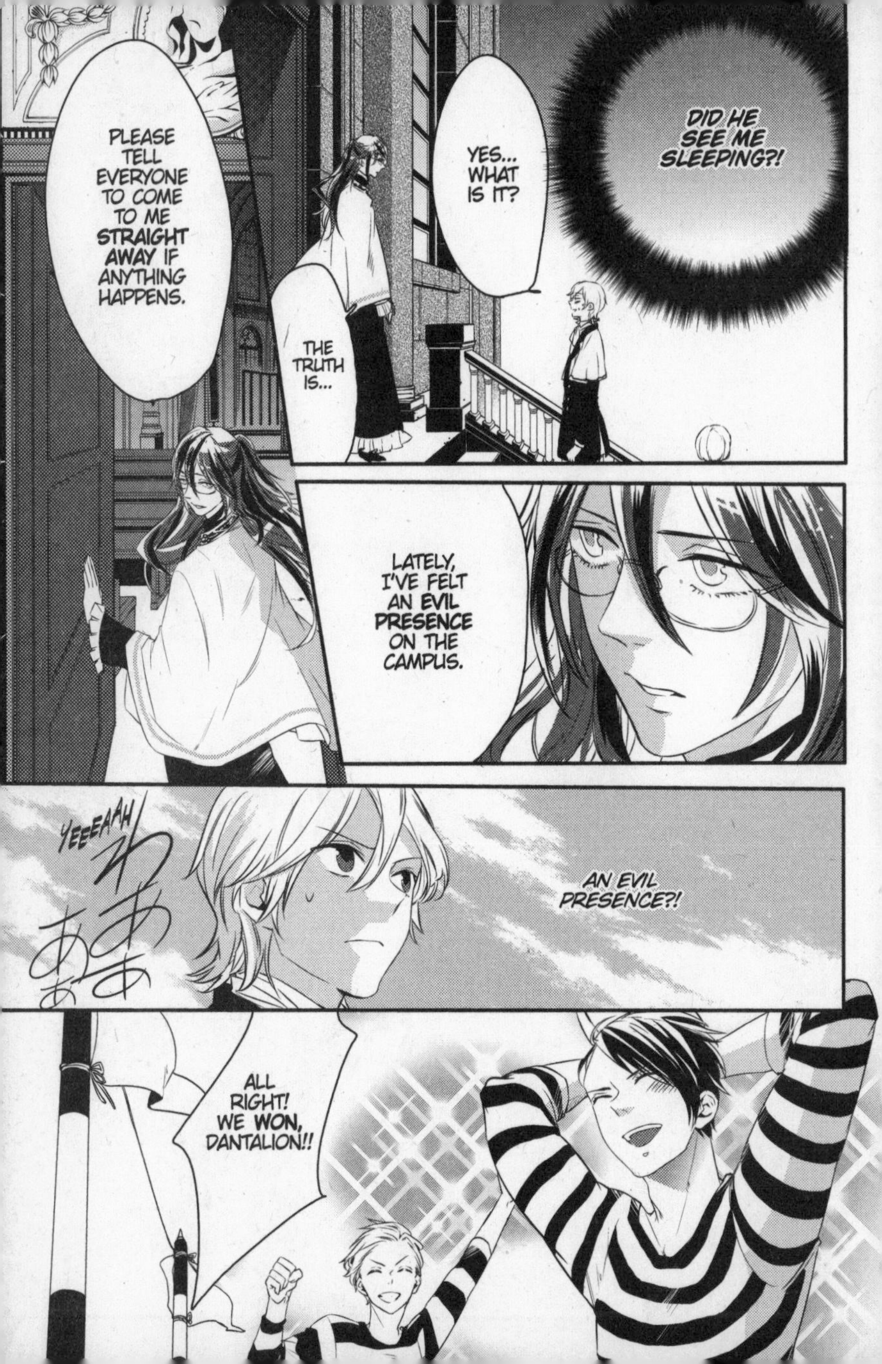
DID HE SEE ME SLEEPING?!
YES... WHAT IS IT?
THE TRUTH IS...
LATELY, I'VE FELT AN EVIL PRESENCE ON THE CAMPUS.
PLEASE TELL EVERYONE TO COME TO ME STRAIGHT AWAY IF ANYTHING HAPPENS.
AN EVIL PRESENCE?!
YEEEAAH
ALL RIGHT! WE WON, DANTALION!!

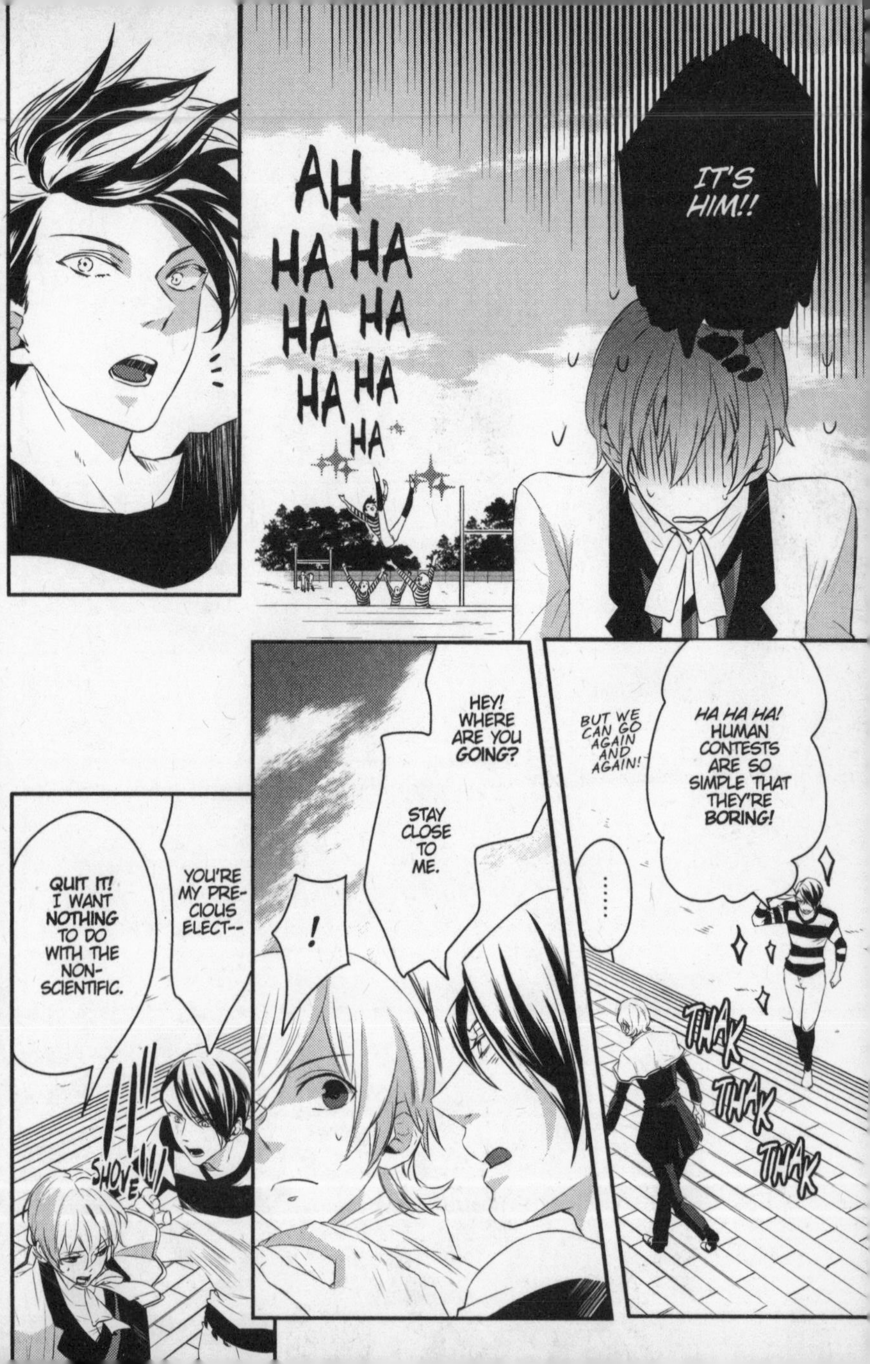
IT'S HIM!!
AH HA HA HA HA HA HA HA HA
HA HA HA! HUMAN CONTESTS ARE SO SIMPLE THAT THEY'RE BORING!
BUT WE CAN GO AGAIN AND AGAIN!
......
THAK
THAK
THAK
HEY! WHERE ARE YOU GOING?
STAY CLOSE TO ME.
!
YOU'RE MY PRE-CIOUS ELECT--
QUIT IT! I WANT NOTHING TO DO WITH THE NON-SCIENTIFIC.
SHOVE

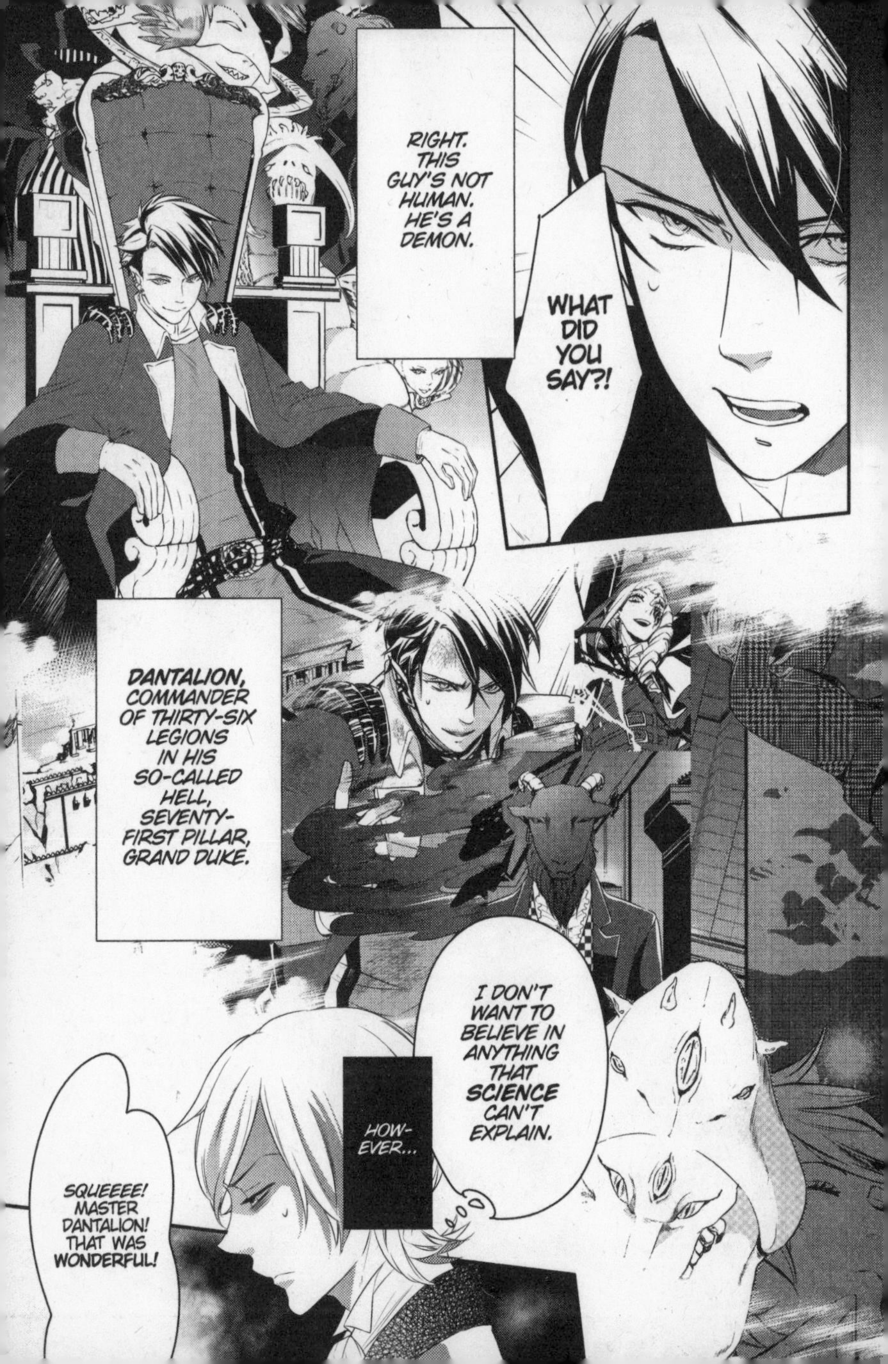
WHAT DID YOU SAY?!
RIGHT. THIS GUY'S NOT HUMAN. HE'S A DEMON.
DANTALION, COMMANDER OF THIRTY-SIX LEGIONS IN HIS SO-CALLED HELL, SEVENTY-FIRST PILLAR, GRAND DUKE.
I DON'T WANT TO BELIEVE IN ANYTHING THAT SCIENCE CAN'T EXPLAIN.
HOW-EVER...
SQUEEEE! MASTER DANTALION! THAT WAS WONDERFUL!

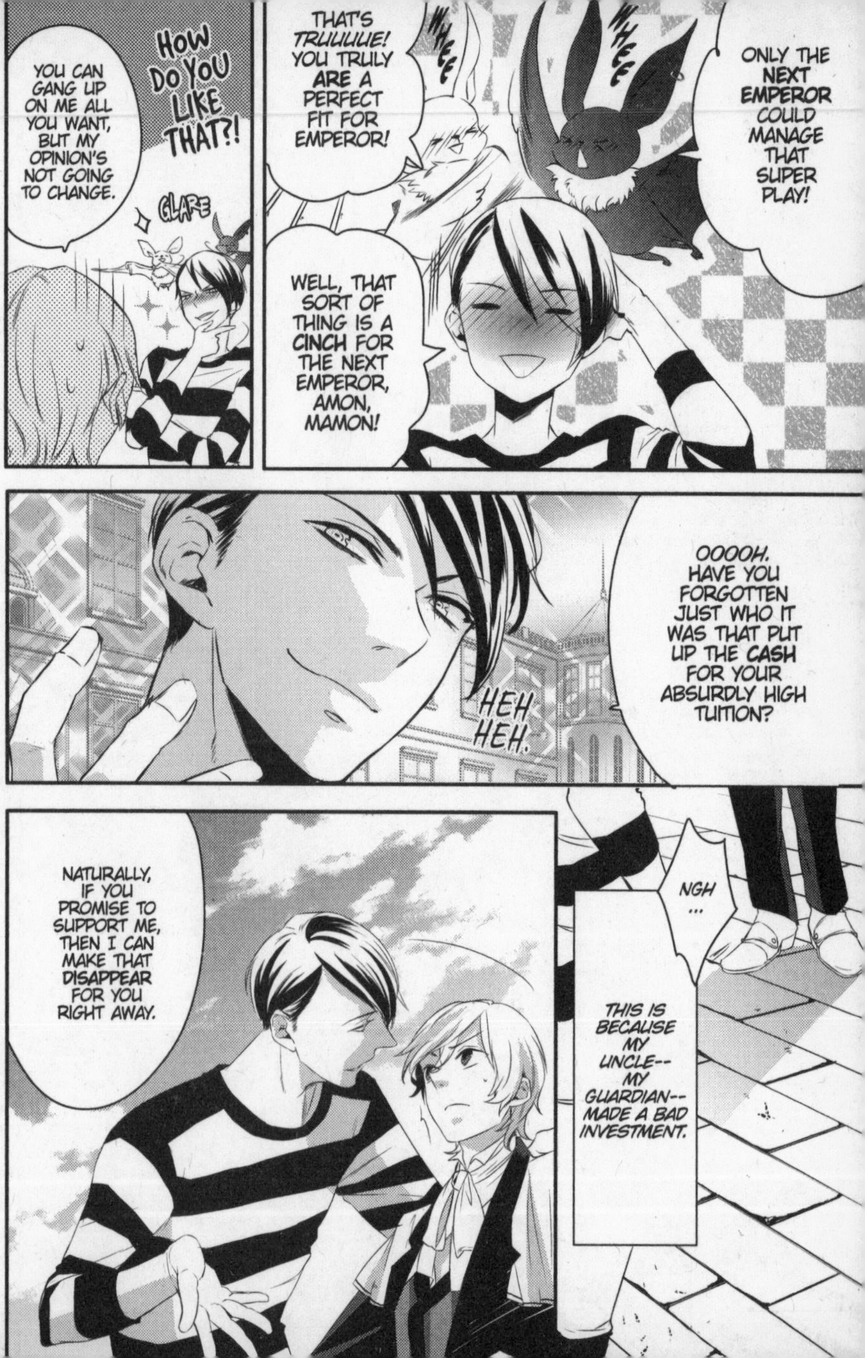
ONLY THE NEXT EMPEROR COULD MANAGE THAT SUPER PLAY!
WHEE
WHEE
THAT'S TRUUUUE! YOU TRULY ARE A PERFECT FIT FOR EMPEROR!
WELL, THAT SORT OF THING IS A CINCH FOR THE NEXT EMPEROR, AMON, MAMON!
HOW DO YOU LIKE THAT?!
YOU CAN GANG UP ON ME ALL YOU WANT, BUT MY OPINION'S NOT GOING TO CHANGE.
GLARE
OOOOH. HAVE YOU FORGOTTEN JUST WHO IT WAS THAT PUT UP THE CASH FOR YOUR ABSURDLY HIGH TUITION?
HEH HEH.
NGH ...
THIS IS BECAUSE MY UNCLE-- MY GUARDIAN-- MADE A BAD INVESTMENT.
NATURALLY, IF YOU PROMISE TO SUPPORT ME, THEN I CAN MAKE THAT DISAPPEAR FOR YOU RIGHT AWAY.

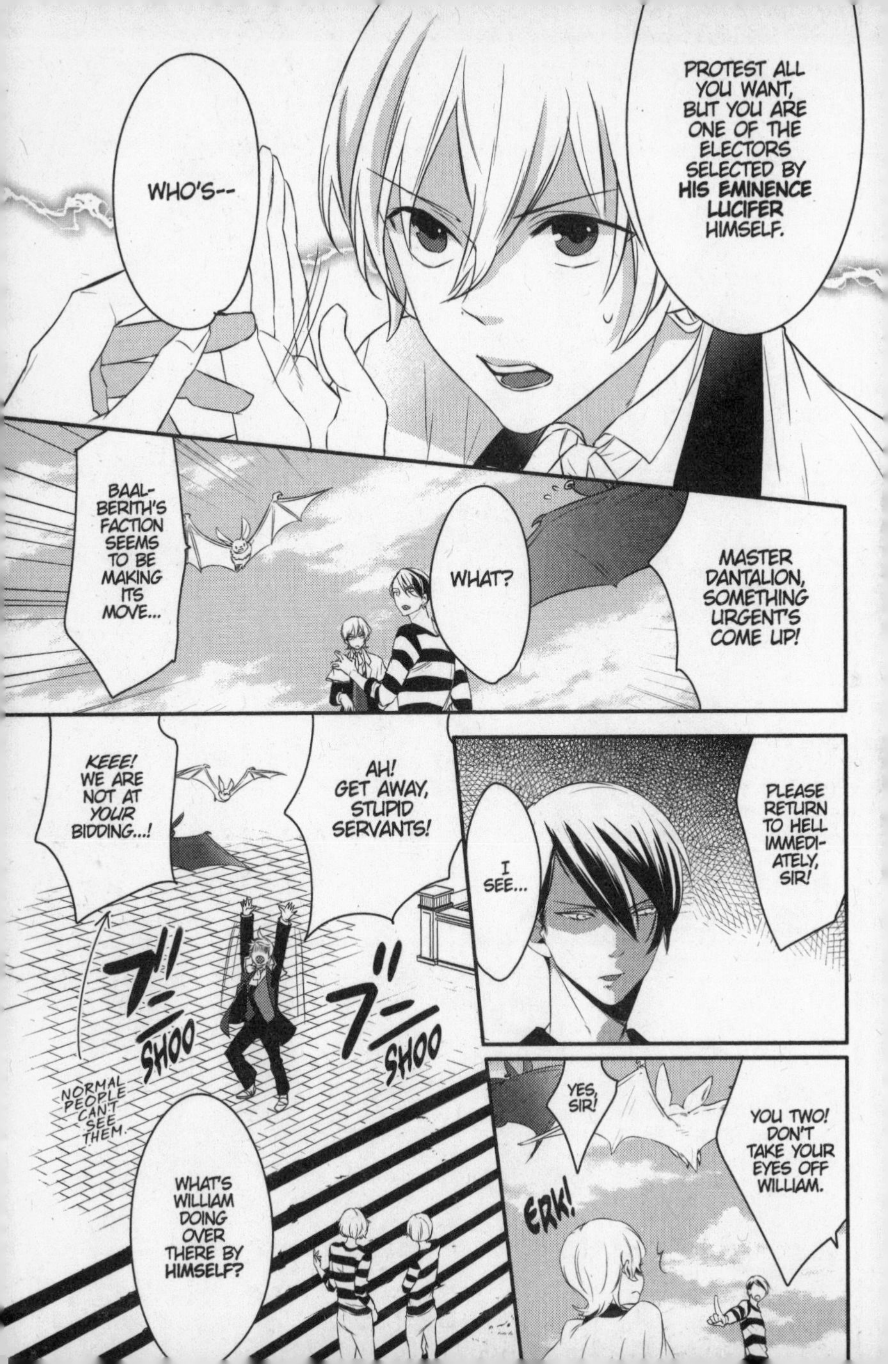
PROTEST ALL YOU WANT, BUT YOU ARE ONE OF THE ELECTORS SELECTED BY HIS EMINENCE LUCIFER HIMSELF.
WHO'S--
MASTER DANTALION, SOMETHING URGENT'S COME UP!
WHAT?
BAAL-BERITH'S FACTION SEEMS TO BE MAKING ITS MOVE...
PLEASE RETURN TO HELL IMMEDIATELY, SIR!
I SEE...
YOU TWO! DON'T TAKE YOUR EYES OFF WILLIAM.
YES, SIR!
ERK!
AH! GET AWAY, STUPID SERVANTS!
KEEE! WE ARE NOT AT YOUR BIDDING...!
SHOO
SHOO
NORMAL PEOPLE CAN'T SEE THEM.
WHAT'S WILLIAM DOING OVER THERE BY HIMSELF?

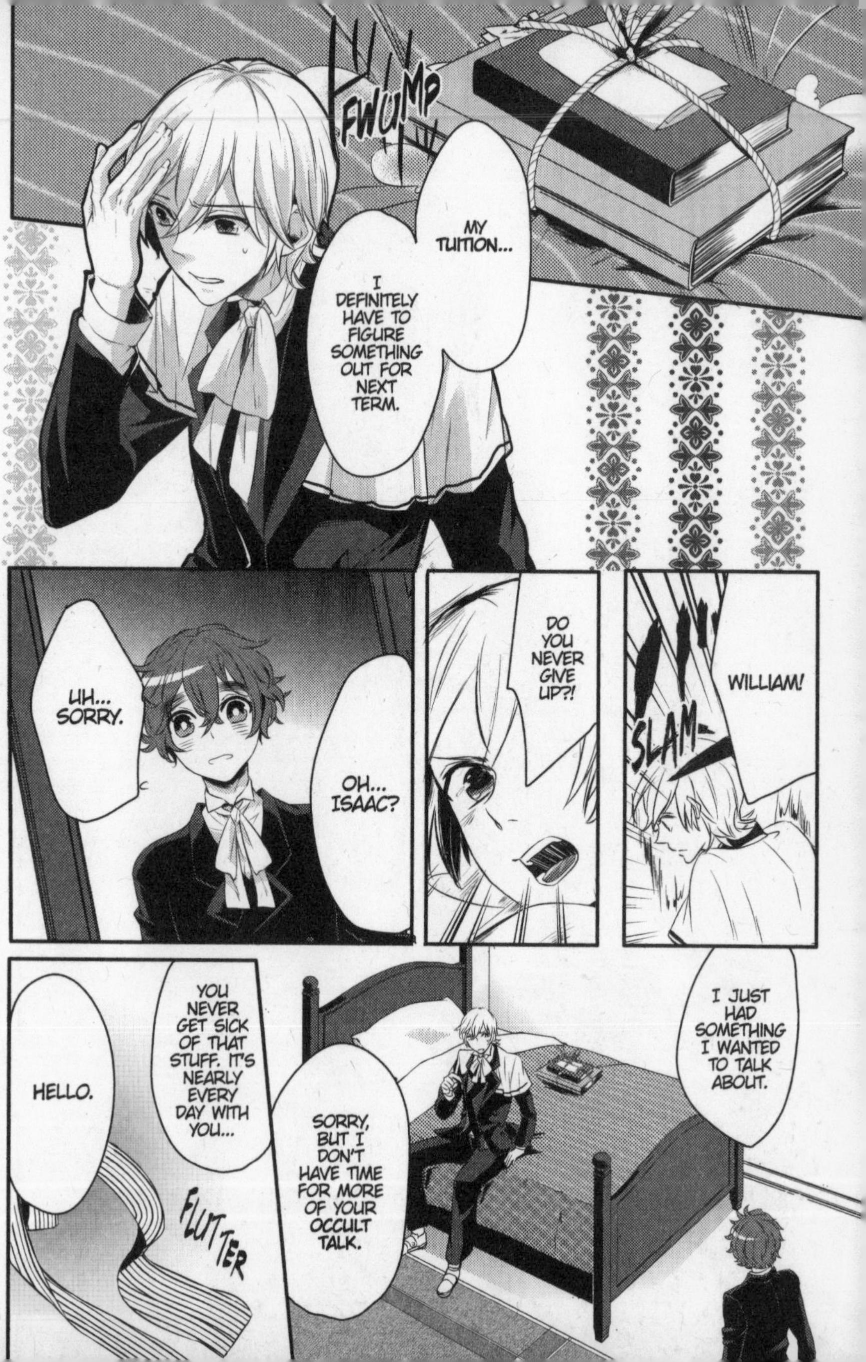
FWUMP
MY TUITION...
I DEFINITELY HAVE TO FIGURE SOMETHING OUT FOR NEXT TERM.
SLAM
WILLIAM!
DO YOU NEVER GIVE UP?!
OH... ISAAC?
UH... SORRY.
I JUST HAD SOMETHING I WANTED TO TALK ABOUT.
SORRY, BUT I DON'T HAVE TIME FOR MORE OF YOUR OCCULT TALK.
YOU NEVER GET SICK OF THAT STUFF. IT'S NEARLY EVERY DAY WITH YOU...
FLUTTER
HELLO.

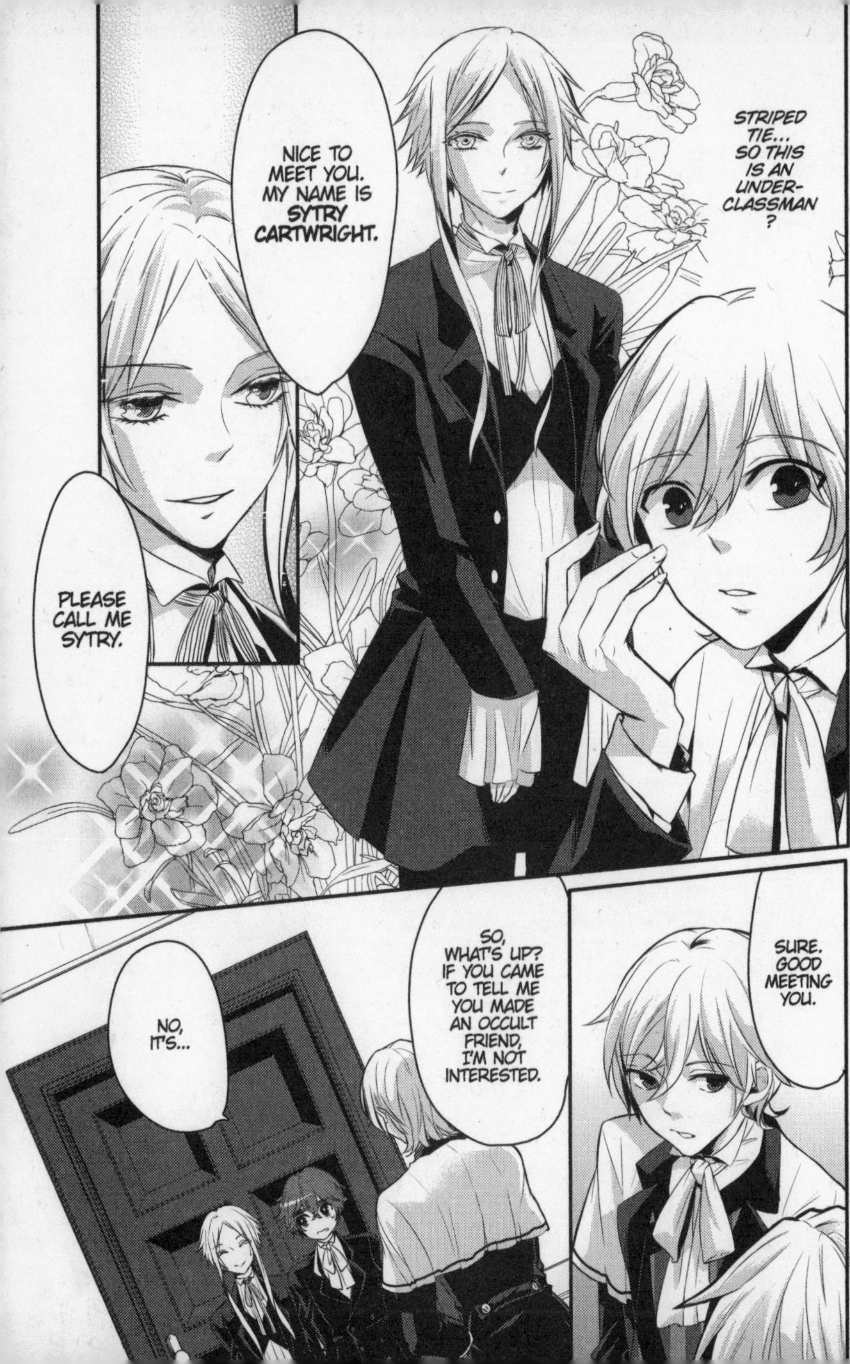
STRIPED TIE... SO THIS IS AN UNDER-CLASSMAN?
NICE TO MEET YOU. MY NAME IS SYTRY CARTWRIGHT.
PLEASE CALL ME SYTRY.
SURE. GOOD MEETING YOU.
SO, WHAT'S UP? IF YOU CAME TO TELL ME YOU MADE AN OCCULT FRIEND, I'M NOT INTERESTED.
NO, IT'S...

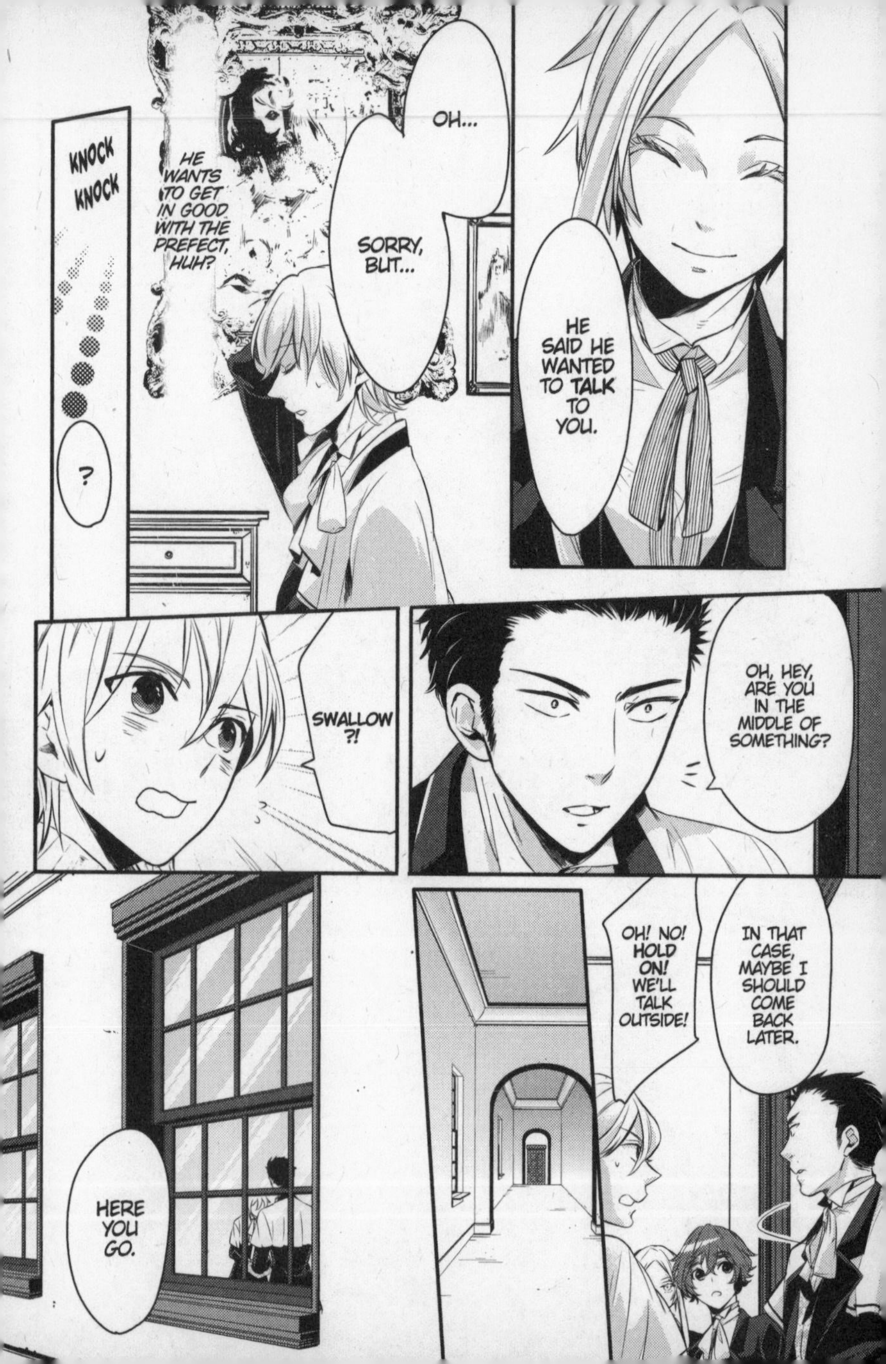
HE SAID HE WANTED TO TALK TO YOU.
OH...
SORRY, BUT...
HE WANTS TO GET IN GOOD WITH THE PREFECT, HUH?
KNOCK KNOCK
?
OH, HEY, ARE YOU IN THE MIDDLE OF SOMETHING?
SWALLOW ?!
IN THAT CASE, MAYBE I SHOULD COME BACK LATER.
OH! NO! HOLD ON! WE'LL TALK OUTSIDE!
HERE YOU GO.

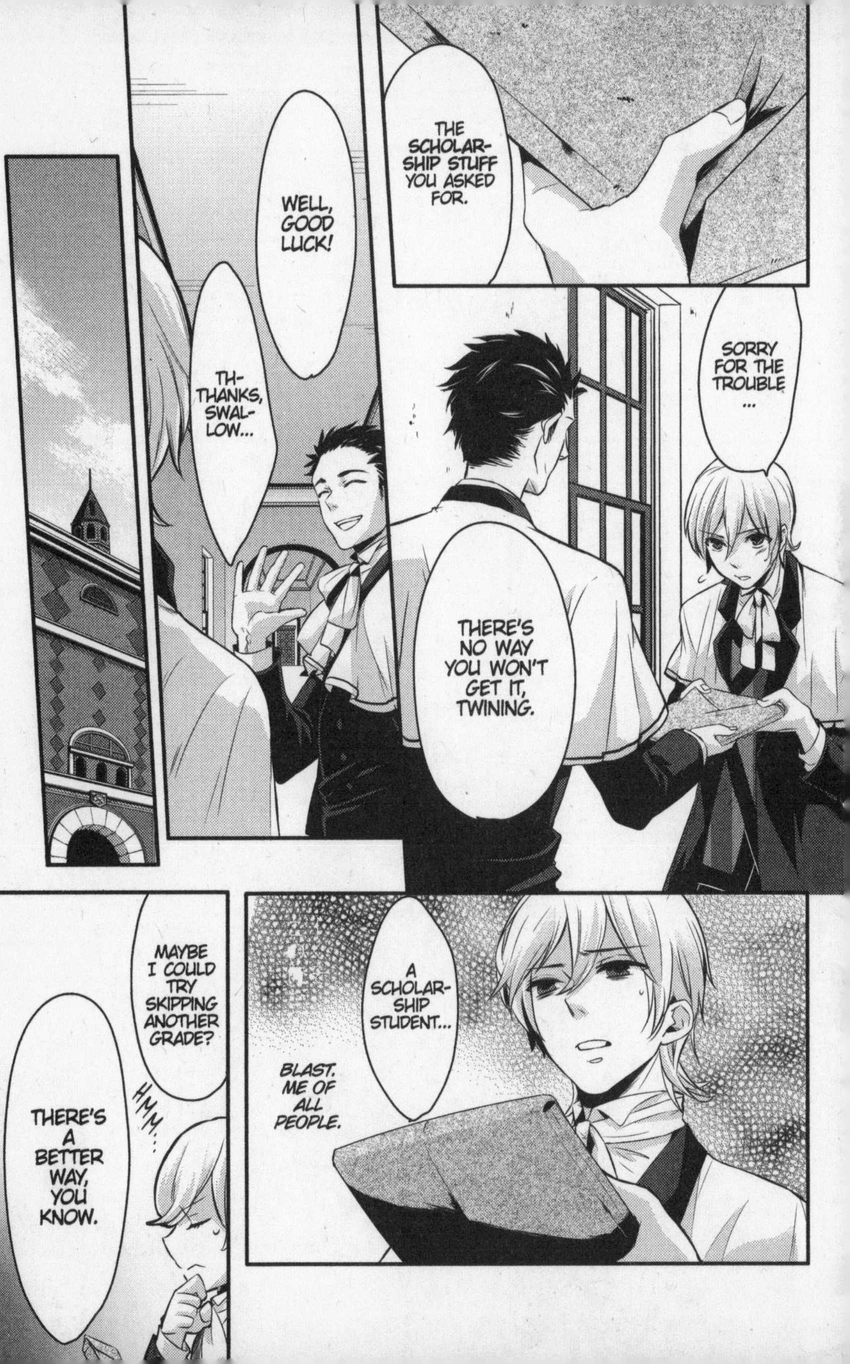
THE SCHOLARSHIP STUFF YOU ASKED FOR.
SORRY FOR THE TROUBLE...
THERE'S NO WAY YOU WON'T GET IT, TWINING.
WELL, GOOD LUCK!
TH-THANKS, SWALLOW...
A SCHOLARSHIP STUDENT...
BLAST. ME OF ALL PEOPLE.
MAYBE I COULD TRY SKIPPING ANOTHER GRADE?
HMM...
THERE'S A BETTER WAY, YOU KNOW.

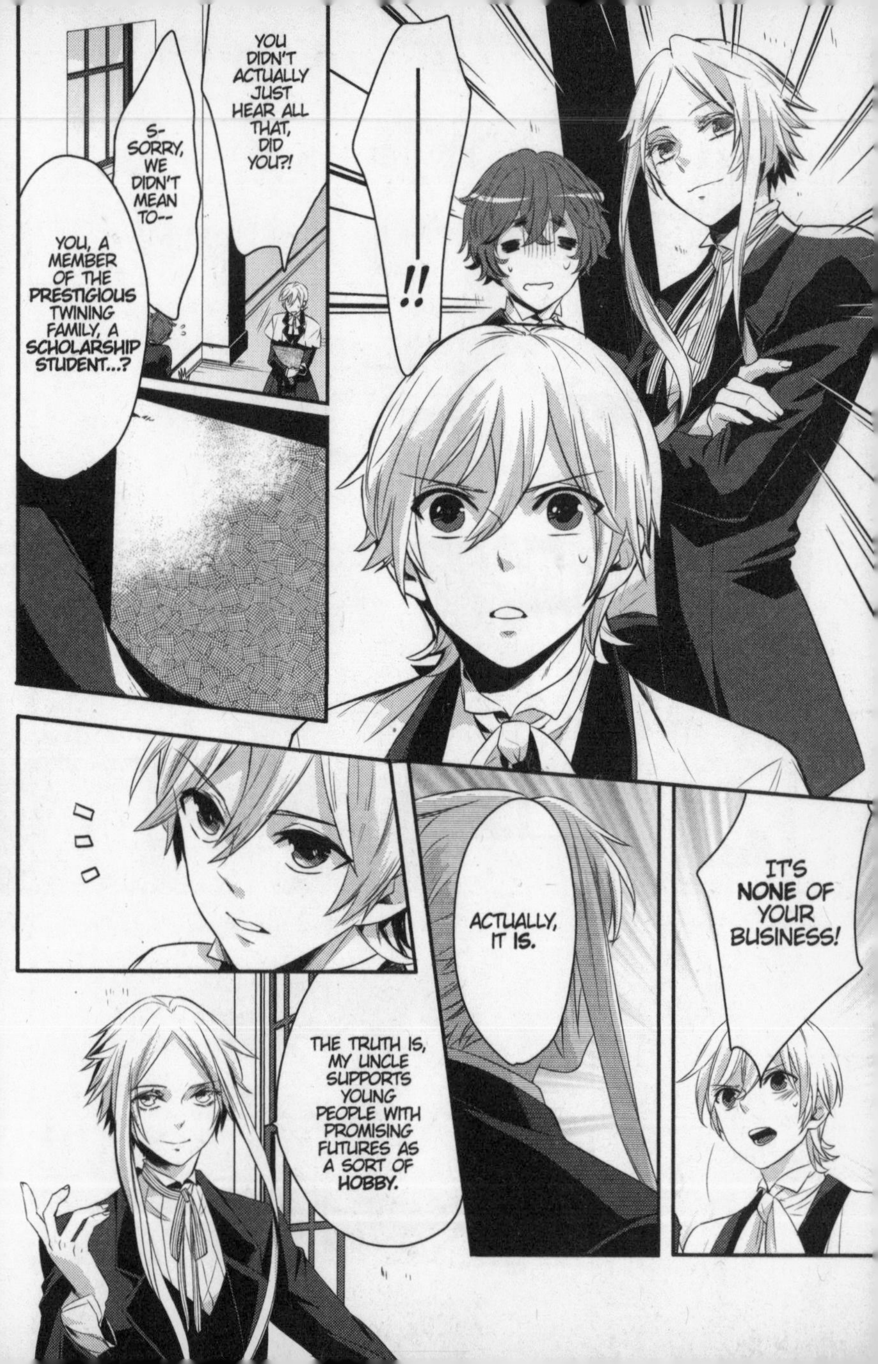
!!
YOU DIDN'T ACTUALLY JUST HEAR ALL THAT, DID YOU?!
S-SORRY, WE DIDN'T MEAN TO--
YOU, A MEMBER OF THE PRESTIGIOUS TWINING FAMILY, A SCHOLARSHIP STUDENT...?
IT'S NONE OF YOUR BUSINESS!
ACTUALLY, IT IS.
THE TRUTH IS, MY UNCLE SUPPORTS YOUNG PEOPLE WITH PROMISING FUTURES AS A SORT OF HOBBY.

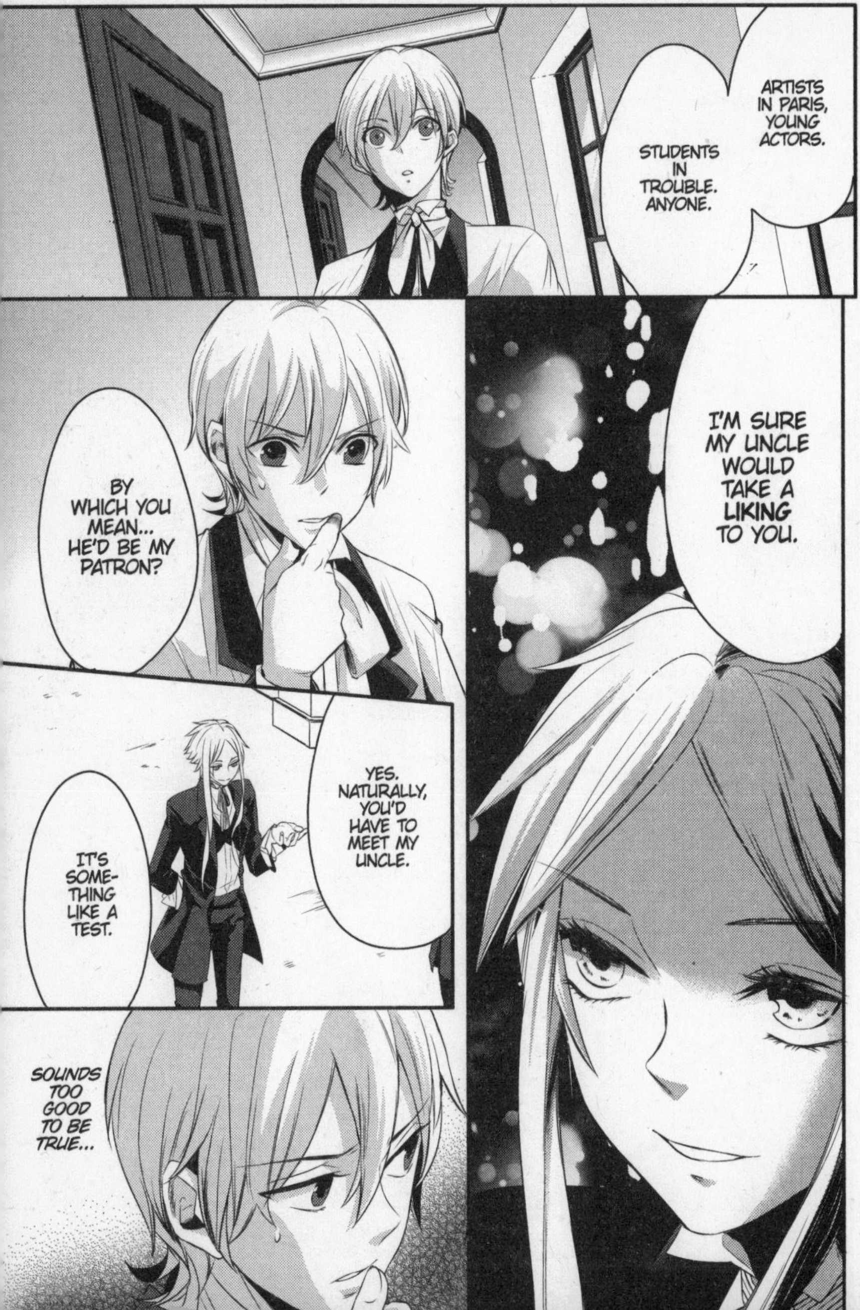
ARTISTS IN PARIS, YOUNG ACTORS.
STUDENTS IN TROUBLE. ANYONE.
I'M SURE MY UNCLE WOULD TAKE A LIKING TO YOU.
BY WHICH YOU MEAN... HE'D BE MY PATRON?
YES. NATURALLY, YOU'D HAVE TO MEET MY UNCLE.
IT'S SOME-THING LIKE A TEST.
SOUNDS TOO GOOD TO BE TRUE...

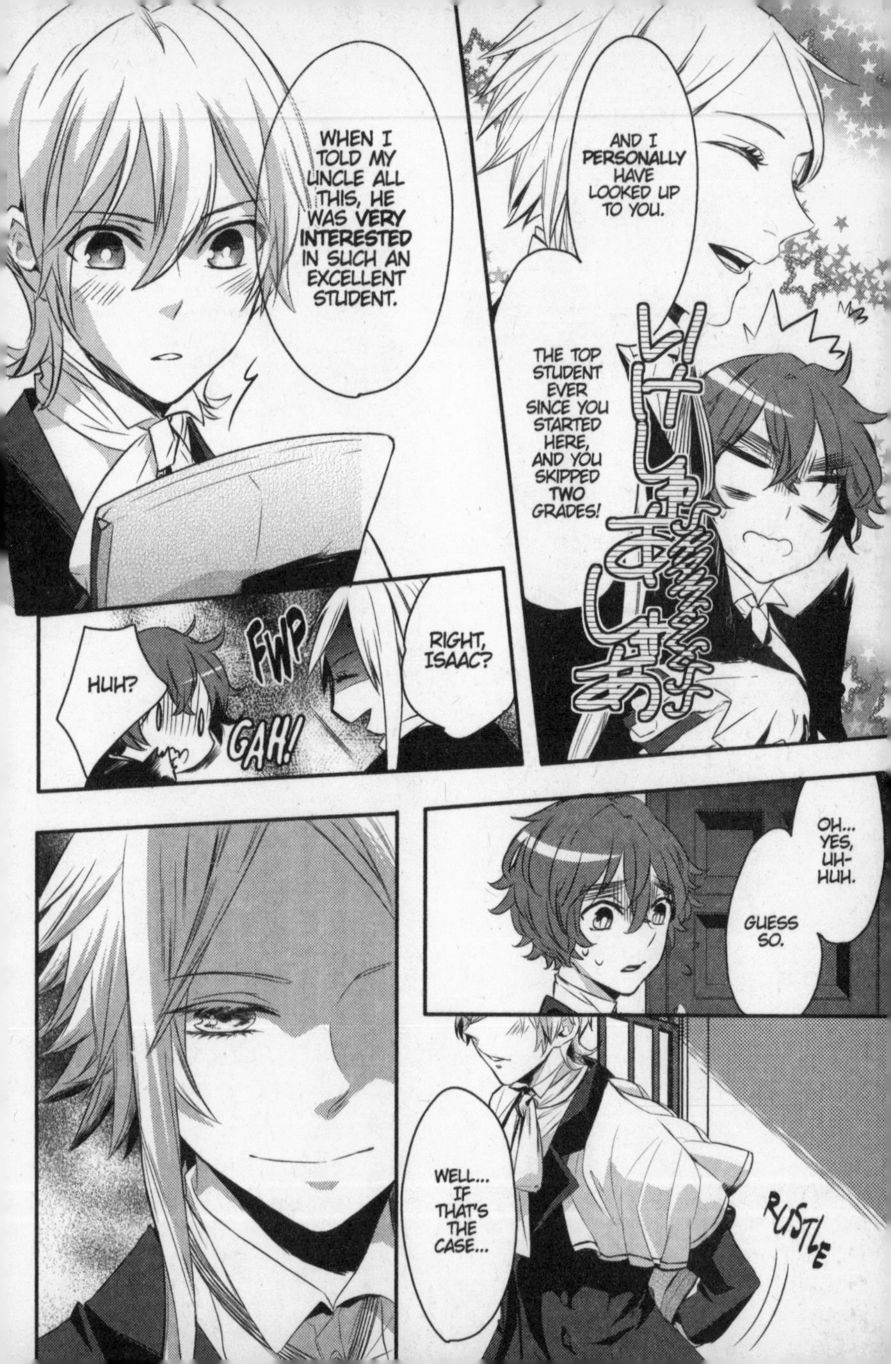
AND I PERSONALLY HAVE LOOKED UP TO YOU.
THE TOP STUDENT EVER SINCE YOU STARTED HERE, AND YOU SKIPPED TWO GRADES!
WHEN I TOLD MY UNCLE ALL THIS, HE WAS **VERY INTERESTED** IN SUCH AN EXCELLENT STUDENT.
RIGHT, ISAAC?
FWP
GAH!
HUH?
OH... YES, UH-HUH.
GUESS SO.
WELL... IF THAT'S THE CASE...
RUSTLE

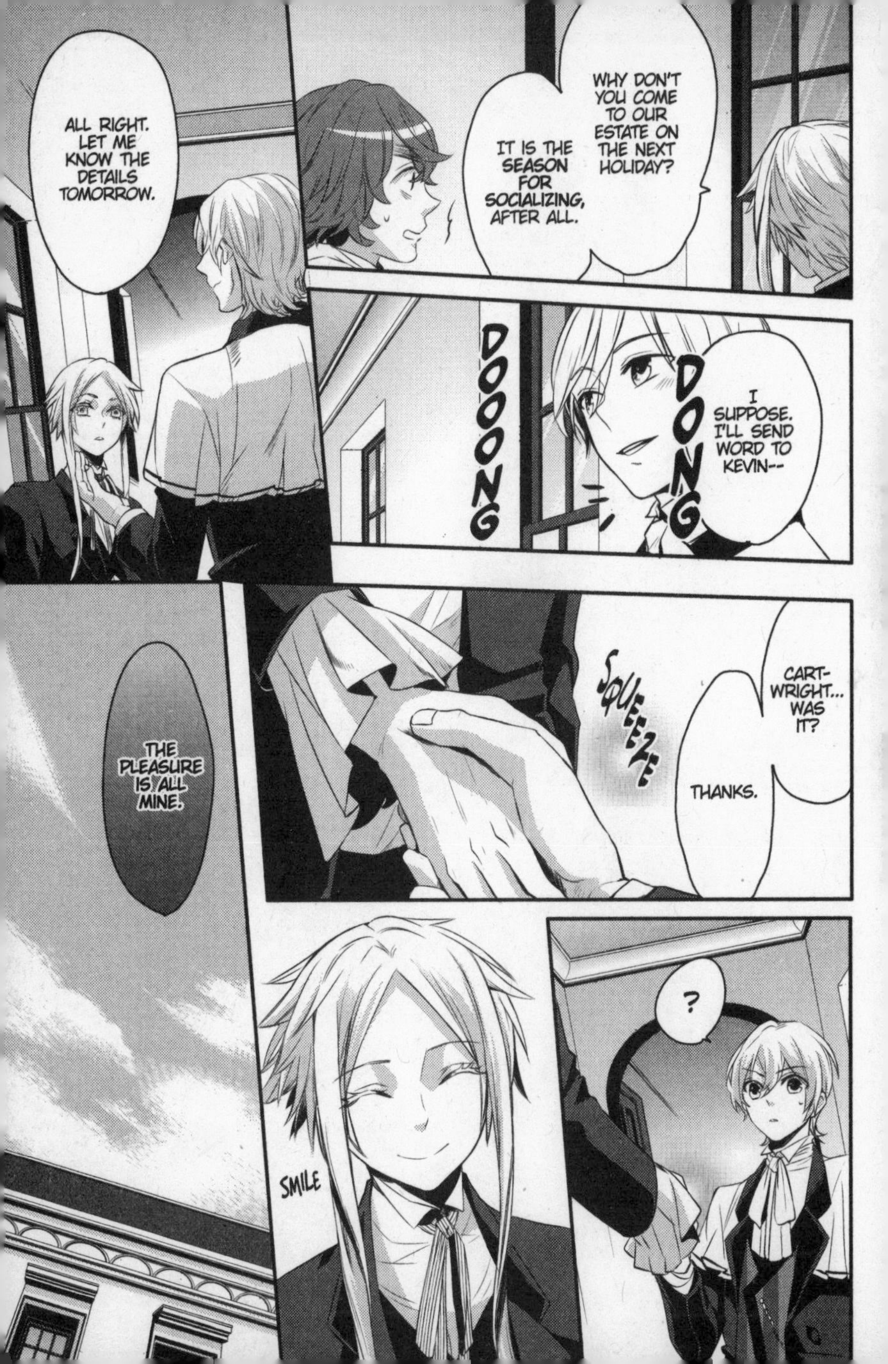
WHY DON'T YOU COME TO OUR ESTATE ON THE NEXT HOLIDAY?
IT IS THE SEASON FOR SOCIALIZING, AFTER ALL.
DONG
I SUPPOSE. I'LL SEND WORD TO KEVIN--
DOOOONG
ALL RIGHT. LET ME KNOW THE DETAILS TOMORROW.
CART-WRIGHT... WAS IT?
THANKS.
SQUEEZE
THE PLEASURE IS ALL MINE.
?
SMILE

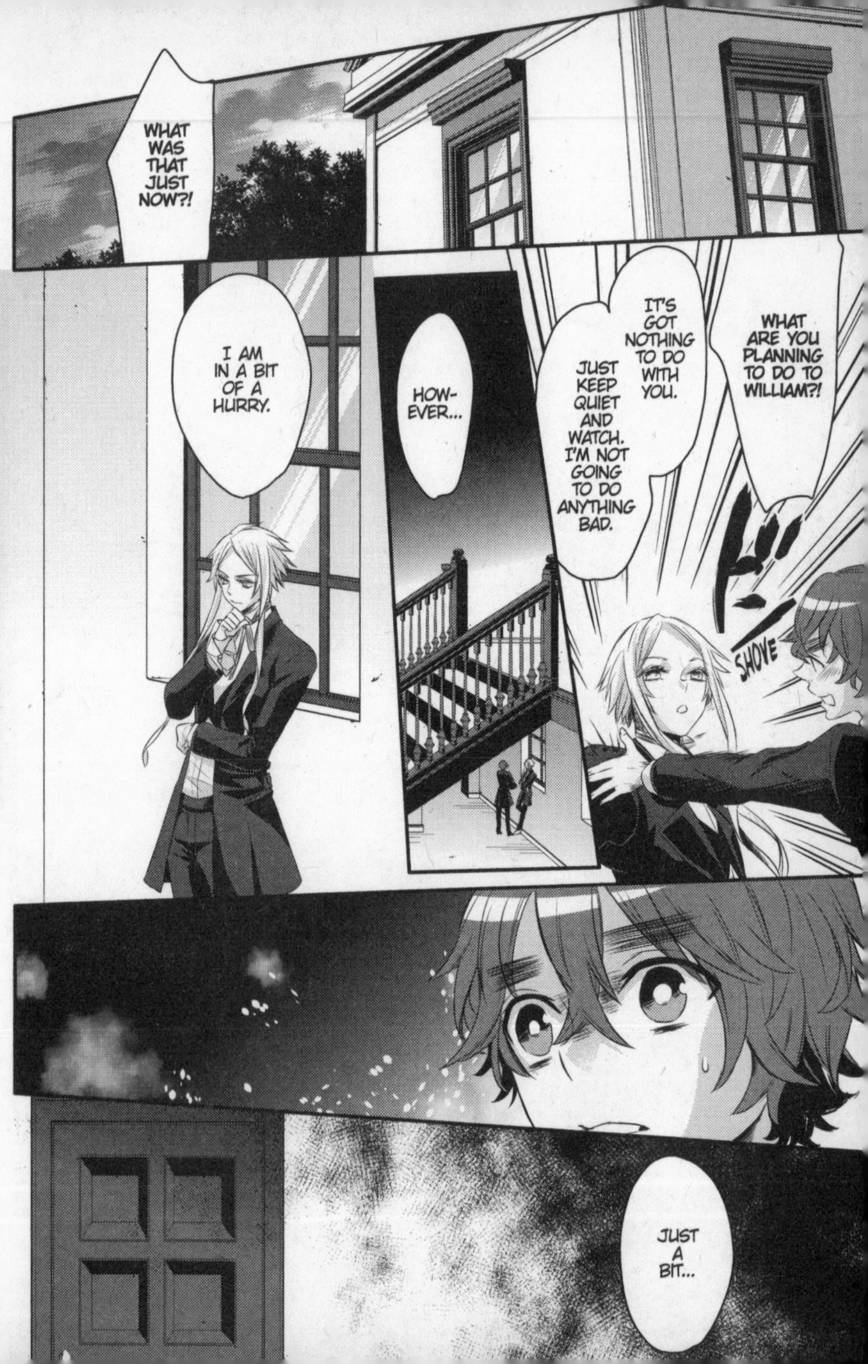
WHAT WAS THAT JUST NOW?!
WHAT ARE YOU PLANNING TO DO TO WILLIAM?!
IT'S GOT NOTHING TO DO WITH YOU. JUST KEEP QUIET AND WATCH. I'M NOT GOING TO DO ANYTHING BAD.
SHOVE
HOW-EVER...
I AM IN A BIT OF A HURRY.
JUST A BIT...

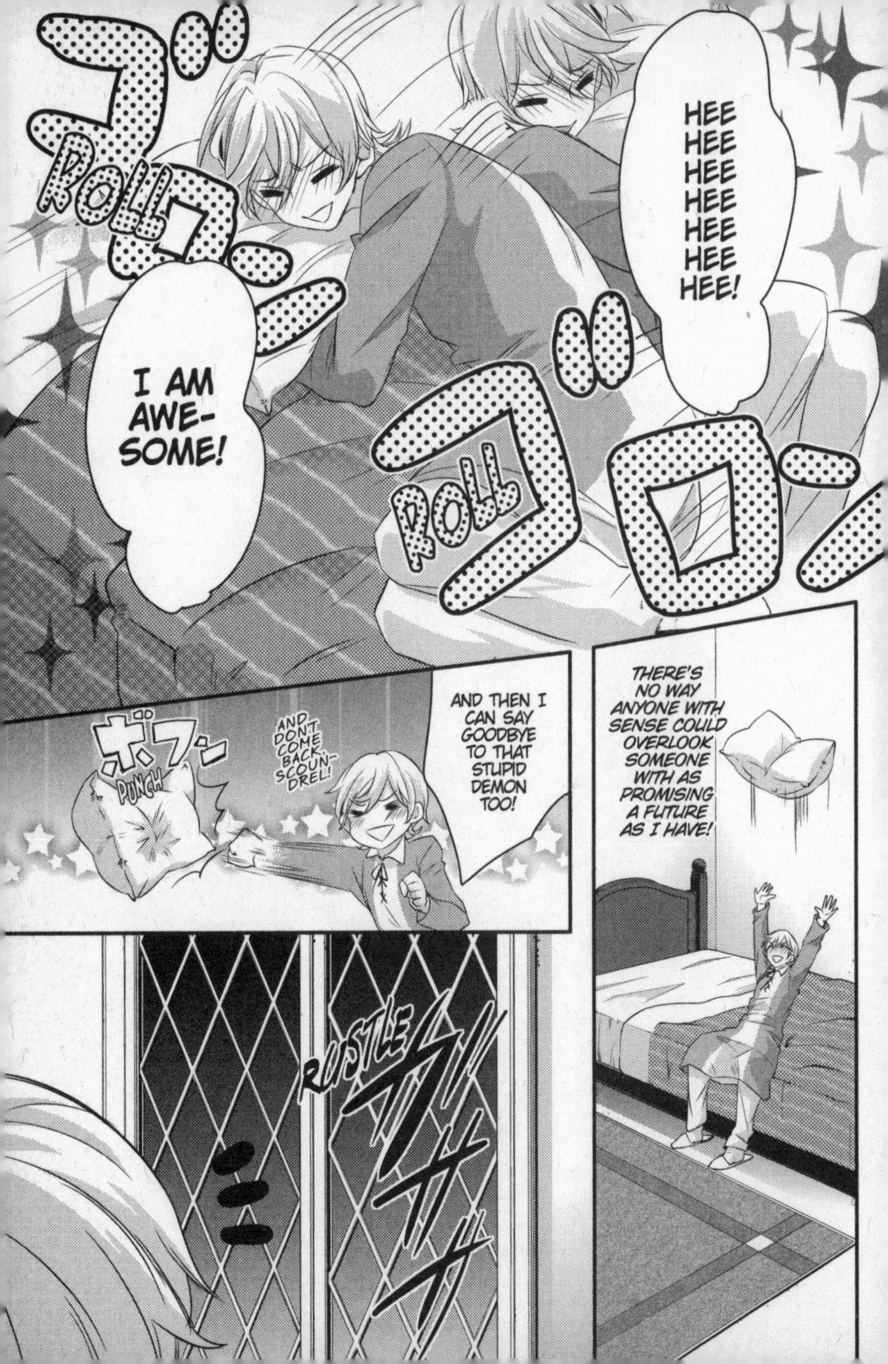
HEE HEE HEE HEE HEE HEE HEE!
I AM AWE-SOME!
ROLL
ROLL
THERE'S NO WAY ANYONE WITH SENSE COULD OVERLOOK SOMEONE WITH AS PROMISING A FUTURE AS I HAVE!
AND THEN I CAN SAY GOODBYE TO THAT STUPID DEMON TOO!
AND DON'T COME BACK, SCOUN-DREL!
PUNCH
RUSTLE

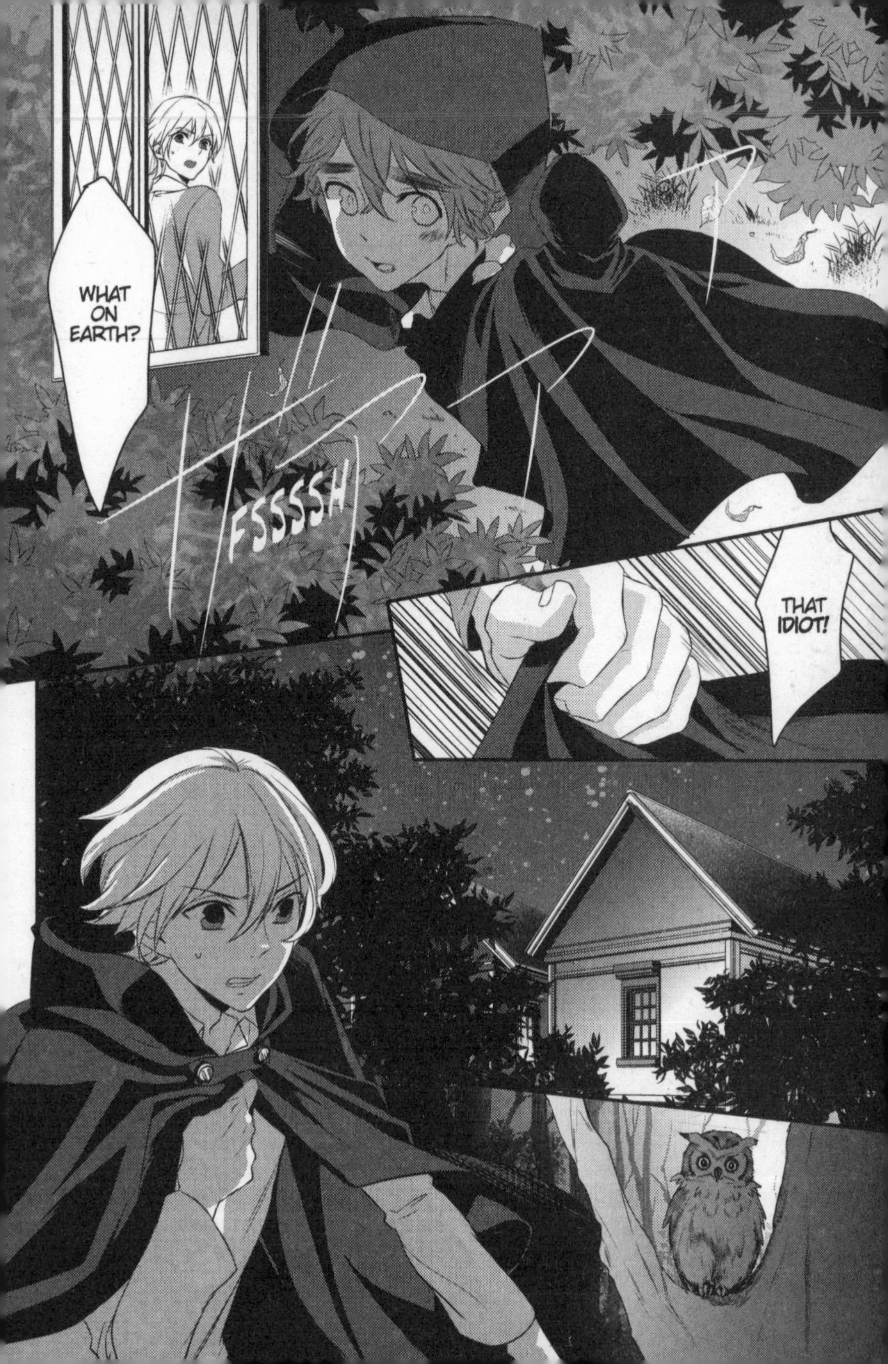
FSSSSH
WHAT ON EARTH?
THAT IDIOT!

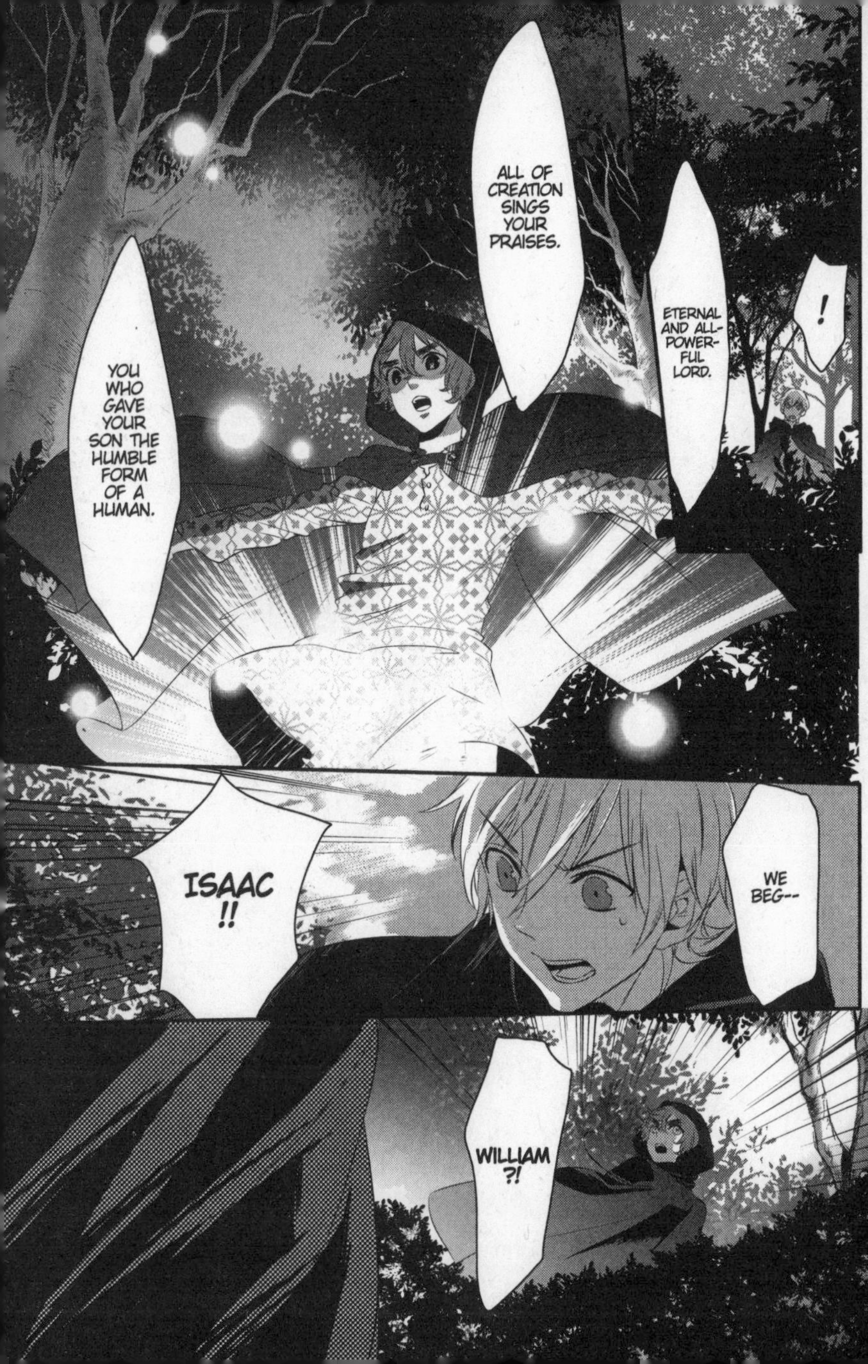
!
ETERNAL AND ALL-POWER-FUL LORD.
ALL OF CREATION SINGS YOUR PRAISES.
YOU WHO GAVE YOUR SON THE HUMBLE FORM OF A HUMAN.
WE BEG--
ISAAC!!
WILLIAM?!

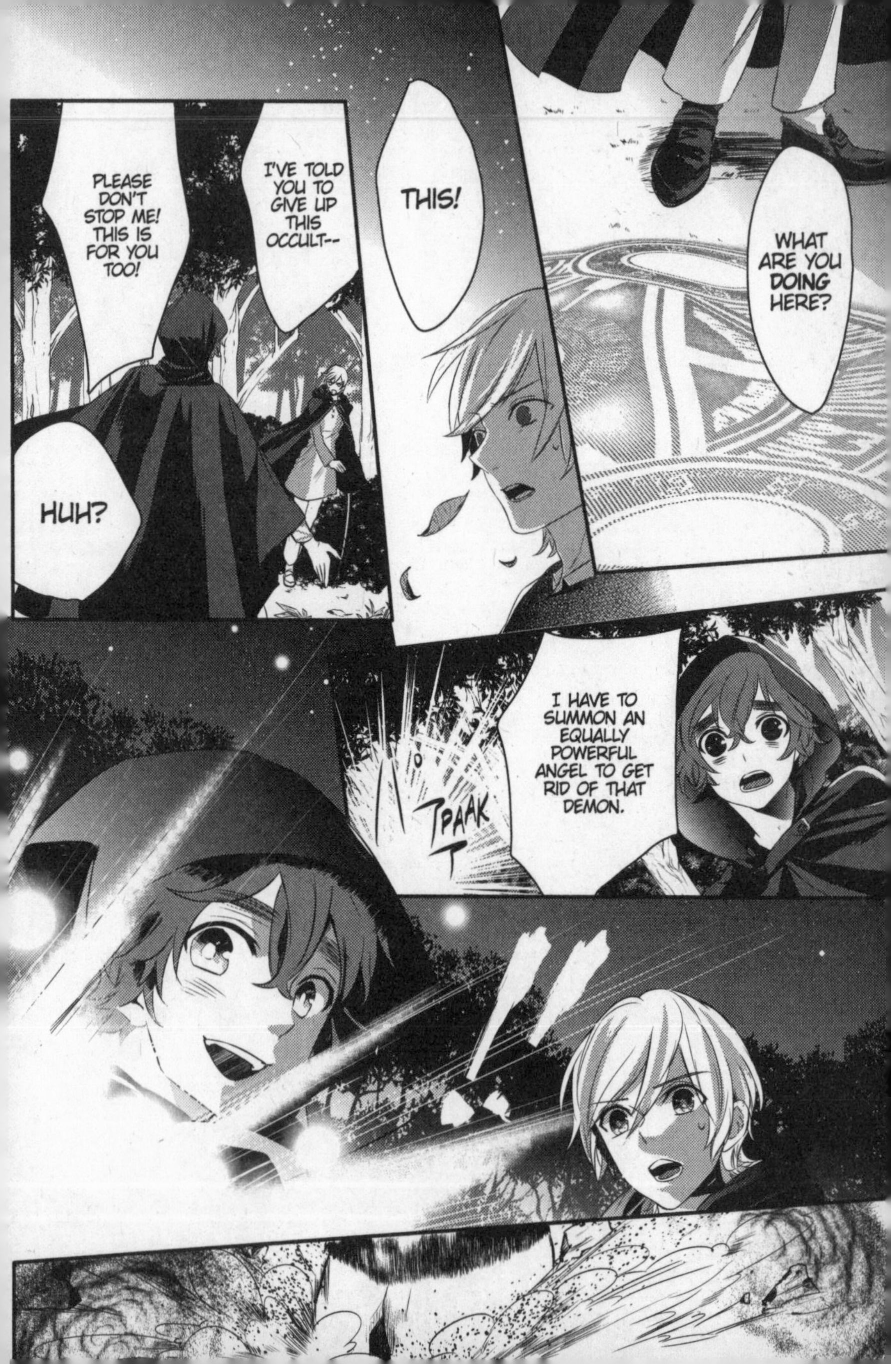
WHAT ARE YOU DOING HERE?
THIS!
I'VE TOLD YOU TO GIVE UP THIS OCCULT--
PLEASE DON'T STOP ME! THIS IS FOR YOU TOO!
HUH?
I HAVE TO SUMMON AN EQUALLY POWERFUL ANGEL TO GET RID OF THAT DEMON.
PAAK

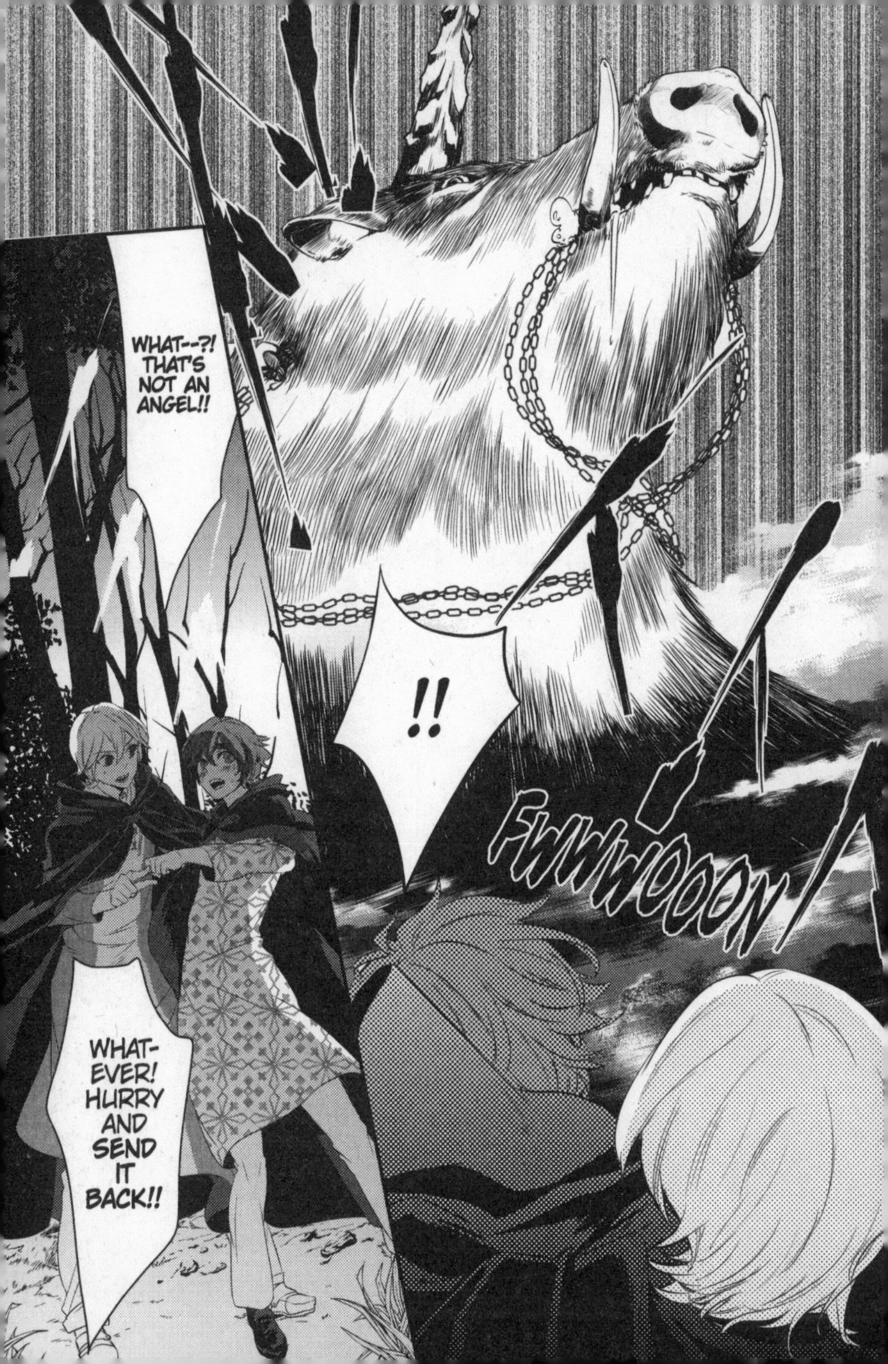
!!
FWWWOOON
WHAT--?! THAT'S NOT AN ANGEL!!
WHAT-EVER! HURRY AND SEND IT BACK!!

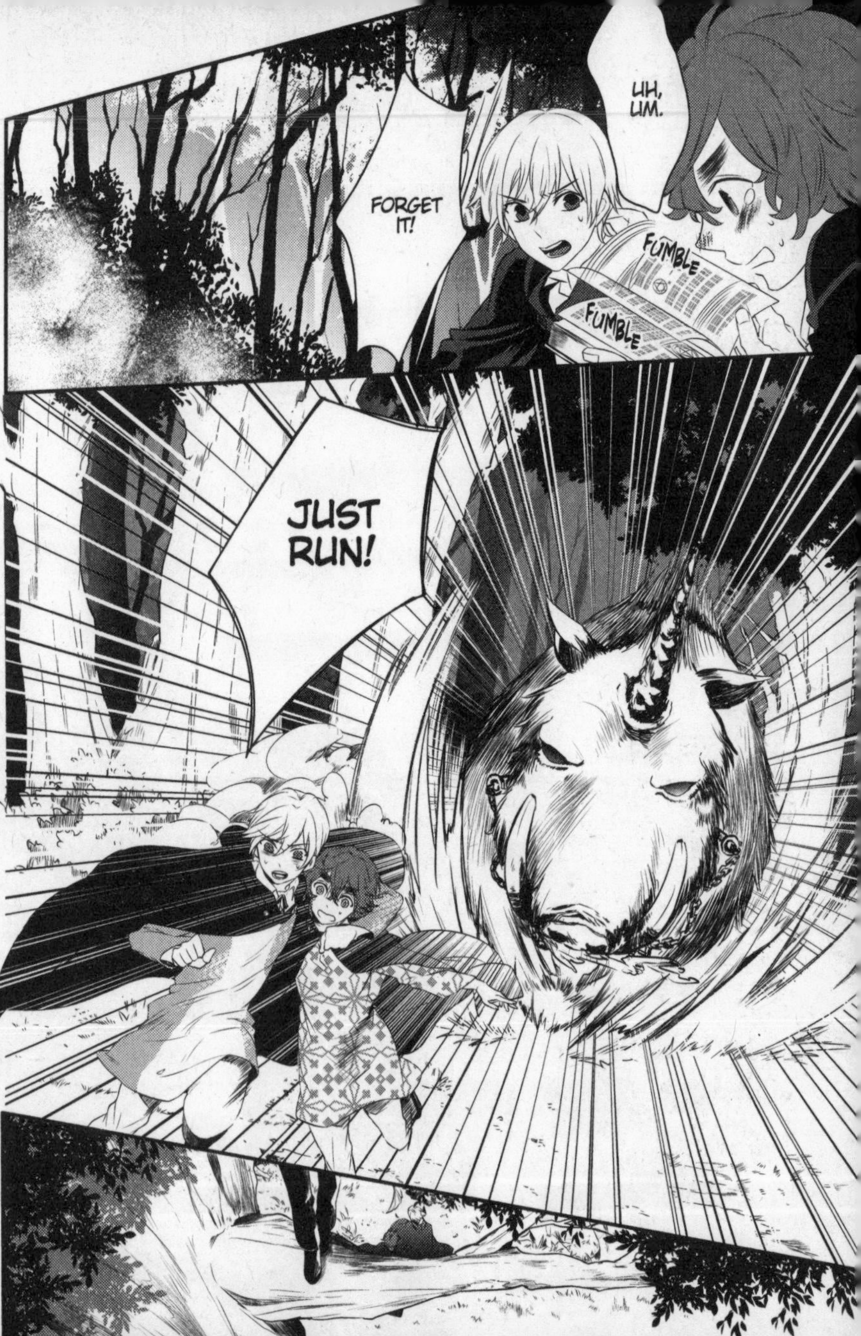
UH, UM.
FUMBLE
FUMBLE
FORGET IT!
JUST RUN!

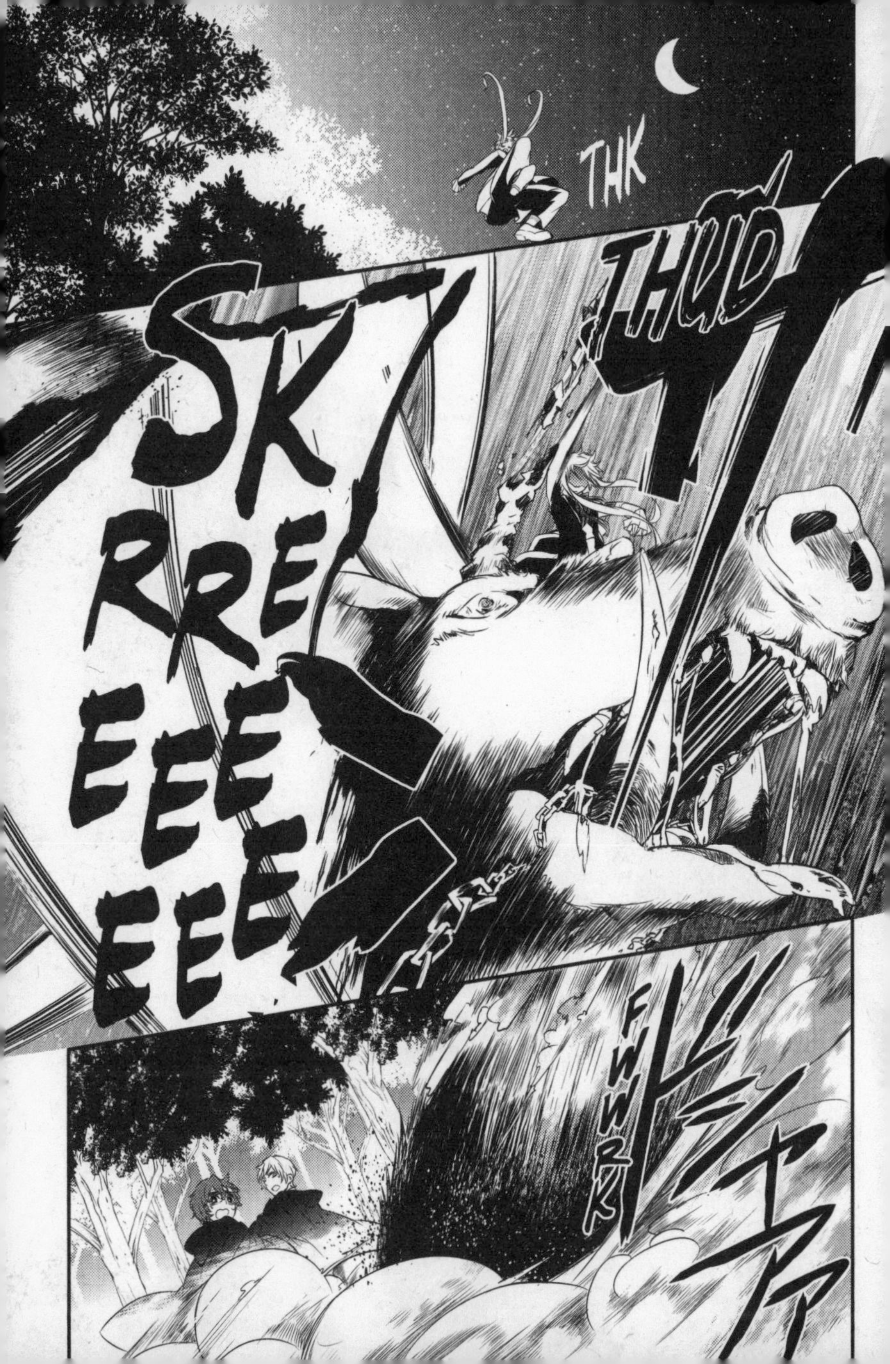

THK
THUD
SKRREEEEEEEEE
FWWRK

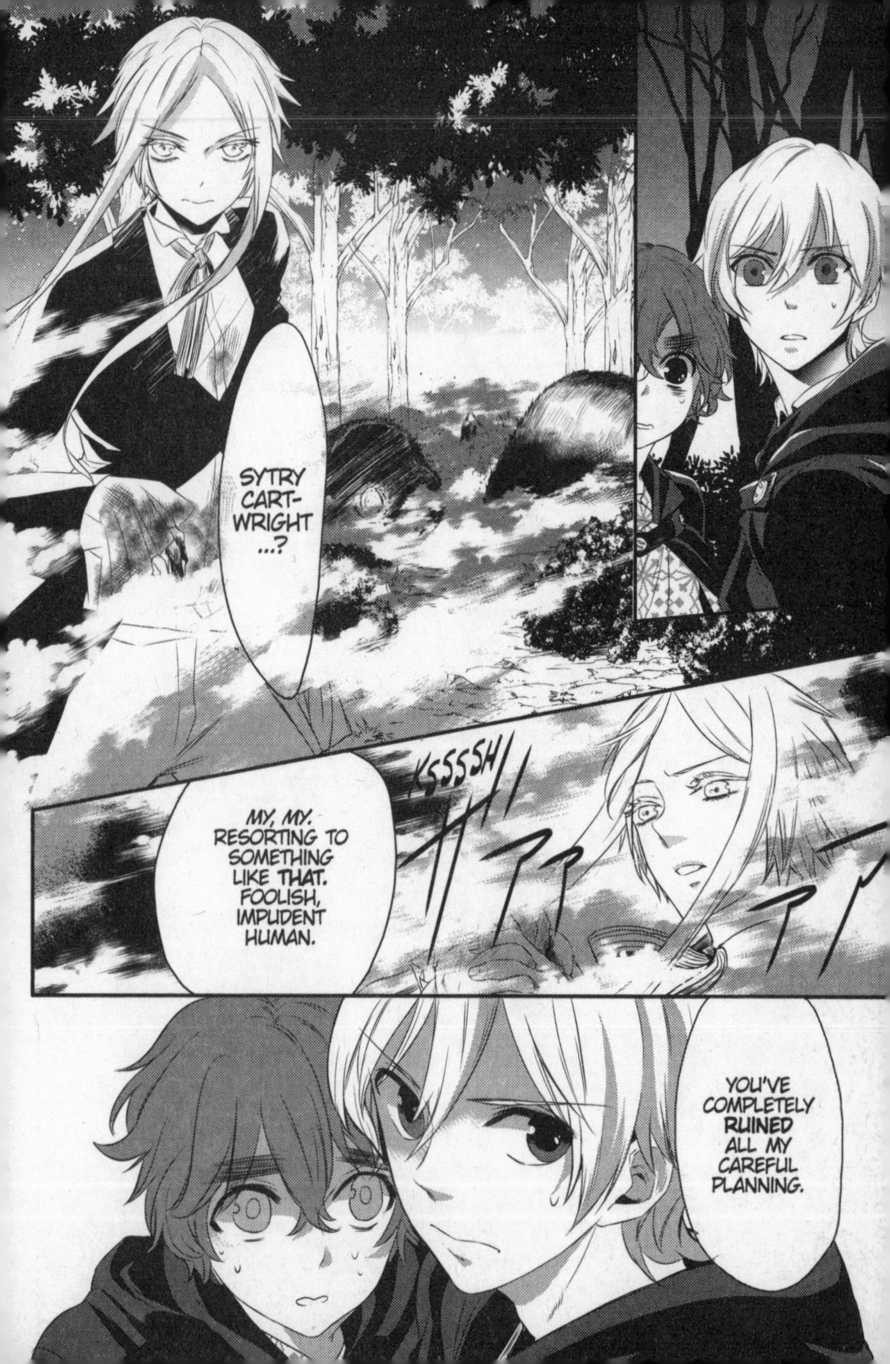
SYTRY CART-WRIGHT ...?
KSSSSH
MY, MY. RESORTING TO SOMETHING LIKE THAT. FOOLISH, IMPUDENT HUMAN.
YOU'VE COMPLETELY RUINED ALL MY CAREFUL PLANNING.

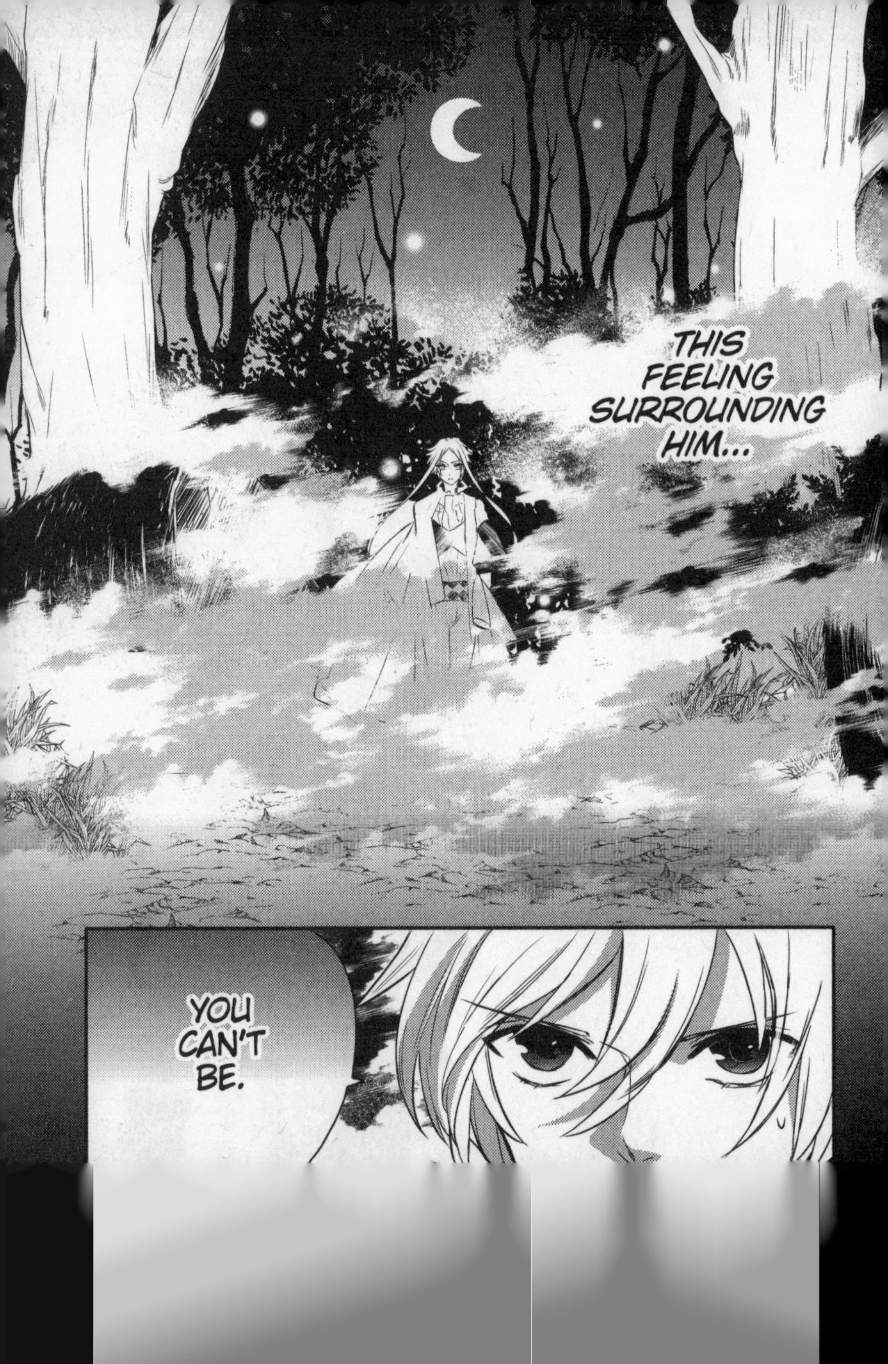
THIS FEELING SURROUNDING HIM...
YOU CAN'T BE.

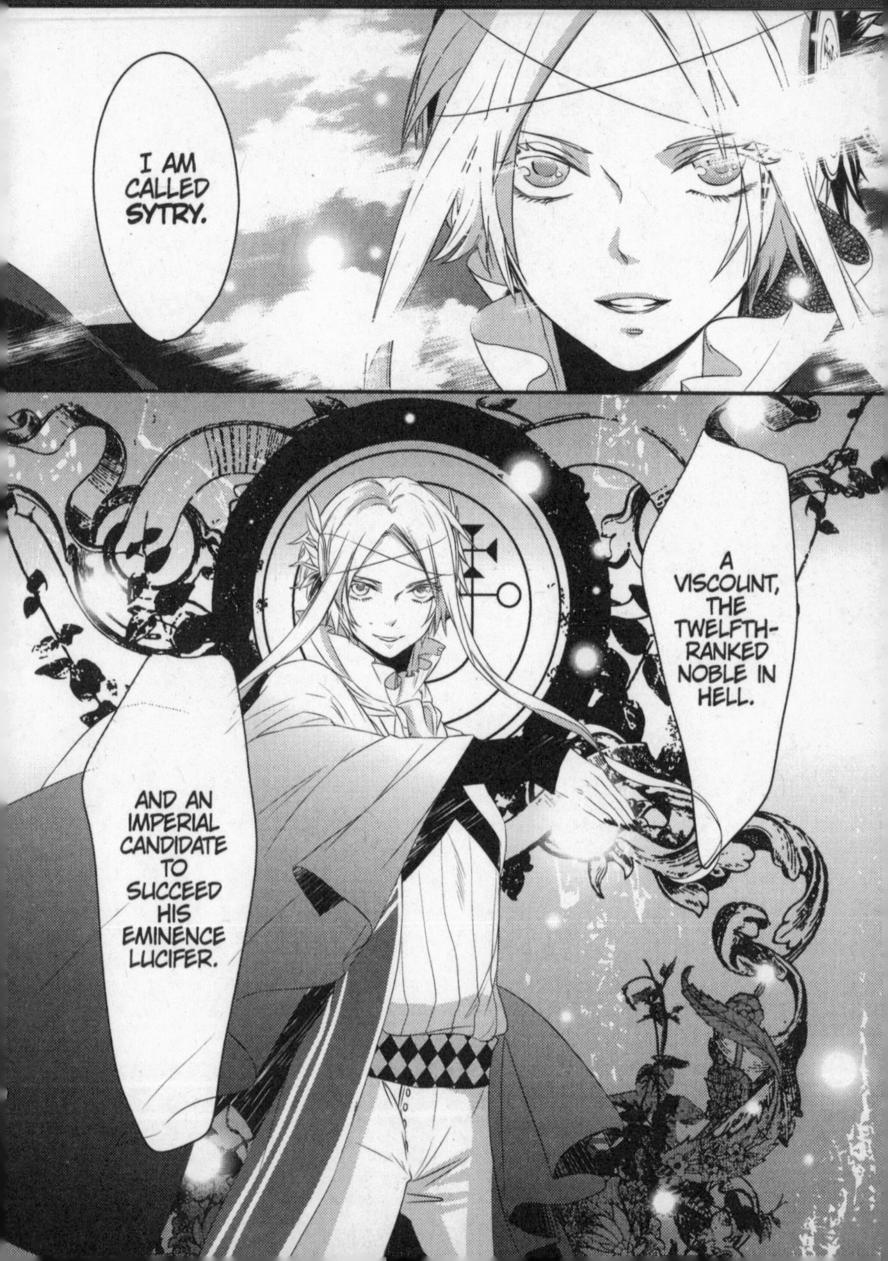
I AM CALLED SYTRY.
A VISCOUNT, THE TWELFTH-RANKED NOBLE IN HELL.
AND AN IMPERIAL CANDIDATE TO SUCCEED HIS EMINENCE LUCIFER.

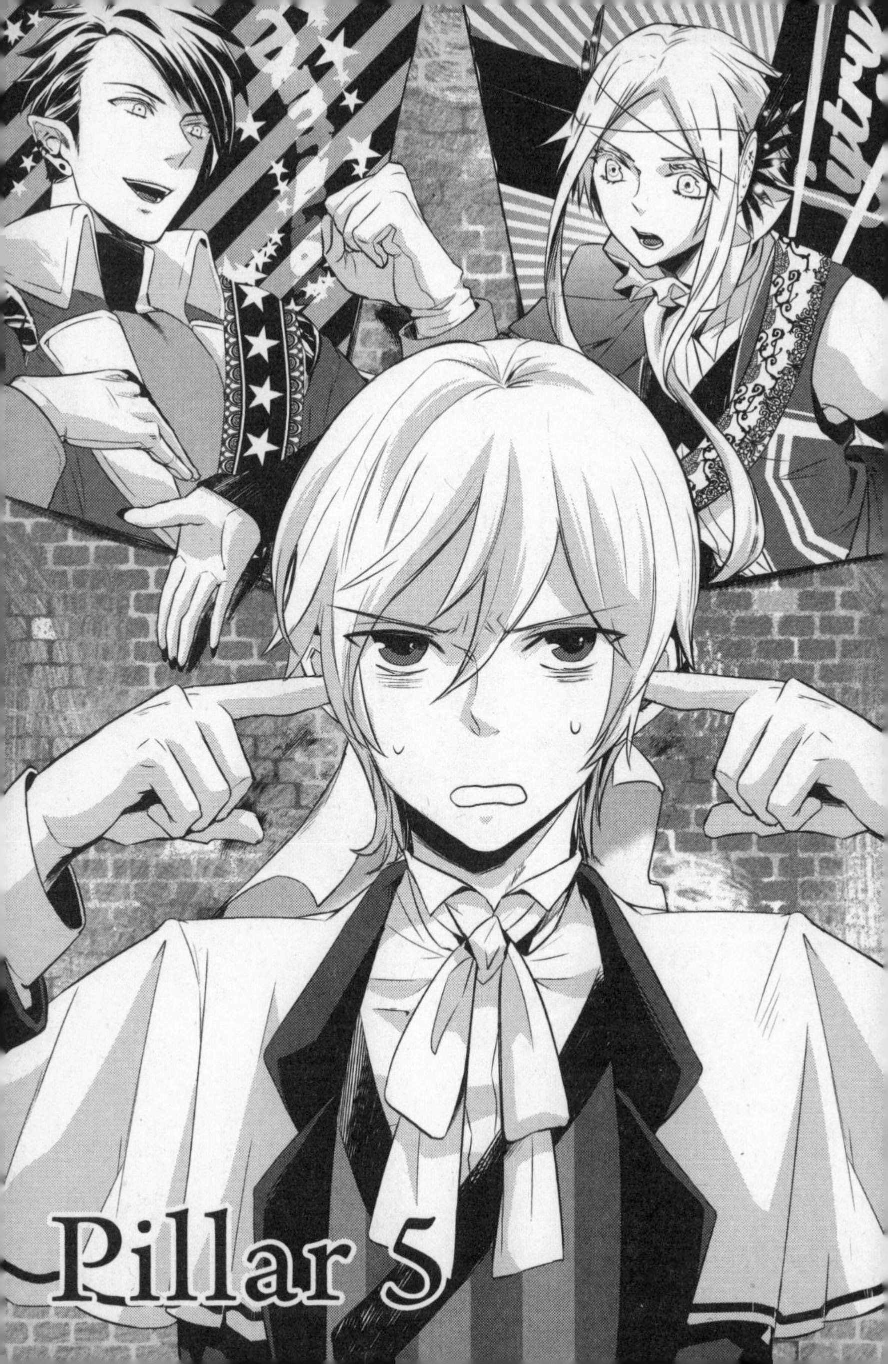
Pillar 5

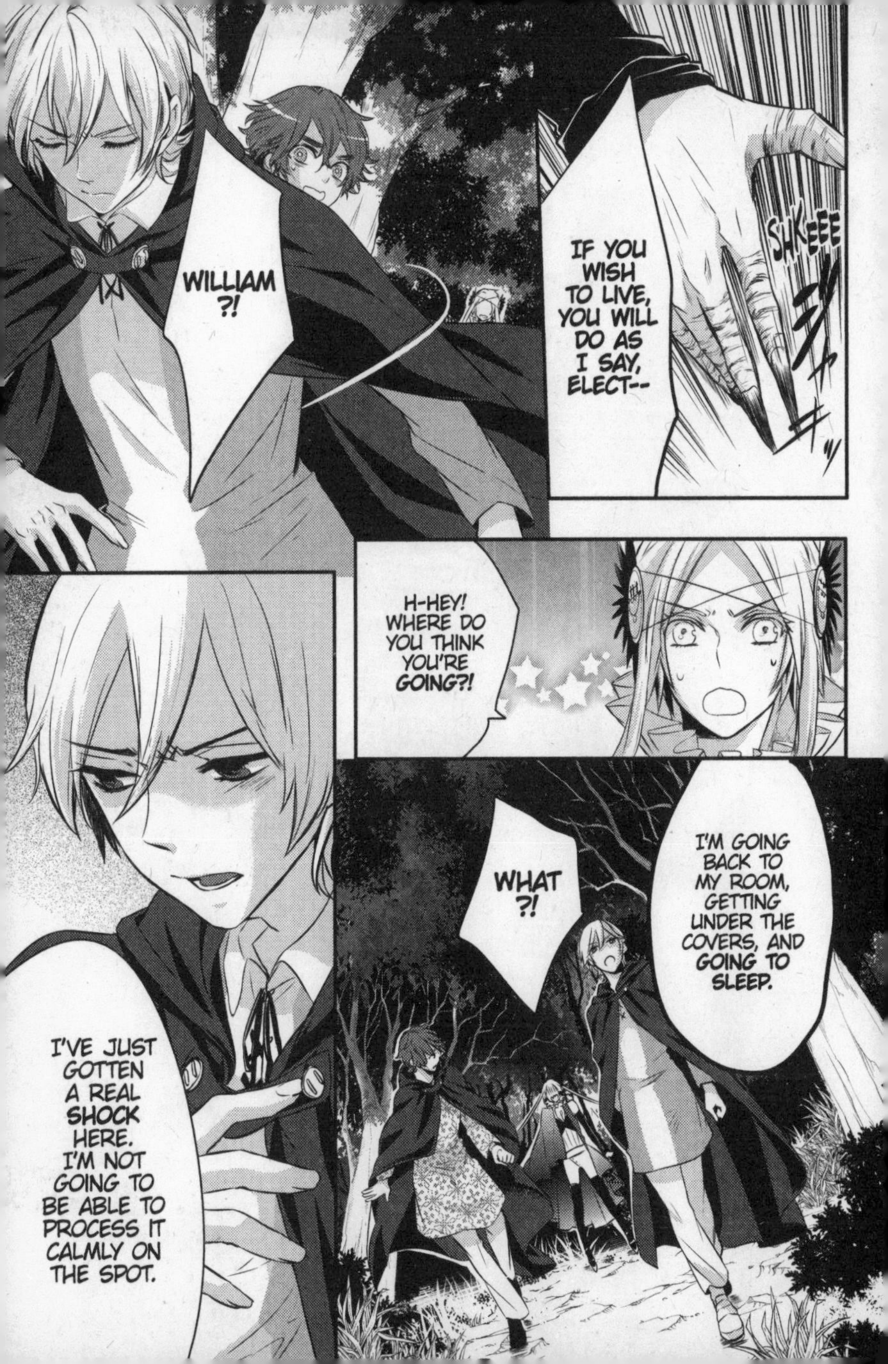
SHKEEE
IF YOU WISH TO LIVE, YOU WILL DO AS I SAY, ELECT--
WILLIAM ?!
H-HEY! WHERE DO YOU THINK YOU'RE GOING?!
I'M GOING BACK TO MY ROOM, GETTING UNDER THE COVERS, AND GOING TO SLEEP.
WHAT ?!
I'VE JUST GOTTEN A REAL SHOCK HERE. I'M NOT GOING TO BE ABLE TO PROCESS IT CALMLY ON THE SPOT.

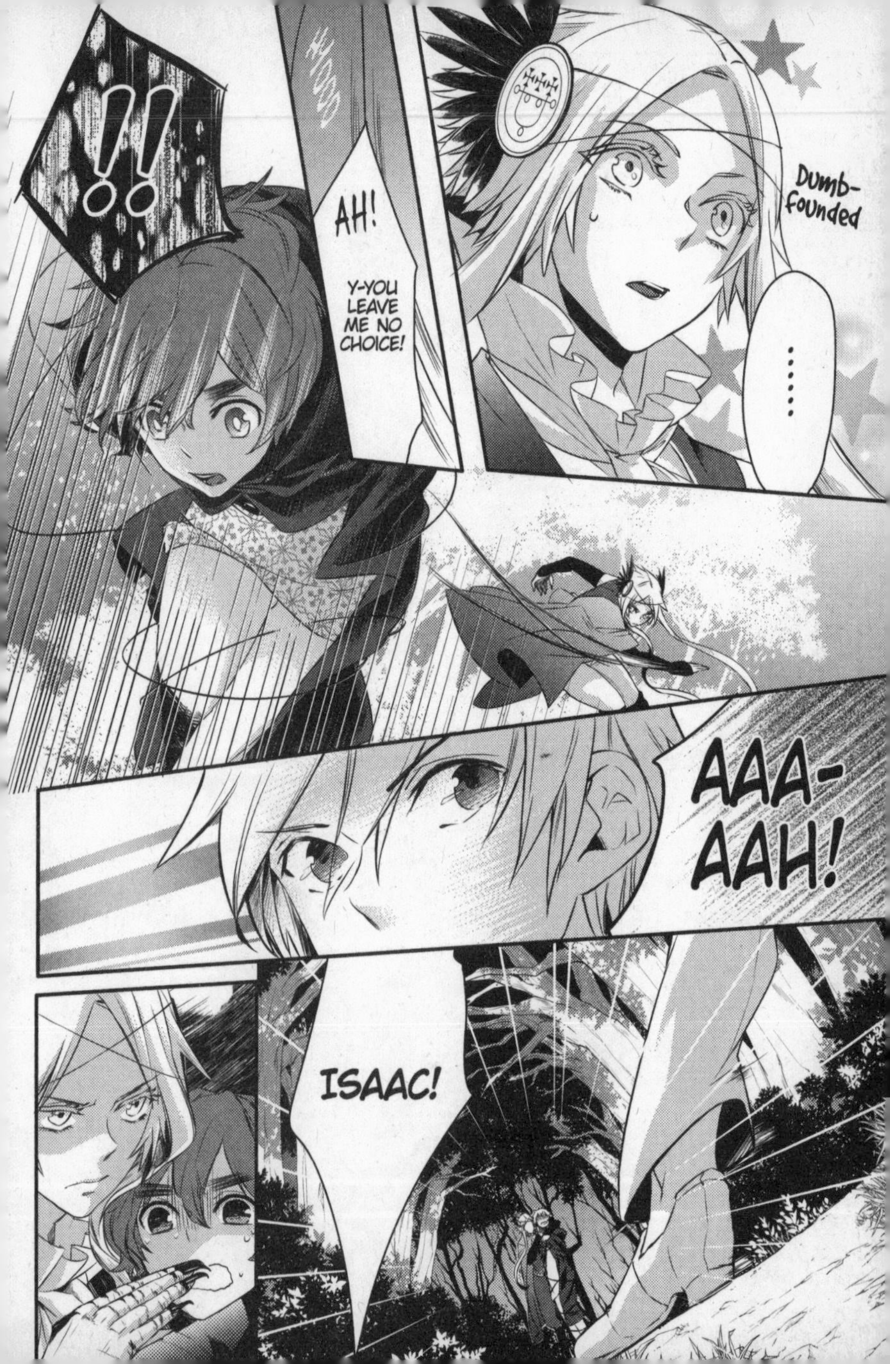
Dumb-founded
......
!!
AH!
Y-YOU LEAVE ME NO CHOICE!
AAA-AAH!
ISAAC!

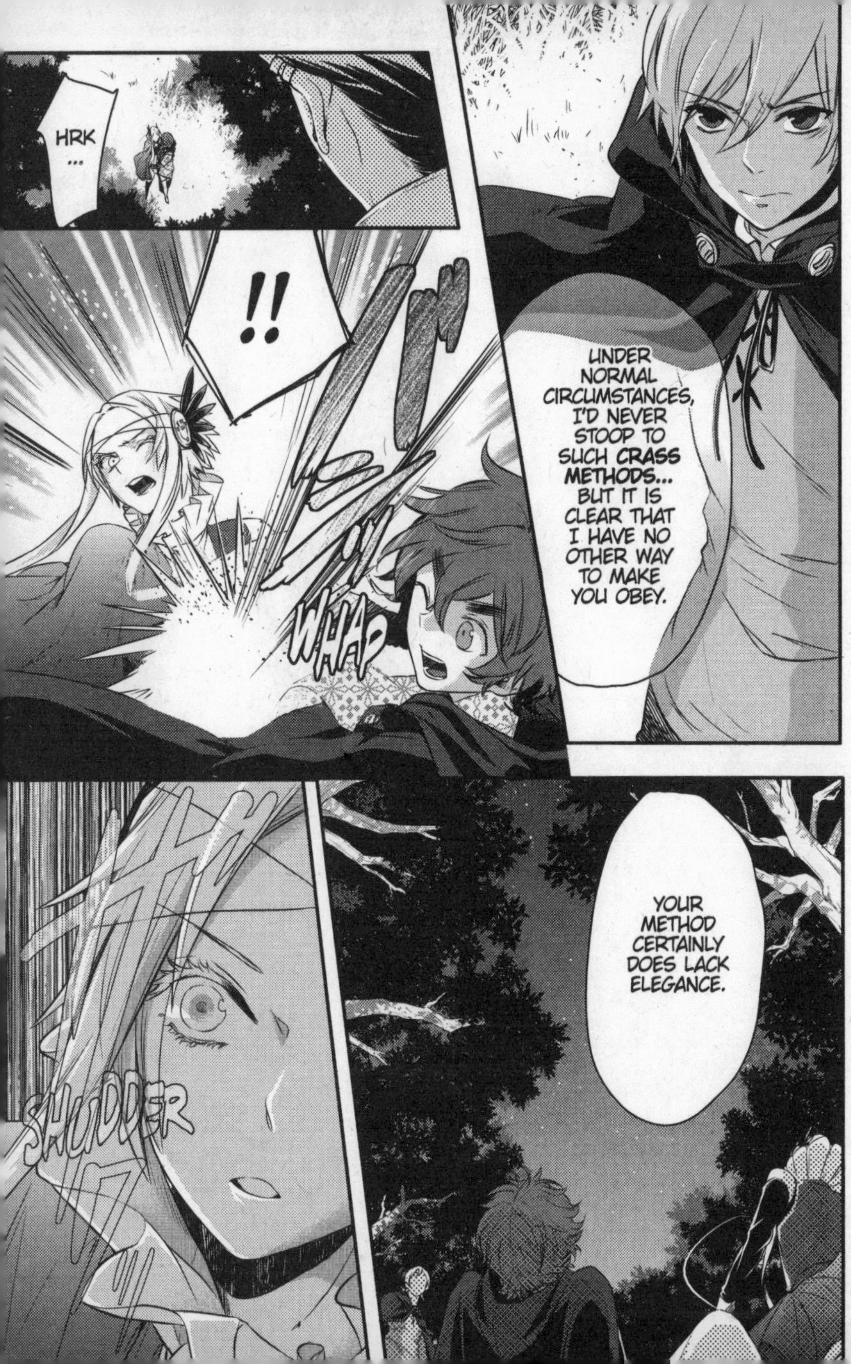
UNDER NORMAL CIRCUMSTANCES, I'D NEVER STOOP TO SUCH **CRASS METHODS...** BUT IT IS CLEAR THAT I HAVE NO OTHER WAY TO MAKE YOU OBEY.
HRK ...
!!
WHAP
YOUR METHOD CERTAINLY DOES LACK ELEGANCE.
SHUDDER

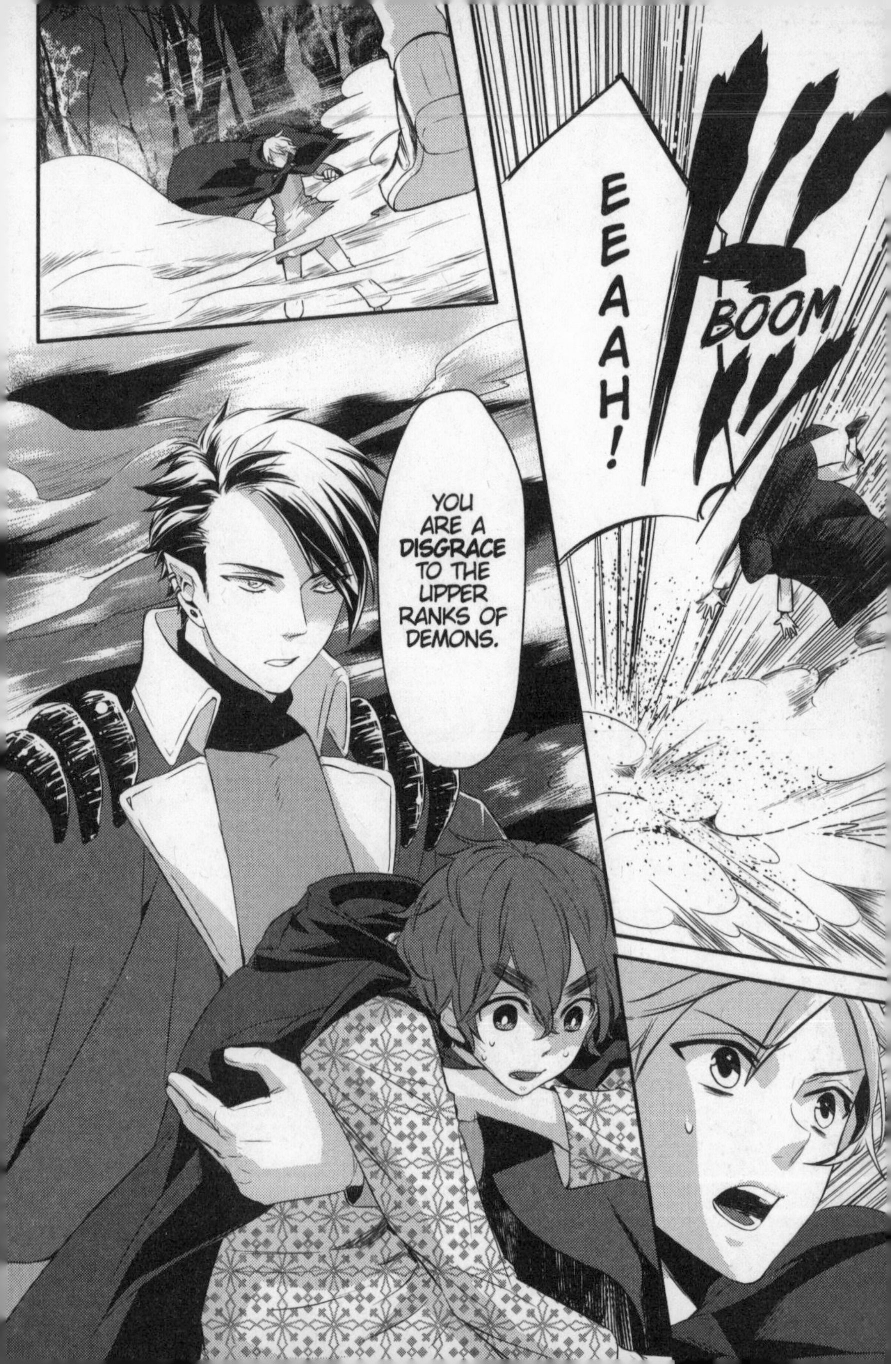
EEAAH!
BOOM
YOU ARE A DISGRACE TO THE UPPER RANKS OF DEMONS.

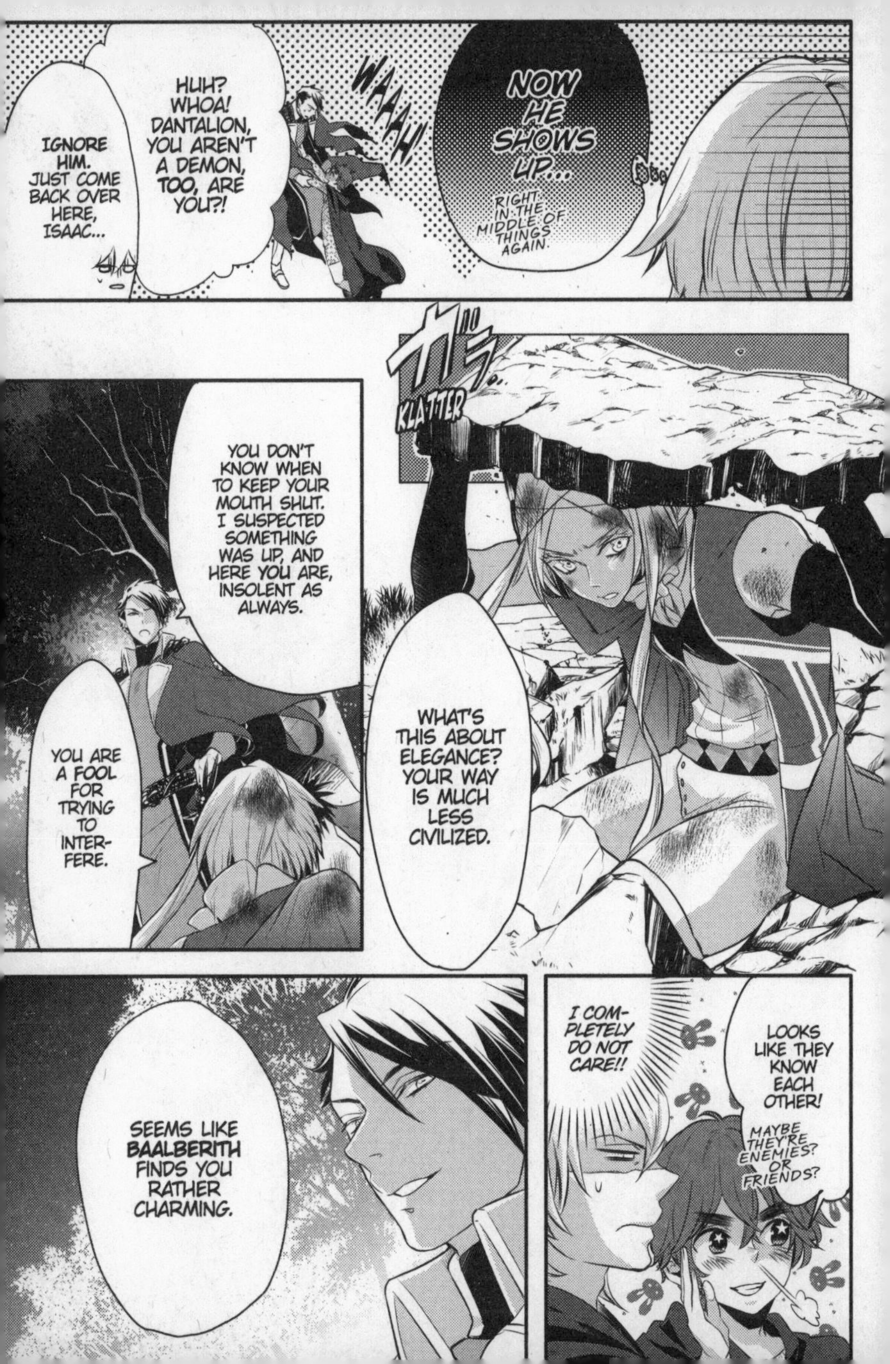
NOW HE SHOWS UP...
RIGHT IN THE MIDDLE OF THINGS AGAIN.
WAAAAH
HUH? WHOA! DANTALION, YOU AREN'T A DEMON, TOO, ARE YOU?!
IGNORE HIM. JUST COME BACK OVER HERE, ISAAC...
KLATTER
WHAT'S THIS ABOUT ELEGANCE? YOUR WAY IS MUCH LESS CIVILIZED.
YOU DON'T KNOW WHEN TO KEEP YOUR MOUTH SHUT. I SUSPECTED SOMETHING WAS UP, AND HERE YOU ARE, INSOLENT AS ALWAYS.
YOU ARE A FOOL FOR TRYING TO INTER-FERE.
LOOKS LIKE THEY KNOW EACH OTHER!
MAYBE THEY'RE ENEMIES? OR FRIENDS?
I COM-PLETELY DO NOT CARE!!
SEEMS LIKE BAALBERITH FINDS YOU RATHER CHARMING.

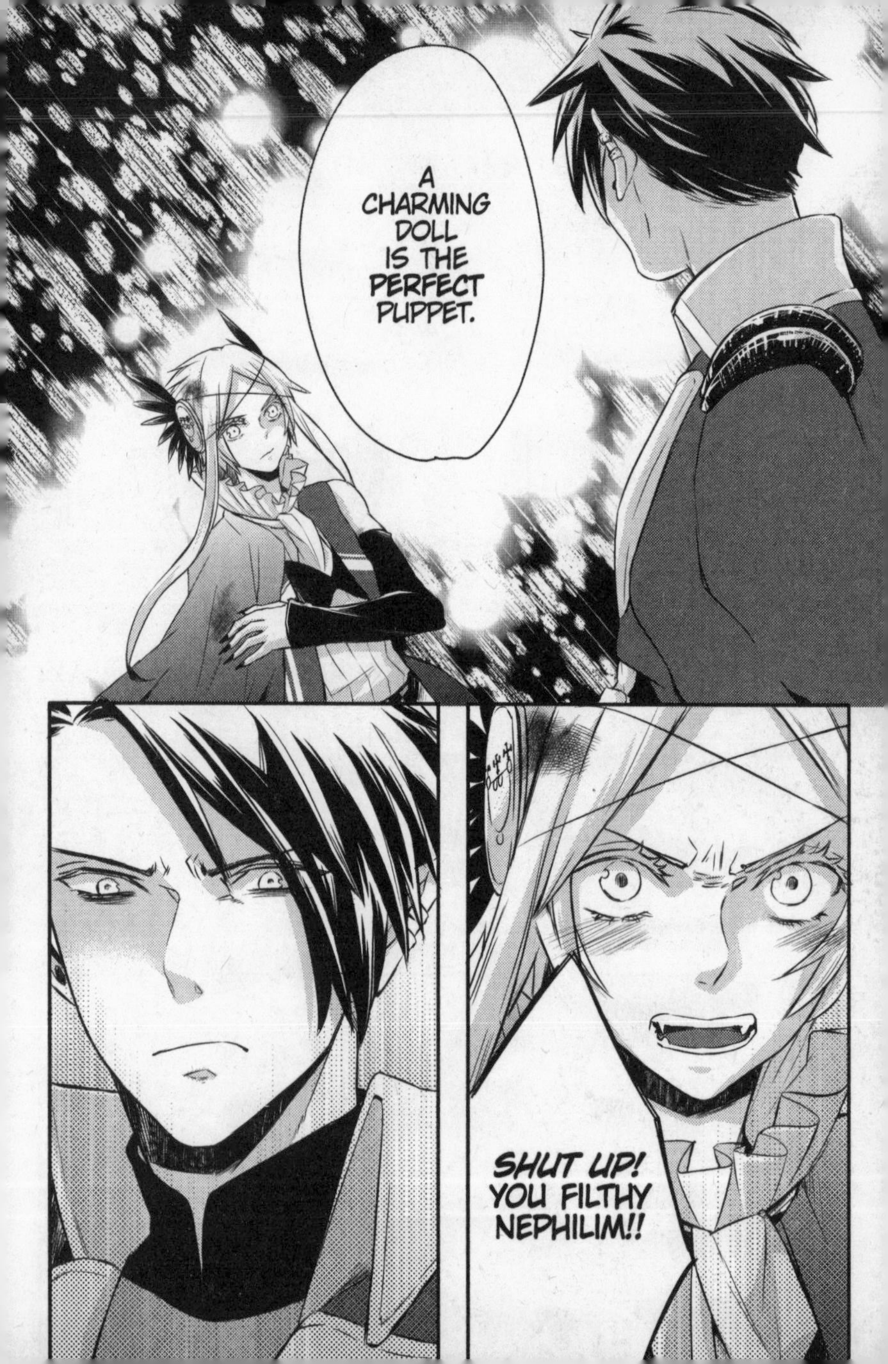
A CHARMING DOLL IS THE PERFECT PUPPET.
SHUT UP! YOU FILTHY NEPHILIM!!

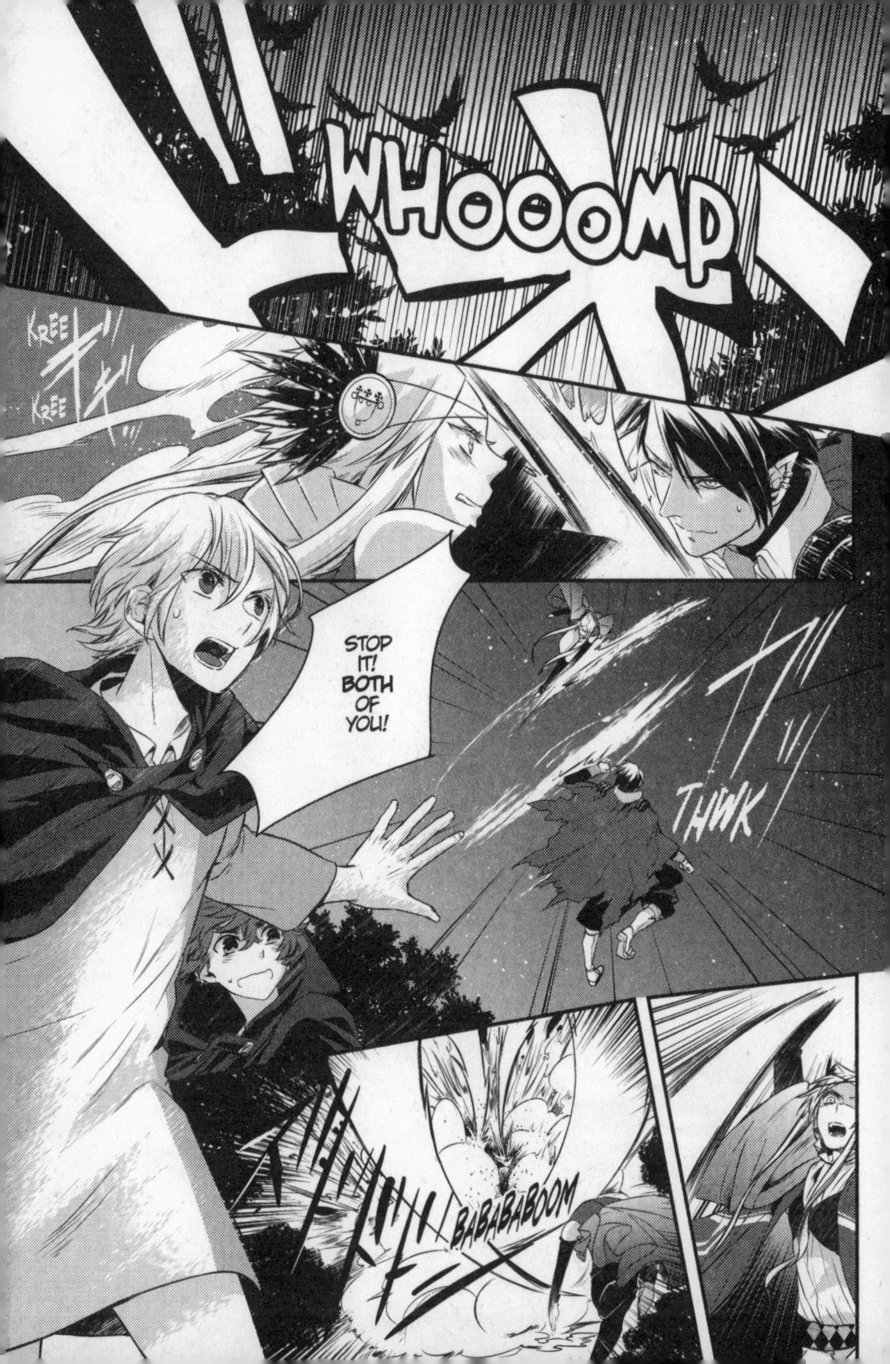
WHOOOMP
KREE
KREE
STOP IT! BOTH OF YOU!
THWK
BABABABOOM

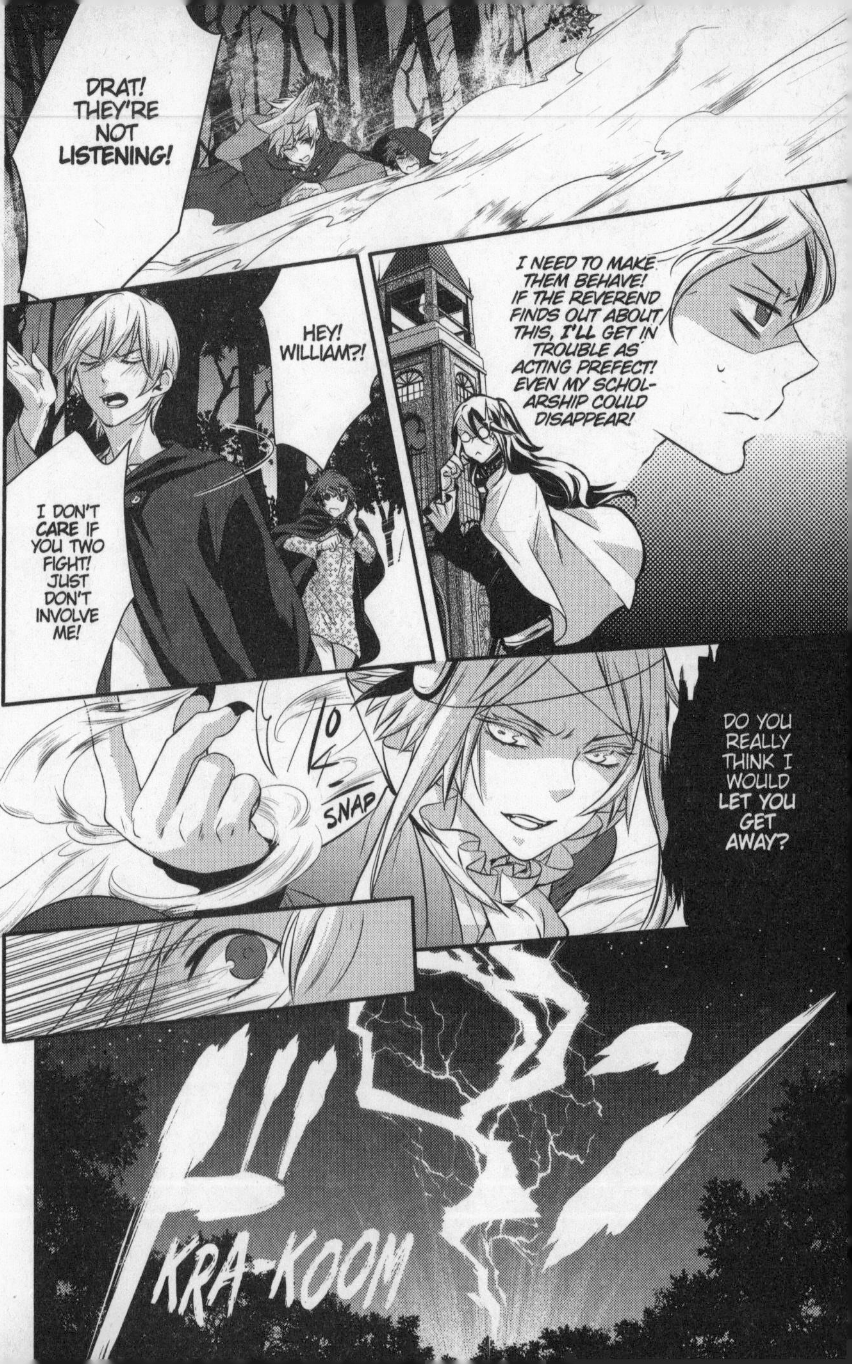
DRAT! THEY'RE NOT LISTENING!
I NEED TO MAKE THEM BEHAVE! IF THE REVEREND FINDS OUT ABOUT THIS, I'LL GET IN TROUBLE AS ACTING PREFECT! EVEN MY SCHOL-ARSHIP COULD DISAPPEAR!
HEY! WILLIAM?!
I DON'T CARE IF YOU TWO FIGHT! JUST DON'T INVOLVE ME!
DO YOU REALLY THINK I WOULD LET YOU GET AWAY?
SNAP
KRA-KOOM

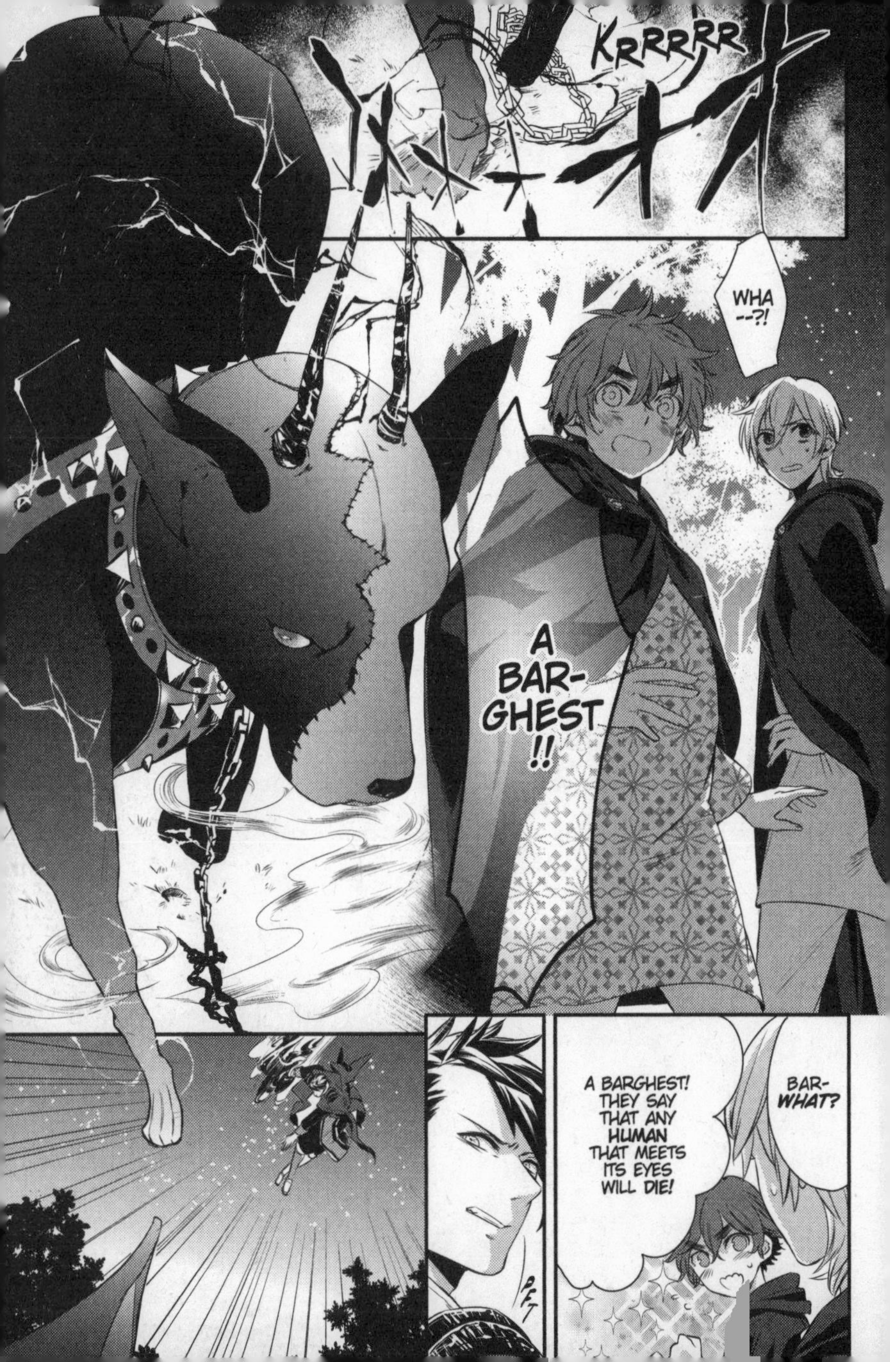
KRRRRR
WHA
--?!
A BAR-
GHEST
!!
BAR-
WHAT?
A BARGHEST!
THEY SAY
THAT ANY
HUMAN
THAT MEETS
ITS EYES
WILL DIE!

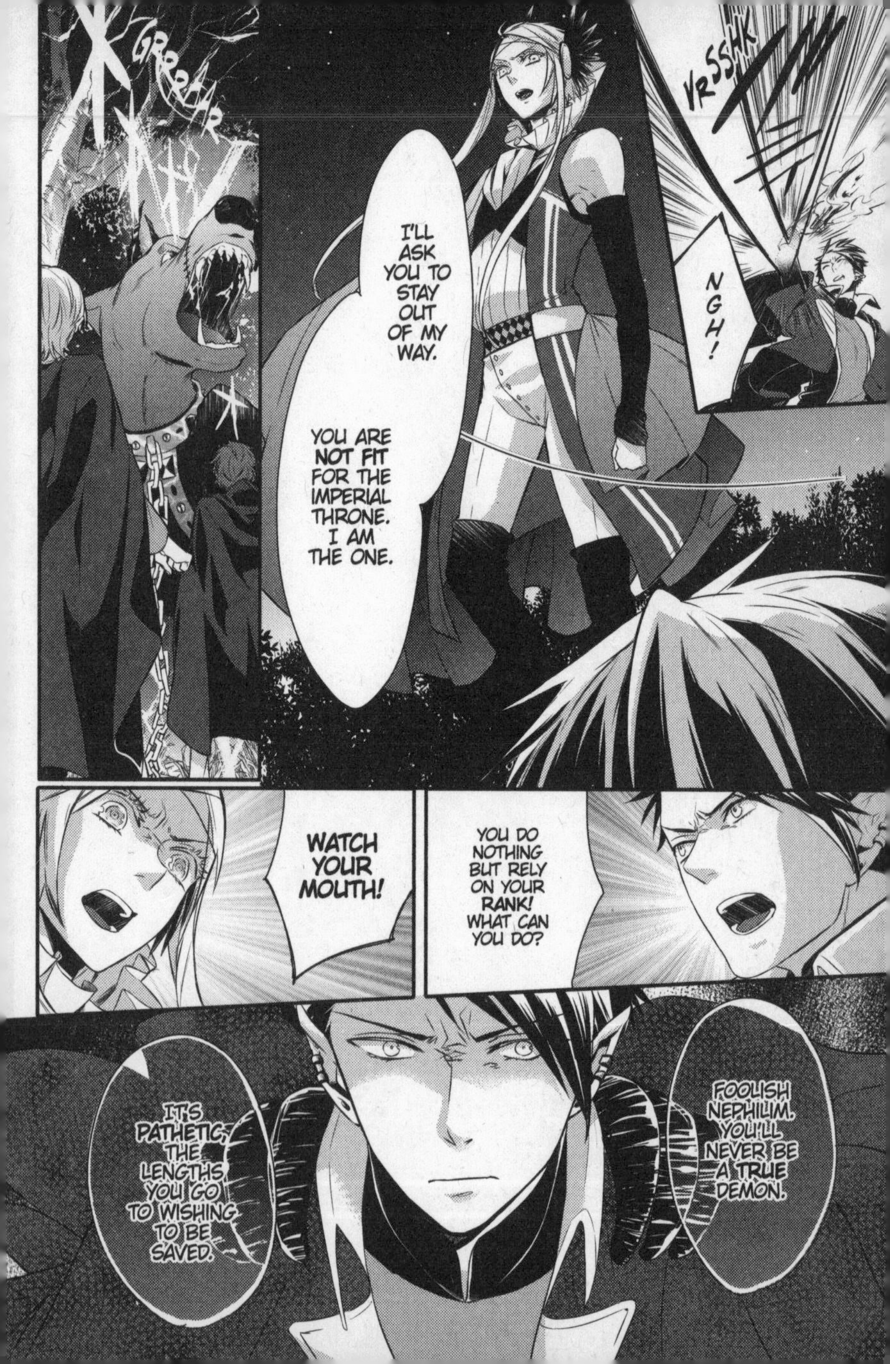
VRSSHK
NGH!
I'LL ASK YOU TO STAY OUT OF MY WAY.
YOU ARE NOT FIT FOR THE IMPERIAL THRONE. I AM THE ONE.
GRRRAR
YOU DO NOTHING BUT RELY ON YOUR RANK! WHAT CAN YOU DO?
WATCH YOUR MOUTH!
FOOLISH NEPHILIM. YOU'LL NEVER BE A TRUE DEMON.
IT'S PATHETIC, THE LENGTHS YOU GO TO WISHING TO BE SAVED.

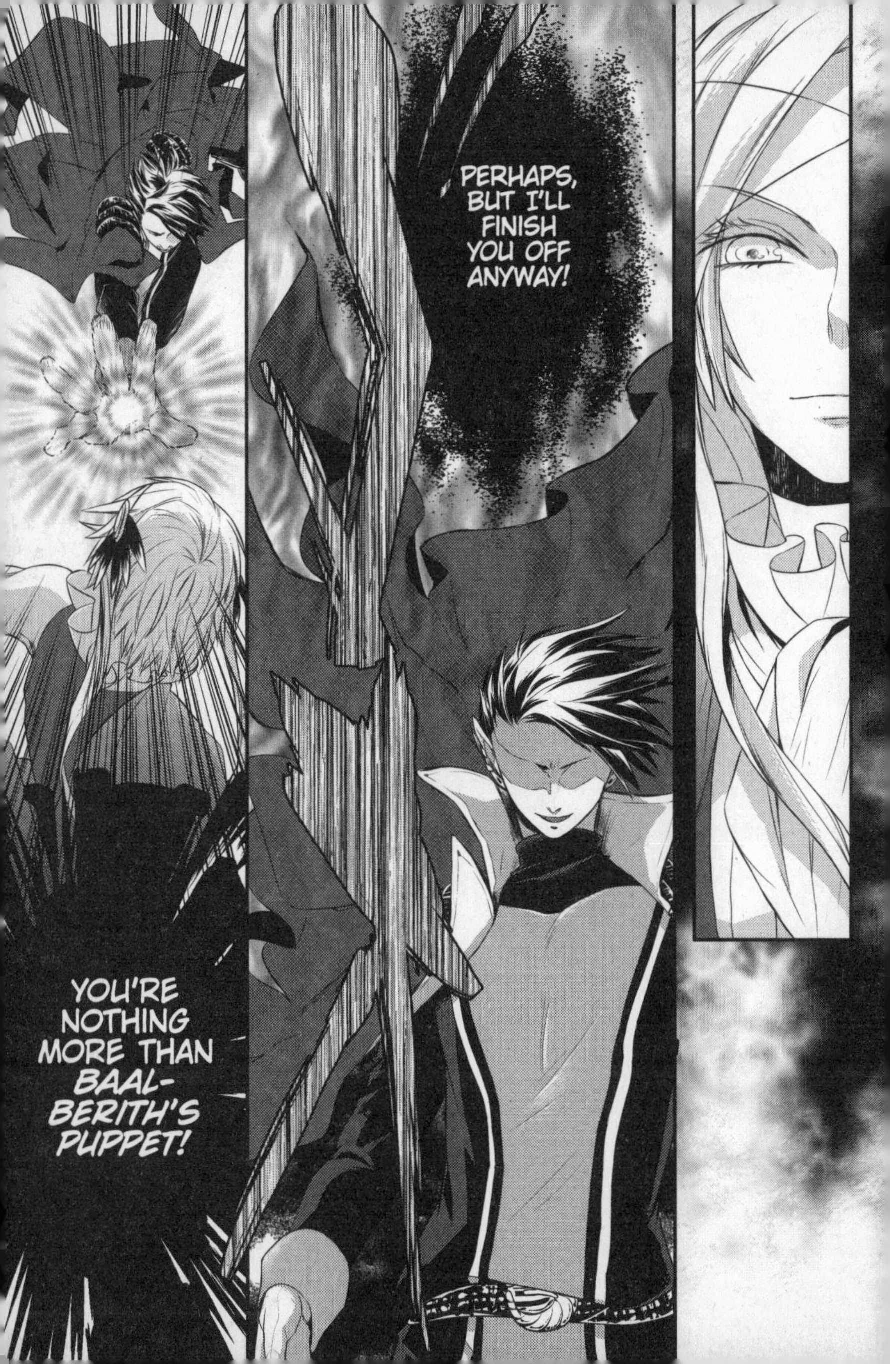
PERHAPS, BUT I'LL FINISH YOU OFF ANYWAY!
YOU'RE NOTHING MORE THAN *BAAL-BERITH'S* PUPPET!

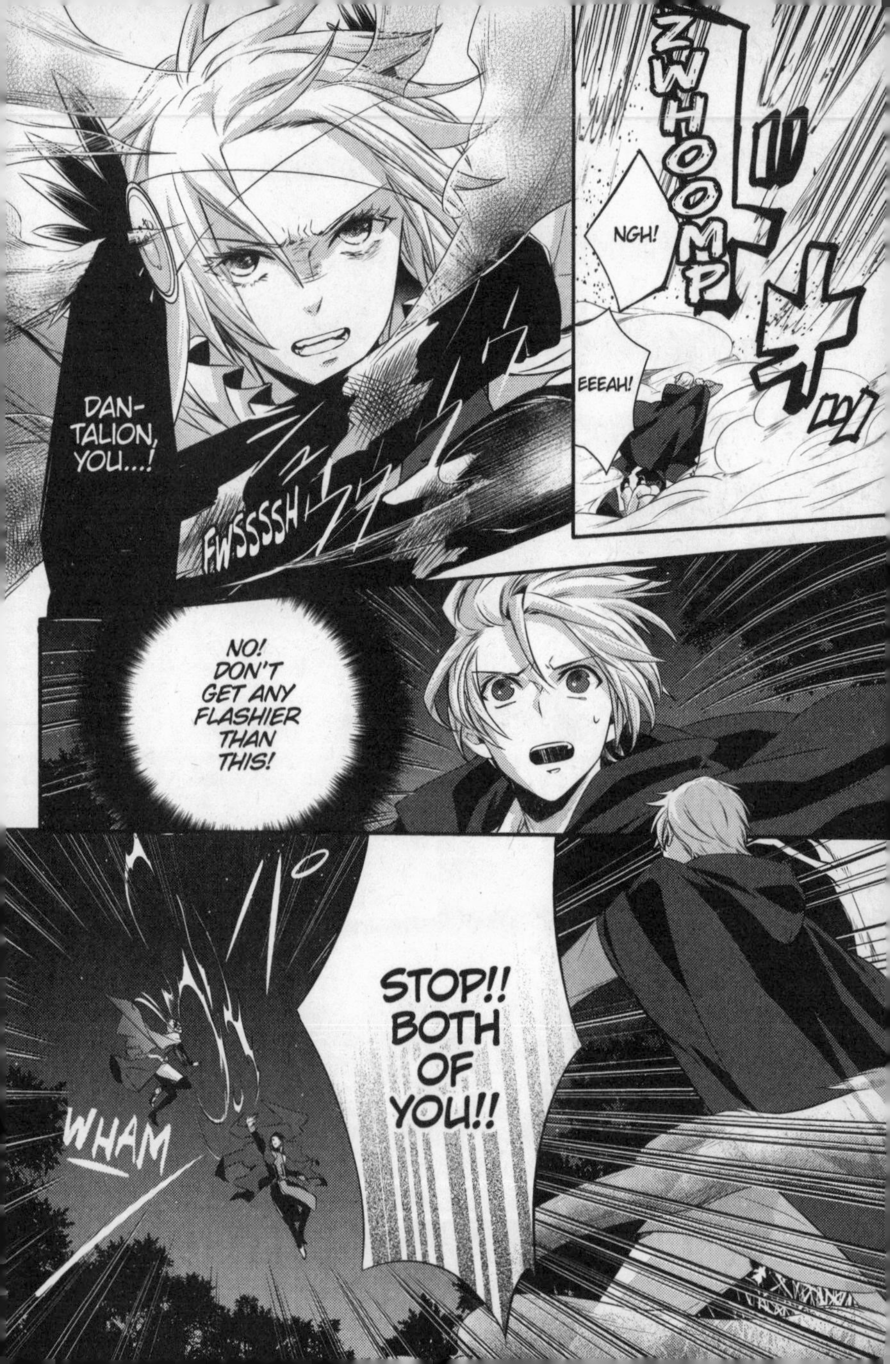
ZWHOOMP
NGH!
EEEAH!
DAN-TALION, YOU...!
FWSSSSH
NO! DON'T GET ANY FLASHIER THAN THIS!
STOP!! BOTH OF YOU!!
WHAM

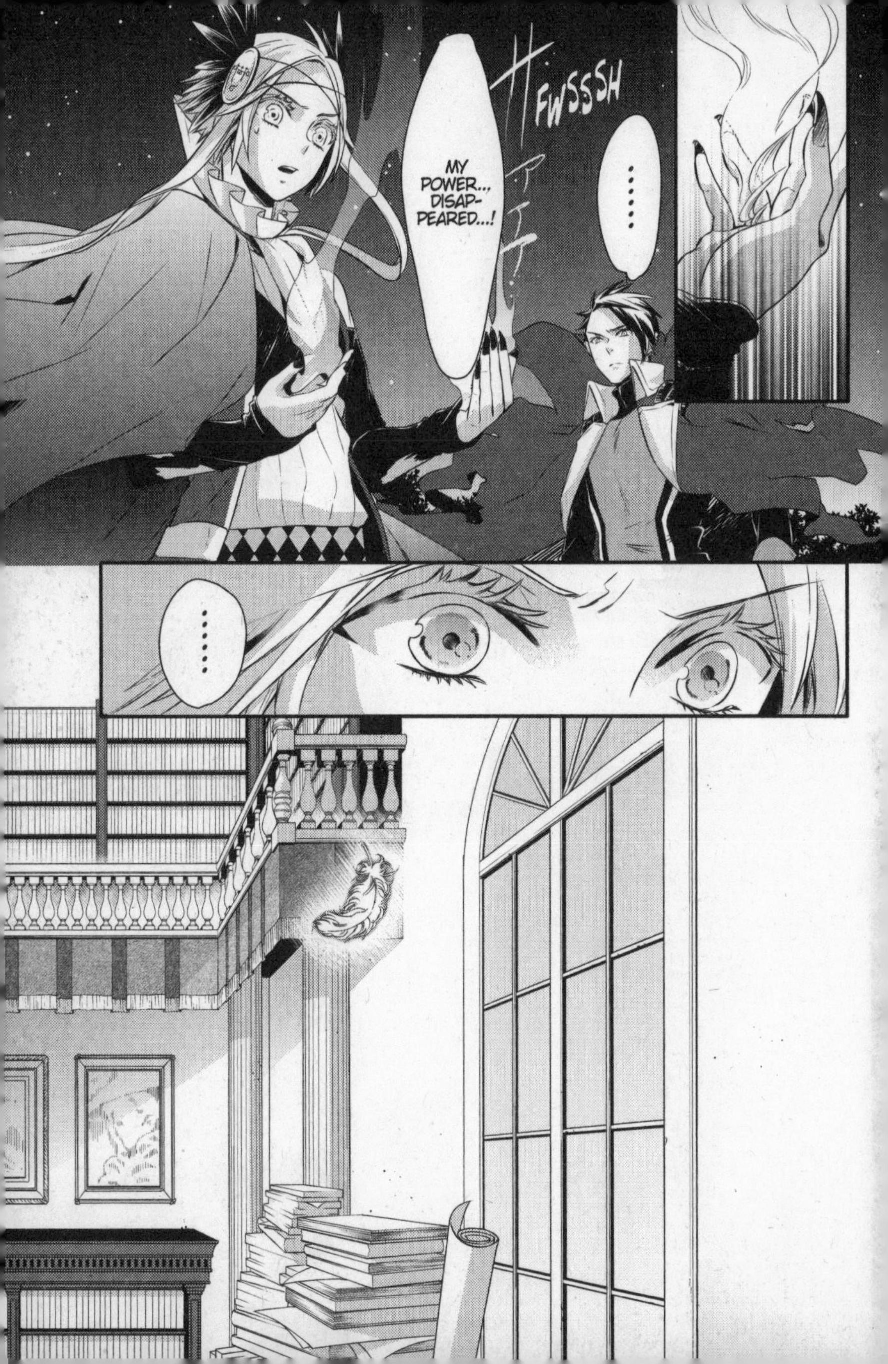
FWSSSH
......
MY POWER..., DISAPPEARED...!
......

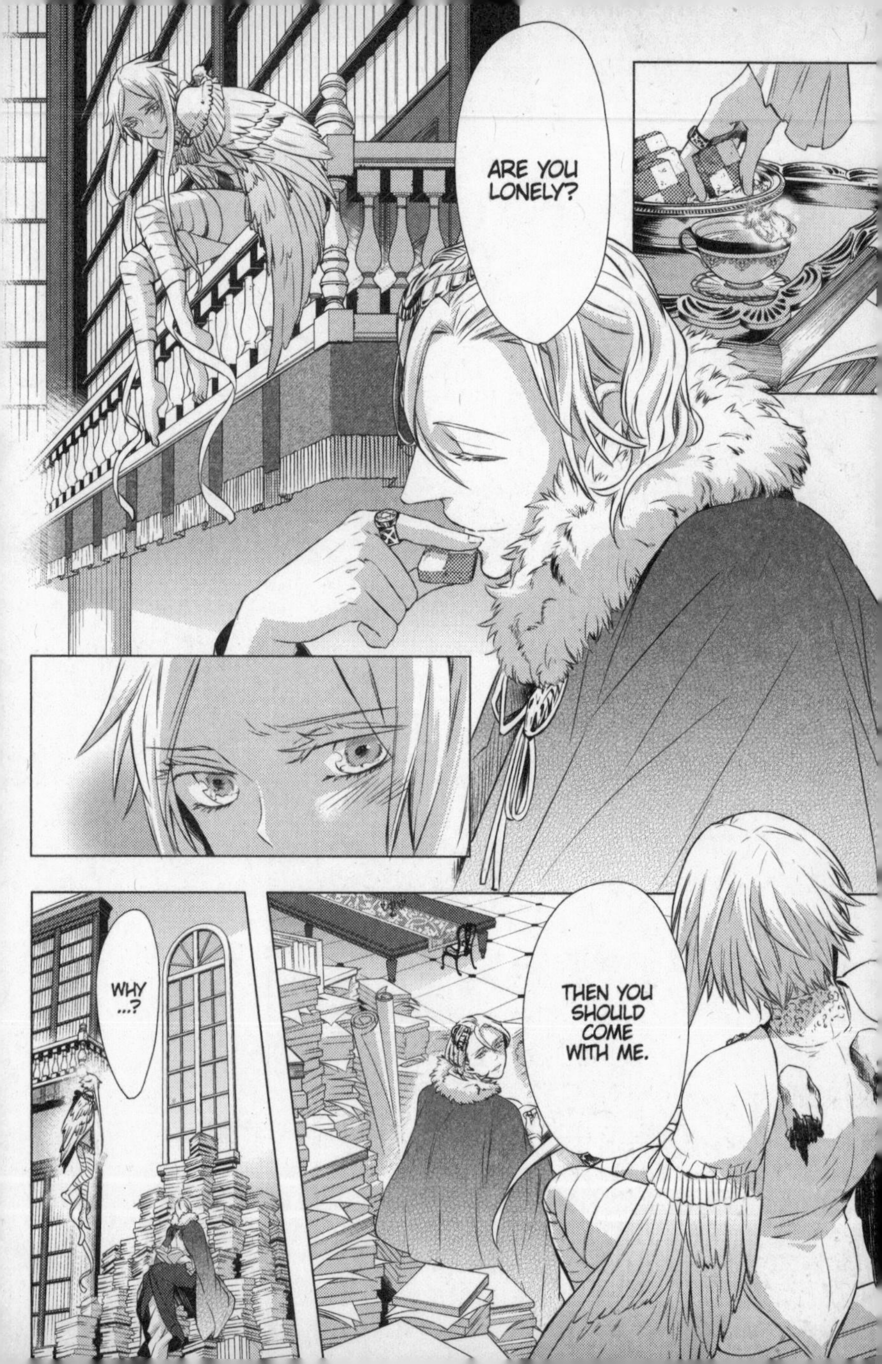
ARE YOU LONELY?
THEN YOU SHOULD COME WITH ME.
WHY ...?

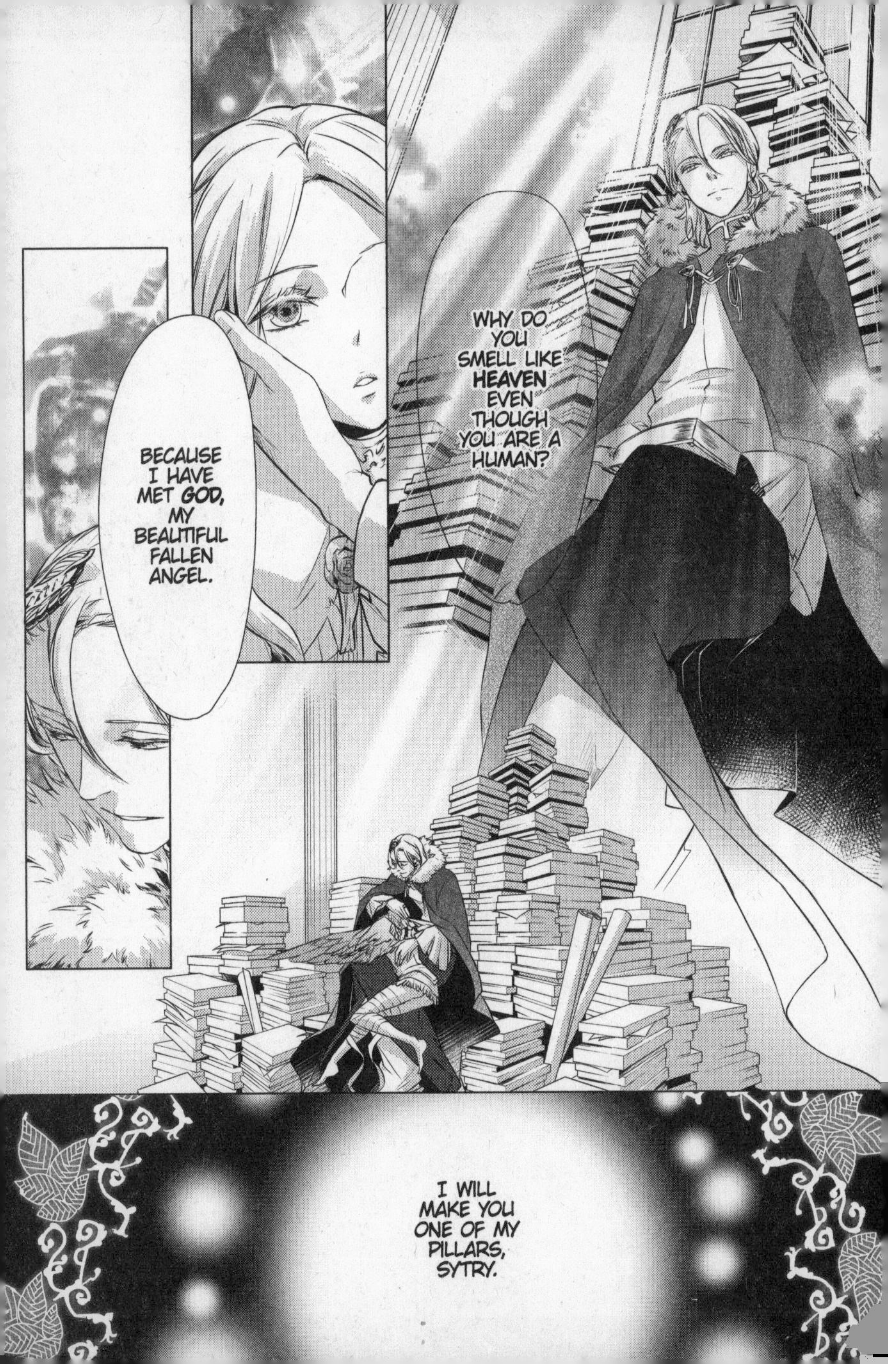
WHY DO YOU SMELL LIKE **HEAVEN** EVEN THOUGH YOU ARE A HUMAN?
BECAUSE I HAVE MET **GOD**, MY BEAUTIFUL FALLEN ANGEL.
I WILL MAKE YOU ONE OF MY PILLARS, SYTRY.

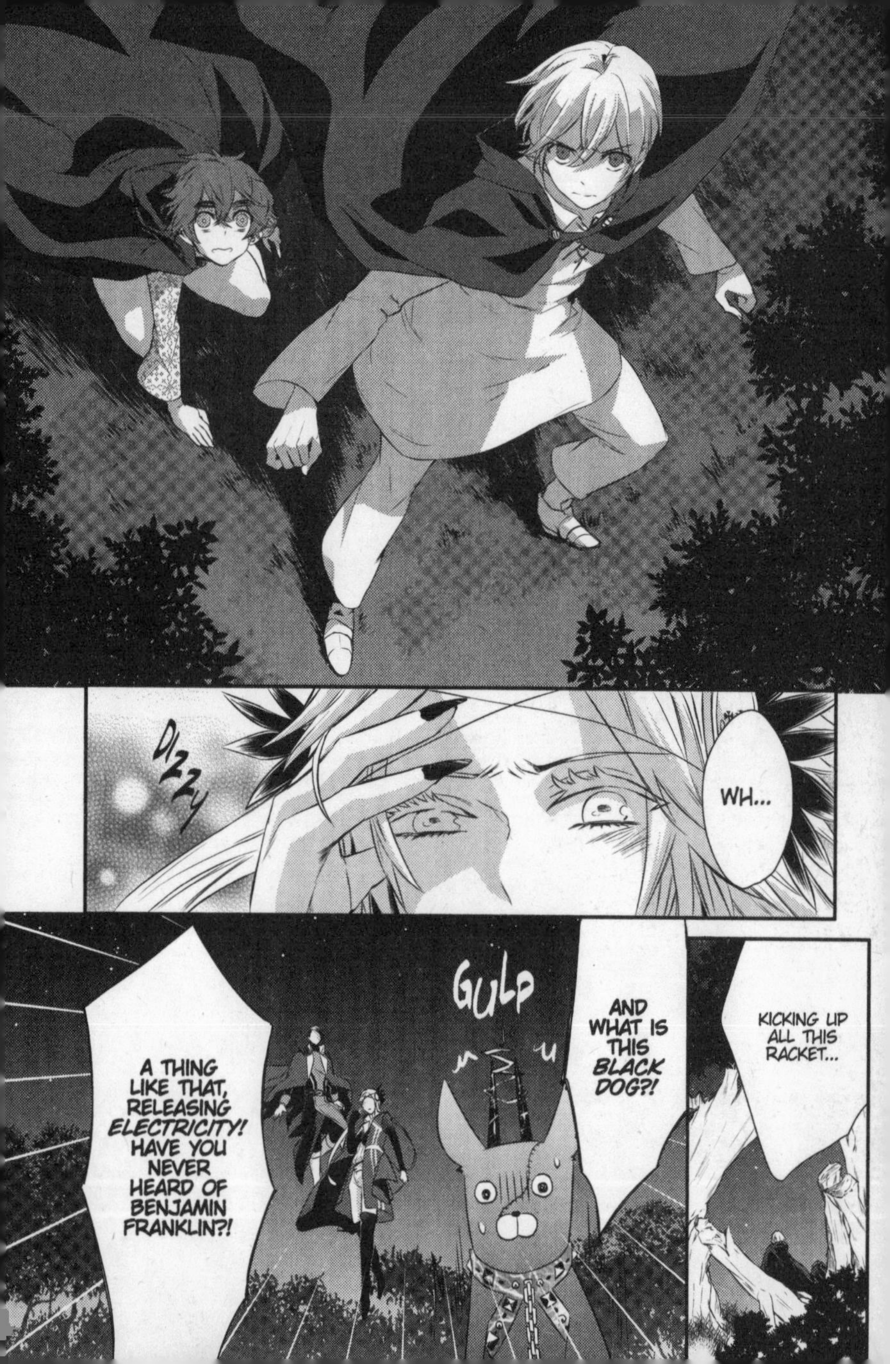
WH...
DIZZY
KICKING UP ALL THIS RACKET...
AND WHAT IS THIS BLACK DOG?!
GULP
A THING LIKE THAT, RELEASING ELECTRICITY! HAVE YOU NEVER HEARD OF BENJAMIN FRANKLIN?!

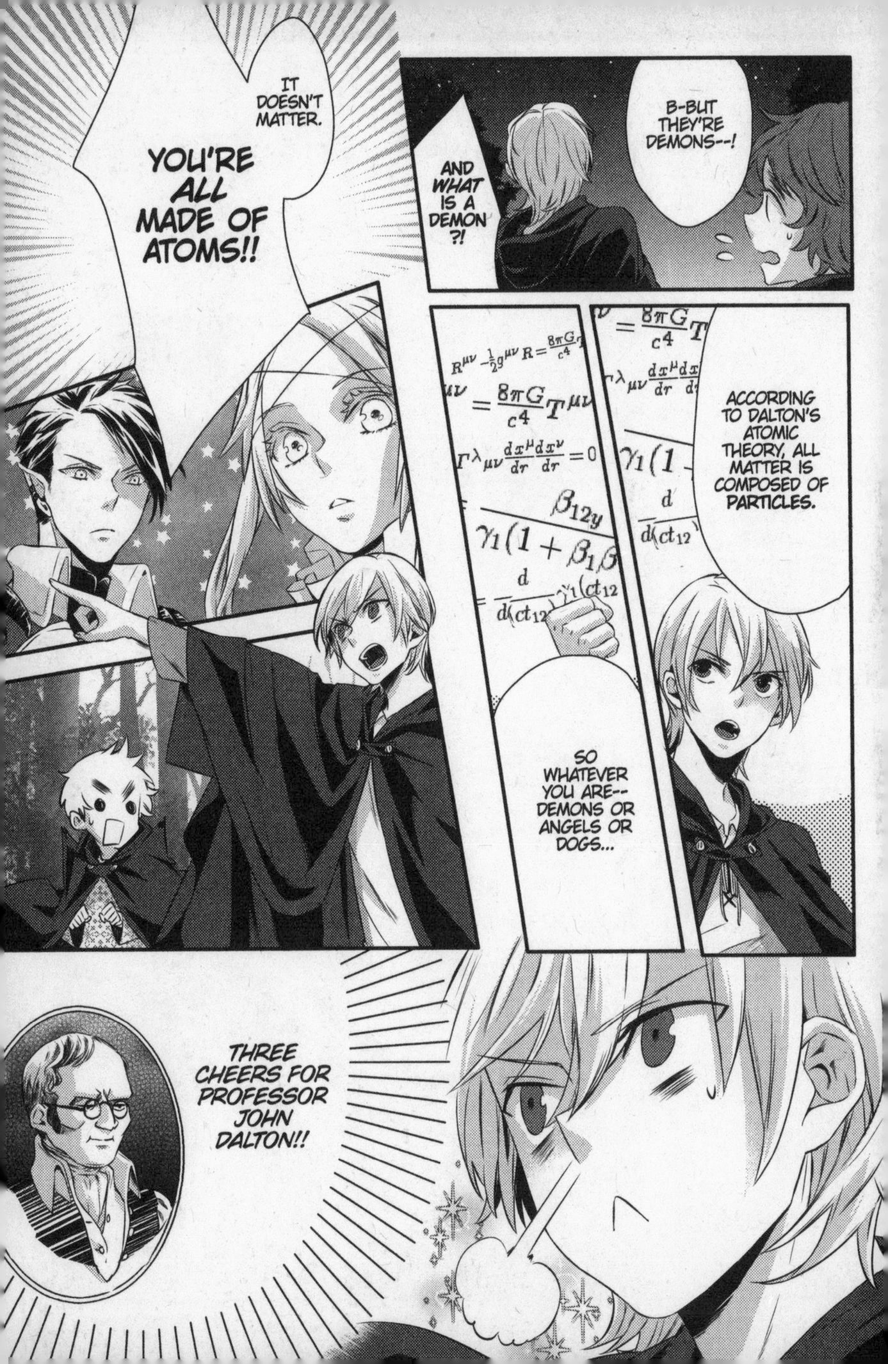
B-BUT THEY'RE DEMONS--!
AND WHAT IS A DEMON?!
ACCORDING TO DALTON'S ATOMIC THEORY, ALL MATTER IS COMPOSED OF PARTICLES.
SO WHATEVER YOU ARE-- DEMONS OR ANGELS OR DOGS...
IT DOESN'T MATTER.
YOU'RE ALL MADE OF ATOMS!!
THREE CHEERS FOR PROFESSOR JOHN DALTON!!

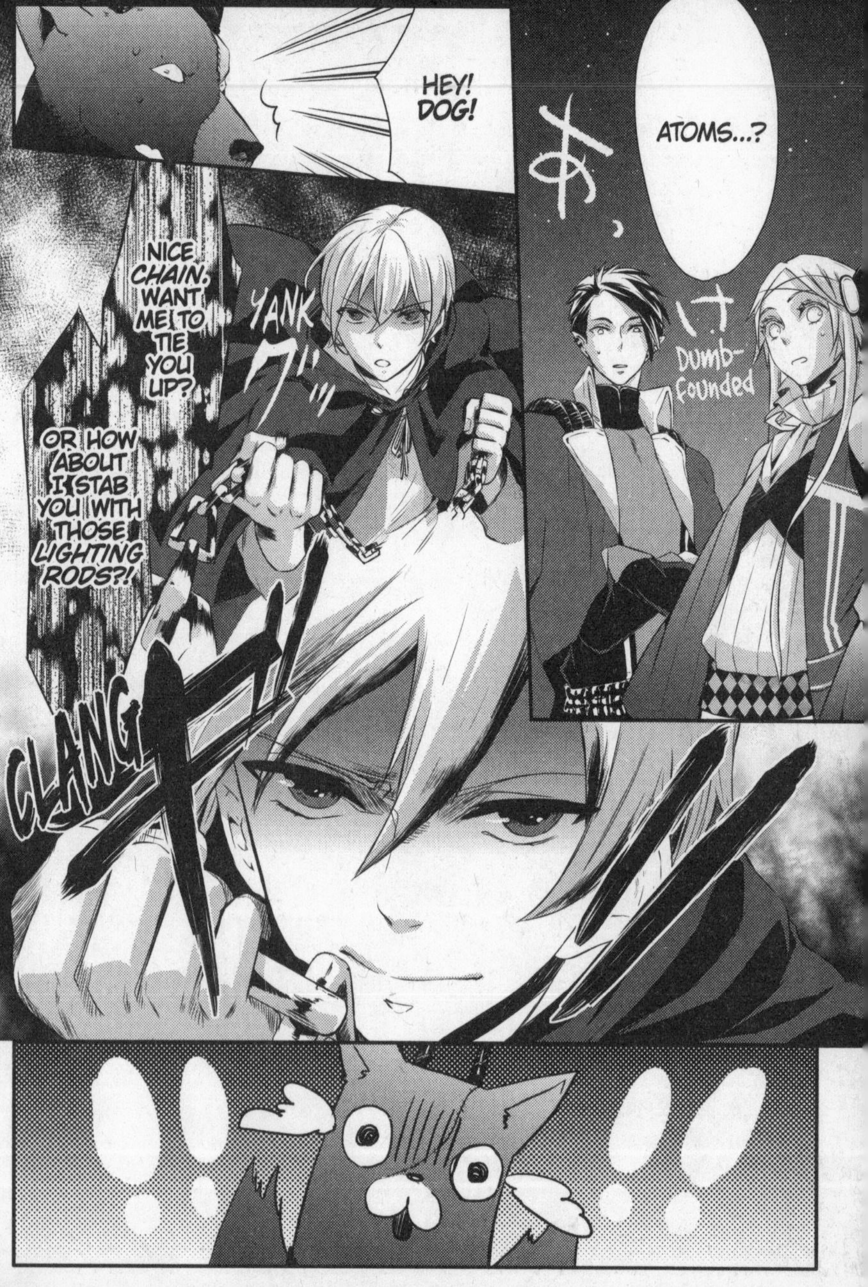
ATOMS...?
Dumb-founded
HEY! DOG!
NICE CHAIN. WANT ME TO TIE YOU UP?
YANK
OR HOW ABOUT I STAB YOU WITH THOSE LIGHTING RODS?!
CLANG
!!

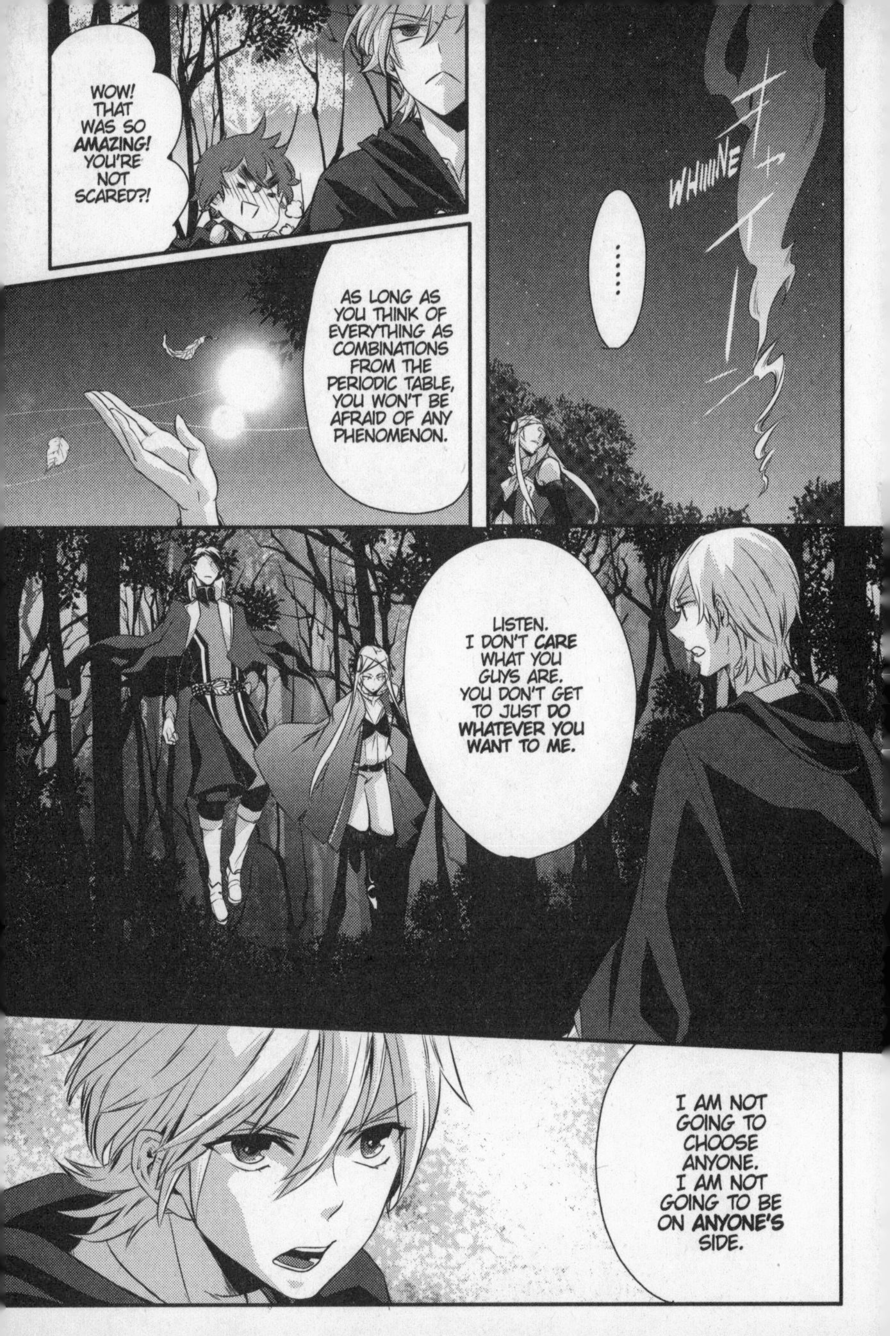
WHIIIINE
……
WOW! THAT WAS SO AMAZING! YOU'RE NOT SCARED?!
AS LONG AS YOU THINK OF EVERYTHING AS COMBINATIONS FROM THE PERIODIC TABLE, YOU WON'T BE AFRAID OF ANY PHENOMENON.
LISTEN. I DON'T CARE WHAT YOU GUYS ARE. YOU DON'T GET TO JUST DO WHATEVER YOU WANT TO ME.
I AM NOT GOING TO CHOOSE ANYONE. I AM NOT GOING TO BE ON ANYONE'S SIDE.

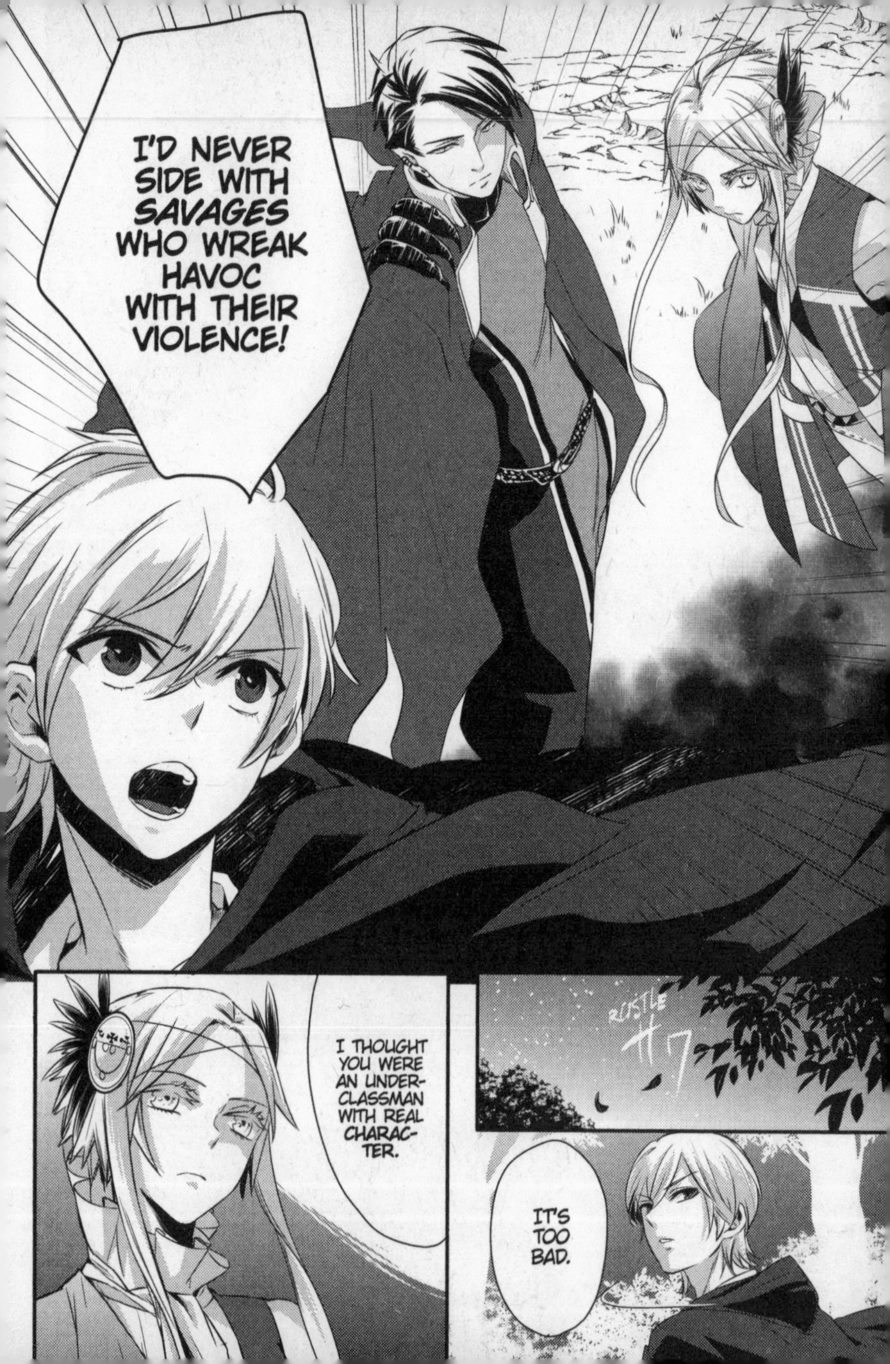

I'D NEVER SIDE WITH SAVAGES WHO WREAK HAVOC WITH THEIR VIOLENCE!
RUSTLE
IT'S TOO BAD.
I THOUGHT YOU WERE AN UNDER-CLASSMAN WITH REAL CHARAC-TER.

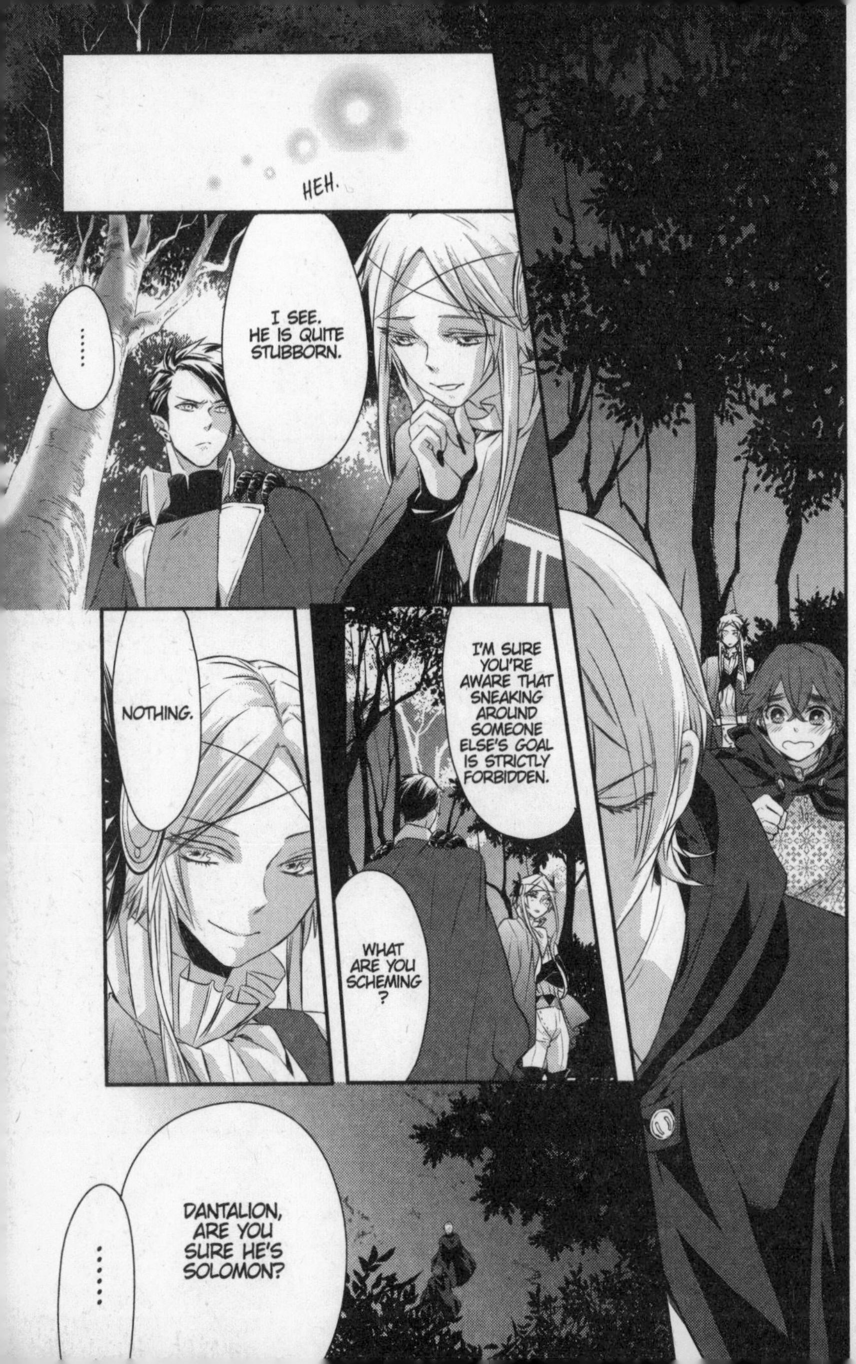
HEH.
I SEE. HE IS QUITE STUBBORN.
......
I'M SURE YOU'RE AWARE THAT SNEAKING AROUND SOMEONE ELSE'S GOAL IS STRICTLY FORBIDDEN.
WHAT ARE YOU SCHEMING?
NOTHING.
DANTALION, ARE YOU SURE HE'S SOLOMON?
......

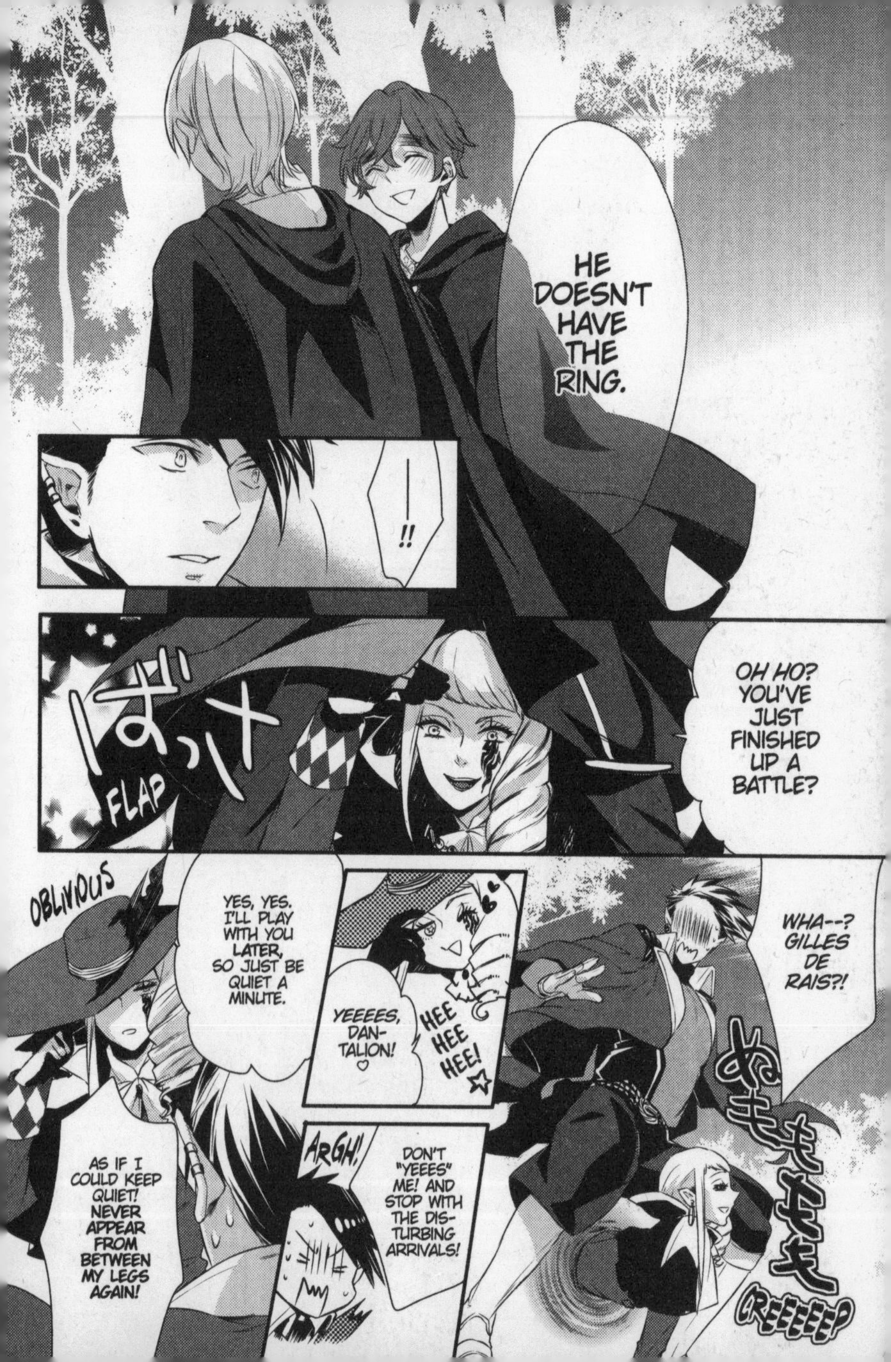
HE DOESN'T HAVE THE RING.
—!!
OH HO? YOU'VE JUST FINISHED UP A BATTLE?
ばっ
FLAP
WHA--? GILLES DE RAIS?!
ぬぅ
CREEEEEP
OBLIVIOUS
YES, YES. I'LL PLAY WITH YOU LATER, SO JUST BE QUIET A MINUTE.
YEEEES, DANTALION! ♡
HEE HEE HEE! ☆
DON'T "YEEES" ME! AND STOP WITH THE DISTURBING ARRIVALS!
ARGH!
AS IF I COULD KEEP QUIET! NEVER APPEAR FROM BETWEEN MY LEGS AGAIN!

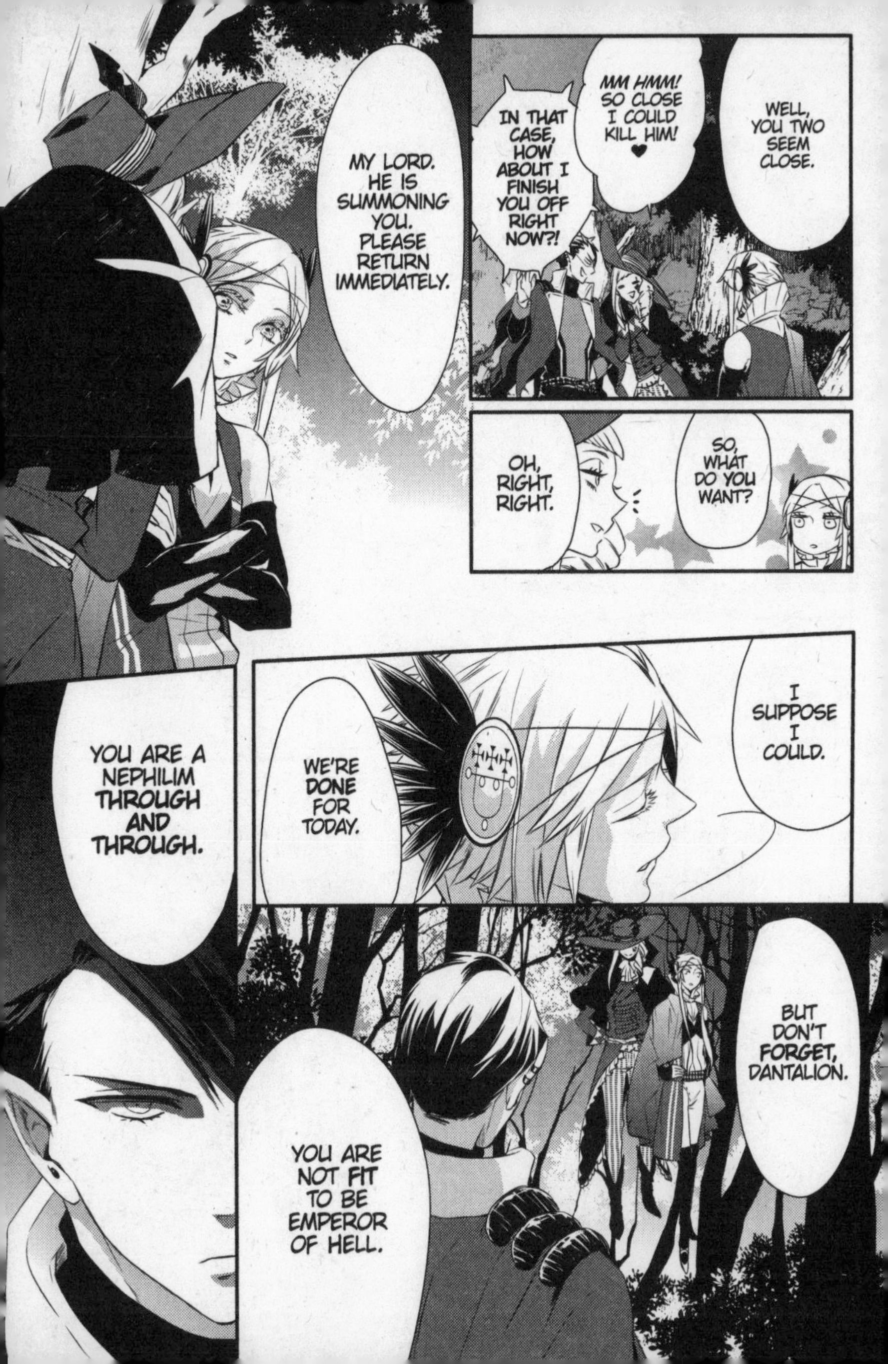
WELL, YOU TWO SEEM CLOSE.
MM HMM! SO CLOSE I COULD KILL HIM! ♥
IN THAT CASE, HOW ABOUT I FINISH YOU OFF RIGHT NOW?!
SO, WHAT DO YOU WANT?
OH, RIGHT, RIGHT.
MY LORD. HE IS SUMMONING YOU. PLEASE RETURN IMMEDIATELY.
I SUPPOSE I COULD.
WE'RE DONE FOR TODAY.
BUT DON'T FORGET, DANTALION.
YOU ARE A NEPHILIM THROUGH AND THROUGH.
YOU ARE NOT FIT TO BE EMPEROR OF HELL.

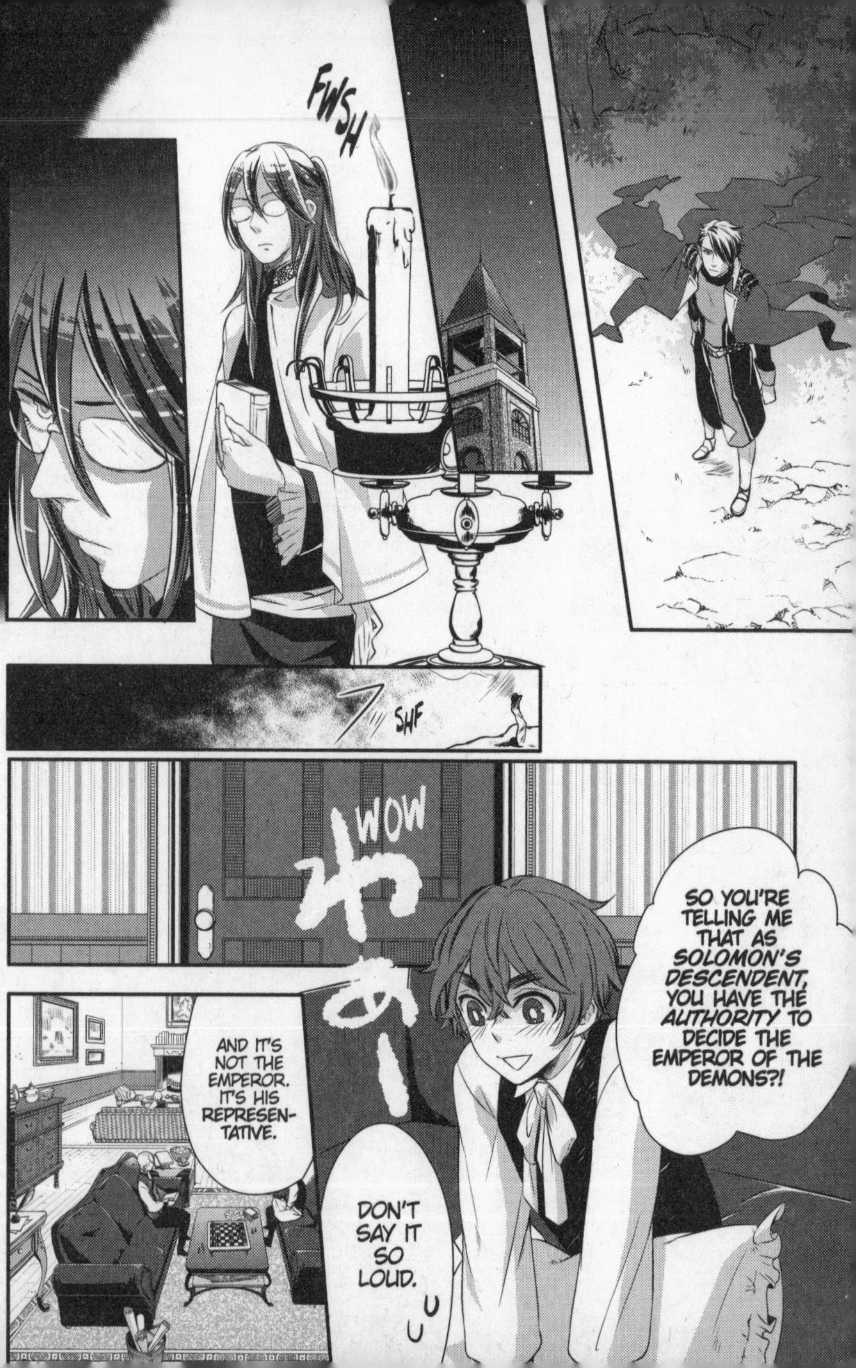
FWSH
SHF
WOW
わあー
SO YOU'RE TELLING ME THAT AS SOLOMON'S DESCENDENT, YOU HAVE THE *AUTHORITY* TO DECIDE THE EMPEROR OF THE DEMONS?!
AND IT'S NOT THE EMPEROR. IT'S HIS REPRESEN-TATIVE.
DON'T SAY IT SO LOUD.
UUU

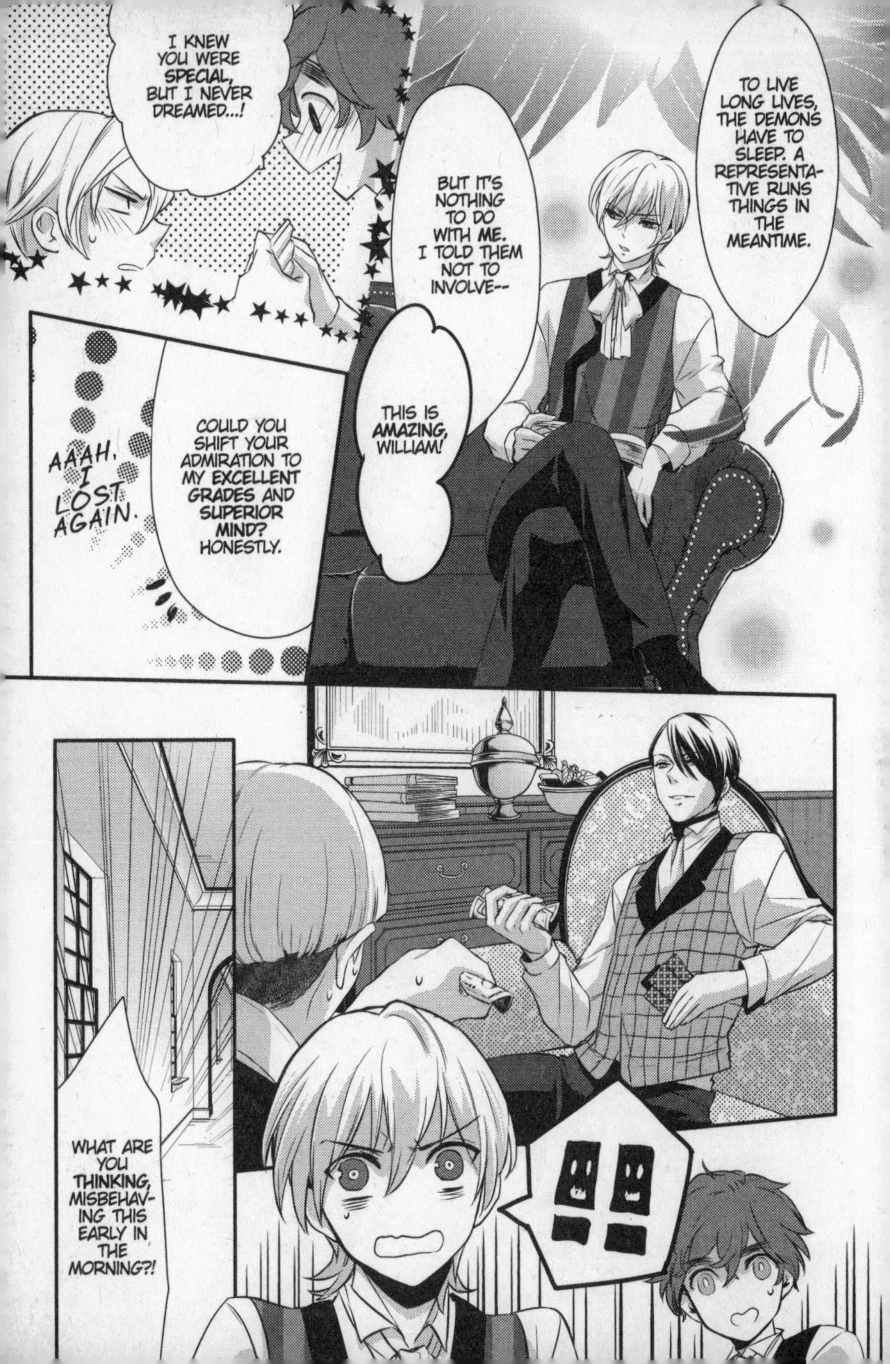
TO LIVE LONG LIVES, THE DEMONS HAVE TO SLEEP. A REPRESENTA-TIVE RUNS THINGS IN THE MEANTIME.
BUT IT'S NOTHING TO DO WITH ME. I TOLD THEM NOT TO INVOLVE--
THIS IS AMAZING, WILLIAM!
I KNEW YOU WERE SPECIAL, BUT I NEVER DREAMED...!
COULD YOU SHIFT YOUR ADMIRATION TO MY EXCELLENT GRADES AND SUPERIOR MIND? HONESTLY.
AAAH, I LOST AGAIN.
!!
WHAT ARE YOU THINKING, MISBEHAV-ING THIS EARLY IN THE MORNING?!

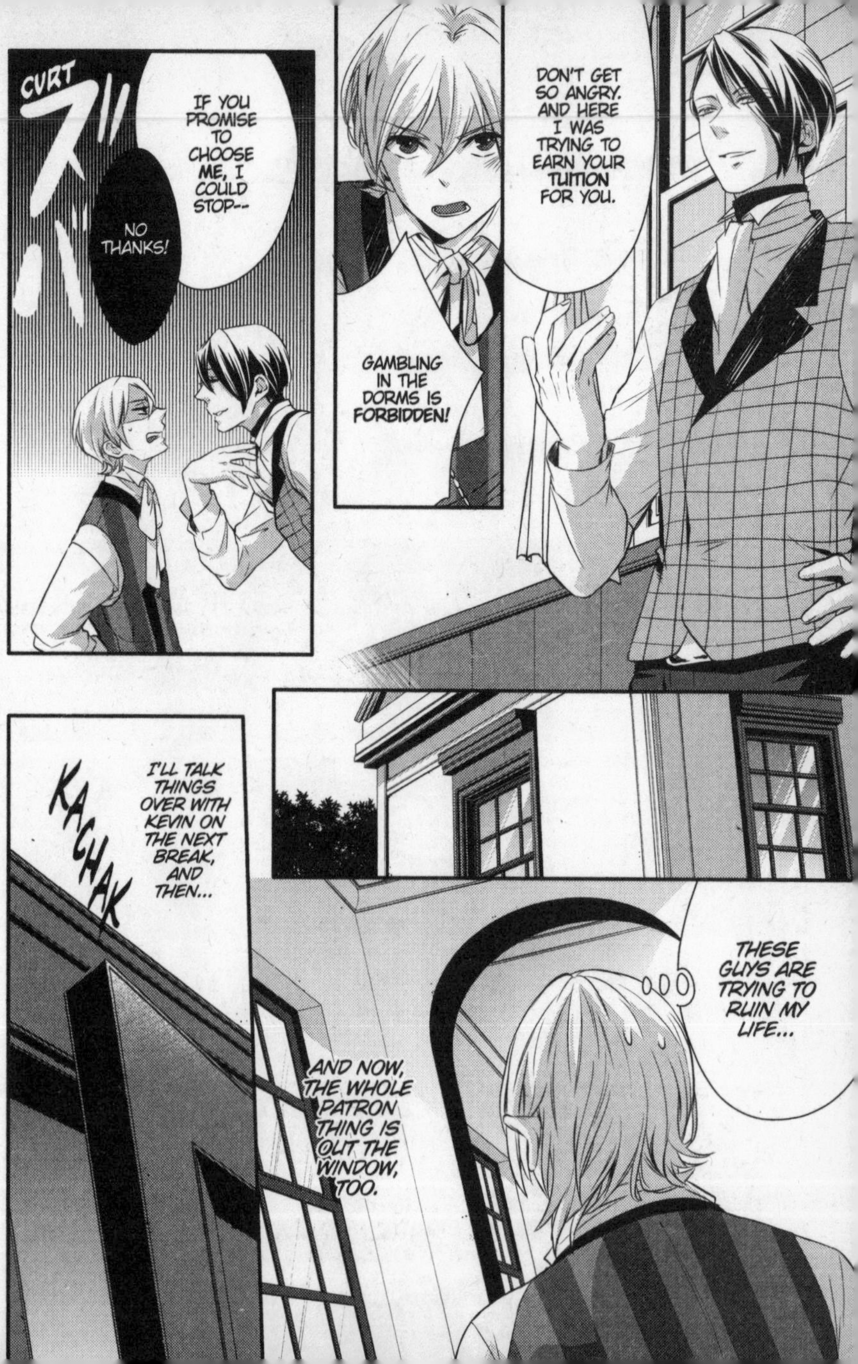
DON'T GET SO ANGRY. AND HERE I WAS TRYING TO EARN YOUR TUITION FOR YOU.
GAMBLING IN THE DORMS IS FORBIDDEN!
CURT
ズバ
IF YOU PROMISE TO CHOOSE ME, I COULD STOP--
NO THANKS!
THESE GUYS ARE TRYING TO RUIN MY LIFE...
AND NOW, THE WHOLE PATRON THING IS OUT THE WINDOW, TOO.
KACHAK
I'LL TALK THINGS OVER WITH KEVIN ON THE NEXT BREAK, AND THEN...

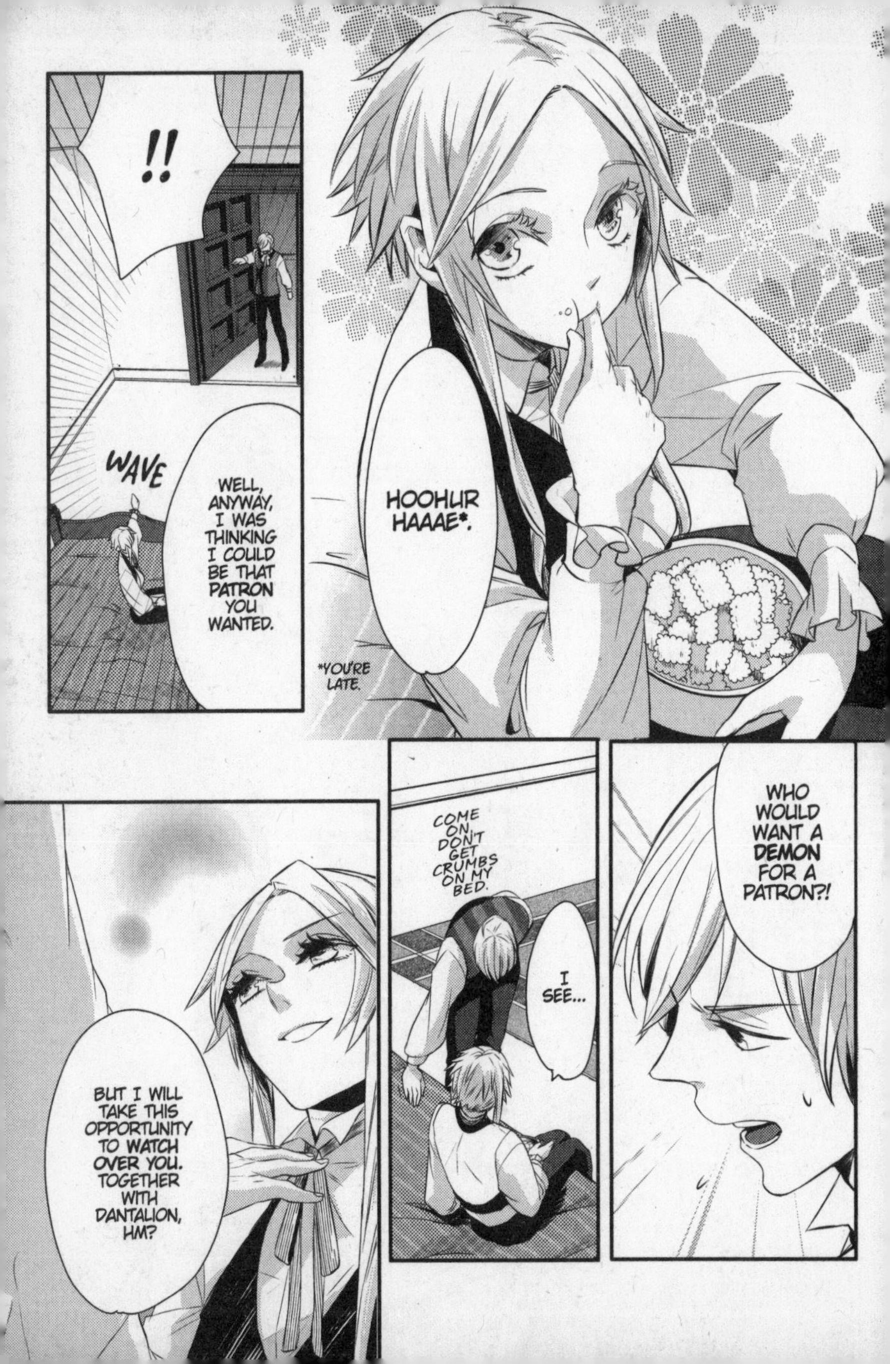
HOOHUR HAAAE*.
*YOU'RE LATE.
!!
WAVE
WELL, ANYWAY, I WAS THINKING I COULD BE THAT PATRON YOU WANTED.
WHO WOULD WANT A DEMON FOR A PATRON?!
COME ON, DON'T GET CRUMBS ON MY BED.
I SEE...
BUT I WILL TAKE THIS OPPORTUNITY TO WATCH OVER YOU. TOGETHER WITH DANTALION, HM?

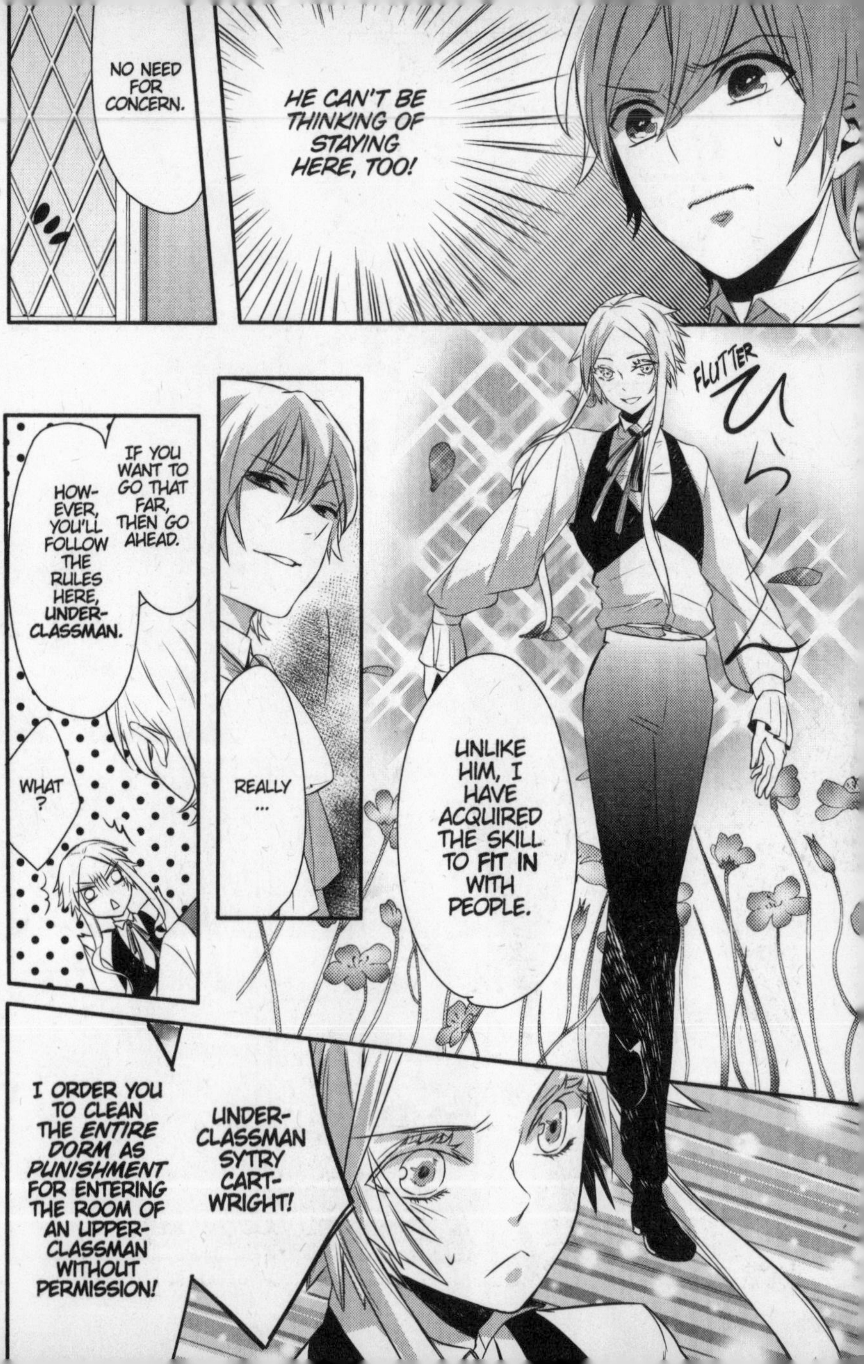
HE CAN'T BE THINKING OF STAYING HERE, TOO!
NO NEED FOR CONCERN.
FLUTTER
UNLIKE HIM, I HAVE ACQUIRED THE SKILL TO FIT IN WITH PEOPLE.
REALLY ...
IF YOU WANT TO GO THAT FAR, THEN GO AHEAD.
HOWEVER, YOU'LL FOLLOW THE RULES HERE, UNDERCLASSMAN.
WHAT?
UNDERCLASSMAN SYTRY CARTWRIGHT!
I ORDER YOU TO CLEAN THE *ENTIRE DORM* AS *PUNISHMENT* FOR ENTERING THE ROOM OF AN UPPERCLASSMAN WITHOUT PERMISSION!

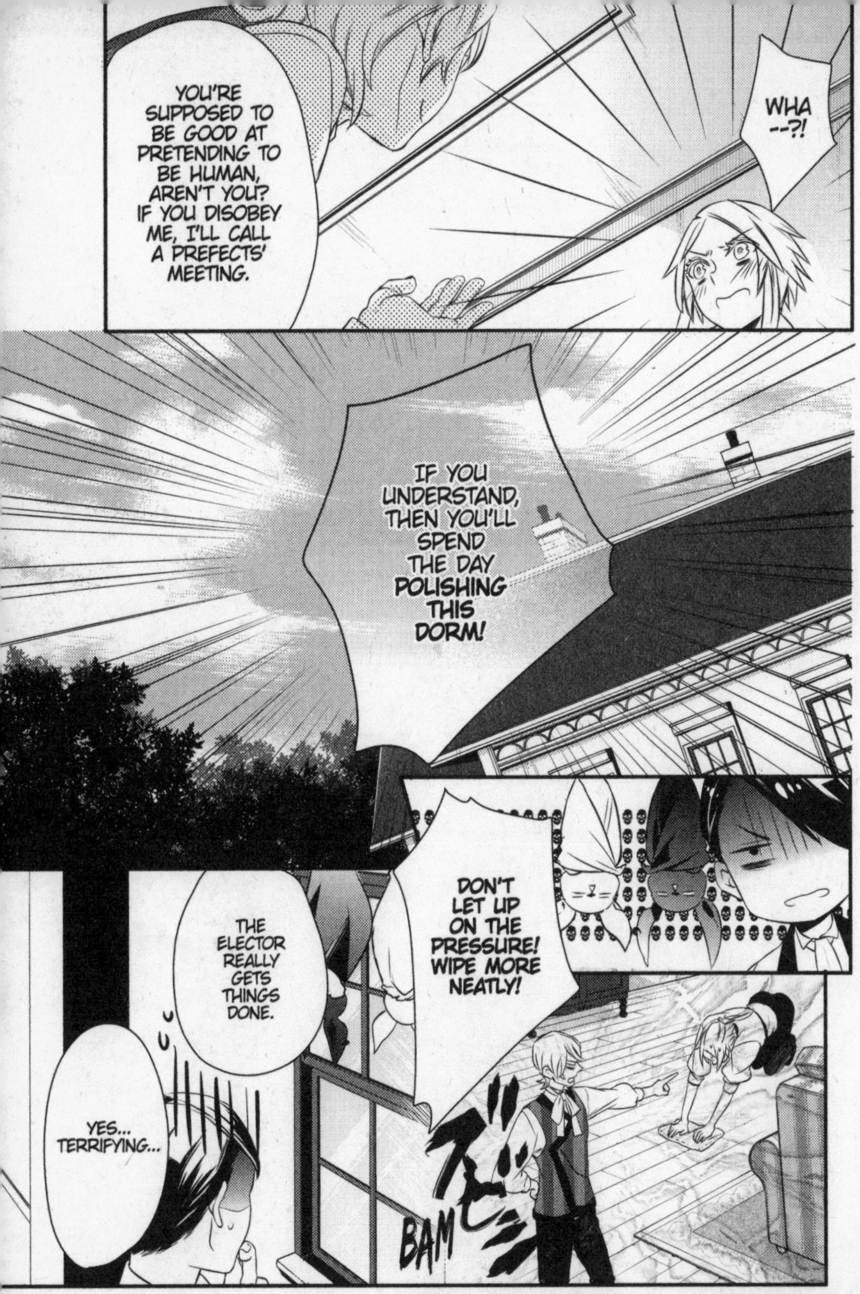
WHA--?!
YOU'RE SUPPOSED TO BE GOOD AT PRETENDING TO BE HUMAN, AREN'T YOU? IF YOU DISOBEY ME, I'LL CALL A PREFECTS' MEETING.
IF YOU UNDERSTAND, THEN YOU'LL SPEND THE DAY POLISHING THIS DORM!
DON'T LET UP ON THE PRESSURE! WIPE MORE NEATLY!
BAM
THE ELECTOR REALLY GETS THINGS DONE.
YES... TERRIFYING...

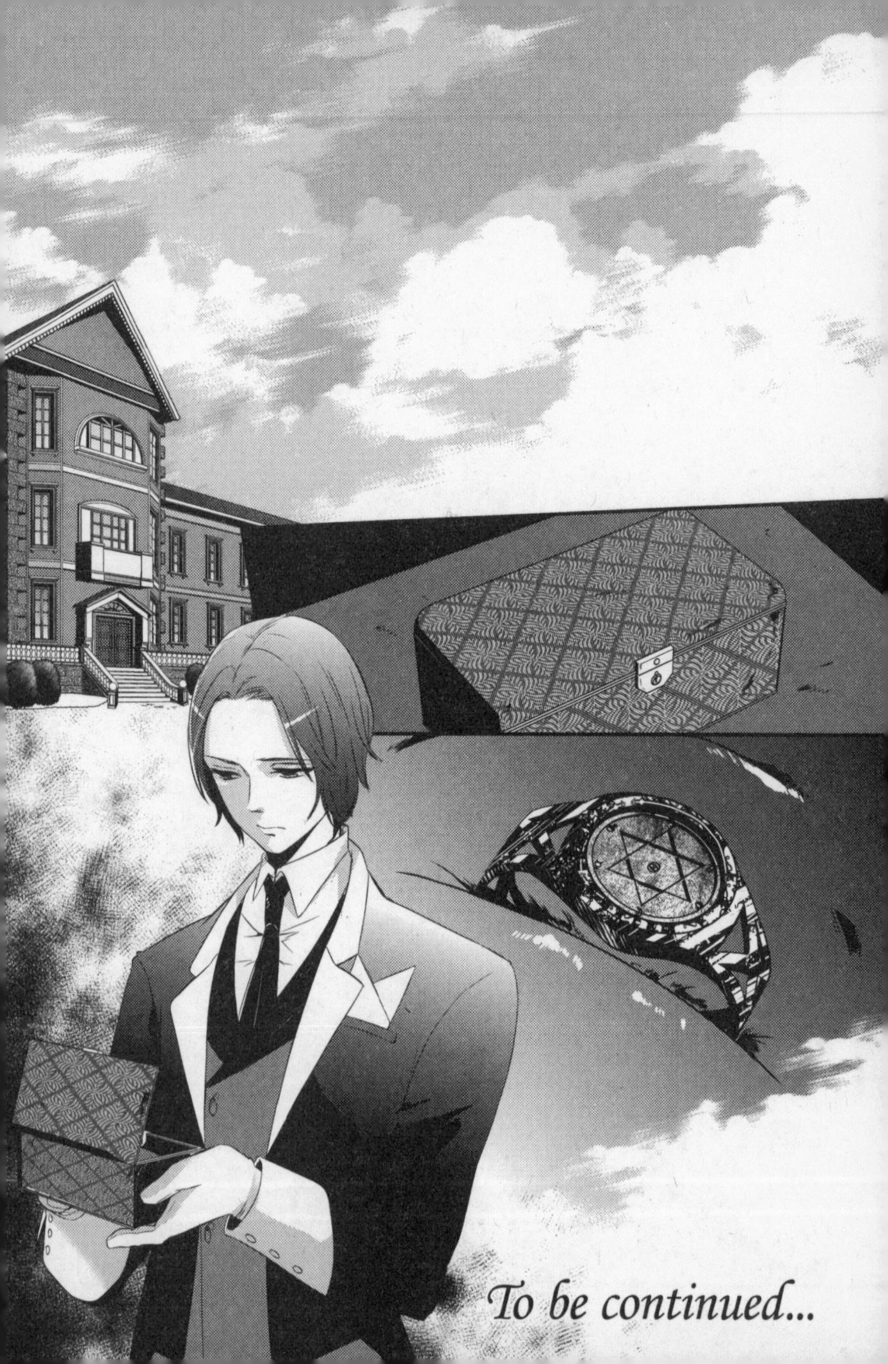
To be continued...

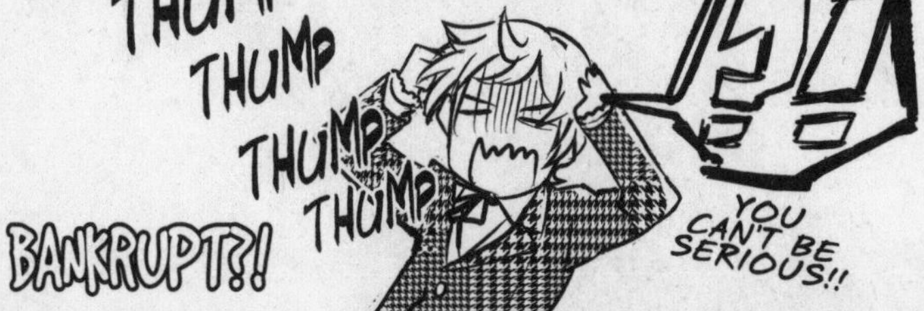
NOOOOOOOOOO!
YOU CAN'T BE SERIOUS!!
THUMP
THUMP
THUMP
THUMP
BANKRUPT?!

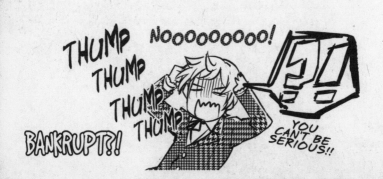

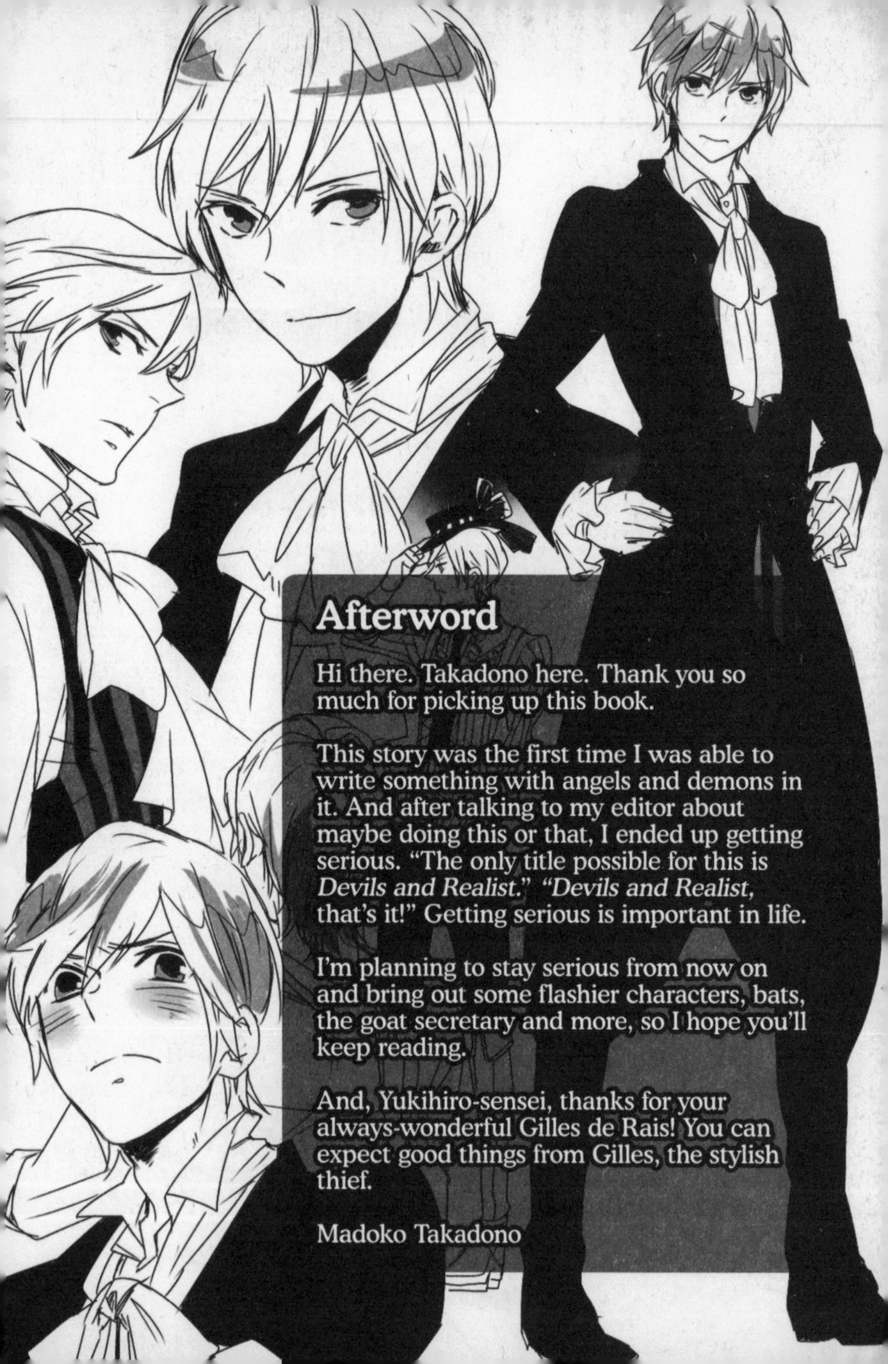

Afterword

Hi there. Takadono here. Thank you so much for picking up this book.

This story was the first time I was able to write something with angels and demons in it. And after talking to my editor about maybe doing this or that, I ended up getting serious. “The only title possible for this is *Devils and Realist*.” “*Devils and Realist*, that’s it!” Getting serious is important in life.

I’m planning to stay serious from now on and bring out some flashier characters, bats, the goat secretary and more, so I hope you’ll keep reading.

And, Yukihiro-sensei, thanks for your always-wonderful Gilles de Rais! You can expect good things from Gilles, the stylish thief.

Madoko Takadono

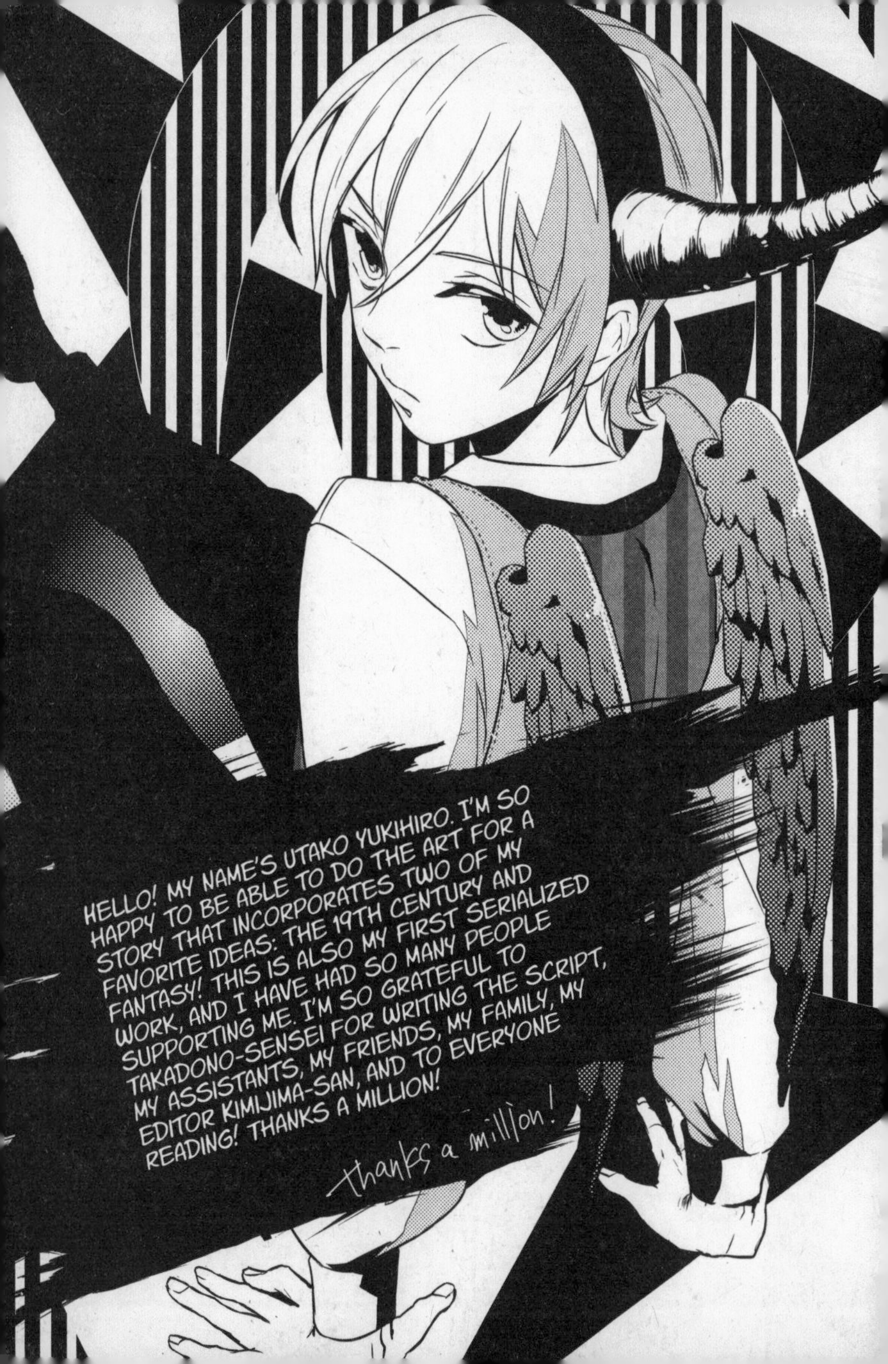
HELLO! MY NAME'S UTAKO YUKIHIRO. I'M SO HAPPY TO BE ABLE TO DO THE ART FOR A STORY THAT INCORPORATES TWO OF MY FAVORITE IDEAS: THE 19TH CENTURY AND FANTASY! THIS IS ALSO MY FIRST SERIALIZED WORK, AND I HAVE HAD SO MANY PEOPLE SUPPORTING ME. I'M SO GRATEFUL TO TAKADONO-SENSEI FOR WRITING THE SCRIPT, MY ASSISTANTS, MY FRIENDS, MY FAMILY, MY EDITOR KIMIJIMA-SAN, AND TO EVERYONE READING! THANKS A MILLION!
thanks a million!

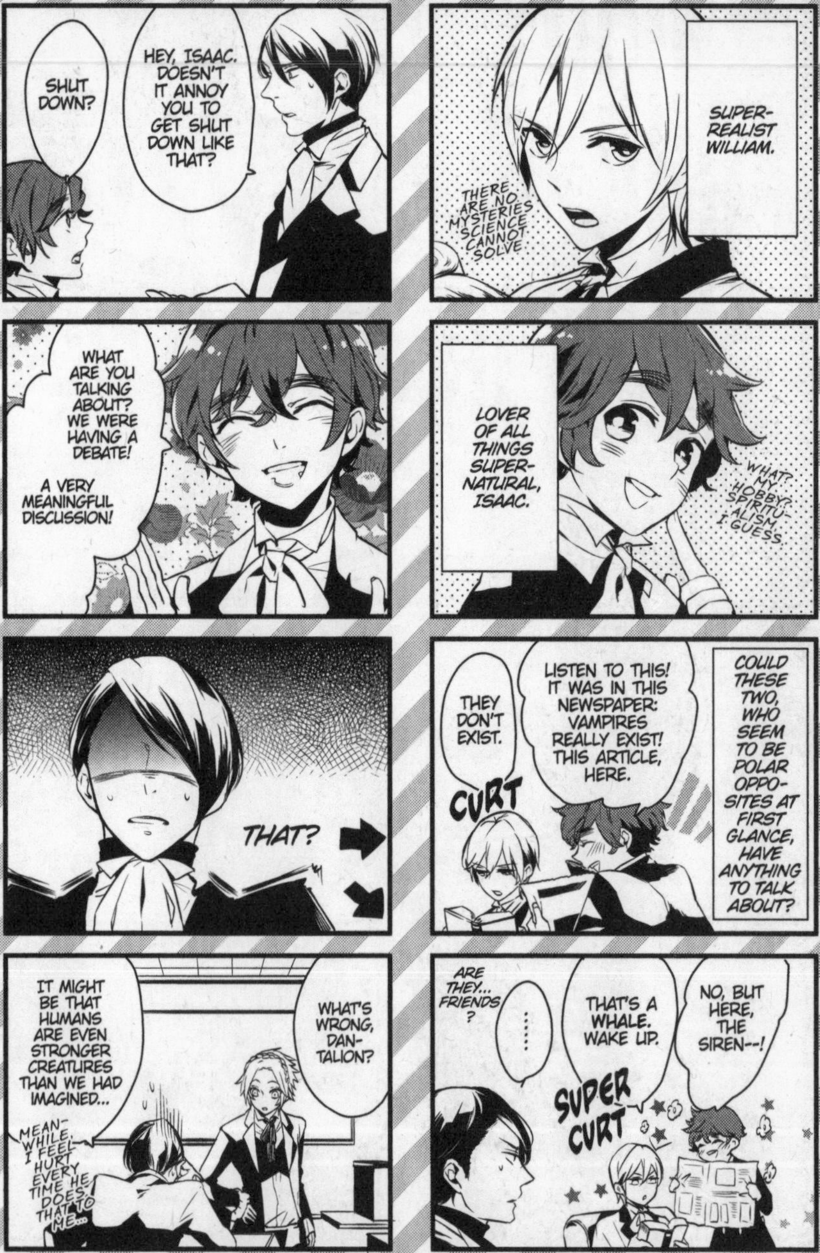
SUPER-REALIST WILLIAM.
THERE ARE NO MYSTERIES SCIENCE CANNOT SOLVE.
LOVER OF ALL THINGS SUPER-NATURAL, ISAAC.
WHAT? MY HOBBY? SPIRITU-ALISM, I GUESS.
COULD THESE TWO, WHO SEEM TO BE POLAR OPPO-SITES AT FIRST GLANCE, HAVE ANYTHING TO TALK ABOUT?
LISTEN TO THIS! IT WAS IN THIS NEWSPAPER: VAMPIRES REALLY EXIST! THIS ARTICLE, HERE.
THEY DON'T EXIST.
CURT
NO, BUT HERE, THE SIREN--!
THAT'S A WHALE. WAKE UP.
......
ARE THEY... FRIENDS?
SUPER CURT
HEY, ISAAC. DOESN'T IT ANNOY YOU TO GET SHUT DOWN LIKE THAT?
SHUT DOWN?
WHAT ARE YOU TALKING ABOUT? WE WERE HAVING A DEBATE!
A VERY MEANINGFUL DISCUSSION!
THAT?
WHAT'S WRONG, DAN-TALION?
IT MIGHT BE THAT HUMANS ARE EVEN STRONGER CREATURES THAN WE HAD IMAGINED...
MEAN-WHILE, I FEEL HURT EVERY TIME HE DOES THAT TO ME...

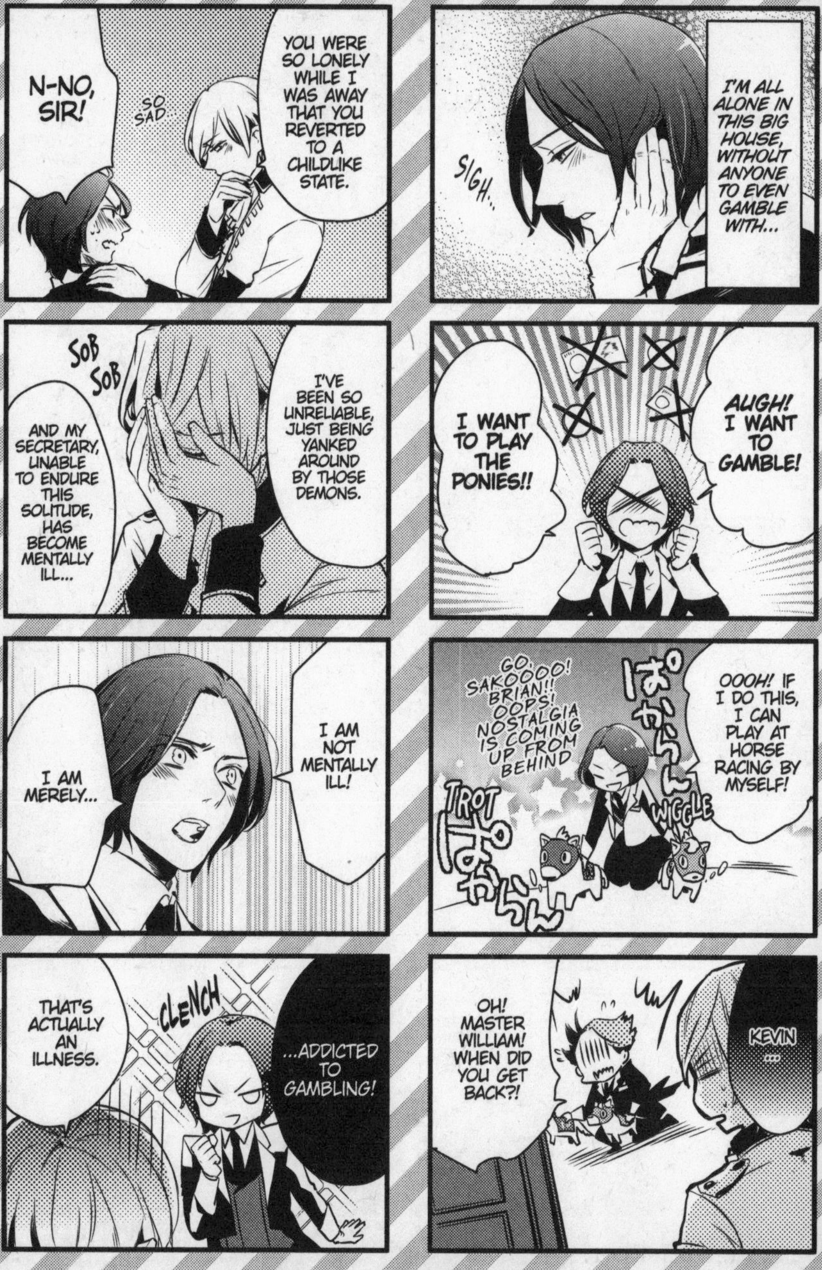
I'M ALL ALONE IN THIS BIG HOUSE, WITHOUT ANYONE TO EVEN GAMBLE WITH...
SIGH...
AUGH! I WANT TO GAMBLE!
I WANT TO PLAY THE PONIES!!
OOOH! IF I DO THIS, I CAN PLAY AT HORSE RACING BY MYSELF!
ぱからん
GO, SAKOOOO! BRIAN!! OOPS! NOSTALGIA IS COMING UP FROM BEHIND
WIGGLE
TROT
ぱからん
OH! MASTER WILLIAM! WHEN DID YOU GET BACK?!
KEVIN...
YOU WERE SO LONELY WHILE I WAS AWAY THAT YOU REVERTED TO A CHILDLIKE STATE.
SO SAD...
N-NO, SIR!
I'VE BEEN SO UNRELIABLE, JUST BEING YANKED AROUND BY THOSE DEMONS.
SOB SOB
AND MY SECRETARY, UNABLE TO ENDURE THIS SOLITUDE, HAS BECOME MENTALLY ILL...
I AM NOT MENTALLY ILL!
I AM MERELY...
...ADDICTED TO GAMBLING!
CLENCH
THAT'S ACTUALLY AN ILLNESS.

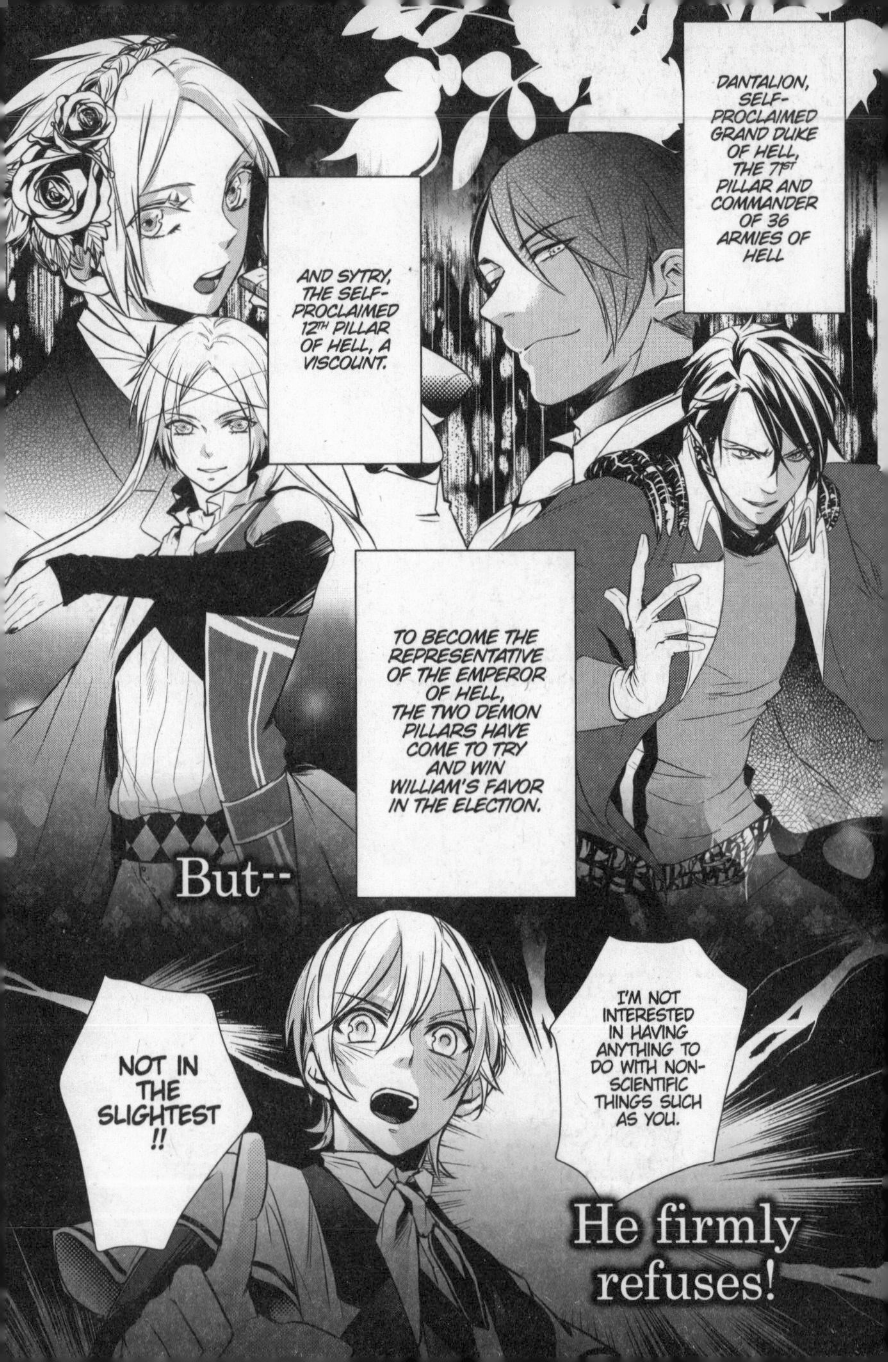
DANTALION, SELF-PROCLAIMED GRAND DUKE OF HELL, THE 71ST PILLAR AND COMMANDER OF 36 ARMIES OF HELL
AND SYTRY, THE SELF-PROCLAIMED 12TH PILLAR OF HELL, A VISCOUNT.
TO BECOME THE REPRESENTATIVE OF THE EMPEROR OF HELL, THE TWO DEMON PILLARS HAVE COME TO TRY AND WIN WILLIAM'S FAVOR IN THE ELECTION.
But--
I'M NOT INTERESTED IN HAVING ANYTHING TO DO WITH NON-SCIENTIFIC THINGS SUCH AS YOU.
NOT IN THE SLIGHTEST !!
He firmly refuses!